Praise for *Settlers on the Edge:*

This highly original work rises brilliantly to the challenge of an extraordinary historical moment in the harshest and most inaccessible region of the Russian North. Niobe Thompson's analysis of social identity, self, agency, and moral economy reveals how successive changes of regime have engendered an accumulation of distinctive identities in which each identity is reinforced by differences of origin, generation, and class.

Among many powerful insights, the author shows how white settlers have used their practical and spiritual engagement with the local landscape to appropriate the widespread northern Native identity marker of belonging, thereby explaining their resistance to programs of resettlement to the south. By following resettled northerners back to their apartment blocks in Central Russia, he shows how, even here, their strategy of survival involves recreating their northern sense of belonging.

This book is a landmark in the anthropology of Russia, of the circumpolar Arctic, and of migration studies.

PIERS VITEBSKY, AUTHOR OF *REINDEER PEOPLE: LIVING WITH ANIMALS AND SPIRITS IN SIBERIA*

Niobe Thompson examines a dynamic period in northeast Russia, spanning its abrupt decline immediately following the break-up of the Soviet Union and the subsequent period of massive investment under a new governor. This is a groundbreaking study done with great insight into the phenomenal changes in Arctic Russia in recent decades. It makes a major, novel contribution to our understanding of identity formation by looking at the region's non-indigenous population.

GAIL FONDAHL, AUTHOR OF *GAINING GROUND? EVENKIS, LAND AND REFORM IN SOUTHEASTERN SIBERIA*

An impressive achievement – among this book's greatest strengths are its solid ethnographic grounding, its thorough grasp of historical process, its lucid and incisive presentation, and its near-seamless integration of description and analysis. It gives a fascinating account of a virtually unknown social world in a sophisticated, yet unpretentious, style.

FINN SIVERT NIELSEN, AUTHOR OF *THE EYE OF THE WHIRLWIND, RUSSIAN IDENTITY AND SOVIET NATION-BUILDING*

Settlers on the Edge

Identity and Modernization on Russia's Arctic Frontier

Niobe Thompson

UBCPress · Vancouver · Toronto

16 15 14 13 12 11 10 09 08   5 4 3 2 1

Printed in Canada on ancient-forest-free paper (100% post-consumer recycled) that is processed chlorine- and acid-free, with vegetable-based inks.

Library and Archives Canada Cataloguing in Publication

Thompson, Niobe, 1973-
Settlers on the edge: identity and modernization of Russia's arctic frontier / Niobe Thompson.

Includes bibliographical references and index.
ISBN 978-0-7748-1467-6

1. Chukchi Peninsula (Russia) – History – 20th century. 2. Migrant labor – Russia (Federation) – Chukchi Peninsula – History. 3. Migration, Internal – Russia – History – 20th century. 4. Acculturation – Russia (Federation) – Chukchi Peninsula. 5. Chukchi Peninsula (Russia) – Population – History – 20th century. 6. Ethnology – Russia (Federation) – Chukchi Peninsula. I. Title.

DK771.C4T48 2008   957'.7   C2008-901772-2

Canada

UBC Press gratefully acknowledges the financial support for our publishing program of the Government of Canada through the Book Publishing Industry Development Program (BPIDP), and of the Canada Council for the Arts, and the British Columbia Arts Council.

This book has been published with the help of a grant from the Canadian Federation for the Humanities and Social Sciences, through the Aid to Scholarly Publications Programme, using funds provided by the Social Sciences and Humanities Research Council of Canada.

UBC Press
The University of British Columbia
2029 West Mall
Vancouver, BC V6T 1Z2
604-822-5959 / Fax: 604-822-6083
www.ubcpress.ca

To Linda

Contents

Illustrations

Figures

Photographs

Preface

Two aspects of the editorial method used in the book require clarification: the transliteration of Russian names and terms and the protection of informants' identities.

This book employs the US Library of Congress system for the transliteration of Russian names and terms, with some exceptions. Where the spelling of a word is already established in popular media and other accounts, I have opted to violate the transliteration system. Thus *Boris E'ltin* is *Boris Yeltsin*, a *Koriak* is a *Koryak*, and the city of *Anadyr'* is *Anadyr* (without the soft sign). When using a Russian term transliterated in the plural, I opt to reproduce the plural endings as they are used in Russian. Thus, a single *vezdekhod* becomes several *vezdekhody*, and a single *muzhik* sits down to drink with a few *muzhiki*. (For a glossary of Russian words, see Appendix 2.)

The identity of many of my informants has been protected using a coding system, in which individuals quoted or cited in the text are assigned the numbers [1] through [66] corresponding to brief descriptions of their gender, approximate age, ethnicity, length of time in the North, and profession (see Appendix 1 for a list of the informants). When the narratives of certain people provide the basis for extended textual descriptions, as, for example, in Chapter 5, surrogate names rather than number codes have been used for stylistic purposes. In certain cases, however, the actual names of informants are preserved in the text, reflecting their status as public figures: elected officials, senior public servants, and well-known media personalities. Furthermore, the names of settlements and towns mentioned in the text have not been changed.

Acknowledgments

I am deeply grateful to the many people in Chukotka and central Russia who opened their doors and, with abundant patience and generosity, shared their knowledge of a world to which I was five years ago a stranger. From the warmth and enthusiasm I met almost without fail, and a great deal of practical assistance given without hesitation, I know that the "law of the North" of which northerners are so proud thrives today. In a part of Russia very difficult to access, I consider the freedom I was given to travel and ask questions without hindrance or conditions little short of miraculous. For this I extend heartfelt thanks and admiration to the administration of the Chukchi Autonomous Okrug and Governor Roman Abramovich, to the governor's special advisors John Tichotsky and Aleksandr Borodin, former deputy governor Sergei Kapkov, and his assistants Aleksandr Eidelshtein, Natal'ia Rakaeva, and Sergei Shuvalov. I am also grateful to the staff of the Chukotka branch of the Russian Red Cross, and in particular its director Ida Ruchina, as well as to the Chukotka branch of the Russian Academy of Sciences and its scientific director Tat'iana Godovykh.

Ultimately, in carrying out this research and making a life in Chukotka, my wife and I came to rely not on institutions, but on the friendships we made with local people, and I regard these friends with great fondness and everlasting gratitude. There would not be much of a story to tell if my fellow *parashiutisty* (firefighters) at Avialesokhrana had not taken us under their (literal) wings, making many journeys possible. In particular, I thank one of Chukotka's most incandescent personalities, a true *severnyi muzhik*, the director of Avialesokhrana Albert Klimentiev (you owe me a liver). Of all the many people in Chukotka who befriended and helped us, I wish to especially thank Vladimir Sirtun and his family, and all the children of his Shkola Strantsvii, Aleksandr and Galina Ganze, Vladilen Kavry, Zoia Tagryn'a, Aleksandr and Nina Mosolov, Vasilii Yakovlev, Petr Klimov, Liudmila Ershova, Vladimir Pereladov, and Pavel and Irina Apletin. I reserve particular gratitude for the people of Vaegi, my adopted home in Chukotka. I also have all the brothers Bogorev, and in particular Viktor – mayor of Vaegi, parashiutist, and riverboat captain – to thank for saving my life more than once, although I've asked myself why it so often needed saving when I was travelling in their company.

In central Russia, the difficult task of tracking down resettled former residents of Chukotka was made possible only through the kind assistance of Teodor Zvizda (in Anadyr), and Vladimir Zakharov (Lipetsk), Stanislav Zhukov (Smolensk), and Mikhail Ivanov (Voronezh).

This book was born thanks to the collective effort and insight of many wonderful colleagues at the Scott Polar Research Institute and the Department of Social Anthropology at the University of Cambridge, and I thank them all. I owe a deep debt of gratitude to Piers Vitebsky, whose intelligence and dedication was a guiding inspiration for this project from its inception, and whose passionate support is very much the reason for its final success.

For their sensitive and insightful comments, I also wish to particularly acknowledge Nikolai Ssorin-Chaikov, Bruce Grant, Nikolai Vakhtin, Patty Gray, Mark Nuttall, Susan Crate, Finn Sivert Nielsen, Sarah Radcliffe, Emma Wilson, Elena Khlinovskaya-Rockhill, Gail Fondahl, and Marilyn Strathern.

In conducting field research and writing for this project over the past five years, I was supported by two Wenner Gren research grants, a Commonwealth Fellowship, and funding from the Canadian Social Sciences and Humanities Research Council. I was free to concentrate on writing this book thanks to a Killam Postdoctoral Fellowship at the University of Alberta. In Cambridge, the Scott Polar Research Institute provided a splendid setting in which to base my research over the years, affording informed critique, unparalleled resources, and the collegiality of afternoon tea in equal measure. I also thank Jesus College for numerous small research grants and for providing a home.

I reserve my deepest gratitude for three people. My mother and father took me with them to a little community in the Canadian North in 1979, where I spent the next seven years falling out of trees, tipping canoes on the lake, leaving my gumboots stuck in the mud, and wishing I were Cree like all my friends. We were newcomers there, but to my great fortune my parents chose to live outside the white cliques and their government-built compounds, and although they would probably not admit it, they inspired many by the way they invested their lives in their adopted home. The concerns at the heart of my research, and the original impulse to go to the Russian North, originate in the northern experiences my parents gave me as a child.

Finally, when my wife married me in 2001, she may not have seen coming a year of life in a struggling industrial town in the Russian Far North. But her patience, love, humour, and forbearance through blizzards, winter darkness, tundra mosquitoes, and my awful vezdekhod driving got me through it all. The work of research and writing was hers as much as mine, and so this book is dedicated to her.

Settlers on the Edge

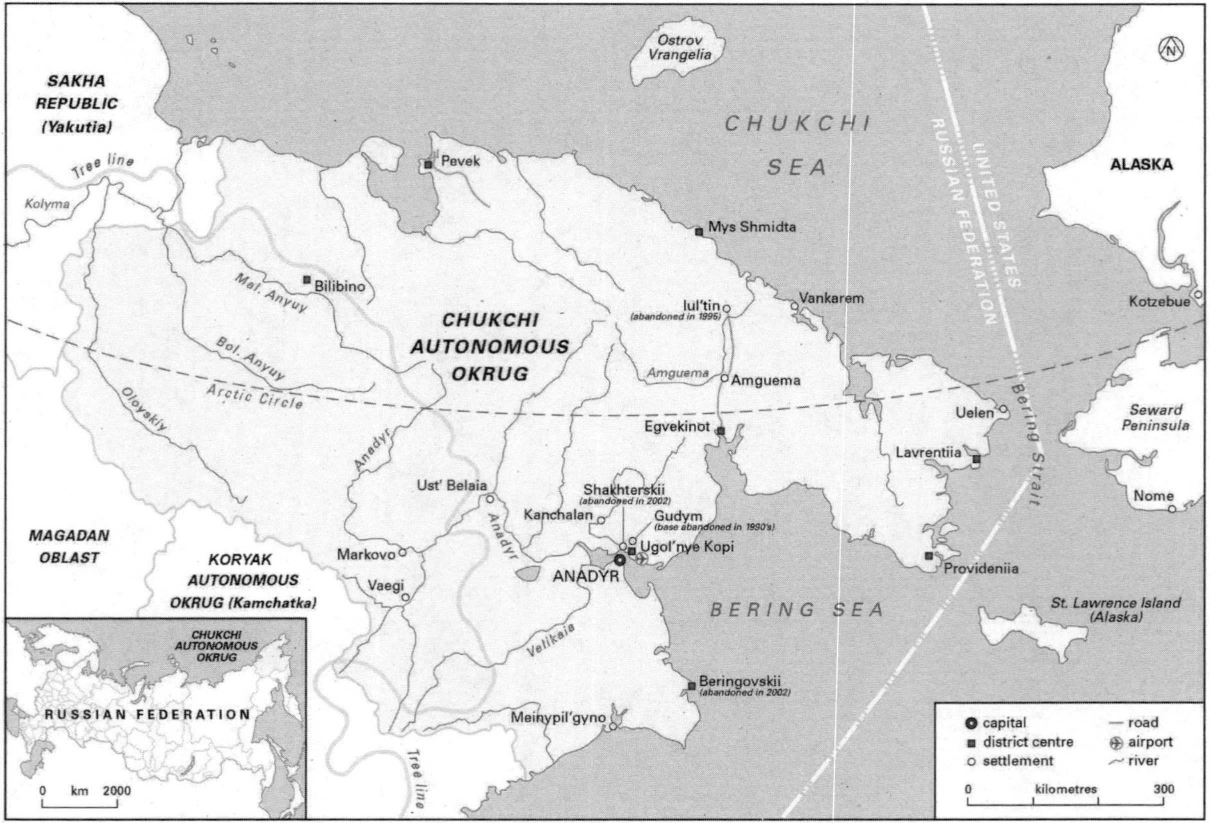

Figure 1.1 Chukotka (Chukchi Autonomous Okrug)

1
Introduction

One of the great untold stories of the Russian North lies concealed behind the unexamined belief that we understand who in these regions is native and who is only visiting. This book is about the people who went to live in Russia's most remote northeast region – Chukotka – as willing participants in the Soviet campaign to master the North, and who to this day constitute its majority population. Although *Settlers on the Edge* is far from unique in choosing the post-Soviet North as a setting, it is the first research to focus entirely on this population and to place in question the assumptions of transience and rootlessness that cling to the northern non-native.[1] The terms normally attached to this figure – *priezzhii* or *prishedshii*, variously translated as either "newcomer" or "incomer" – hardly suggest the depth of history Soviet-era migrants now possess in the North, even in those regions most recently settled by Russians.[2] In fact, the experiences of migration have with time yielded palpable senses of belonging in place, and the "newcomer" of an earlier period has become the "settler" of the present day. Migrant workers who arrived with an expectation of their own transience in the North, but who remained there decades later, gradually responded to the opportunities and challenges of northern life by putting down roots.[3] Not all the original migrants to the North underwent such transformations; in fact, staying only briefly was more common. But the point, for those who might attach a stigma of eternal outsiderness to the "newcomer," is that though dislocation and rootlessness were common to all northern migrants, they were almost never an aspiration. Indeed, migrants, whether they left after a short stay or remained to build a life, were almost universally in search of that most elusive quality in Soviet life: a secure and *settled* existence.

In its final three decades of power, the Soviet state engineered a remarkable project of voluntary mass settlement in the Russian Far North. For migrants to these regions, the conditions of life were exceptional not only in the sense one might expect, beset by isolation and a harsh climate, but also, in the era after Stalin's death in 1953, the lives of northern settlers were exceptionally privileged. A regime whose ostensible purpose in building communism was to efface class antagonisms and eventually to eliminate class distinctions altogether, in fact created in the North a new formation of class privilege. Having turned its back on the prison-labour system, that regime found material incentives to be a much more powerful instrument than coercion for driving the settlement and development of the country's North. While the average citizen fought a losing struggle with chronic shortage and meagre income during the years of "stagnation" (roughly 1965-85), newcomers to the North were protected by an excellent system of supply and were awarded a range of special benefits. In fact, by construing life in the North as a kind of sacrifice, the state could privilege northern workers twice over. Not only were they publicly celebrated as the avant-garde of socialist construction – civilizers and modernizers on the natural and cultural frontier – their purported sacrifices removed their material entitlements from scrutiny. Northerners thus enjoyed luxuries normally reserved for the Soviet nomenclatura: living in the "cognac zone," they flew to Moscow to shop for furs and perfume, took their holidays on the Bulgarian coast, and retired in their fifties to custom-built colonies in the Baltics.[4]

The farther from the Soviet metropolis northern workers settled, the greater the privileges that accrued. So it was that in Chukotka, a region on the farthest northeast periphery of Soviet territory, settler prosperity reached a fabled extreme. Isolation and distance in this place – as far as one can travel from Moscow and remain in Russia – have always shaped the experience of settling there in extraordinary ways. So remote is Chukotka that it remained outside the effective control of the tsarist state, and the organization of its indigenous reindeer herders into state farms was completed only in the 1950s, two decades after Soviet collectivization began (Znamenski 1999). Unlike in more accessible regions of the North, settlement there did not take the form of a gradual history. As late as 1930, 96 percent of those living in Chukotka were indigenous, most of them

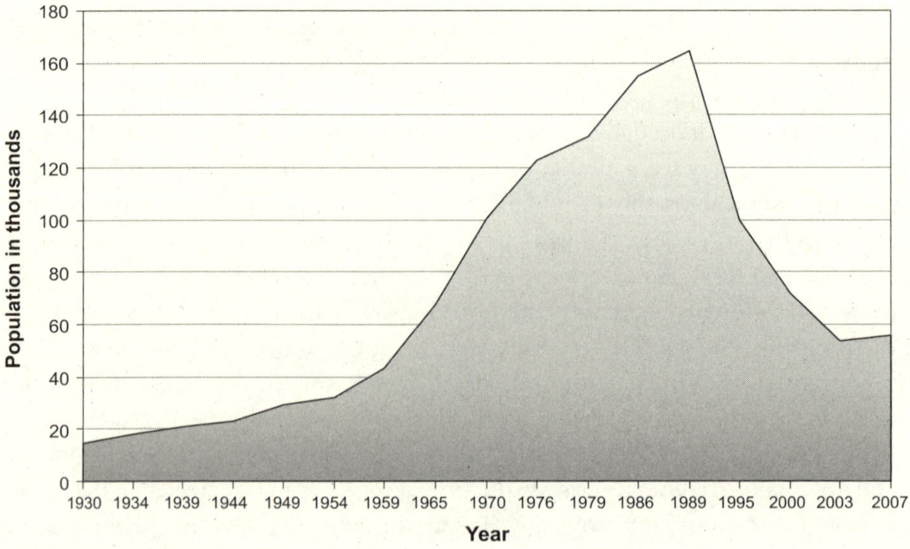

Figure 1.2 Total population in Chukotka, 1930-2007
Sources: Goskomstat CAO (1998); Goskomstat CAO (2001); Kotov et al. (1995); interviews with CAO administration officials, 2003

Chukchi. Only post-war mass settlement shifted the balance. Between 1959 and 1970, Chukotka boasted the highest rate of in-migration of any region in the Soviet Union (Kaiser 1994, 176-77), and by the time Soviet power collapsed in the late 1980s, native people comprised only 10 percent of the population (FSGS 2004) (see Figures 1.2 and 1.3). Underpinning this exceptionally concentrated wave of settlement was Chukotka's status as a kind of ultimate northern territory. Not only did it fall into the highest echelon in the Soviet ranking of north remoteness, which the state used to calculate the generosity of northern pay and other benefits, Chukotka's position on the very edge of the Soviet space, within sight of America, lent this place a particularly intoxicating aura of romance.

The Soviet state fell apart in 1991. The experience of daily life in post-Soviet Chukotka was so grimly in contrast to that of the years before this sudden fracture that we might think of this territory as preternaturally fated to extremes. The Soviet collapse extinguished the regime's belief in (and its capacity to support) mass settlement, and the exaggerated privileges of the newcomer were liquidated with merciless symmetry thereafter. In Russia's "era of transition," there was little sense of transition in Chukotka. Instead, the end of Soviet power seemed a conclusion. The entire edifice of modern industrial life fell apart, towns were abandoned, the northern supply system disintegrated, and people began, quite literally, to starve. The majority of the population fled to central Russia, so that now Chukotka had the highest rate of out-migration in the country. For a people whose

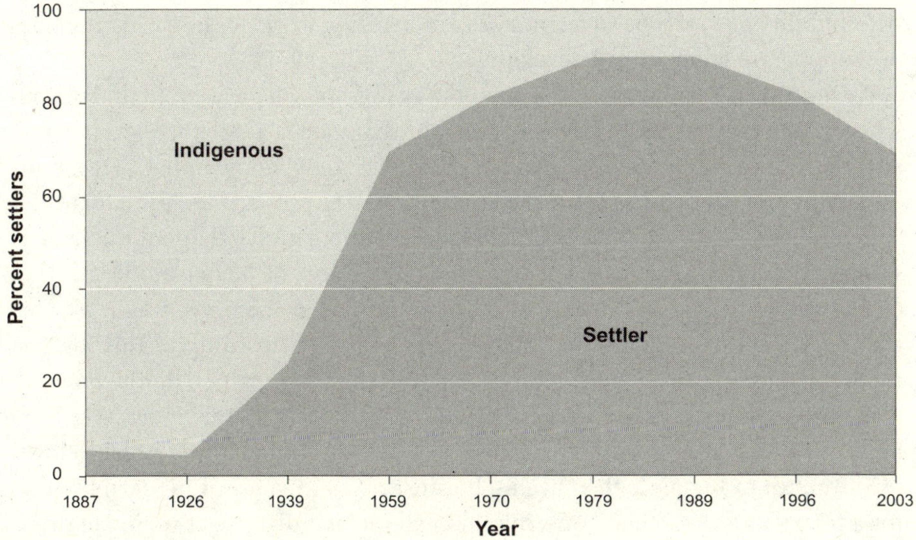

Figure 1.3 Settlers as a percentage of total population, 1887-2003
Source: Kotov et al. (1995); Gray (2005); interviews with CAO administration officials, 2003

sense of history was shaped by the teleological doctrine of technological and cultural progress, time seemed to reverse. For Chukotka's settlers, modernity had been an idea inseparable from the conveniences of central heating and air travel; life deprived of them felt like falling backward. And indeed, such was the case, for the energies of modernization – manifest in the institutions of acculturating and administrative change, technologies of transport and production, and optimism in the urban system – retreated out of this place, back into the core, like a tide.

That was the 1990s. By the time I began visiting Chukotka in 2001, the modernizing tide had come back in. In the way of this place, it had returned with exceptional and spectacular force, and the most "fallen behind" *(otstalyi)* of Russia's regions was leaping, in many senses, to its leading edge. At the turn of the twenty-first century, the forces of capital accumulation and selective westernization shaping urban Russian life, and defiantly redefining what it meant to be modern, suddenly chose Chukotka as their testing ground. The region became a stage on which oligarchic power contested presidential power, and where some of the marvellous profits of Russia's re-emerging resource economy came to rest. Just as outsiders had made of the local domain and all its inhabitants a construction site of modernization in the Soviet era, now a new generation of "experts" and "specialists" was arriving from distant cities to refashion local life. Perhaps this had little to do with the interests of local people, or even with the economic potential of this territory. It might even have been true that by calling this frantic project of change a "modernization," outsiders were doing more to transform their own distant lives than those of locals. But clearly, the event of their arrival confirmed once again the susceptibility of a peripheral territory in a globalizing world to the oscillating tides of that phenomenon we call development.

We must continually return to Chukotka's geographical position to understand its contemporary fate. The frame of thought that names a territory "peripheral" stigmatizes the local as fixed in place and left behind by innovation. Correspondingly, what or who comes from the centre bears the modern identity. Identities slip, however, and that is the problem and the opportunity shaping the lives of settlers in Chukotka. Because a doctrine and project of Soviet modernization emanating from Russia's metropolitan core produced them, we might assume that Soviet-era in-migrants were indivisible from it. According to this logic, if modernizations have an ephemeral presence in the Far North, so do their agents; if they did not leave as the Soviet modernization subsided, this must have been because poverty prevented them. Those who remain from that period, it follows, are loyal not to the *place* they live in, but instead to the *idea* of modern life that for a time was lodged there, offering them all the blandishments of Soviet privilege. These ideas are fundamental to much of the received wisdom informing policy discussions on the population problems of the Russian North today. Many commentators in Russia and abroad consider the settler presence in the post-Soviet North to be anomalous, a costly structural distortion inherited from another time.[5]

In reality, the newcomers of the Soviet era were *detached* from their modernizing roles and identities by the post-Soviet "demodernization." The exigencies of survival largely emasculated the old Soviet settler sense of self. This is a notion quite foreign to citizens of the West, for whom participation in a history of progress toward modernity (if only an ideational journey) has rarely been in question. Nevertheless, it happens. As James Ferguson (1999, 243) warns, globalization "creates new, up-to-date ways of not only connecting places, but also of bypassing and ignoring them." The demodernizing experience is relatively common outside the world's most powerful metropoli, and in those places where these recessive histories are freshest, we encounter people who once defined themselves as modern, and indeed as makers of modernity, now disconnected from such projects.

In Chukotka, the newcomers of the Soviet era derived a sense of themselves from their participation in a mission to "master the North" – *osvoenie severa.* Newcomers were prosperous, skilled in modern techniques and ideologies, hypermobile, and situated as much outside the North as in it. They lived a suspended and transient existence, in which the challenges of life in remote arctic conditions were ameliorated by importing a remarkable diversity of goods and conveniences from far away. But as that way of life disappeared, they either left the North (a difficult process) or were forced to survive without the scaffolding of colonial privilege.

As the decade of post-Soviet crisis ended, the arrival of a subsequent tide of modernizing change revealed the extent to which the experiences of survival have transformed Chukotka's settlers. As in the past, this newest modernization was animated by a binary logic of "newcomer" and "local," "modern" and "left behind," but now indigenous people were not alone in occupying the local category. Soviet-era migrants who still lived in the region had, to their own surprise, now joined natives in the ranks of the local and left behind. In this new era of outsider-led development, they now witnessed the projects of modernity with as much confusion and apprehension as, a generation earlier, their native counterparts in Chukotka had experienced. This uncomfortable, and quite new, sensation was a potent signal of passage over a vital threshold.

Stripped of the idea and the powers of colonial mission, these newcomers of the past had become the locals of the present. Having fallen out of the state of privileged suspension that Soviet policy had afforded them, they had settled into new lives in which, for most, getting by required a close attention to what support their immediate communities and landscapes could afford them. Yet, although the emasculation of their colonial identity was sudden, the accumulation of social capital and local knowledge in the North on which they based their survival was not; it long preceded the Soviet collapse and it continued after. A careful examination of how, over time and through changing historical circumstances, these in-migrants gradually shifted their loyalties away from the ideas and practices of outsiderness and came to root their lives in local, northern places, produces a picture of the settling process. This finding is profoundly important to our understanding of the contemporary Russian North: up to now, social scientists, and by extension state officials and planners, have argued that irrevocable senses of belonging are the preserve of the indigenous and métis populations of the Far North. But in recent years, increasingly ambitious attempts to depopulate these regions by removing the in-migrants of the Soviet era have encountered popular resistance.[6] I hope this book will supply an explanation.

A Case for the Settler

Addressing a major conference of social scientists in 2004, British anthropologist Tim Ingold offered a "Manifesto for the Anthropology of the North" (2004), challenging the profession to engage with all residents of the region. He urged his colleagues to examine how *all* people of the North "are linked to landscapes and localities, in the formation of personal and collective identities." Ingold's challenge was certainly authoritative within the profession, but not singular. The same year, *Sibirica* published the proceedings of a roundtable meeting of Russian and Western anthropologists in Halle, Germany, proposing a critical reassessment of Siberian ethnography. One of its key recommendations is worth quoting in full: "This idea – that the social anthropology of Siberia should not only be limited to the indigenous peoples, that other categories of the population should also become objects of study, that even urban populations in Siberian cities should become a subject of social anthropological research to no less a degree than villages and nomadic groups – ran as a red thread through many of the discussions" (Gray, Vakhtin, and Schweitzer 2003, 204).

It might appear self-evident that anthropology should show interest in the full range of actors in any social field. Yet, in social investigations of the post-Soviet North, this is not so. Its non-indigenous population is rarely examined in any depth. In fact, the possibility that a settler population with lasting attachments to the Arctic might have emerged from among the many migrants who moved north in the Soviet era has until now never been seriously discussed.[7] Instead, social scientists have bypassed the northern industrial town on the way to the native village, producing over the past decade a rich and varied body of research on the indigenous experience. No doubt, the assumed transience of settlers, in contrast to the rootedness of native people, raises the question of their long-term importance to life in northern communities. The two most common terms in currency – *priezzhii* (newcomer) for settlers and *mestnyi* (local) for natives – reproduce the idea that there are two kinds of people in the North, the recently arrived, and by implication, the soon to leave, and the eternal native, who will always remain. Moreover, Siberian ethnography is blinkered by its traditional tendency to judge human phenomena through the prism of ethnicity and to propose ethnic difference as the sole basis of northern identities.

Responding to this imbalance, Otto Habeck (2005b), in his introduction to a recent edited volume on identity in Siberia, urges an emerging generation of anthropologists to move beyond the "primacy of the 'ethnic.'" The ethnicity fixation in northern research certainly helps to explain its traditional choice of subjects: with our eye on the ethnic, we miss the settler.[8] Aware of the diverse and diasporic origins of this population, we assume that, whereas native settlements are the site of fairly bounded cultures with detectable senses of collectivity and community, for settlers, close affinity with community and the land are mere ideas, remnants of nostalgia residing in a mythic village past on the Russian "mainland" – the *materik*. In the absence of ethnographic scrutiny, it is only natural that settler populations become reduced by default to aggregate formations, inchoate accumulations of transient labour, almost, dare we say it, without culture (although settlers are nevertheless somehow presumed to maintain hegemonic neo-colonial positions within northern societies).

We might have expected the collapse of Soviet ideology to have stimulated a reassessment of the "suitable subject" in northern ethnography. However, in this matter there has in fact been a remarkable continuity with the past. The entrance of foreign anthropologists into previously closed Russian field sites and, moreover, their collaboration with Russian colleagues, certainly represented a fundamental break from the Soviet ethnographic tradition. As Habeck (2005b) and Gray, Vakhtin, and Schweitzer (2003) observe, Soviet preoccupations with "traditional" cultural forms, problems of ethnogenesis, the categorization of fixed etnosy, and the cataloguing of disappearing material and spiritual culture were superseded after the collapse by a dedication to *contemporary* issues in indigenous life, which naturally repositioned anthropologists as more activist and partisan figures within their respective ethnographic sites (Slezkine 1991; Schindler 1991; Basilov 1994). But, whereas Soviet methods and ideologies were challenged, the Soviet ethnographic tradition, shaped by its early founders Shternberg, Jochelson, and Bogoraz, and elaborated by such eminent scholars as Kreinovich, Popov, Prokof'ev, Dolgikh, Potapov, Bromlei, and Okladnikov, apparently succeeded in configuring the contemporary North as an *indigenous* social field.

Consequently, in the first post-Soviet decade, when the output of well-funded Western social scientists far outpaced that of Russia's own academic community, interest in the indigenous subject monopolized the field. Among the most prodigious specializations were investigations of reindeer husbandry and herding cultures (Vitebsky 2005; D. Anderson 2000; Golovnev and Osherenko 1999; Stammler 2004), gender relations in indigenous communities (Rethmann 2001; Vitebsky and

Wolfe 2001; M.M. Balzer 1992), property rights and indigenous entitlements (Fondahl 1995, 1998; Osherenko 1995; Schindler 1994), rural and indigenous political mobilization (Gray 2005; Wilson 2002), nationalism and ethnic identity (Argounova 2001; Balzer and Vinokurova 1996; Grant 1995), shamanism and indigenous religious revival (Vaté 2003; Vitebsky 2002; M.M. Balzer 1999), and postcolonial discourse and the meaning of indigenous tradition (Habeck 2005a; Ssorin-Chaikov 2003; Schindler 1997; Krupnik and Vakhtin 1997). This field of literature, though defined by a common geographic referent, is already too broad to review in detail. But, in the region with which this study is concerned – Chukotka – the domination of indigenous studies (or more accurately a lack of interest in the non-indigenous subject) is equally apparent. Anna Kerttula's (2000) fieldwork in the late perestroika period led to the first monograph on post-Soviet Chukotka, in which "newcomers" in the coastal community of Sireniki serve as a foil for her description of Yup'ik and Chukchi lifeways. Dire socio-economic conditions in Chukotka's indigenous communities were the focus of several studies, including those by Alexandr Pika (1996), Harald Finkler (1995), and Joëlle Robert-Lamblin (1993). Particular interest has attended the uneven record of indigenous "cultural revival" and indigenous politics, evident in articles by Igor Krupnik and Nikolai Vakhtin (1997), Debra Schindler (1997), Patty Gray (2000), and Petra Rethmann (2004), and culminating in Gray's 2005 book assessing native political resistance in the 1990s.[9]

One of the most powerful contributions to arise from the study of Russia's northern peoples concerns the way in which native belonging is situated in practical skills of land use. This vein of research has also strongly shaped our perceptions of the settler presence in the North. Accounts of indigenous ways of life point to landscape, and in particular activities such as hunting and travelling within it, as a primary constituent of personal and collective identity, in a manner consistent with writing on belonging and landscape in other regions (Brody 1981, 2000; Nuttall 1991; Vitebsky 1992). Here, practical interactions with local environments decisively constitute the concepts of "northern belonging" and "indigenous homeland," which find their articulation in descriptions of "ecological senses of belonging" based on practices of "dwelling on the land" or "skills of dwelling" (Ingold 2000; D. Anderson 2000). When native people's interests are threatened, they often invoke political claims of "indigeneity," which derive their power from traditions of local interaction with a specific territory, practices of harvesting local resources, and the threat of cultural failure if that bond is severed.

Nothing therefore arouses our skepticism of northern settlers as a viable object of study as forcefully as their purported lack of connection to the land. European incomers are invariably portrayed in this way, as aliens to the tundra, people who, if they move out of their urban environments at all, do so to harvest natural resources in a utilitarian and short-termist fashion. Anna Kerttula (2000, 29) describes settlers as "a group devoid of cultural or spiritual connection to the village and its surrounding environment. They were the perpetual outsiders." Alexander King (2002), drawing from research in neighbouring Kamchatka, posits a dichotomy of native Koryak and settler Russian perceptions of nature: for settlers, nature is wild, an emptiness, an alternative to civilization, whereas for the Koryaki, nature is itself a civilization, marked and known through practical engagement. According to King, because settlers essentialize nature in romantic discourses, they can never understand their natural surroundings as a source of identity and belonging in a fully native way. King himself connects his arguments to earlier northern ethnographies (Nuttall 1992; D. Anderson 2000; Ingold 2000), which identify in their native subjects a specifically indigenous manner of belonging in their homelands, landscapes they imbue with personhood, so that humans exist in a mutual neo-social entanglement with the mountains, streams, reindeer, and trees around them.[10] In Chukotka, Patty Gray employed the contrasting environments of the northern city (Anadyr) and the tundra as a framework for understanding the differences between settler and indigenous perceptions of nature. Gray (2005, 141) remarks, "Incomers, by contrast [with natives] longed to be anchored to one site and to walk among monstrous and immovable structures." According to Gray, they viewed the tundra in purely utilitarian terms: "incomers saw the tundra as a source of mineral wealth, or as a vast 'backyard' for weekend hunting or fishing."

These accounts provide an impressively fine-grained examination of the indigenous experience. But we should not expect to find ethnographic depth in their descriptions of the "newcomer." That is not their authors' desire; by enlisting a non-indigenous presence as a kind of counterfoil, they succeed instead in more clearly defining the true object of their attention – the native figure. In the process, this technique flattens and ultimately reifies the settler identity. In the way of ethnographic fieldwork, anthropologists rely on what their closest sources tell them, not only about themselves, but also about the kinds of people they define themselves against. Patty Gray, for example, cultivated relationships within the indigenous intelligentsia of Chukotka's capital in order to develop her very thorough 2005 study of indigenous political mobilization in the region. It is precisely from members of this community that I later heard the most vociferous denunciations of the *priezzhii mentalitet* (newcomer mentality), the essence of which Gray records in her writing. These individuals openly shared their enmity toward the settler presence in Chukotka (which I usually failed to detect among non-elite natives in the villages), grounded in the belief that Russians lacked a meaningful affinity with the northern landscape. But as Gray (2005) observes, one of the features of modern life in Chukotka is that so many indigenous people no longer move over the tundra and sea, and now confine themselves to urban spaces. This is often particularly the case for members of Chukotka's native intelligentsia, whose professional lives (and tastes) are far removed from those domains in which they might observe settlers in direct contact with the land. So why should we invest in them the authority to speak for an experience and a way of life that is not theirs? That would be like asking Russians in the arctic town about reindeer herding: the answers would be stereotypical. What would we learn about settlers if we finally went directly to them, asked them, watched them, and lived with them in their adopted northern settings?

This was the task I set myself. My purpose was to consider the experience of settlers not as the embodied agents of modernizing change, nor as the "perpetual outsiders" that indigenous-centred accounts purport them to be, but as people with a measure of sovereignty from the colonial histories in which they participated. The "settler experience," after all, has been one not only of privileged inclusion, but also of brutal exclusion. The tidal patterns of modernizing change have, in the end, generated among settlers a rather cynical regard for the promises of modernity in the Far North, alongside the ability to draw sustenance from local sources of security when distant ones have disappeared. As people charting a course through the vagaries of the modernizing cycle, settlers have responded in their own individual ways. One of the clearest benefits of this exercise, therefore, is the challenge it presents to the monotypic rubric the "newcomer" in the North presently inhabits. It permits us to understand the diversity of identities – of lifestyles, attachments to place, plans for the future – that breathe with life beneath the conflated idea of this population.

Settlement in Context

Chukotka is a territory roughly the size of Sweden and Norway combined, culminating at the farthest northeast corner of the Eurasian landmass and separated by the Bering Strait from Alaska, a distance of forty kilometres at its narrowest (see Figure 1.1). Straddling the Arctic Circle, its warmest coast bordering the northernmost fringe of the Pacific Ocean, Chukotka has a severe climate. Annual average temperatures range from minus 4 to minus 14 Celsius, and winter temperatures reach minus 45 on the coasts and minus 60 inland. The eastern coast, on the Bering Sea, is the windiest region in Russia, with average winds above 55 kilometres per hour for almost six months a year and annual storms that bring sustained winds of over 140 kilometres per hour. Chukotka's modern capital, Anadyr, lies on the mouth of the Anadyr River at the edge of the Bering Sea, and at 65 degrees north is roughly on the same latitude as Fairbanks (Alaska) and Oulu (Sweden), but farther north than Reykjavik (Iceland), Nuuk (Greenland), and Iqaluit (Canada). Low mountain ranges, dominated by the Aniusk-Chukotka uplands, which separate the Pacific and Arctic Ocean basins, cover most of Chukotka's territory. The entire region is within the permafrost zone, tundra and transitional northern taiga cover the landscape, and though some hardy varieties of cabbage, potato, and onion will grow in open soil in the southern interior, farther north and along the coasts, heated greenhouses are required to support vegetable growing during the short two-month summer (Kotov, 1995).

Although the Bering Strait region has witnessed successive human migrations dating back to 70,000 BC, and the Chukotka peninsula has been home to the Chukchi and Yup'ik for at least thirty-five hundred years, Europeans appeared in this territory only in the seventeenth century. Semen Dezhnev, a Cossack explorer, reached Chukotka by ship in 1649 and established a fortified camp for overwintering (an *ostrog*) on the upper Anadyr River, in the territory of the Chuwan Yukagir. Although his successors attempted to establish a permanent presence in order to collect fur tribute *(iasak)* from the native population, robust resistance from inland and coastal Chukchi, and the region's acute isolation from the closest Russian settlements, resulted in a century of violent setbacks and periodic withdrawal. Indeed, although the so-called Chukchi Wars (1729-64) visited a series of Cossack invasions of genocidal intent on the Chukchi, Yup'ik, and Koryak populations of the region, they cost far more to the state than they yielded in tribute. After successive sackings and razings, the Anadyrsk ostrog was finally abandoned in 1694. Thereafter, in an effort to bring peace to the territory (and in admission of the impossibility of subjugating such a remote and pugnacious foe), Catherine II granted the Chukchi both immunity from iasak and a unique status among northern peoples: "not completely dependent" subjects of the empire. The subsequent withdrawal of Russian forces compromised their allies the Yukagiry and created an inland vacuum into which the reindeer-herding Chukchi quickly expanded. Only in the middle decades of the nineteenth century did Russian missionaries and settlers again appear in the region, and a community named Markovo was established on the banks of the Anadyr River ten kilometres from the old Anadyrsk ostrog. By this time, permanent Russian settlements existed along the Kolyma River, to the west of present-day Chukotka, and by the 1880s, roughly four hundred Russian and métis settlers were living in a handful of settlements along the Anadyr (Dikov 1989; Vdovin 1965; Znamenski 1999).[11]

Chukotka was never fully part of the Russian empire; the semi-sovereign status of its native peoples was only one indication of the tenuous influence of the imperial state in this remote territory. During the eighteenth and nineteenth centuries, the Chukchi reindeer-herding culture reached a modern apogee of influence and productivity on the lands that constitute present-day Chukotka. In their deer, nomadic herders possessed almost all the necessities for life on the tundra; trade with coastal peoples supplied other requirements (the fat of marine mammals, walrus tusk, whalebone). Living in a harsh and unpredictable climate, they moved across vast distances in response to changing weather and fluctuating pasture health. For the inland way of life, these qualities assured a degree of resilience, and indeed prosperity, far greater than the first Russian settlers enjoyed. The herding economy produced a more reliable and nutritious supply of food, and a fuller complement of animal parts and furs, than the sedentary trading, hunting, and fishing lifestyle of the Russians and their métis descendants living in riverside settlements. The immobility of these settlements was a matter of weakness. Because their inhabitants were fixed in place, when arctic conditions affected the abundance of game and fish, and the Chukchi failed to visit them, they starved. Even at the turn of the twenty-first century, when the ethnographer Waldemar Bogoras (1904-9, 95) visited Chukotka, their vulnerability was evident: "The possession of reindeer herds makes the material life of the nomadic Chukchi more stable, especially when compared with the precarious subsistence of most of the fishing and seal-hunting tribes in this neighbourhood, not excepting even the Russians and Russianised natives."

Because of this, the gradual Russification of indigenous cultures evident in Siberia and other parts of the North did not occur in Chukotka; instead, it was the Chukchi who acculturated the Russians. Settler women married into nomadic herding families, at least partly to secure a reliable source of food and skins for their sedentary relatives. The Chukchi language served as a regional lingua franca, underpinning the trading economy in which Russians, Chukchi, Eveny, Yukagiry, Koryaki, and coastal Yup'ik participated (Krupnik 1993). Russian traders further west on the Kolyma pleaded with Chukchi herders to patronize their trading fairs, in competition with European and American trading posts on the coasts. And Russian Orthodox Christianity failed almost completely to penetrate Chukchi territory, where shamanist beliefs reigned until well after the arrival of the Soviets.

At the close of the nineteenth century, whaling ships, gold prospectors, and fur traders coming from Canada and the United States shifted the linguistic and economic centre of gravity still farther from Russian influence. When an overland journey from the imperial capital to the Russian settlements on the Kolyma still took years, whaling ships along Chukotka's coasts were hiring indigenous whalers and guides, and American traders were establishing a network of commercial posts. A pan-Bering whaling economy developed in the late nineteenth century, reaching as far east as the Mackenzie Delta in Canada's North. The US dollar and the English language soon became new media of exchange along the coasts, encouraging Chukchi herders to realign their trade away from the annual Russian markets inland. Thereafter, English-speaking agents monopolized Chukotka's entire commercial trade in furs until they were pushed out by Soviet authorities in the 1920s (Znamenski 1999).

Not until 1923, when Soviet power was finally consolidated across Chukotka, could Russians begin to challenge the economic and cultural autonomy of the reindeer Chukchi. This process was slow at first, lagging behind other regions of the North, and the European population remained a negligible minority for decades after the Revolution (it was 4 percent in 1930). Collectivization was completed only in 1949, and it took a further decade to fully appropriate the Chukchi herds and sedentarize their owners in collective farms *(kolkhozy)*. During that time, many herders successfully resisted Soviet authorities by driving their herds deep into isolated areas, and they were captured only when secret service troops (the Narodny Komissariat Vnutrennikh Del or NKVD) and warplanes were sent to suppress them.[12] Nevertheless, as the state gained the upper hand, the powers of mobility over this isolated landscape that the nomadic Chukchi once possessed passed into the hands of European in-migrants.

Mobility was the hallmark and the instrument of domination on this landscape. Just as it gave the Chukchi the advantage over Russian settlers in the nineteenth century, the power of movement was vital for the consolidation of Soviet authority and settler privilege in the twentieth century. In the early years, steamships and motorized riverboats, powerful all-terrain vehicles (*vezdekhody*), and ultimately airplanes brought cultural commissars deep into Chukchi territory. Later, the technologies of transport supported the collectivization of herds and the sedentarization of herding families in new Soviet villages. Finally, as Soviet transport matured, and remoteness no longer presented an impediment to the flow of goods and people into and within Chukotka, a new generation of Soviet settlers assumed complete administrative and cultural mastery in Chukchi territory. Chukotka's nomadic people, whose mobility on the tundra a generation earlier guaranteed their economic and cultural dominance, now became dependent on a new kind of settler, more mobile than any the territory had yet seen.

Under Soviet administration, Chukotka's native population was targeted for "cultural enlightenment" and enlisted to support industrialization, supplying Russian settlements with reindeer and sea-mammal meat, fish, and furs from state farms. To maximize their contributions, Soviet authorities implemented a series of "rationalizing" measures, beginning with the sedentarization of nomadic herders up until the early 1950s and culminating in the mid-1960s with policies of amalgamation *(ukrupnenie)* that merged settlements into larger villages (Dikov 1989). In the process, a number of traditional coastal settlements along the Bering Strait were liquidated, partly due to their location in a sensitive border region near the Soviet Union's Cold War enemy across the water. As the traditional herding and hunting way of life was reorganized under state control, native people lost ownership and managerial authority over their reindeer and all other forms of indigenous property to settler specialists. Dispossessed natives became state employees under the supervision of settlers, and their children were taught by settler teachers in village schools, many of which were residential. One of the more devastating consequences of these changes was the systematic and intentional immobilization of the nomadic Chukchi. Now their movements were managed and facilitated by European outsiders, on whom they came to rely for survival. The Sovietized herding system destroyed the self-sufficient clan-centred mode of nomadism by separating male herders on the tundra from their female counterparts, who now lived and worked in the villages. The successor to the herding clan – the mostly male herding brigade – now required a constant supply of food, clothing, medicines, and instruction from the village centre. Naturally, the skills of the settler specialist were vital to maintaining these arrangements, and Russian helicopter pilots, vezdekhod drivers, and *kolkhoz* managers ferried herders from tundra to village, supplied the brigades, and collected the meat.

As in the Soviet North generally, the industrialization of Chukotka progressed in two phases: by forced labour until 1955 and by voluntary labour thereafter. In 1941 (well after the emergence of slave labour camps in less isolated parts of the country), prisoners of the gulag system began to mine uranium, tin, tungsten, and gold, and built the port towns of Egvekinot and Pevek. After Stalin's death and the subsequent dismantling of the prisoner-labour system, Soviet authorities resorted to a regime of "northern benefits" *(severnye l'goty)* to incentivize northern residence and attract voluntary labour to Chukotka. Incentives included high pay, long holidays, early retirement, and, with time, far better living conditions in northern towns than in central Russia (Yanovskii 1969).

The mass settlement of Chukotka was concentrated and intense. During roughly three decades, beginning in 1960 when the geographic organization of northern benefits was formalized in state law and ending with Soviet collapse in 1991, the population rose by over four times, from 41,000 to a peak of 164,700 (see Figure 1.2). Not included in the peak population figure were large numbers of military personnel stationed in permanent bases throughout the territory. Although many settlers came to administer and teach Chukotka's indigenous peoples, these projects of cultural "lifting up" actually comprised only a small fraction of the work the growing settler population was recruited to carry out. The villages remained a predominantly indigenous domain, whereas most in-migrants settled in Chukotka's capital, Anadyr, and a rapidly growing constellation of district centres and industrial "towns of the urban type," where they worked in mining and geological exploration, marine and air transport, construction and food production, communications and the media, retail and distribution, and the security services. Supported by a complex and vastly expensive system of transport and supply bringing goods to the territory by ship from the eastern terminus of the Soviet railway in Vladivostok and by air from all corners of the Soviet Union, they enjoyed most of the perquisites of urban Soviet life. Yet, so remote did Chukotka remain, and so totally reliant on sea and air transport to maintain its growing urban population, that it could well have been an island. Indeed, that is precisely how its settler residents viewed their position on the edge of Soviet territory, and so they called the rest of the country "the mainland" – materik.

The territory remained a subordinate unit – an "autonomous okrug" – of Magadan Oblast until shortly after the collapse of the Soviet Union in 1991.[13] Then, local Communist Party elites led by the Chukchi head of government, Vladimir Etylin, grasped the spirit of federal devolution we know as the "parade of sovereignties"

Figure 1.4 Soviet Far North
Sources: Slavin (1967); Heleniak (1999)

by declaring Chukotka's secession from Magadan. Although Etylin's leadership held promise for the fulfillment of indigenous political hopes in Chukotka, his opposition to President Yeltsin's reformist administration soon dashed them. In late 1991, Yeltsin appointed a non-indigenous ally, Aleksandr Nazarov, as the reformist head of administration (a role later formalized as governor). Nazarov effectively ran the okrug administration from 1992 until 2000. Under his leadership, Chukotka underwent a severe crisis of living standards and witnessed an exodus of skilled labour, the failure of shipping deliveries upon which the okrug's isolated communities relied, and the mass liquidation of state enterprises. Nazarov's autocratic and corrupt administration simply compounded Chukotka's crisis. Federal loans to renew the gold-mining sector evaporated from administration accounts, and Nazarov introduced a virtual barter economy by withholding budget funds transferred from Moscow. By the late 1990s, Chukotka was suffering through a major humanitarian disaster, with starvation in the settlements, high suicide rates, and epidemic alcoholism (even while Nazarov supported a professional football team in Moscow). Little news of these dire conditions reached beyond Chukotka's borders, because access to the okrug for Russians and foreigners alike was strictly controlled, and independent organizations, many based within the indigenous community, were harassed or co-opted by Nazarov's administration and other state structures (Krupnik and Vakhtin 2002; Gray 2005). The region was trapped in a vicious circle: crisis fuelled out-migration, but out-migration only deepened

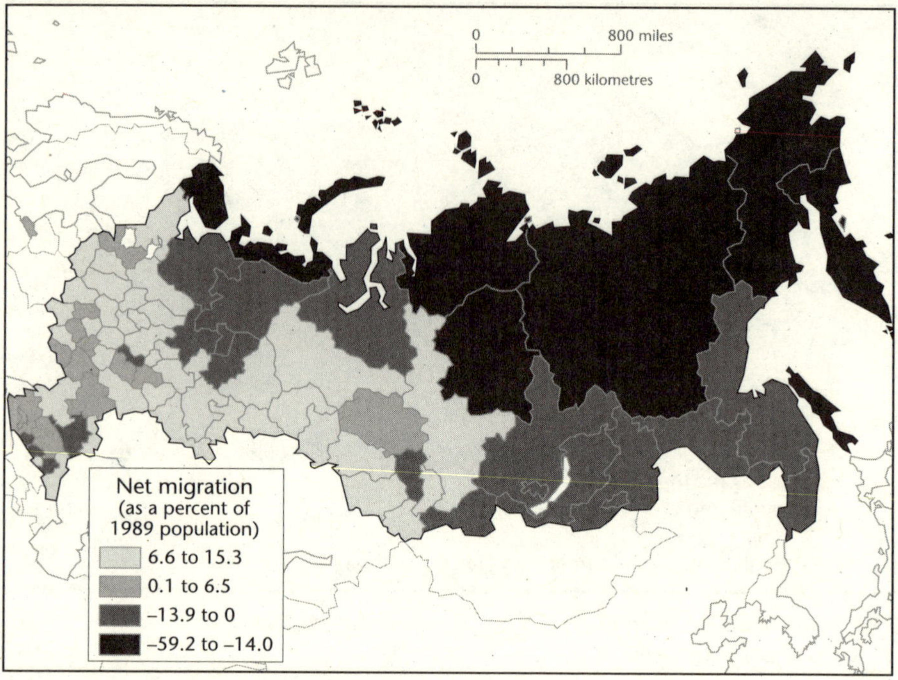

Figure 1.5 Net migration by region in Russia, 1989-2002
Source: Heleniak (2003) (used with permission of the author)

the crisis. By 2000, so many had left that Chukotka's population had dropped by over half, to seventy-five thousand (FSGS 2004), and among the eighty-nine regions of the Russian Federation, only in war-torn Chechnya were living standards worse ("Annual Ranking" 2000).

The post-Soviet crisis underlined Chukotka's marginal position, peripheral to the projects and attentions of the emergent Russia. The departure of so many skilled settlers constituted the draining away of Moscow's power and interest in the Far North: this was a de facto retreat of the state. But the Russian centre was not so thoroughly dismantled during this decade as it seemed at the time. Federalist devolution, the privatization of public assets, and the ruin of state institutions and prestige simply masked the ferment of countervailing energies, which by the end of the 1990s sat prepared for a new centralizing *dirigisme* under the leadership of President Putin. To revitalize the powers of the federal state, Putin of necessity confronted a group in whose hands wealth and influence had concentrated in spectacular abundance under his predecessor: Russia's new class of oligarch industrialists. Beginning in 2000, the movement of a large number of Putin's protégés into federal power structures rapidly eroded the oligarchs' ability to shape policy at the highest levels and thereby secure political protection for their large but vulnerable business empires. Putin proceeded to persecute the oligarchy with *realpolitik* determination, penalizing any kind of political resistance by stripping its leading members of their holdings and forcing several of them into exile. Under siege at the centre, their lines of access to power crumbling, Russia's oligarchic structures began to search elsewhere for bases of support and protection. This triggered an oligarchic flight to the regions and, in parallel with President Putin's consolidation of power in Moscow, the capture of regional administrations became a defining feature of life across the Russian North. Chukotka – depopulated, isolated, and desperately impoverished – naturally presented an easy target. Chukotka had once offered a paradigmatic mode of life in the Soviet North – that of the hyperprivileged northern settler. Now, the arrival of oligarchic money and power in the post-Soviet era subsequently thrust Chukotka to the leading edge of a new era of northern development, another chapter in the tidal cycle of change.

In December 2000, one of Russia's wealthiest oligarchs, Roman Abramovich, was elected governor of Chukotka, initiating an administrative revolution alongside an ambitious and strikingly expensive program of modernization. This election, in which a young and wealthy businessman from Moscow moved into high political office on the Russian periphery, was the first in a series of landslide victories for resource magnates in other regions, including Taimyr and Evenkia. In all three cases, the character of reform followed the oligarchic pattern of conflating public administration with corporate institutions and methods, so that the divisions between government and the oligarchic companies that funded and animated them were blurred. In Chukotka, Governor Abramovich enlisted the resources of his Moscow-based oil company, Sibneft, to fill the absence left by the region's failed public administration and moribund economy. In his first five-year term in office, Abramovich's Sibneft and other allied companies funded virtually the entire regional budget, while his team carried out a program of complete social and economic renovation, promising to "return an acceptable way of life" to the region (Abramovich 2001). The capital, Anadyr, became the focus of an extraordinary rebuilding exercise, involving thousands of Turkish, Canadian, and Muscovite shift workers. Abramovich's rural development programs resurrected the indigenous economy by returning to the Soviet state farm system, while rebuilding villages, some in their entirety. To alleviate the burden of isolation, the aviation and the shipping-supply systems were revived, complete with subsidized helicopter flights linking remote villages with district towns and the capital.

This most recent modernization was, as in the Soviet past, a campaign of reformative investment whose energies originated in a distant metropolis. And, like past modernizations, Abramovich's project was vested with the interests and preferences of a new generation of newcomers, people of the city sent north to shape local realities according to their own interpretations of modernity. Young and well-educated "experts" and "specialists" left the Moscow headquarters of Sibneft and sister companies to staff Chukotka's new regional administration. They assumed leadership roles within all the key reforming agencies and institutions, and proceeded to recruit a second and third layer of subordinate specialists from outside the North to support them. But, as in any project of development, the arrangements of authority and the nature of investment in fact elevated the "modernizer" at a much greater speed than the "modernized." So it was that for this modernizing cadre, and for Abramovich himself, the remaking of Chukotka was foremost a project of self-transformation. If this region became a vast philanthropic canvas upon which Abramovich and his followers could model a new way of life, their efforts were at heart self-directed. At the very least, Chukotka furnished a site on which Abramovich could shed his robber baron reputation and visibly clarify his loyalty to the Putin regime, which by 2004 had become a requirement of his own survival.

Outsider-led, technocratic in its culture, and neo-Soviet in its specific visions of progress, Abramovich's campaign did not include Chukotka's established settlers within its vision of reform. Yesterday's modernizers were the "left behind" of today. As Abramovich's followers saw it, the remaining settler population and the industrial settlements they inhabited constituted a final remnant of the failed and discredited Soviet brand of development (*osvoenie*). By extension, they believed that settlers stood in the way of a new, more efficient, and more sustainable mode of development. Living in a region with no functioning economy, so remote that the cost of living was the highest in Russia, settler-modernizers of the Soviet era had now become a kind of human ballast – in the words of Abramovich's senior planners, "the debris of the past" *(ostatki proshlego)*. Their ties to the North were no help. Their participation in Soviet history simply marked them as remnants of the past and suggested their incapacity to participate in modernizing projects of a new era.

So it was that Abramovich's followers saw modernization as a project of two parallel objectives: building a new Chukotka for those irrevocably *of* the North (native Chukchi and Yup'ik), while cutting the costs of development by removing those northerners who, in the modernizers' view, had no home there. The new administration developed an ambitious strategy to resettle large numbers of non-indigenous residents to central Russian cities, while liquidating a series of "non-viable" settlements *(besperspektivnye poselki)*. To reach a sustainable number, Chukotka's population of seventy-five thousand at the time of Abramovich's 2000 election would have to fall (his planners predicted) to roughly thirty-five thousand (the proportion of settlers to natives thus falling from 80 to 57 percent). Predictably, many settlers' own life plans differed quite radically from the role Abramovich's followers assigned to them. They contested the very terms of modernity, resisted their objectification as the human debris of a failed (Soviet) project, and, most forcefully of all, expressed their attachments to the North while pointing out the absurdity of "returning" to a life elsewhere.

This, more or less, is the history of recent settlement in Chukotka; these are the circumstances that first brought migrants there in large numbers and that have structured their lives to the present day. My narrative returns to this history in detail, teasing out the consequences for settler senses of self and place of such a tumultuous and disorienting ride through time. Indeed, the chapters of this book follow the structure of a chronology, because at the centre of its concern is the progress of settler identities through a series of discrete historical experiences. But, before setting off, I wish to provide some critical frames of understanding, with which a reader can begin to consider the settler experience in Chukotka in more universal terms.

Settlement in Theory

I explained in the opening pages how recent critiques of Siberian ethnography, and indeed circumpolar ethnography in general, are issuing the salutary challenge to broaden the scope and to attend to the full diversity of northern populations. This is an important task, since it is precisely the examination of the *non-indigenous* experience in the Russian North that can help to mature and deepen this still nascent school of study. There are three distinct bodies of theoretical ferment within the larger anthropological discipline into which the figure and history of the settler in the North affords an entrée. The first relates to our understanding of modernization, a notion of progress that, under examination, fragments into a mass of questions on the subjectivity of modern and left-behind identities, the uses of the modernization discourse in the battle for domination, and the role of geographies of power and powerlessness in sustaining the "modernizing cycle." The second ties into the debate on the nature of the Soviet everyday and the powers of the Soviet state occasioned by the vastly greater resources now available for producing social histories of Soviet life. In short, this is the revisionist questioning of hitherto dominant conceptions of Soviet statehood. The third area of theory moves over some of the most notoriously labyrinthine territory of anthropological inquiry: the problem of identity. Let us consider each of these in more detail.

Modernization

This book could be read as an examination of successive campaigns of modernization and their human effects in a discrete northern territory. Unexamined, the term "modernization" operates as lexical shorthand for the diverse and numerous projects outsiders have imported into northern Russia's local contexts, whether in the Soviet era or more recently. Under scrutiny, however, "modernization" pulls us toward its origins in an evolutionary paradigm, one that attaches to the imported manager a modern status and situates the local way of life further down a single continuum of progress. This study might also be considered an investigation of localism, a system of beliefs and a way of life that resist the authority of outsider knowledge within the local domain and cherish forms of accumulated knowledge adapted to the immediate setting. As these two points of view meet, we find both the idea of modernity and the nature of modernization subject to starkly contrasting interpretations. Thus, what in recent years the followers of Governor Abramovich might have considered modernizing projects of bringing up to date, established settlers understood as competing, and even *regressive,* practices. Although the word *modernizatsiia* (modernization) circulated in all Chukotka's social domains after Abramovich's arrival, across local kitchen tables it often carried ironic and morally ambivalent meanings.

I can live with these contradictions. The power of this term lies precisely in its ambiguity, and its multiple meanings invite us to a closer inspection. Even at its surface, as an unquestioned rhetoric, modernization evokes a long history of social renovation and class conflict in Russia. Indeed, after the (apparent) rejection of Soviet ideology, Russians still remain steeped in teleological interpretations of the world. The fixedness of concepts such as *kul'tura* (culture), *obrazovanie* (education), *vospitanie* (cultivating or raising), and osvoenie (an imperial brand of mastery) is the product of a centuries-long self-perception of peripherality, of learning from the West, of challenging Western power on its own terms, and then wilfully diverging from standards of Western civilization.[14] This is perhaps why Russian literary and popular discourses betray an obsession with Russia's borderline position between Europe and Asia, and about its unsteady relationship with the West. Cycles of modernization and reform, punctuated by stagnation and backwardness, are *emic* Russian characterizations of their own history, particularly since Peter I. The very persistence of the Russian aspiration to modernity has solidified ideas of backwardness, progress, and falling behind within a mythical structure.

We should not view this as a purely Russian development. In his ethnography of industrial decline in Zambia, James Ferguson (1999, 14) underlines the universal appeal of the modernization idea: "the myth of modernization (no less than any other myth) gives form to an understanding of the world, providing a set of categories and premises that continue to shape people's experiences and interpretations of their lives." Paradoxically, in contemporary Chukotka, even those disadvantaged by a present-day modernization were, as the modernizers of an earlier era, still caught in its mythical grip. Those settlers who rejected the intrusions of the "expert" outsider often simultaneously narrated hierarchies of modern and backward in their characterizations of town and settlement, Russian and Chukchi, and the "cultured" and "cultureless." In a case of "nested orientalism" (Ssorin-Chaikov 2003), the targets of modernizing change perpetuated the teleological mentality of which they themselves were victims. The modernization myth itself did not trouble them; their only argument was with the possibility that they occupied the same primitive rung of development as their indigenous neighbours.

As an optimistic logic of progress, therefore, the idea of "modernization" opens our eyes to inequality, to differences in status between the *peredovoi* and the otstalyi (the "leading edge" and the "fallen behind"). The spectacular separation in cultural and economic power between Russia's metropoles and its provinces is perennial, an imbalance duplicated in Russia's historical position adjacent to, but not within, dynamic and industrializing Western Europe. If some historians have characterized Russia as the original "developing nation" (Shanin 1985; Gerschenkron 1970), others have identified campaigns of "catching up" and the pattern of "compressed development" as a resulting compensation (see Lewin 1987; Kotkin 1995; Tucker 1990). Accounts such as Aleksandr Gerschenkron's view all of Russia in unitary terms as an undeveloped nation. However, I prefer characterizations of Russia (since at least the early eighteenth century) as a *differentiated* territory, a space within which are found both the agents and the targets of development.[15] Russia's geographic disparities have always been mirrored in class separation, since it was the socio-economic resources deriving from extreme privilege that enabled the urban Russian elite to easily absorb nation-building ideas from the more developed nations of Western Europe (and latterly the USA). Turning to consider their provincial counterparts, whose way of life they found foreign to the point of unintelligibility, Russia's urban elite have many times embarked (in a fitful way) on projects to implant "modern" lifestyles and technologies in their rural periphery. So, though some characterize modernizing efforts beyond the Russian city as a strictly colonial practice (Gray 2000), it seems that modernization in the provinces can more usefully be understood as a series of "catching up" projects, in which Russia's urban middle classes periodically strike outwards, endeavouring to integrate hinterland populations into a more homogeneous Russian "civilization." This is not to disregard the economic-extractive aspect of modernizing programs, but metropole-led osvoenie – or "mastering," in a territorial and cultural sense – has been perpetually at the heart of Russian (and Soviet) state building.

As the diffusion of ideas, technologies, and "modern" people to a peripheral locality, the idea of modernization is inseparable from problems of distance and mobility. Chukotka, a periphery par excellence, affords a particularly vivid demonstration of this relationship. In a place of such marvellous expanses, where distance achieves an extreme and all-shaping influence over human affairs, we can see movement as power and immobility as dependence and vulnerability. The tidal cycle of modernizing change in the Russian Far North continually sets up polarities of the mobile and immobile (signified in modernization's discourse as the "modern" and the "fallen behind"). Modernity is always a condition of, in one or another respect, fastest, easiest, farthest movement. This is only logical, because distance itself is conditioned by power. Zygmunt Bauman (1998, 12) puts it nicely: "far from being an objective, impersonal, physical 'given,' 'distance' is a social product; its length varies depending on the speed with which it may be overcome (and, in a monetary economy, on the cost involved in the attainment of that speed)." When the first Russians settled on the banks of the Kolyma River, at the western edge of Chukchi territory, they lived as an underclass, dependent on the exquisite mobility of reindeer herders to periodically rescue them from starvation. And the destruction of this herding culture was finally effected only at the point that Soviet technologies of transport conquered the distances of the tundra (two decades *after* Stalin decided on this task).

In the last three decades of Soviet power – a time of mass settlement in Chukotka – mobility remained a critical diagnostic of power and a mark of modern identity. In the North, and everywhere in Soviet life, classes and communities defined themselves in part by the speed at which they moved. Soviet power may have liquidated the burden of distance in the Russian North, but not for everyone. In the process of assembling a sense of themselves as modernizers, newcomers seized a monopoly on the powers of movement. So extraordinary was the Soviet transport system that they could inhabit multiple settings, living in remote northern settlements but also in central Russian places and even, in a sense, in the airplanes, ships, and trains in which they so often found themselves. Many newcomers in fact *embodied* the technologies of transport because it was their job in the North to maintain and pilot the myriad vessels that, like the arteries of a body, oxygenated industrializing Chukotka. If modernity equalled mobility, the power of movement was also hoarded and rationed out with frugal care to the fallen behind, so as not to erode the exclusivity of the modernizing community. After all, an important aspect of Soviet modernization was the *immobilization* of native herders and hunters. Sedentarized in villages and made dependent on Russian helicopter pilots and barge captains, natives progressively lost the knowledge and the resources they once commanded to travel over their landscape independently.

Later, in the era of Roman Abramovich, modernity was refashioned and reassigned to a new population – Abramovich's followers – who arrived to make their own particular claims to modernizing authority. Once again, mobility operated as a key marker of power, but now in different and more extreme ways. The settlers of the Soviet era, regardless of their movements, had formerly built communities of place, possessed of a palpable sense of locality (a sense, in Ferdinand Tönnies' [1957] formula, of *Gemeinschaft*). Theirs was in many respects a traditional society, in which much of the life of the community was face to face, unmediated by technology. But Abramovich's followers operated almost completely "out of place," almost always in a state of multiple locatedness. They represented, in Bauman's (1998, 19) words, "the 'dephysicalisation,' the new weightlessness of power." As I will relate in the last chapters of this book, Roman Abramovich epitomized the hypermobility of a new global elite, literally always in motion and living within high-speed vessels of transport. He also granted his followers, particularly those in his inner circle, this speed of movement. His regional administration was in many places at once, both northern and metropolitan; its internal conversations formed webs across vast spaces, and its workers only "camped" in the North, flying on chartered jets and helicopters between the spaces of work in Chukotka, Moscow, London, and elsewhere. As an oil billionaire, Abramovich needed security and protection, and his ceaseless movement would make it difficult for his enemies ever to locate him. But the state of hypermobility was also an instrument for defining the boundaries of the group because no one in Chukotka who was not admitted to Abramovich's circles could possibly travel at these speeds and over these distances. This shows, in the same way as the history of the mobile Soviet settler, that each social class has, quite literally, a speed of its own. As Pierre Bourdieu (1985) might observe, mobility amounts to a practice of distinction.

If a modernization is at heart an exercise of self-definition and boundary marking for its agents, how important is its *nominal* objective, namely, bringing a selected people and a place up to date? I give an answer in the final chapters of this book. But, before we read that far, it is useful to begin thinking of Abramovich's modernization, in its immoderate scale, cost, and timelines, as really just another Soviet Five-Year Plan. It possessed that universal architecture common to any of the traditional Russian projects of catching up. Campaign-style modernization of this kind relies on a perception of local conditions as so disastrous that they must be improved *at all costs.* Once declared, a campaign sublimates the normal range of considerations to a single core measure of success (which was, in the case of contemporary Chukotka, financial viability). The prestige of the campaign – its charismatic appeal to those it seeks to enlist – derives from its transcendent claims, its promise to deliver more, and faster, than anyone thought possible. Yet, the impossibility of such claims should be obvious to anyone not deeply intoxicated by the spirit of the campaign. In a way that both James Ferguson (1994) and Nikolai Ssorin-Chaikov (2003) have observed of other contexts, it is precisely the *inevitability* of failure that drives the modernizing-and-entropy cycle in places such as Chukotka. This is so because failures of modernization defer the moment of lasting improvement and thus postpone the point at which "development" assistance is no longer required. The failed development schemes of today will necessitate the development plans of tomorrow. This logic remains intact in the Russian North despite the outer shifts in regime and ideology. Indeed, if the grossly overambitious Soviet plans for industrializing Chukotka were impossible to sustain, the scale of Abramovich's modernization (and in particular the costs) likewise seems to presage another failure.

I am not terribly concerned with the question of sustainable development; in comparison with the creative strategies of adaptation in the stories of rooted settlers, the very idea seems oxymoronic. What outsiders have brought to Chukotka in the name of development has perennially proved unsuitable until locals have with time adapted imported innovations to *severnaia spetsifika* (the particular circumstances of the North). If modernization carries an implication of transience (transient people, transient projects, transient hopes), the more significant questions must lie in the ground effects of the modernizing cycle in the lives of local people. How, in other words, are these people at times attached and at other times detached from the projects of modernity, and what room does this turbulence leave for their sovereign efforts to claim an identity and a place to call home?

Soviet State Power

A familiar obsession in the historiography of the Soviet period is to examine the potency of the Soviet state – the sources of its legitimacy and its organizational capacities. Originating in the work of historians and political scientists, the "totalitarianism-revisionist" debate later met with new and transcendent interpretations realigning the focus toward the experience of everyday life, which only a more anthropological approach to research could accommodate.[16] This innovation came just as the Soviet Union quite unexpectedly collapsed, and it reconfigured the landscape of inquiry to account for the apparent weakness of the state by the point of perestroika. Drawn from the very few on-the-ground ethnographies of late-Soviet life then in existence, a revisionist argument emerged to reject the idea of a unitary and effective Soviet state apparatus, characterizing it instead as a weak and uneven fabric sitting atop a society fragmented into neo-feudal domains.[17] According to this line of argument, the "shortage economy," which the Hungarian economist Janos Kornai (1992) described as the inevitable and permanent result of central planning, engendered conditions that neither individual citizens nor the regime itself could survive without resort to the support of more or less sealed communities of mutual aid: a society of networks. For Caroline Humphrey (2002) and Katherine Verdery (1996), the institution – the *vedomstvo* – whether a collective farm, industrial enterprise, or bureaucratic agency, was therefore the basic organizational unit of Soviet life. The state above became, in this interpretation, an increasingly impotent force, emanating forms of symbolic power, espousing rhetoric in place of doctrine, recommending rather than commanding. But, as Finn Sivert Nielsen (2007) argues in his closely observed ethnography of urban survival in stagnation-era Leningrad, the formal institution was not the only building block of the "stateless" Soviet society. Protection was also afforded at the informal level by circles of acquaintance. Nielsen maps privilege and poverty within geographies of intimate and unmediated interaction, revealing an "archipelago" of social islands, each surrounded by a limbo of material scarcity impoverished of productive human intercourse. Nielsen (2007, 97) writes, "the whole country is segregated into Islands, enclosed by more massive Barriers the more benefits they give. One cannot simply move to Leningrad. Rural migrants are 'hunters' looking for the Place where the good life is and hoping to work themselves closer to its wellsprings."

Nielsen's allegorical language of "islands," "barriers," and "hunters" finds a close relative in Alena Ledeneva's (1998) account of informal network exchange, shaped by the rules of Russian *blat* (pull, or connections). Such practices of exchange have often been characterized as the perpetuation of peasant-village habits in the daily life of the new socialist city (see Kotkin's "little tactics of the habitat," 1995; Jowitt's explanation of *pile* in socialist Romania, 1992). Taken as a whole, these accounts characterize Soviet society as intensely cellular – a Balkans of outwardly defensive networks – in which loyalties were immediate and personal, rather than patriotic and state directed. The formal structures of state power, in correlation, became increasingly distant from the lives of ordinary people. Thus, Nielsen (2007, 19) contends that as bureaucratic lines of command declined into terminal sclerosis, Soviet citizens were forced into a netherworld of informal exchange, a "society outside society." The state, so goes this line of thinking, had lost its powers of large-scale organization, whether in the economic or the cultural domain, long before its symbolic edifice collapsed in 1991.

Such a Potemkin-village characterization of the late-Soviet state rests on the proposition that average Soviet citizens understood this and that they navigated the daily paradoxes of this reality by moving between two modes of being: official but mendacious involvement in public rituals of citizenship, and honest, candid participation in the private and confidential spaces of everyday life. To recite the doctrines of Soviet ideology in public fora – published writing, public meetings, academic examinations – had no meaning beyond the expression of membership, of obedience, and of knowing the rules. Whether or not so vivid a gulf between the public and the private, between unofficial "truth" and official "lies," actually existed in the minds and actions of typical Soviet people remains open to question. A great deal of evidence suggests that daily participation in the rituals of public life actually exerted a friction. There was a discomfort with such hypocrisy that resulted, in the words of the émigré sociologist Vladimir Shlapentokh (1989), in a mass "phenomenon of retreat" into private worlds immune to Soviet ideology.[18]

I do not propose to challenge the various orthodoxies of Soviet historiography, but I do point out that, as always, a view from the periphery can uncover remarkable insights into the problems of the centre. In so many ways, the experience of the northern settler in the stagnation era stands uncomfortably at odds with the ethnographic record of life in the Soviet city. The success of mass settlement appears to suggest that Soviet power could, until the very end, effectively operate in the High Modernist mode; after all, northern osvoenie was a spectacular example of large-scale social engineering. The enthusiasm of the northern settler for the tasks of industrializing the North and "lifting up" its peoples was surely incompatible with mass cynicism toward the objectives of the Soviet project. Does this ethnography of the northern settler then overturn the conclusions of Nielsen, Verdery, Jowitt, and Shlapentokh on the weakness of the state? No. Instead, as the first chapters argue, the case of northern settlement reveals how this state recognized its own deficiencies, and with remarkable adroitness exploited them in the pursuit of those goals of state building it most cherished. The regime accomplished this not by banishing shortages and ameliorating the sense of anomie in mainstream Soviet life, but rather by harnessing the frustration of its citizens and recognizing this sentiment as, in fact, a desire for alternatives. That is what the late-Soviet North became: an alternative, in material, cultural, and moral terms. The success of mass settlement is thus, paradoxically, a testament both to the *power* of the late-Soviet state and to its quickly accelerating decrepitude.

Questions of Identity

In Chukotka, the idea of northern belonging among settlers was forged in the crucible of a history of dramatic reversals. The chapters of this book thus alternate between the examination of this history, broken into three distinct episodes – late-Soviet, post-Soviet, and Putin-era Russia – and an ethnographic consideration of the effects of historical circumstances on the self-perceptions of settlers. This is also a study of collective identity, and moreover a diachronic portrait of an identity shifting through time. But caution is required, for the concept of "identity" can be so rich in meaning that it can seem at the same time meaningless. If the very term is to serve as anything more than, in the words of Roger Brubacker (2004, 61), a "suggestive oxymoron," some qualifications are in order.

Let us start with the observation that people are usually busy characterizing and categorizing themselves, and are doing so in response to the efforts of others to project characterizations upon them. Settlers in Chukotka are the original products of the modernizing cycle, and their identities were in part produced and upheld by the structures of cultural and material privilege inherent to Soviet-era osvoenie. What then happened to those identities when the forces of modernization slackened? How did settlers perceive themselves when they ceased to participate in modernizing projects? To answer these questions, we must first recognize that there is always a degree of slippage between the way people view themselves and the circumstances in which they actually find themselves; self-perceptions are as vulnerable to nostalgia and dreams of the future as they are to the experience of the present. But just as self-understandings fall behind the times or race ahead of them, they also respond to the present in surprising ways. People do not necessarily accept assigned identities (for example, as modern Soviet civilizers), and sometimes the experience of being categorized within an identity animates altogether contrasting self-definitions. The terms "settler" and "newcomer" offer a case in point – both reify a fictitious homogeneity of experience and disposition, while papering over the actual diversity of human trajectories within the population to which they refer. Ultimately, we require some understanding of that complexity in order to detect the particular trajectory of "settling" and coming to belong in northern places in a durable way.

Adrift in the turbulent ebb and flow of the modernizing cycle, the settler has been continually challenged to renovate and re-establish sources of self-understanding. One framework for understanding the settler response to historical events draws on a voluntarist conception of the self, able to shift through social identities and realign affiliations in an opportunistic fashion. This interpretation borrows from intentionalist interpretations of human agency, among them Ernest Goffman's (1959) theorization of the person as an internal quality hidden behind a mask-like social face. This is a view of social identity as deliberate performance, with its roots in the work of A.R. Radcliffe-Brown (1957) and G.H. Mead (1934), and its modern incarnation in Anthony Giddens' (1988) proposal that identities are created in public contexts by the accomplishments of intentional selves. These views are controversial, however, because the voluntarist interpretation is hounded by thorny questions about the limits of individual sovereignty in real-world contexts (the "structure-and-agency" debate).

To resolve this tension – to recognize both volitional sovereignty and the location of individuals within social textures constraining their performances – some have argued for making a clear distinction between "social identity" and "self." According to Martin Sökefeld (1999), the self is the location of agency and reflexivity, which in a socialized individual is endowed with durability and sameness through time. In counterpoint to the unified self, social identities are faces turned to the social field. They are the plural and shifting presentations of an inner volitional agent. With a clear distinction between self/agent and social identities/presentations/performances, the possibility of both sameness and transformation in a single person becomes comprehensible. In Sökefeld's account, identities are collective cultural constructs, and selves possess limited, but clear, opportunities for adopting and discarding them in particular social settings. Applied in Chukotka, such an actor-focused account offers a means of understanding how individual settlers might respond to shifting reifications of, for example, Soviet ideology or Governor Roman Abramovich's promise of progress.

But, as anthropologists so often observe, the nature of the ethnographic method is such that you are unlikely to find in the field what you first expected. My own experience convinced me to set aside theories of the sovereign self and a methodology focusing exclusively on micro-social practice. Instead, the operation of *aggregate* identities – the cultural groupings within the ethnographic setting – and their influence on individual choice emerged as the most salient conceptual feature. As I returned to Chukotka over the span of five years, it became ever clearer that individual settlers, particularly those well established in their communities, were deeply entrenched within enduring collective identities more or less invulnerable to major renovation. To shape-change, to cross boundaries between one collective identity and another, and to turn away from a public identity often built up over many decades, usually amounted to an impossible hypocrisy in the context of Chukotka's small communities.

For this reason, settler and modernizer identities are best examined within theories of *community* and *group boundary marking*. We could describe a community in practical terms as a population whose members are integrated within a network of reciprocity and mutual reliance, and who possess the means to understand their commonalities as constituting a cultural whole. This is not to say that settlers, or indeed incoming "experts" of the Abramovich era, have ever inhabited collective identities with fixed and structural permanence. Rather, as Fredrik Barth (1969) has observed, collective identities are produced and reproduced by interaction across group boundaries, a process of relational definition that itself constitutes the reality of difference. This interpretation of collective identities as social constructions, later elaborated by Benedict Anderson (1983) and Eric Hobsbawm and Terence Ranger (1983), offers a view of the individual as neither voluntaristic nor as "caught" in structure. The stock of attributes and behaviours that members of a community display are instead what Anthony Cohen (1985) refers to as "social symbols" and Barth terms the "idioms of identity," the expression of which constitutes either outsiderness or belonging, or rather, the limits of the collective boundary. The internal attributes of a community – for example, its faculties of reciprocal giving and socio-economic self-regulation – are naturally supported by a sense of group identity, which could hardly exist without a knowledge of these limits. This leaves us with a dual theory of community, simultaneously characterized by internal similarity or "culture in common" and relational difference mediated by group boundaries.

The "remodernization" of Chukotka by Governor Abramovich challenged the legitimacy of vestigial and nostalgically informed settler identities (as modern people, as a cultural avant-garde, and even as "true" people of the North). The intrusion of the outsider expert into the local domain and the execution of modernization projects (such as community closures and resettlement to the south) sparked, in a reactive way, an emboldened sense of belonging among locals. This effect has been demonstrated in other settings, to be found in a range of ethnographies that have in common a concern for "peoples at the fringe" – communities contending with threats of effacement originating in distant metropolitan centres (for example, Vidich and Bensman 1968; Elias and Scotson 1965; Cohen 1985, 1987; Emmet 1982; Strathern 1981). Cohen (1982, 6), whose research was set in the Shetlands fishing settlement of Whalsay, observes that "practices of cultural identification" are particularly evident in "peripheral communities" located at the margins of industrialized metropoles. In places like these, threats from outside become a vital constituent of self-awareness for the community. In their classic text on the nature of "community," Colin Bell and Howard Newby (1978, 290) remark, "Our membership of communities is largely unconscious unless it is threatened; otherwise one just belongs, and generally irrevocably so." They introduced the notion of "communion," a heightened awareness of community membership, as a kind of *defensive* celebration of group boundaries. Sustained as it is by intense affective bonds, "communion" is related to the Weberian concept of charisma, whose effects recede as its emotional powers become routinized. It is this unstable and ephemeral aspect of communities on the defensive that bears most relevance to the situation of settlers in Chukotka, faced as they were (from 2001 onward) with a radical but momentary program of modernization.

It should be very clear that this study of settler identity concerns more than simply the moments of communion – the short-lived celebrations of collective feeling when under pressure from without. Just as meaningful a question relates to how, in more prosaic circumstances, communities are constituted and maintained by the practices of their members. There is no doubt that constructivist theories of community offer the best analytical toolbox for understanding collective identity in certain circumstances. Many anthropologists would eschew positivist descriptions of community altogether and attend only to the meanings people attach to membership. For example, Anthony Cohen's (1985) epistemological questioning of the nature of community rests within an analysis of the symbols group members employ to signal, first, their own membership, and second, the boundaries delineating outsiderness, which he characterizes as the internal and external "definitions" of community, respectively. Such theorizations are particularly helpful for understanding the social separation of local and outsider in Chukotka's contemporary capital, Anadyr, which I characterize with a borrowing from Canada as a condition of "two solitudes" (MacLennan 1945).

But I do not agree that community life, and in particular the boundaries of a community, should be considered strictly in symbolic terms. Things and acts become symbols only when their referential meaning is recognized. Practices native to a community carry overtly symbolic meaning only at certain moments in the progress of community life (typically, when local people are contending with an outside threat). Yet, as long as the norms of community life – the routine practices of mutuality – are sustained, they alone constitute compelling grounds for membership. So we see that the forms of reciprocal support deriving from everyday "neighbourliness" animate the social life of the community and delineate its boundaries, while at the same time carrying the potential for the mobilization of an *idea* of the group and its boundaries *in exceptional circumstances.* It is for this reason that I give equal attention in this study of the settler to discursive boundary marking (symbolic differentiation) and the practices of day-to-day survival, including land use and practices of exchange.

The everyday logic of community life – let us say the "content" – is still best viewed from the perspective of exchange theory, for which we owe a debt to Marcell Mauss (1990), Michael Taussig (1980), and Marshall Sahlins (1972). Particularly relevant is Mauss' characterization of gift-giving as an enactment of community, a practice symbolic of the cherished relationships within its social limits. If Mauss located his theories in studies of "primitive societies," Caroline Humphrey (2000) and Nikolai Ssorin-Chaikov (2000) have helped to "deprimitivize" the gift (and barter) by demonstrating its salience within industrial societies (settings that Mauss and Taussig actually considered the province of commodity exchange). Because the gift holds a hidden presumption of mutuality, giving and helping are critical drivers behind the circulation of goods within any self-sustaining community. This was certainly the case within Chukotka's settler communities, where participation in the practices of exchange served as a boundary marker and source of identity. In this regard, the notion of "generalized reciprocity" is particularly useful for characterizing the importance of exchange among settlers and for explaining its perpetual quality. Generalized reciprocity describes practices of giving that are on the surface unconditional but that nevertheless set up an expectation of return, albeit delayed, and are presented in a non-commensurate form (Bourdieu 1983). Reciprocity is "generalized" in the sense that participants in a community of exchange may give to one and get from another: there is a sense that what you put in comes back to you in the end.

Theories of social capital also enrich our understanding of exchange practices, particularly as a means of accounting for the *variable* intensity of community life. If social capital amounts to the stock of social connection within a population (Putnam 2000; Coleman 1988), it follows that communities can be variously well endowed or impoverished. Social capital theory also illuminates the relationship between the pragmatic activity of exchange and the symbolic life of discourses such as "trust" and "generosity." Mutual trust and generosity are central aspects of the settler tradition, key tenants of the code of the North, for survival in the harsh and isolated conditions of northern communities relies on a continual resort to mutual help. But, in truth, the norms of generosity and welcoming have always to some degree been constrained by everyday scarcity in the North, particularly during the post-Soviet crisis. Because of this, there is a need to interrelate cultures of exchange and mutual aid to the persistence of boundary marking in settler communities. Again, Finn Sivert Nielsen's (2007) ethnography of survival in late-Soviet Leningrad comes to the rescue, with its model of "islands" of intimate acquaintance, protective of their members and hostile to penetration, floating on the sea of shortage-plagued stagnation-era life. Similarly, the blat networks of Alena Ledeneva's (1998) portrait of Soviet-era society testify to the density of exchange within informal networks. Although neither Nielsen nor Ledeneva employ the terminology of social capital theory, they effectively introduce this tradition to the anthropology of Soviet life by demonstrating that Soviet society was never weak in social capital (*pace* Jowitt 1992), only that it was organized in an intensely cellular fashion.

A final and decisive aspect of "community" relates to the problem of *belonging*. Identity can be so many things, expressed so variously: it can, for example, relate to gender, age, social class, or occupation. But here, if we are interested in the problem of how people "settle," we must look to the manner in which modes of social and geographic *location* become sources of self-understanding. In a process of settling, European migrants to Chukotka were able to discard their transient dispositions and their attachments to faraway homes and eventually situate their personal and collective identities firmly within their immediate environment. This conceptual realignment was vastly accelerated in Chukotka by the abrupt dislocations of historical circumstance. For example, hardship after 1991 winnowed the population, leaving more committed northerners in its aftermath. But because of the way of life it made necessary, the experience of survival also catalyzed a latent sense of belonging among settlers. In parallel with the end of transport, practices of survival in northern settlements *localized* people – whether indigenous or not – constricting and concentrating their everyday onto an immediate social canvas and the nearby landscape.[19] There ceased to be a resort or a reference of much meaning beyond the local, but fortunately the local could also be richly sustaining.

With this is mind, I cannot help but argue that the story of the settler, fixed on the northern landscape, has a place in the lively discussion of indigeneity within anthropology (indeed, within *Current Anthropology*).[20] The reader must decide whether to view this ethnography in such polemic terms as those in which these debates are voiced. But it should be read as open-minded interrogation of "nativeness," one that attempts to transcend the deadening terms of debate that now shape the discourses of indigenous rights and that still assign identities of native and colonizer in a zero-sum fashion. I much prefer the wisdom found in deeply ethnographic questionings of indigenous identity, characterizing nativeness as no more than, but neither less than, practical *experience* in a particular landscape. This is not a controversial idea; many accounts of northern indigenous peoples in Canada, Greenland, Scandinavia, and Russia point to landscape, and moreover to land use, as a primary constituent of identity constructions (for example, Vitebsky 2005; King 2002; Sharpe 2001; D. Anderson 2000; Ingold 2000; Brody 1981, 2000; Brightman 1993) in a manner consistent with writing on belonging in other regions (Feld and Basso 1996; Hirsch and O'Hanlon 1995). In what we might simply call the ethnographic (as opposed to the political) approach to indigeneity, practices of hunting, gathering, worshipping, or travelling on the land lead to an entanglement of landscape features and personal histories, so that individuals become "written on to the land" (Nuttall 1992) and land becomes written in the minds and on the bodies of its people.

Although these accounts of embedded identity or belonging to place focus on indigenous figures in the North, there is no reason not to consider within the same rubric rooted practices of dwelling found among settlers. Indeed, my ethnography of the settler culminates in its final pages with a description of practical ties to land and local community life, arguing that senses of belonging spring from and are refreshed by such entanglements. A sense of settler belonging may, at certain times in Chukotka's history, have seemed more a discursive than practical characteristic – and is thus better examined in the light of those works on community emphasizing relational positioning, boundary marking, and hostility to the outsider (such as Cohen 1987; Vidich and Bensman 1968; Elias and Scotson 1965). But in Chukotka, as I predict is true elsewhere in the Russian North, "belonging" is also a property of the settler identity that both precedes and outlasts the effervescent sense of solidarity provoked by intrusions and threats from outside. My own "ethnographic present" in the Abramovich era may be just such an effervescent moment, but this is nevertheless a historical, diachronic account of changing collective identities. Just as I refer to a past in which the settler had less need to define the boundaries of the group, so I anticipate a future after Abramovich's modernization in which this is again the case.

Part 1
The Soviet Years, 1955-91

2
Northern Settlement and the Late-Soviet State

> There were no supplies, there was sheer demand.
>
> – Joseph Brodsky, *Less Than One: Selected Essays*

Mass voluntary settlement in the Far North coincided almost perfectly with the Soviet Union's economic and ideological stagnation, the three-decade-long senescence of state power that ended with its complete demise in 1991. Slow decline was the retroactive diagnosis of a generation of revisionist studies, whose aim it was to account for the unexpected weakness of the Soviet state and, by extension, for its precipitous collapse.[1] They revealed how the reality of everyday socialism for most Soviet citizens was plagued by acute and perpetual shortage, while the state under Brezhnev had lost its prestige as a manager of the economy. By the stagnation era, which began in the late 1960s, networks of bureaucratic and personal loyalty were rapidly replacing the formal levers of administrative command, creating conditions in which the entire edifice could appear to suddenly fold in on itself. As the reserves of ideological enthusiasm waned and daily hardships mounted, ordinary Soviets were forced into a subversive relationship with the state, animating domains of activity not only illegal but also invisible in official discourse (Shlapentokh 1989; Nielsen 2007). This fuelled a degree of cynicism toward official ideology and the grand projects of the state from which, it seems in retrospect, no recovery was possible.

Where, in this picture, is the privileged settler of the Far North? How can we reconcile the revisionist portrait of stagnation-era life and the dysfunctional state with the spectacular success of mass northern settlement? How is it that this phase of northern development, which stands as a supreme achievement of state-led social engineering, spans the very period when the state supposedly lost its powers of managerial and charismatic control?

The settlers of Soviet Chukotka, or any other region of the Far North, may have lived at the edge of Soviet life, but their importance for understanding this era is central. Out of an examination of settler privilege emerge two insights that condition our understanding of late-Soviet life and challenge revisionist characterizations of the senescent state. First, we see that despite its incapacity to protect the ordinary citizen from chronic shortages, the stagnation-era state in fact possessed a considerable reservoir of administrative effectiveness until its final demise in 1991. The regime systematically rationed and channelled those resources it controlled toward the domains of endeavour most critical to its interests, including the military, scientific research, sport, and northern development. These policies generated pools of relative prosperity and productivity that most studies of Soviet life bypassed or failed to detect because of the closed and often secretive nature of these projects. Such a zone of privilege and state functionality was Chukotka; settlers in this remote region enjoyed the highest degree of northern benefits, but they also lived within a restricted border area inaccessible to ordinary Soviets. Second, the state found ways to transform its economic decrepitude into a source of strength. The selective manipulation of shortage and abundance gave the regime a tool for harnessing and directing the frustrations of ordinary citizens. Although chronic shortage was a failure of the state to fulfill its official commitments, shortage was also a deliberate tool that served state goals, in particular as a driver of migration to northern regions.

If mass settlement in Chukotka fell within a clearly delimited thirty-year period, there were likewise features of state power and everyday life in the Soviet Union that lent these years the quality of a recognizable era. The threshold year was 1956, when Krushchev officially renounced aspects of Stalinist rule, thereby setting in motion a terminal weakening of the state and initiating a degree of public ambivalence toward the Soviet project. Krushchev demystified Soviet power and, by simultaneously removing coercion from among the principal levers of administrative control, created spaces in private life where a critical reconsideration of Soviet reality became possible. Dissent of an overt and political nature was still effectively suppressed, but with an official recognition of state fallibility, participation in its rituals assumed an increasingly hypocritical aspect, as the gap widened between ideological rhetoric and the reality of Soviet life. By promising rapid economic growth and the end of everyday hardship, Krushchev patched over the holes in state legitimacy that his reflexive criticism had opened up, but this bought only immediate relief at the expense of state prestige over the long term. The stagnation that followed under Brezhnev, which in economic terms was evident already by 1970, generated a corrosive cynicism toward the rhetoric of Leninist ideology and toward the practical capacity of the Soviet state to govern and manage.

The post-Stalinist leadership compensated for the erosion of revolutionary enthusiasm and the repressive powers of the centralist Stalin-era administration by making two key concessions. It accepted limitations on Moscow's exercise of state power, adopting a model under Brezhnev of devolving significant administrative authority to regional elites (the "trust-in-cadres" policy) and in doing so, tacitly institutionalizing bureaucratic corruption in exchange for loyalty and stability. The result was both a diffusion of power from Moscow to regional elites and an increasing personalism in public administration (since less could be done to prevent it), both of which blunted the managerial authority of the centre and accelerated the fracturing of the Soviet economy.[2] In an atmosphere of deepening public cynicism regarding the promises of official ideology, the regime secured the loyalty of ordinary workers by embracing material incentives, making full use of a system already partly in place in the Stalinist era. With the powers of coercion removed, and the motivational powers of Leninist ideology compromised by corruption and hardship, higher pay and better living conditions amounted to the only effective remaining tool of labour control. This resulted in a kind of state-worker contract in the final years of the stagnation era, which the émigré sociologist Vladimir Shlapentokh (1989, 95) succinctly described: "Ultimately, the Soviet people have won the battle with the government in the economic sphere, forcing the latter to adjust to the economic behaviour of its citizens and to realise that this behaviour cannot be controlled solely with ideological means."

By the last decade of Soviet power, these concessions had generated a remarkable level of inequality in Soviet life, without ultimately securing labour discipline or preventing the explosive growth of an illegal second economy.[3] The Siberian sociologist Tatiana Zaslavskaia (1984) published the first studies of class stratification in this era, and Shlapentokh, already writing from the West, pointed to the failure of average incomes to keep up with rising prices, alongside the emergence of a new class of illegal entrepreneurs operating outside the official economy and compensating for chronic shortage by introducing their own products and services on the black market. We have some insight into the everyday reality of Soviet life at this time through the work of the Norwegian anthropologist Finn Sivert Nielsen (2007, 4), who produced a unique ethnographic portrait of urban survival in early 1980s Leningrad.[4] He described a hollowing-out of the formal workplace, as ordinary citizens were forced into a netherworld of informal exchange, moonlighting, smuggling, and the illegal production of goods. The workplace, where progressively less work was actually done, provided cover for lives located more and more in this "society outside society." Unable to survive on the basis of what could be earned and bought in the legitimate state-sanctioned economy, Leningraders turned to informal exchange within networks of acquaintance and mutual reliance, in which personal ties rather than state commands determined the flow of goods and services. To describe the texture of this society, Nielsen developed a metaphorical language, evoking a geography of relative security and hardship, scattered like an "archipelago of islands," each surrounded by a limbo of material scarcity, a zone of hostile and unpredictable interaction between strangers. Nielsen's allegorical language of "islands," "barriers," and "hunters" suggests a mode of survival in desperate circumstances, and life in the Soviet city became a kind of foraging exercise. Indeed, by the early 1980s, the average Soviet spent nearly five hours every day searching for goods and services, much of the time standing in queues.

It was by this point misleading to speak of the state in normative terms as a unitary structure of centralized administration. The patchwork of insular circles of mutual aid that Nielsen described, and the foraging expeditions of "hunters" that moved between them, also had their analogue at the institutional level. The only state enterprises capable of fulfilling their production quotas were those able to insulate their workers from shortage within institutional zones of security they erected. Meanwhile, the movement of goods between enterprises relied on personalized relations rather than state commands. The cellular texture of social life that conditions of survival engendered naturally shaped the modes of intercourse in daily life, which was characterized by indifference or hostility between strangers in the public domain, in contrast with intense bonds of loyalty and generosity within circles of acquaintance. The figurative territory that Nielsen named "limbo," filling the space between social "islands," was dangerous and sterile, for the key to "obtaining" (a term with obsessive familiarity to the late-Soviet citizen) lay in personalized relationships, not formal ones.[5]

This picture of stagnation life in the Soviet city stands radically at odds with the northern settler experience. That the lives of these settlers were so fundamentally unlike those of most citizens living on the Russian "mainland" serves as a remarkable comment on the powers and preferences of the Soviet regime. While Nielsen's Leningraders operated in the shadow economy and abused state resources just to survive daily hardship, settlers in the North led prosperous lives within a fully *licit* relationship with the state. Their way of life in this zone of abundance in turn helped to preserve their faith in the managerial and ideological prestige of the Soviet project. In contrast with conditions of stagnation, northern development charged ahead, so that the official rhetoric of progress seemed fulfilled in daily life. Prosperity moulded the very "shape" of northern urban life; settlers' shared membership in the project of northern mastery, and the relative absence of scarcity, prevented the atomization of settler society into defensive and insular islands, as in mainstream Soviet cities. Consequently, this particular population was bonded by a sense of solidarity stretching beyond circles of acquaintance, unlike in much of Soviet life. For them, "community" was an expansive and embracing sentiment.

Settlement as a Practice of State Building

If these conditions of life were so unusual in late-Soviet Russia, it is because they depended on a system of northern benefits – including superb transport, high pay, and an excellent supply of goods – of baroque complexity and extremely high public expense. In fact, northern settler society might be understood as one of the most expensive formations of privilege the Soviet leadership ever sanctioned. By 1989, when the entire circumpolar North contained a population of only 10 million, 8 million lived on Soviet territory (Heleniak 1999). The annual subsidies and benefits conceived to keep this population in place equalled roughly 6 percent of Soviet GDP. Why was the Soviet leadership prepared to devote so large a share of national wealth to maintain the settler way of life? How did the Far North come to figure so centrally in the Soviet state-building project?

Anadyr in winter, 1970s
Archives *of the Heritage of Chukotka Regional Museum*

Settlement and industrialization in the North were shaped by a multi-faceted policy of "mastering" (osvoenie), which designated northern territory as a storehouse of natural wealth critical to the Soviet Union's economic development and sovereign survival. If, to exploit this wealth, social inequalities were deepened and the effacement of class distinctions was postponed, this was an acceptable sacrifice. After all, successive Soviet leaders shared a common concern: fear of hostility abroad and the need for rapid industrialization, in order to meet the threat posed by foreign powers. In the context of this drive for security, "mastery of the North" *(severnoe osvoenie)* emerged as a Moscow-centric doctrine of resource exploitation, which treated natural resources and northern native peoples alike in utilitarian terms.

The history of the osvoenie policy is the subject of a range of studies (Bradshaw 1995; Bond 1994; Gregory and Stuart 1986). There are several reasons why, among all the regions of the circumpolar North, a unique emphasis on mass settlement emerged in Soviet Russia. Clearly, the exploitation of natural resources was central to the Soviet strategy of export-led growth, and so the North was, in the words of economist John Tichotsky (2000, 78), "hard-wired to international markets." The orientation of northern natural resources to export trade belies the traditional assumption that Soviet development in the North was, regardless of the considerable costs, necessary to assure complete economic self-sufficiency (the autarky argument) (Bradshaw 1995; Bond 1994). In fact, northern development there was in many senses perfectly aligned with the classic pattern of colonial rent extraction from an internal resource frontier, as observed in other northern regions such as Canada.[6] Moreover, Soviet reliance on a small set of resource exports, and in particular gold, helps to explain the lengths to which the regime went in developing mineral-rich Chukotka, the most remote and inaccessible territory in the Soviet Union.

If resource exports buttressed Soviet economic security, settlement and industrialization on the resource frontier also addressed the military vulnerability of the state's northern flank. Nowhere was this task more critical than in Chukotka, which faced Alaska across the narrow Bering Strait. In the Cold War era, Chukotka was a key outpost, where policies of osvoenie assumed distinctly strategic and defence-oriented forms. The region harboured long-range bomber groups, ballistic missile platforms, armoured divisions, and at least one underground weapons factory. Viewed through the prism of defence strategy, rapid civilian settlement along sparsely inhabited borders fulfilled the axiom that "every resident of the North is a potential defender of the Motherland."[7]

No encompassing understanding of northern osvoenie is possible without addressing its cultural and ideological prejudices, without which the huge costs entailed in building a settled North might have precluded large-scale settlement.[8] Northern osvoenie satisfied ideological objectives in several ways. For a young and experimental Soviet regime, a North empty but for small and scattered indigenous groups operated as a kind of untouched canvas on which could be inscribed completely new and distinctly *socialist* forms of life. Siting towns on the northern frontier was thus a politico-ideological exercise demonstrating the superior organizational and motivational powers of the revolutionary-socialist state. Just as important was the North's value as an instrument of propaganda, operating somewhat like a vast model collective farm for the benefit of visiting fellow travellers from the West. These not only included a range of influential journalists and travel writers (Smolka 1937; Gruber 1944; Mowat 1970), but also members of the Western political class, including American vice-president Henry Wallace, who visited the Kolyma in 1944 (Wallace 1992), and the future Canadian prime minister Jean Chrétien, who returned in 1971 from a tour of the Siberian North impressed by "20th Century progress" and hoping that Soviet achievements would inspire Canadians to "recognise more of the possibilities of [their] own north" (Slipchenko 1972).

Finally, the Soviet state deliberately promoted the idea of osvoenie as a cultural policy, a benighted campaign to enlighten the native peoples of the North and elevate their standard of living. According to state propaganda, this was a monument to Soviet-socialist magnanimity and a straight-across sacrifice of state resources. The Canadian novelist Farley Mowat (1970, 304) was certainly impressed;

he toured the Soviet North in the 1960s in the company of the Chukchi writer Yuri Rytkheu and concluded, "Soviet physical accomplishments in Siberia are unmatched for their brilliance of conception and execution. The Soviets have, in not quite half-a-century, attained effective mastery over the entire region." Ironically, once proposed, the missionary version of northern osvoenie formed so convenient a platform for criticism from abroad that it was accepted without question by many Western observers, who employed it to excoriate the Soviets for their policies of indigenous extinction (see Forsyth 1992; Slezkine 1994; Vitebsky 1996). In fact, though ideology certainly played a part in driving northern development, critiques constructed in these terms failed to address the quite utilitarian calculations underlying "civilizing" programs of native development. The manner of Soviet interference in traditional indigenous ways of life was in fact intended to harness native peoples to the emerging industrial economy. The ideology of cultural progress was simply a reifying cover for this process. The modernization of indigenous lifestyles was aimed at converting subsistence economies to surplus-producing ones, whose beneficiary could only have been the burgeoning industrial population of settlers.[9] This is clearly reflected in the experience of natives in Chukotka, who found themselves organized into "rational" systems of production directly tied to the industrial economy.[10]

The interpretation of northern osvoenie as foremost a "hard policy" of resource extraction offers a similarly powerful explanation for the eventual shift from prisoner to voluntary labour in northern regions. By the early 1950s, Stalin's vast gulag archipelago had outlived its utility as an engine of economic growth. Forced labour may have been useful in laying the foundations of industry in the early years of northern osvoenie – building roads and ports, and mining alluvial gold deposits – but a more sophisticated and better-motivated labour force was required for anything approaching an advanced industrial economy. By the time of Stalin's death, the cost of maintaining the forced-labour system exceeded the profits it generated, and the limitations of the coercive approach to industrialization were well understood by the Soviet leadership (Gregory and Lazarev 2003; Applebaum 2003). Although Khrushchev's condemnation of Stalinist labour policy was dressed in moral imperatives, there were clear economic justifications for it. This marked a threshold in northern life; by late 1956, the forced-labour era in the Soviet North was over.

The Uses of Class Envy

Although the coercive mode of social engineering had conclusively failed to produce economic results by the time of Stalin's death, the urgency of the osvoenie project itself had in no way abated. It was in this context that, in an era of post-war austerity reaching into the late 1950s, the North suddenly emerged from behind the shadow cast by Stalin's gulag to become, in popular Soviet perceptions, a zone of material abundance and special labour privileges. The transformation was remarkably rapid. If, earlier in the decade, the North was still largely a destination for the regime's enemies, by its end a northern posting was considered a reward reserved for the Soviet labour elite. The literary critic Vera Dunham (1976, 38) remarked on this shift evident in post-war Soviet fiction: "Perhaps only in the Arctic zone were five-star cognac and perfume exempt from scrutiny. Anything went there, in any quantity, of any quality. Truly of the future, luxuries were politicised into incentives for free-frontier explorers and resettlers."

By openly broadcasting the emergence of an exclusive social stratum of northern settlers who enjoyed access to a cornucopia of luxuries normally available only to the nomenclatura, the Soviet regime was adopting a new set of levers to drive forward northern development.

The incentives system in the Soviet North was not a *de novo* policy introduced by the Khrushchev-era leadership. Rather, it was a natural application of labour policies already apparent throughout the Soviet economy and in evolution since the first Five-Year Plan (1928-32). Industrialization and the security of the Soviet regime, the two intertwined objectives of the Stalinist state-building project, required control over all means of capital, foremost among them labour itself. To achieve this, a return to many pre-Soviet social forms and conventions was unavoidable. This was a process Stalin himself initiated, and the retreat from Bolshevik principles of proletarian solidarity began as soon as Soviet industrialization commenced in earnest. In pursuit of social control, his regime installed a culture of rewards and privileges alongside the threat of coercion and repression, a development that immediately engendered a renewed stratification of privilege within the workforce.

General rationing was introduced in 1929, creating a hierarchy of access to scarce goods that favoured workers in key sectors – heavy industry and transport – as well as the strategic areas of defence and security. They received "special rations," much superior to those allocated to white-collar workers, whereas the rural population and politically suspect groups fell outside the rationing system altogether (Osokina 2001). As industrialization advanced, the bureaucratic management of distribution through rationing expanded, and hierarchies of access to deficit goods were articulated throughout Soviet society, always to the benefit of the most important enterprises and sectors. By the mid-1930s, a system of state-managed distribution emerged to further separate and protect privileged workers within a hierarchy of consumption. Rationed and scarce goods were channelled to closed stores and cafeterias within the workplace, accessible only to employees; the quality and range of products reflected an official estimation of the enterprise's importance. "Closed distribution shops" (initially called *zakrytye raspredeliteli* or *zakrytye rabochie kooperativy*) proliferated throughout state enterprises, bureaucratic departments, and Soviet cities, and each offered a carefully controlled range of goods to its "membership."[11] In this way, shortages were structured to bypass the most favoured segments of the working population.

A significant shift in sanctioned attitudes attended this development, in which materialist consumption and the esteem of luxuries enjoyed an official rehabilitation. As patterns of forced industrialization and collectivization were routinized, materialist consumption became a sanctioned ideal, a development reflected in the evolution of the notion of *kul'turnost'* (cultured behaviour) to valorize consumerism as "cultured." Along with literacy, knowledge of opera and ballet, and a familiarity with the urban setting, Soviet kul'turnost' required a refined eye for consumer goods, holidays, and food products. The end of rationing in 1935 was accompanied by the arrival of shops modelled on Western temples of consumerism such as Macy's in New York, and the public elevation of "model consumers," typically skilled engineers, enterprise managers, Stakhanovites, and members of the cultural elite (Hessler 2000). This shift was reflected in Stalinist slogans of the time, such as "We are achieving abundance!" and "Life has become better, comrades! Life has become more fun!"[12]

Materialist aspirations naturally soon far outstripped the reality of actually lived socialism. A cult of consumption had appeared within a society with very few avenues for its practical fulfillment. Yet, it seems this disjuncture was entirely deliberate: insatiable bourgeois aspirations provided one pillar of a psychological and bureaucratic system of social control, the other two of which were the persistence of shortage and restrictions on mobility. Because the state controlled access to deficit goods through bureaucratic distribution, it could privilege certain social groups while persecuting others, thus providing a mechanism for allocating labour resources and shaping migration without resort to overt coercion. The cult of consumption directed social concern toward obtaining goods. Shortage amplified the intensity of that quest while limiting public expectations. Finally, control over the movement of Soviet citizens by means of the *propiska* (residency permit) system and the strategic positioning of "closed distribution systems" over priority areas of economic and political activity (defence, steel production, "culture work") fixed labour in place and ensured its loyalty and productivity.[13] A residency permit literally became a meal ticket.

As it matured, closed distribution created and sustained a new Soviet class system to replace that dismantled by Bolshevik revolution and repression. As Elena Osokina (2001) has observed, privilege and class in Soviet society had little to do with income and everything to do with *access* to scarce goods. Those with heightened rights of access were equivalent to affluent and propertied individuals in Western societies. Social class was therefore dependent not on the mode of production, as Marxist ideology would claim, but on the mode and degree of consumption. The Soviet variant of social class was in large part determined by a *spatially organized* hierarchy of supply, and the closed distribution system became a structural prop of this system, cementing the layering of material inequality. With the propiska system in place, Moscow and Leningrad emerged as vaguely defined zones of closed distribution, while a network of smaller interlocking and often nested zones spread throughout society and over the entire territory of the Soviet Union. Among the best known were the special research colonies for elite military scientists established during the Cold War, the location and even existence of which were never officially acknowledged.[14]

Closed Distribution and the Far North

In the late-Soviet era, no zone of closed distribution was so vast and geographically distinct as the North. If the state's objective in managing shortage and abundance was to attract the most skilled and loyal workers into priority spheres of economic activity, and to seal those spheres from penetration in order to maintain their privileged status, nowhere was the geographic organization of privilege clearer. Shortage in everyday life fuelled a widespread desire to migrate north, but the propiska system enabled the state to carefully regulate admission to these regions. Indeed, as for the Soviet Union as a whole, the internal passport system was vital for maintaining the integrity of the North as an exclusive zone of abundance and for ensuring that it received only the most skilled and reliable workers. In the case of the most desirable zones, where benefits were highest and living conditions most prosperous, the barriers to entry were greater still. This was the case for Chukotka, where entry was controlled by the Interior Ministry and applicants were vetted by the KGB. To gain a residency permit (propiska), an official summons *(vyzov)* was required from a local enterprise or government department, which undertook to supply accommodation and employment. Citizens with criminal records were ineligible, a specialized education was usually required, and references of good character were sought, preferably from a Communist Party sponsor. An alternative route to obtaining a propiska was via the system of distributing graduates from institutes of higher education (called literally "distribution", or *raspredelenie)*. In many professions, the top two or three graduates in each class would have the right to request a northern posting, and regions of the extreme Far North such as Chukotka were usually the most desirable destinations of all. This was true not only for geologists, but also for bookkeepers, meteorologists, medical doctors, shop managers, journalists, forest-fire fighters, and almost any other practical discipline in demand in the North.[15]

The first legislation awarding special incentives to certain grades of skilled workers in the North was in force as early as 1932, but the incentives regime reached maturation only in the 1960s (Rozin, Khlystova, and Shchegel'skii 1975; Ivanov 1991). In 1960, the North was divided into two zones – the "Far North" and "regions equated with the Far North" – with the most remote territories such as

Chukotka placed in the former category, where workers were awarded the most generous benefits (Popov-Cherkasov 1981; Armstrong 1965). On paper, the key benefits were higher pay, longer holidays, better pensions, earlier retirement, and priority housing entitlements. There was some variation in pay and other privileges within the workforce, but the experience of a geologist who came to Chukotka in 1971 was fairly typical for settlers of the time:

> When I moved to Chukotka, my dad was getting 97 rubles a month working as an accountant in a farming equipment plant in central Russia. When I arrived, just out of army service and with a geology degree, I went to work for the geological survey in Egvekinot, and I got a base monthly salary of 150 [rubles], plus the northern territory bonus *[koeffitsient]* of 150. In addition to that, whenever we were in the field on survey, which was 100 percent of the time for young geologists like me, we got a field bonus *[polevye]* of 50 percent of base salary. So from the first day, I was making about 350 a month, almost four times more than my dad would ever make on the materik. Every six months you worked, you would also qualify for a northern service bonus *[nadbavka]*, which by the end of the first three years equalled your base salary. So by the time I first went back on holiday to see my family, I was making about five hundred a month. To put that into perspective, I could eat a big lunch with three courses at the central cafeteria in Egvekinot for under a ruble, and the flight back to Moscow cost me 210.
>
> Then there were the holidays and breaks. We got about fifty-five days in annual leave, whereas my dad got fifteen. I liked to save my holidays and take them every three years, when I could take five straight months and travel all over the country. That was fine, because like most of us, I was travelling back to the materik for short periods between my holidays. That's because anyone who worked in the field was on a shift system: I worked for fifteen days in the field, and had fifteen days off back in town. If we were on a longer expedition, they lumped the shifts together and gave us a month off afterwards. Of course, that was more than enough time to fly out – I knew people who would fly to Moscow just to catch a performance at the theatre. [64][16]

Northern workers also retired at least five years earlier on a supplemented pension, and many categories of worker, including police and KGB officers, underground miners, and seamen, could retire on a full pension after twelve years of northern work. In principle, if they chose to return to the materik, they were placed at the head of the queue for a new flat in the regions to which they relocated. However, the process of allocating flats was usually so corrupted that a more reliable method of securing accommodation was to build it oneself. In this respect, northern workers were again unusually privileged, because in the 1970s and early 1980s they had the special right to form associations with the power to contract state enterprises and even private labourers *(shabashniki)* to build condominium residences *(kooperativy)* in any part of the country they chose. Using their considerable savings, former residents of Chukotka built high-quality flats in the Moscow region, along the Black Sea, and in the prosperous Baltic republics (where many still live today).

These legislated entitlements produced an extreme and highly enviable standard of living for northern settlers. But, as any veteran of the North will attest, formal benefits such as pay were only part of the appeal of the North. In the "shortage economy," protection from scarcity was far more important than pay, and standard accounts of northern development are therefore mistaken in their emphasis on the pull of the "long ruble" (Armstrong 1965; Mote 1998). As I will explain in the coming pages, it was the promise of abundant and available food, the lack of queues in the shops, a flat of one's own, and at the same time exceptional access back to the materik by virtue of cheap northern aviation that pulled workers north.

Privilege in Practice

In the first decade of mass voluntary settlement (1955-65), there were still only modest grounds for speaking of a privileged northern worker. On the debris of the recently closed labour-camp system, the Soviet leadership could not overnight create a population of prosperous and well-housed northern settlers. Nor did it have to. Material incentives, as they were introduced, did not need to be elaborate to be effective; it was necessary only to create a zone of *relative* prosperity in the North. As long as living conditions were better than elsewhere in the country, demand for northern settlement was high. These were the last years of post-war reconstruction, and the stock of living space had not yet recovered in those parts of the country devastated by fighting. In the late 1950s and early 1960s, recruitment for northern settlement proved easy among a generation growing up in the ruins left by war. In the official rhetoric of the era, these were pioneers – *entusiasty* – animated by a sense of mission and enthusiasm for "opening up the North" compensating for the suffering that came with settling the undeveloped North. But there are still plenty of entusiasty in the North today, and despite the persistence of the rhetoric of willing sacrifice, their personal recollections reveal a different story. A seamstress from Minsk who moved to Chukotka in the early 1960s recalled, "It wasn't a matter of enthusiasm, but of famine. Byelorussia had been occupied by the fascists and was completely destroyed. [After the war] we ate grass, gathered cornhusks in the fields, picked edible plants in the forest. [In coming north] we were running away from hunger" [4].

Living conditions in northern regions remained difficult into the 1960s. As for the prisoner labourers a decade before, northern postings to Chukotka in these years often came with the proviso that migrants build the very settlements they were intended to inhabit. The material and psychological conditions of pioneer life there could still come as a shock. The daughter of an entusiast settler who came to Chukotka in the late 1950s to work as a school director recalled that, in the 1950s, "there was something called *'orgnabor,'* when a workgroup was formed in a factory or a village. They would take these so-called volunteers, who they called entusiasty or *komsomoltsy* [members of the Soviet Communist Party youth branch], and send them all to the North. There was a group sent to Ust'-Belaia [a Chukchi village on the middle reaches of the Anadyr River], eighteen people, and in the end only two survived their time there. It's not easy to say what killed them – impossible conditions, accidents, drinking ... They were just thrown out there to build civilization and abandoned" [7].

Nevertheless, the prospect of a decently paid job and, most importantly, a place to live, was enough to tempt many young recruits to the North. A retired senior geologist who settled in Chukotka in 1956 related how for the first four years he lived with his wife and two children in mobile survey camps. By their fifth year he was leading large geological expeditions in the interior, and his family was allocated a one-room flat in the district centre. By the standards of the day, they considered themselves privileged. He had been rewarded a northern posting in a geological enterprise after coming first in his graduating class. The life his family led in the North of the late 1950s, he recalled, was more prosperous and secure than anything he had experienced in childhood, part of which he spent under German occupation outside Leningrad [5].

Difficult living conditions in the first years of mass settlement nevertheless generated a problem bedevilling northern development thereafter – high labour turnover *(tekuchest')*. Although settlement continued unabated, many northern enterprises found it impossible to retain staff, particularly since the pace of investment meant that almost every organization in the post-Stalinist North was in a constant state of expansion. Northern migrants joined a "flowing population," transient and lacking loyalty to a single workplace (Yanovskii 1969), while northern enterprises themselves engaged in a kind of benefits bidding war to attract skilled workers. Yet more threatening to northern development objectives, conditions in mainstream Soviet life under Krushchev (1956-64) were rapidly leaving the era of post-war recovery and austerity behind. This was the era of the Thaw (roughly 1958-64), which the typical Soviet citizen experienced not so much as a period of intellectual permissiveness, as a time of abundance in the shops, when it finally became possible to obtain a new one-family flat.[17] Conditions of life on the materik now threatened to catch up with those in the ostensibly "privileged" North. Krushchev's consumerist policies, if taken too far, would erode a pillar of state power – the persistence of shortage in everyday life.

To maintain the idea of the North as a prosperous frontier within an increasingly affluent society, the Soviet leadership was forced to broaden the incentives to migration. In 1959, Krushchev had made a speech in Vladivostok, in which he spoke in utopian terms about northern settlements covered by plastic domes and warmed by sunrays deflected by Soviet satellites (Armstrong 1965). His point was serious; the leadership was protecting the northern osvoenie objectives by signalling its intention to keep northern living standards moving well ahead of the Soviet average. And so it was that long-time settlers in Chukotka remember the early 1960s as a crossing point, when the settler way of life ripened into its affluent halcyon. Before this time, pay had been good. But now the state was investing in *quality* of life, building a truly settled North where newcomers could raise families and finally "really live" *(zhit' po-nastoiashemu).*

The Hollow Ruble and the Importance of Supply

Hindered by a lack of fieldwork access, northernists have in the past identified the "long ruble" – meaning the wage increment and cash bonuses – as the primary attraction to migrant workers.[18] Certainly, a low income was widely perceived in the stagnation era as a primary cause of hardship for ordinary Soviet workers, and Vladimir Shlapentokh (1989) refers to a series of sociological studies from the 1970s and 1980s showing that low salaries were a driving motive in changes of employment and decisions to migrate. Similarly, recollections of the long ruble run like a red thread through the narratives of settler life in stagnation-era Chukotka. Although prices were fixed in the Soviet economy, and essential food and goods were affordable, holiday travel, luxury clothing and jewellery, and durables such as televisions, furniture, and washing machines were very expensive by the standards of an average Soviet income. In the 1970s, as shortages worsened, the growth of the shadow economy amounted to de facto inflation, as consumers were forced to pay black market prices to obtain goods. For settlers in Chukotka, a typical monthly household income (two full-time earners) was 800-1,000 rubles, in comparison to 150 in central parts of the country, and since costs were only marginally higher in the Far North, northerners had vastly higher spending power and could rapidly save large sums.[19]

It was not true, however, that a northern income four to five times higher than the average translated into a proportionately higher standard of living in material terms. In the Soviet shortage economy, there were few opportunities to spend the full amount of money northerners earned; the only major items for which they could legitimately save – flats, country cottages, and cars – were difficult to obtain.[20] Because northern shops were well supplied, this vastly devalued the worth of those items that were readily available; a former geologist from Chukotka's Iul'tinskii District recalled

> a sea of cognac – we only drank cognac there. Vodka just didn't have any appeal – tea with cognac, coffee with cognac, cognac on the tundra, cognac with breakfast ... My

> friends often came over when my wife was on holiday on the materik or at work. We lived on the first floor – we'd open the window and watch a video, and drink cognac from crystal glasses. And we'd say a toast, drink, and toss the glasses out the window into the yard. There was a mountain of broken crystal outside my window, and that was the usual thing. When we ran out of glasses, we just walked down to the shop and bought another box of them. And back to the flat for more! [64]

Because northerners could find little practical use for their exceedingly large incomes, they often displayed a cavalier disregard for money. Although many informants today cast this behaviour in a romantic and anti-materialist light, it could only have emerged at a time when everyone had more than enough. A former geologist remarked,

> I remember one bachelor geologist living in the dormitory in Selchan, and he had a big bulletin board on his wall labelled "*nam pishut*" (what they write us). It was covered with telegrams from our colleagues on leave on the materik, saying things like, "Vitia, I burned through 500, send me 200" or "Vitia, I'm broke, send me enough for the plane ticket back." In other words, the romantic approach had nothing to do with saving money for the long run – it was about working hard and going on holidays, having a great time, spending everything, and coming back to the North to work for another year. [3]

Another recurring set of narratives concerns the avaricious settler, a type for whom saving the long ruble was a driving motive, a behaviour considered antisocial and indeed deviant. Very often, informants would divide the categories of northern migrant into the money-grubbers and the romantic anti-materialists, placing themselves in the latter category. One long-time geologist remarked, "To be honest, I never had much time for the Ukrainians, who only came here to *zakhrobit' khroshi,* as they say (pull the bucks)" [1]. A common variation on this theme is the story of a man, whose name no one can quite recall, who

> came up to work as a truck-driver on the Egvekinot-Iul'tin road, hauling ore concentrate – one of the best-paid jobs you could get. He never took a holiday, doubled up his shifts, and scrimped on everything – he lived on nothing but oatmeal and canned beef *[tushenka],* which he bought in bulk from the geological survey warehouse. After about fifteen years, he turned in his keys, withdrew his fortune from the savings bank, and packed it into a suitcase. Now he was going home to really *live*! Well, he was waiting at the airport in Anadyr for his flight to Moscow, and he thought, why not have a little drink to celebrate? He went into the cafeteria, drank a glass of vodka, and dropped down on his suitcase full of rubles dead of a heart attack. [1]

Neither official Soviet morality nor popular Russian culture have ever particularly recommended the pursuit of wealth, and so in narrating the past in this way, contemporary settlers may be covering materialist motives with a moral gloss (what sociologists call the desirable values effect). But settler attitudes to high pay in the Soviet years also suggest that money in this society operated in a manner very different from that to which citizens of capitalist states are accustomed.

The role of money throughout the Soviet space, where privilege depended on *access* to scarce resources, was problematic, and as shortages worsened, so did the utility of the ruble. When a long queue formed outside a Soviet shop, passersby would ask not what was for sale, but "what are they giving out?" *(chto daiut?)*. Having money was not the same thing as a right to buy; there was only the state-sanctioned right to give. Whereas money in a free market is a signal of value, the Soviet Union had a demonetized economy, in which bureaucratic commands replaced consumer demand in driving the movement of goods and services. Moreover, unlike in a free market, Soviet money was not a completely portable asset, able to command value wherever it was taken. The geography of closed distribution meant money was most powerful within the domains to which a citizen belonged: an army officer with rights to special medical treatment and excellent food shops in Chukotka could not easily cross into the geological survey's domain of distribution and access.

The weakness of the Soviet ruble affected northerners as well. Although serious problems of shortage did not reach the Far North until perestroika (1985-91), settlers often lived with a foot in central regions of the country, where the scarcity of goods *(defitsit)* was an essential part of life. This presented a problem to northerners hoping to use their high northern incomes to build a life back in central Russia, a very common aspiration. Well-paid northerners always had enough money to cover the nominal side of any purchase, but they increasingly found that money was only a necessary, but not sufficient, condition for "obtaining."[21] Even with their large savings, settlers began to experience problems in arranging the construction of condominiums in central Russia. The queue for obtaining cars also lengthened interminably, and settlers were well aware of how much time their mainland counterparts were spending in their everyday lives searching and queuing for essential goods. Watching stagnation from a distance, many settlers made the entirely reasonable choice to remain in the North, drinking cognac and dressing in their furs and pearls. As time passed, the Far North's well-stocked shops served to remind local residents how different life remained in these regions. Indeed, the lack of acute shortages soon eclipsed the formal benefit of earning the long ruble as the cornerstone of settler prosperity. One informant recalled, "When I came to Chukotka and went into a shop for the first time, I thought, 'This is communism, finally!' You could just walk in and lay your hands on sausages of any sort, cured fish, conserves of fruit and vegetables ... and listen! No one was in a panic!" [6]

These are the words of a heating-systems engineer who grew up in post-war Smolensk. During his Brezhnev-era youth, he remembered, everyone called the rail line to Moscow the "sausage train" because taking an overnight journey to the capital was the only way of obtaining food no longer on the shelves in the provinces. While in university, he met and married a Russian woman from Chukotka and settled there after graduation.

The incredible abundance of supplies that so overwhelmed him was the achievement of an immensely complex and costly system of northern supply, which shipped, trucked, and flew practically all the food and goods the northern population consumed from central and southern regions of the country. In Chukotka, whose main port in Anadyr lies over four thousand kilometres sailing from Vladivostok (the eastern terminus of the trans-Siberian rail line), supplies for an entire year had to reach the region during a shipping season of less than three months. Despite the expense and difficulty, shops in Chukotka were well stocked, and until the very last years of perestroika (1988-91), the region was virtually unaffected by the problems of shortage that plagued Soviet life on the materik. Settlers certainly understood the crisis of shortages outside the North; the abundance of supply in Chukotka and the absence of queuing are still remembered as one of the best aspects of northern life: the words "*snabzhenie bylo otlichnoe*" (the supply of goods was excellent) possess a near ritual quality in narratives of the settler experience.

Employees of certain powerful enterprises and administrations had access to a still-further degree of abundance generated by their institutional powers of distribution and supply. As the administrative capital, Anadyr furnished the most varied cultural amenities, the biggest shops, and the best air transport in the region. Yet, across from the civilian population, on the north shore of the mouth of the Anadyr River, lay the valley of Gudym, the site of a secret base buried under a mountain and holding a vast store of military hardware, sensitive communications installations, and even an arms factory designed to be impervious to nuclear attack. Every civilian resident of Anadyr knew that, as good as the general distribution system was in the town, these military bases were even more exclusive zones of supply. A former construction engineer in Anadyr recalled that "We had great shops – you could get apples and oranges year round, as many as you wanted. But in the closed military shops – well, you had to see it to believe it. They had pineapples and bananas!" [14]

In another settler town, Egvekinot, residents could find daily essentials in the shops, but the local branch of the geological survey, the Ekspeditsiia, shipped its own supplies for furnishing geological expeditions. A former geologist remembered, "we really had no shortages in general. There was a brewery, a dairy, fresh milk, and eggs. There was furniture for sale in the shops! But you know, I always got my supplies from the stores of the Ekspeditsiia – everything just sat there for us to take. So smoked sausage, for example – this was sometimes hard to get even in Chukotka, but we could take it from the stores by the case. There was fruit, canned meat, butter, barrels of salmon roe, and never less than five kinds of imported cigarettes." [64]

The Liquidation of Distance

Another very important consideration for workers migrating to the most isolated region of the Soviet North was the excellent system of reliable and cheap air transport. Chukotka may have been remote, but because the state cross-subsidized a network of flights reaching every settlement and linking the region to major cities on the materik, the burden of distance was effectively lifted. Extreme remoteness became rather a rhetorical condition, useful for buttressing settlers' self-perceptions of difference and their sense of entitlement to the special rewards of northern residence.[22] But, combined with exceptionally long annual leave and the extended breaks between shifts that many workers enjoyed, northern aviation offered settlers a level of mobility truly remarkable by Soviet standards. Paradoxically, settlers often remarked that they sought mobility in coming north: rather than giving them a life in arctic isolation, resettlement supplied the money and holidays to travel throughout the entire Soviet Union. The mobility of the average settler could thus support a considerably more cosmopolitan lifestyle than that enjoyed by most residents of major Soviet cities. This quality, however, did not often translate into mobility *within* the North, or even within Chukotka's territory, particularly for those with sedentary jobs in the towns and capital. Instead, settler corridors of movement would usually take them out of the North at every opportunity, where they travelled for pleasure, maintained networks of kin and friendship, and prepared for a future back on the materik. It is still common to find settlers with decades of experience in Chukotka and flats full of souvenirs from Eastern Europe and Central Asia who have no experience at all of the tundra beyond Anadyr.

Problems of Housing

Of all the perquisites of northern settlement, the promise of *zhilploshchad'*, literally "space to live," was one of the most highly valued. Mass industrialization and the growth of Soviet cities were initially aided by Stalin's density housing policy, forcing the partition of individual-family flats into communal housing. When concerted state efforts to alleviate housing shortages finally began in the late 1950s, only a third of newlyweds and 6 percent of young single workers had their own flats (Klopov 1985). The situation was different in the North, where employers issuing an official summons (vyzov) guaranteed their recruits housing. For the post-war generation, the prospect of obtaining a flat to start adult life and raise a family was critical for maintaining the appeal of northern settlement. The importance authorities attached to housing, in comparison with other northern benefits, was directly reflected in the Soviet policy of building fully serviced and permanent settlements in the Far North. For sympathetic commentators abroad, the appearance of a large and settled population in the Soviet North, which had no equivalent in other circumpolar regions, appeared to dovetail with the ideological principle that living standards should be made uniform throughout the entire socialist space (Mowat 1970; Smolka 1937; Armstrong 1965). In fact, the permanent style of development, which characterized even the remotest settlements in Chukotka, including industrial mining towns near deposits of tin, gold, and coal with clearly finite lifetimes, reflected the power that zhilploshchad' held for Soviet workers. While the hollow ruble gradually reverted to a mere symbol of northern prosperity, the idea of living in one's own family flat continued to burn brightly in the dreams of aspiring migrants until the very end of the Soviet era.

So difficult was it to build housing at a pace to match the rate of migration that zhilploshchad' was one formal benefit the Soviet state struggled to grant in full. Although many migrants immediately received modern and comfortable two- and three-room flats on the day of their arrival, others struggled for years to claim the housing promised them. In Chukotka, swiftly expanding enterprises were often short of labour, but desperate housing shortages prevented them from recruiting workers. Only the larger and better-financed organizations had the power to build or acquire housing, and thus, only they could attract the best workers. To illustrate, the Chukotka branch of the Russian Academy of Sciences, which expanded into a major institute in the 1980s, constructed two large apartment buildings over that period. With this large stock of housing, the institute rapidly attracted an academic staff of thirty-five, including two *doctory nauk* (Doctors of Philosophy with habilitation degrees) and fourteen *kandidaty nauk* (Doctors of Philosophy), all of whom were enticed to abandon posts in Moscow and other large cities and settle in Anadyr, still a town of under ten thousand inhabitants [12].

This confirms one principle of the closed distribution system – powerful enterprises could use their allocative privileges to attract workers, draining the labour market surrounding them but protecting their own interests. For less valuable workers, or for those working within politically weak organizations, it was much more common to spend the first years in Chukotka living in communal flats or hostels, converted barges dragged onto land, and even enormous pipe sections and abandoned airplanes adapted into makeshift homes. Institutional affiliation was also more important than professional status. Chukotka's head dentist (from the mid-1980s), who first came to Anadyr in 1969 with a prestigious higher education, managed to obtain a two-room flat only after fifteen years; the dentistry service, as he put it, suffered from a lack of "pull" [13]. By comparison, I spoke with several former construction workers in Anadyr who received two-room flats from their employer, the once powerful Anadyr Construction Trust (Anadyrstroi), within a year of arriving.

Late-Soviet Anadyr, showing Arktika apartment buildings, 1980s
Archives of the Heritage of Chukotka Regional Museum

The struggle to secure housing illustrates that Soviet Chukotka, far from being a homogeneous zone of abundance and prosperity, in fact contained significant disparities of privilege. This belies the rhetoric of egalitarianism and solidarity pervading the narratives of present-day settlers, which present a picture of social relations as conspicuously non-hierarchical (see Chapter 3). Certainly, boiler stokers and Party officials alike patronized the same well-supplied shops in Chukotka's towns, received equally inflated wages, and took equally long annual leave in resorts on the Black Sea. Both enjoyed a measure of official esteem in the hierarchy of Soviet workers and were envied their northern propiska by their mainland counterparts. But, in casting all settlers as members of a discrete and elevated social class – an elite category of Soviet labour – we should resist the presumption that a classless population existed within its boundaries. Just as the late-Soviet North comprised a zone of privilege in Soviet society, and Chukotka was in turn more privileged than other less remote parts of the North – one closed distribution system encased within another – so were found many smaller and more exclusive zones of privilege nested within Chukotka's own borders. Although gaining admission to Chukotka was itself a considerable achievement, migrants to the okrug were then faced with a highly differentiated patchwork of institutions and territories, some offering much better access to scarce goods than others. Unequal access to housing was testament to this fact. Whereas conditions of general prosperity masked the actual existence of a stratified hierarchy of privilege within settler (and indeed indigenous) society, this quite suddenly changed with the Soviet collapse. Thereafter, as we will see in coming chapters, the place each northerner occupied in the old Soviet hierarchy directly shaped his or her destiny in the post-Soviet era.

The Effective State and Settler Difference

By going beyond the standard accounts of northern settlement and the incentives system, and talking face to face with settler veterans of the Soviet experience, we learn that formal incentives of northern residence eroded into symbol long before the in situ attractions of the settler lifestyle. What good was the long ruble when less and less was for sale back in central regions of the country? Early retirement and return to the reality of stagnation-era life on the materik, as many settlers came to understand on their long holidays outside the North, was becoming by the 1980s a rather dreadful prospect. The growing difficulty of obtaining a flat there, never mind a car or a plot of rural land, rendered return not just distasteful but unrealistic. For settlers, the gap was only widening between their quality of life in the North and the experience of survival they witnessed outside.

But then, this was the system of closed distribution at work – the direct result of state efforts to structure shortage. The weakness of money in particular points to the distinct *locational* rigidity of Soviet labour, a symptom of economic sclerosis on one hand, and yet a source of state power over the movement of its population on the other. The logic of a closed distribution system, after all, began with the interests of the state project upon which it was sited – in this case, the industrializing and elaborately defended territory of Chukotka – and the privileges of those workers inhabiting the zone flowed strictly from the needs of that project. The free movement of workers, if perhaps healthy for the economy in general, was toxic to the specific projects at the centre of each closed distribution system. The rewards of residence reflected the need to fix workers in place and thereby protect the state's cherished goals of severnoe osvoenie. This is precisely why, especially as the larger Soviet economy stagnated, settlers living in northern towns well supplied with *defitsitnye* goods found it difficult to export their privileges to central Russia. These settlers, who, without moving into the shadow economy, quite effortlessly inhabited an elite social class, were members of that class only *while they inhabited the North.* Their status was not freely convertible, and they could not cash in their northern privileges for a better life elsewhere. This geographically fixed system of privilege, in turn, incentivized a long-term commitment to northern life.

In conversations with long-time settlers, one encounters a hidden world of far less tangible reasons for choosing the northern life. There were, and are, *qualities* of settler life foreign to calculations of material benefit but vital for understanding the relative permanence of the Soviet in-migrant population in Chukotka. This is the subject of the next chapter, but what I wish to emphasize here is the manner in which settlers' experience of prosperity, which could not have existed without the support of an effective state apparatus, shaped their relationship with the institutions of state power.

This is to say that, if settlers witnessed a manifestation of the state in its most dynamic, benevolent, and commanding form, their experience translated into a particular conception of the Soviet project that was quite unlike the cynical regard shared by growing numbers of ordinary citizens. The limitations of the centrally planned economy, further crippled by pervasive corruption in bureaucracy, converted Soviet life into a gruelling exercise in foraging: the individual retreated from the official workplace into the shadows of the second economy and the personal obsessions of Finn Sivert Nielsen's (2007) *uzkie krugi* ("narrow circles" or "small cliques"); state enterprises in turn erected self-defensive barriers in an internecine bidding war for scarce labour and materials, the behaviour of Verdery's late-Soviet vedomstvo. So crippled had the command economy become that on the seventieth anniversary of the Communist Revolution (in 1987), the Soviet Union resorted to large imports of grain, meat, butter, and fruit from abroad to create the impression of normality.

Even the state monopoly on distribution, on which it relied to uphold the geographic hierarchy of privilege and thus protect its cherished projects, was finally compromised by corruption and the black market. The flow of goods and services in Soviet cities moved into channels beyond state control, heavily dependent on networks of acquaintance, while official jobs became increasingly a platform for illegal trading, smuggling, and favour peddling.[23] Inequality and the emergence of a new class of wealthy shadow-economy entrepreneurs and corrupt *apparatchiki* recommended to ordinary Soviets the rewards of subverting the official economic order. The failure of state control over economic life also encouraged a more general hostility to the Soviet project and its ideology, and the movement of Soviet citizens into spaces of everyday private life and social intercourse beyond official control reflected a terminal fracture in the bonds between state and individual. In all domains of life where this was possible, Soviets were going where the state was not.

Chukotka presents a radically contrasting picture. To its settlers, the state still appeared capable of fulfilling the Leninist prophecy of a prosperous future. Unlike on the materik, prosperity derived from a legitimate and uncorrupted relationship with the state. Conditions in the "zone of abundance" obviated the need for a shadow economy in the region, although settlers could use their high incomes to obtain prestige items on the black market during their holidays. Prosperity likewise generated a sense of solidarity among settlers, who, unlike the residents of stagnation-era Leningrad, were not forced to live within narrow and barricaded circles of mutual reliance to survive. Although some northern enterprises were powerful patrons, awarding their employees with resources scarce even by local standards (flats, novels), there was no real "limbo" of scarcity (in Finn Sivert Nielsen's conception) to threaten the survival of settlers.

If the most defining characteristic of Soviet stagnation was a gradual failure of the state, the recollections of settlers evoke a contrary reality, in which the charisma and efficacy of the state were not stagnant but in fact ascendant. The history of mass settlement in Chukotka reveals the quite remarkable ability of the Soviet regime, in certain strategically selected domains, to make a virtue of its failings. As stagnation-era society assumed a more cellular, fragmented texture afflicted by shortage and the exhaustion of state-building ideology, the regime harnessed these destabilizing forces and tailored the incentives for northern migration to match them, duplicating the informal "island" in Soviet life by creating an officially sanctioned zone of privilege in the North. Soviet Chukotka, like other northern regions, became a vast domain closed to outsiders and extraordinarily effective at provisioning those within its boundaries. At the same time, the cosmopolitan mobility of the settler sensitized this population to the realities of life outside the North, which simply served to cement settler loyalties to northern communities. As shortages of all kinds, material and ideological, assumed ever-deeper extremes and forced ordinary Soviets into a subversive relationship with the state, a twilight zone of illegal exchanges, and cynical non-participation in formal rituals of citizenship, life in late-Soviet Chukotka took its own trajectory. Until the very demise of Soviet power, it remained a domain of particular state *functionality.*

3
Arctic Idyll: Living in Soviet Chukotka

Veteran settlers in the Russian North will usually tell you that they never meant to stay. In their plans, the North was to be a brief chapter, a period of sacrifice and adventure leading to a better life back on the mainland. From the 1960s, it took three years of northern residence to attain the full northern salary and annual leave. "Three years, maximum six," they remember promising themselves, and then back south to use their savings on a car, a flat, perhaps a rural dacha. This was a common story, but many others changed their plans, and after working three years, subsequently stayed on in the North for a working lifetime. State-supplied northern benefits, which incentivized long-term settlement, clearly played a role. But material privilege alone cannot account for the size and permanence of the settler population that, by the point of Soviet collapse, vastly outnumbered northern indigenous peoples and continues to do so even after fifteen years of rapid out-migration.

There were advantages to settler life hardly connected to official northern benefits, advantages invisible to those without direct experience of the Soviet North. Both foreign observers and Soviet experts on the North have failed to understand that settler privileges extended beyond the long ruble and the well-stocked village shop in ways that were never advertised in central regions of the Soviet Union. But, to explain how requires a reconstruction of the *sensation* of settler life and the moral and ideational frameworks upon which it rested. This exercise relies on the collected stories present-day settlers tell about their lives in the Soviet era, and so, in contrast to the examination of northern prosperity, this leads us into the territory of ethnographic history. This methodological shift also occasions a shift in scale, from the entire Soviet Russian North to a particular part of it. The stories I collected are mostly set in Chukotka, a region whose settlers are in many ways paradigmatic of the larger non-native population in the Russian North (see Introduction). From this point onward, this is our setting.

In Chukotka, settlers found exceptional resources for personal renovation, and they found them at a time in Soviet life when attention to personal needs attained the aspect of a mass obsession. After all, economic and managerial failure was only part of the general stagnation of Soviet power; the revolutionary state was also losing its ideational momentum. The Brezhnevite compromise, which devolved power downwards to regional and local elites and granted the individual a degree of immunity and privacy, reflected ideological exhaustion and a lack of will even at the centre to perpetuate a "continual revolution." The promises of socialist rhetoric were by this point so evidently hollow (remember that Khrushchev had promised fully developed communism in ten years) that the obligations of citizenship now entailed routine and unbearable hypocrisy for many ordinary Soviets. As a corrosive anomie took hold, particularly among the post-war generation coming of age during Krushchev's Thaw and its Thermidorean aftermath, the Far North was reimagined. Shedding the aura of a revolutionary frontier lit by the ideological fervour of volunteer-enthusiasts, it became an idea of escape, a geographical antidote to modern Soviet life. On one hand, it is true that the appeal of prosperity and abundance in the North during the Soviet era signalled the materialist turn in society and its uses in projects of social engineering. But on the other, the mass appeal of northern settlement as a way of fleeing the Soviet everyday reflects just as meaningfully on the condition of the state and its projects.

The appeal of the North from a distance is one question. Another concerns what settlers actually found there. In Chukotka, by their own accounts, settlers discovered the resources to live more purposeful lives, the freedom to direct their daily efforts toward projects free of cynicism. The "purposeful life" was animated by three particular aspects of settler privilege, and though they could never have arisen independently of the conditions of material prosperity, they were less tangible rewards than those advertised in the Soviet regime's official package of benefits, which have been given credit for the success of mass settlement. They were certainly difficult to detect from a distance. Instead, they were a pleasant discovery for new arrivals and an invisible glue bonding ever-growing numbers to the North in a permanent way.

The first of these was the least anticipated: a quality of freedom. We now understand how the Brezhnev-era state, afflicted with sclerotic decrepitude in many domains of life, nevertheless achieved a near complete managerial command in the Far North. Northern workers lived in an economic environment animated by an effective and commanding state. If shortages were pushing ordinary Soviets into subversive activity outside the official economy in order to survive, the benefits of northern prosperity held the settler more or less within a legitimate relationship with the state. Yet, in a life that was so effectively prescribed, controlled, and legitimated by state power, we find a paradox: the Far North was also, for settlers, a domain of remarkable *statelessness*. Even as the state secured their lives in material ways, it permitted extraordinary freedom from the rituals of official public life and permitted the flourishing of unofficial spaces of freedom. Within limits, settlers could do what they wanted in their private lives and, even more significantly, in their involvements with others, and so personal interests and spontaneous initiatives shaped modes of leisure to a degree unattainable for ordinary Soviets. Understandably, the benevolent regard with which many settlers held the Soviet project resulted not only from their perception of its efficacy, but also from their freedom to inhabit a relatively expansive and unscripted private realm.

In addition to this, settlers shared a common sense of mission, an awareness and experience of their own agency in a development and modernization project with both the untamed northern landscape and its "primitive" indigenous peoples as its objects. This was of great consequence for people whose personal and family histories bore the trauma of unceasing projects of social engineering in the early and middle years of the Soviet experiment. In the North, settlers were finally the agents of change, not the victims. They were experts, they imported metropolitan technologies and lifestyles, and their roles in northern osvoenie made them powerful. In short, they were renovated by their position in a colonial project.

Finally, this sense of common mission, incubated in the paradoxically stateless spaces of freedom, and supported by material prosperity, generated an exceptional fabric of community. No account of the settler past fails to recall the kindness, generosity, and mutual concern that held northern communities together. This quality of daily life furnished settlers with a sense of social location, it protected them from the hazards of the arctic climate and remote isolation, and it produced a feeling of commonality. This sense, and in particular a belief that northern communities were stronger and kinder than any to be found on the materik, led their members quite quickly to think about themselves as people of Chukotka, rather than visitors with a home far away.

These aspects of settler life have never been addressed in accounts of northern settlement focusing on material prosperity. Nor do they feature in any of the existing ethnographic literature on life in the Soviet and post-Soviet North, simply because these accounts have never examined the lives of settlers in any depth. But the intangible, invisible advantages of northern life in fact became the most meaningful reference points for Soviet settlers – for thinking about themselves and their place in Soviet society, for orienting their loyalties to place, and with time, for informing their responses to the collapse of the Soviet project. Unusual circumstances engendered communities with an unusual sense of difference. This sense of difference – what we might call a settler identity – is not simply a curiosity of the Soviet past. Rather, it constitutes one of its most influential survivals, a fact of sociality still strongly shaping the contemporary North. The idea among settlers that they collectively constitute a discrete culture rooted, in this case, in Chukotka's landscape, operates as a bulwark of resistance. It resists, as we will see in the second half of this book, policies of modernization premised on the classification of Chukotka's settlers as merely a dislocated population, a collection of people without a special relationship to the North or any kind of collective and distinctly northern identity.

The Return of Privacy

Social histories of Soviet life often point to the end of the Stalinist surveillance state and the beginning of Brezhnev-era stagnation as a threshold moment, after which it became possible to speak of an "informal public sphere," a realm of independent and spontaneous social activity more expansive than the private realm of the "kitchen-table salon." Its counterpart, the "official public sphere," where the forms and content of social interaction were controlled by the state, continued to play a pervasive role in daily life, but now the boundaries between the unofficial and the official had shifted. Whereas sociological understandings of the public and private, deriving from the work of Ferdinand Tönnies (1957) and Émile Durkheim (1964), had been foundational to conceptualizations of modern society generally, only with studies of Soviet life was the distinction between official and unofficial public spheres introduced.[1] This new distinction was occasioned by the extraordinary efforts of the Stalinist state to penetrate the private domain and to render so much of everyday life a surveilled and scripted public performance that large amounts of social time came to be structured by the rituals of citizenship.[2]

By persecuting private life, scripting social interaction within the social *kollektiv*, and mandating how the individual should spend time outside the workplace, the state laid the basis for an inevitable reaction once its coercive powers slackened. During the post-Stalinist Thaw, this reaction took the form of an irrepressible attention to the domestic, the intimate, and the personal. Private life, and the correlative pursuit of personal fulfillment, became a kind of *Zeitgeist* for the post-Stalinist era. With Khrushchev's denunciation of Stalinist excess, this spirit quickly asserted itself in the cultural production and daily activities of the Soviet people. The state still monopolized the script in the official public sphere, as the 1966 show trial of the dissidents Yuli Daniel and Andrei Sinyavksy made clear. But individual initiative could be put to use in a grey zone, public and social in character yet still relatively free of state control, and a lively "alternative script" on Soviet reality flourished in this space, to which the rich body of stagnation-era political jokes can testify. As this domain expanded, so that neither the regime nor the ordinary individual could possibly deny its role in everyday life, an officially tolerated hypocrisy attended the mandatory participation in the rituals of official life. But, in a proportional reaction, honesty and authenticity – in relations with others and in directing personal energies – became cherished values, and next to the struggle for everyday survival, this quest for honesty achieved an obsessive importance in the stagnation era.

Vladimir Shlapentokh (1989) called this the "privatisation of Soviet society" and the "phenomenon of retreat." He was referring to the mass withdrawal of energy and belief from the state and the realignment of individual interest toward private life, already clearly evident in the work of the most prominent post-Thaw novelists, including the "Village Prose" writers Valentin Rasputin, Vasilii Shukshin, and Viktor Astafiev, and the neo-realists Yuri Kazakov, Vladimir Makanin, and Yuri Bondarev. In all their works, the individual experience and the search for personal meaning and fulfillment completely crowd out official public life, and the official aims of the Soviet state are practically invisible. Shlapentokh pointed to the emergence of a crypto-political "civil society" in the unofficial public realm, and subsequent studies of everyday life in the stagnation era explored other directions in which the retreat from public life generated forms of private initiative. Oleg Yanitskii (1993), for example, identified Soviet-era environmentalism as a meaningful precursor to independent political activity. In practice, the search for personal meaning and fulfillment usually took apolitical forms, since the state maintained its capacity to suppress overt dissent. Instead, people absorbed themselves in collecting, music, drinking, drug-taking, science, the mythological, the magical, and the exotic, and testing the limits of individual strength in extreme sport, including alpinism and exploration. The intimate realm, where relations were most resistant to ideology and surveillance, seemed to be the most cherished of all, evident in the cult of friendship and the explosion of interest in the erotic.[3] The spaces of freedom within which the individual could indulge these interests proliferated in the 1970s and 1980s. These included cultural centres, which hosted a universe of clubs and circles *(kruzhkii)* no longer closely watched by state authorities, cafés and "intelligentsia salons," and the "hanging-out" domain of the counterculture *tusovka*,[4] and wild nature, where escape took on a literal aspect. Nevertheless, the state demanded its due, and unstructured time remained a relatively scarce resource (this is why, as the writer Joseph Brodsky [1986] remembered, so many of the literary intelligentsia strove to be night watchmen).

If the privatization of Soviet life amounted to a tidal movement of personal energies away from the projects of the state, and set a generation of Soviets in search of opportunities for self-realization, life in the Far North furnished them in abundance. In the recollections of present-day settlers, Soviet Chukotka accommodated an extraordinarily rich unofficial public realm. A sense of solidarity among settlers, enthusiasm for northern life and its various challenges and projects, and a kind of benevolent retreat on the part of the state lent everyday life a cherished quality of "honesty" and "authenticity." A former drilling technician who moved to Chukotka from eastern Ukraine at the beginning of the 1970s put it this way: "We lived in a kind of spiritual oasis, an untainted paradise. There was purity and simple honesty in human relationships, as though we were all of one mind and one breed – kind, noble, creative. This is why I lived here, not because of the long ruble" [16].[5]

When settlers speak of purity and simple honesty, what do they mean? Surely, it is a kind of shorthand for the distinctly different ways in which northern life permitted, or encouraged, them to interact. It is abundantly clear that settlers perceived the North as an alternative space, and going there as a way of rejecting the hypocrisy in everyday Soviet life and radically realigning personal energies toward self-realization. But here we return to the already familiar paradox of northern development: the remarkable ability of the state to find sources of strength in its weaknesses. If we doubt the power of the Soviet state to turn popular resistance to the advantage of its cherished projects, we have only to consider the remarkable benefits northern osvoenie harvested from the cynicism of a generation of skilled graduates during stagnation.

Romantic Questing

The economy of shortage may have been the engine of post-war northern settlement, but a kind of moral and spiritual scarcity in mainstream Soviet life also drove many of its inhabitants to the geographic fringe. A member of the artistic community of Chukotka's capital, Anadyr, who came to the region in the early 1980s, recalled,

> I was just terrified of becoming like my parents – married, two children in a two-room flat, making do on 120 rubles [a month]. You know the old Soviet joke about the man who goes away on a business trip, gets drunk on the last night, and ends up on the wrong plane home? He lands in another city, but everything is identical, so he hails a taxi and asks for 25 Engels Street. He arrives, goes to the fourteenth floor, his key fits in the door, the flat is just like his, he has a shower, and then some strange woman walks in and he finally realizes something is out of place. OK, this was one of our jokes, but we laughed because it was so true. [65]

As an antidote to the urban everyday, the North was imagined in highly romantic terms: *romantika severa* (the romance of the North) was a soup of preconceptions, among them extreme remoteness and harsh climate, the indigenous and the exotic, and ecological and human purity. Settlers in the present often assert that they came to the North not for the money, but for the "smell of the taiga" and "for the northern mist," echoing the sentiments of a widely known song of the 1960s, which included the line "But I'm going – I'm going for the mists, for dreams and the smell of the taiga."[6] The Far North was about as far away as a young graduate could get from the Soviet metropolis; it was the next best thing to foreign travel, which was out of the question. In this sense, Chukotka held a particular appeal; as one long-time settler explained, "If I was going north, I wanted to go as far north as possible, I wanted to experience the extreme" [25]. For a generation fascinated with the West, somehow it mattered that Chukotka was practically touching America, regardless of the fact that it lay behind an impenetrable "ice curtain." All the same, romantika severa was never a particularly subversive commentary on Soviet state power. The romantic allure of the North, albeit tied to a rejection of the Soviet project in its urban variants, entirely coincided with the interests of northern osvoenie. Alongside the portrayal of abundance and material privilege, romantic stereotypes were continually cultivated and recirculated in official accounts of northern life. Ironically, state policy and popular anti-establishment sentiments were mutually constitutive.

Vstrecha (*The Meeting*), depicting a stylized encounter between the Russian artist and Chukotka's native Chukchi, date unknown
Woodblock print, artist V. Istomen

Longing for the North was seeded at an early age, and for most, that stimulus came in the form of northern literature, a wildly popular genre throughout the Soviet period. A westerner might underestimate the importance of reading for Soviet youth, but we should recall Brodsky (1986, 28), who remarked, "In its ethics, my generation was the most bookish in the history of Russia ... Books became the first and only reality, whereas reality itself was regarded as nonsense or nuisance." Yet, even this future dissident, as a boy, was reading through a canon of literature approved by the state. Indeed, the Soviet regime always considered reading an indispensable means of penetrating the private life of its citizens (it viewed reading illegal *samizdat'* literature as a particularly grave threat to authority). As the state sought to disrupt the private sphere, the individual retreated into solitary pursuits, and this elevated the novel as a key accessory of genuine leisure. But few spaces were in fact so carefully controlled as the Soviet novel, or rather, no novels reached the shelves whose messages did not align with the interests of the regime.

Fiction was, according to the literary critic Vera Dunham (1976), a key medium of communication between the state and the citizen, and novels clarified to readers both what the system required of them and where the limits of possible action lay.

Adults migrating north in the 1960s and 1970s had grown up in the Stalin era, when stories of Soviet explorers were a critical fuel for lighting the Komsomol (the Party's youth branch) spirit and encouraging "voluntary" service in the Far North. With the formation of Glavsevmorput, the massive state-planning organization for the North, the Soviet Union launched a series of scientific and exploratory northern expeditions whose successes inspired Soviet readers. Heroic aviators, scientists installed on pack-ice drift stations, the mariners of the new Northern Sea Route, and meteorologists living year-round in the remotest northern stations were covered with public glory in the press (McCannon 1998; Horensma 1991).[7] The efforts of the *Cheliuskintsy* mariners, the *Papanintsy* polar explorers, and the *Chkalovtsy* arctic aviators, all part of a planned assault to scientifically measure northern conditions and subsequently build a permanent Soviet presence, are still familiar to middle-aged Russians today.

Literature of the Stalin era construed the Arctic as a stage for collectivist endeavours, overtly serving the cause of building socialism, securing the state's boundaries, and elevating the international prestige of the Soviet Union. But, by the time mass settlement commenced after Stalin's death, the embourgeoisement of Soviet values and the post-Thaw *(ottepel')* personalist turn had recast *romantika severa.* Under Brezhnev, the notion of building communism in the near future was, with the state's tacit approval, kicked into the tall grass by a new generation of novelists, poets, and bards. Again, Brodsky (1986, 26) spoke for his generation when he wrote, "We emerged from under the postwar rubble when the state was too busy patching its own skin and couldn't look after us very well. We entered schools, and whatever elevated rubbish we were taught there, the suffering and the poverty were visible all around. You cannot cover a ruin with a page of *Pravda.*"

The manner in which prospective settlers imagined the North shifted as well, from a savage frontier awaiting the civilizing efforts of enthusiastic young experts to a repository of alternative values and exotic cultures. Now many migrants were discarding the sanctioned notion of bringing Soviet modernity to the North and instead anticipating an entirely new and unaccustomed way of life. Going north dovetailed perfectly with the phenomenon of retreat, for this expanse seemed to offer the ultimate stage for personal quests of self-realization. Migration became an act of personal submission, in which fresh arrivals looked for redemption via the wisdom of the northern old-timer *(starozhilets)* or the exotic Chukchi hunter. In turn, if the technocratic promise of Soviet planning fell to earth under Brezhnev, the North was idealized as a zone of pre-technological purity, where direct contact with "nature" was still possible, a literary sentiment promoted by the Village Prose writers *(derevenshiki).*

Although Chukotka was never an empty frontier, as southern migrants to the region quickly realized, the presence of indigenous populations hardly disrupted their romantic notions of the North.[8] The novelist Yuri Rytkheu, a native of Chukotka's Arctic coast who was educated in Leningrad, was among the best-known authors to present indigenous tradition as a cultural package that European outsiders, instead of seeking to change, might learn from, a sentiment perfectly in line with the introspective turn of the Brezhnev era. The Rytkheu novel that most settlers can remember, entitled *A Dream in Polar Fog,* was published in 1968; set in the early twentieth century, it features a young Canadian sailor stranded in what is evidently the Chukotkan coastal village of Uelen who renounces his past, marries a local woman, and adopts the Chukchi way of life.[9] Soviet readers could easily see turn-of-the-century Canada as a trope for any urban and industrialized setting, including the stagnation-era reality in which they found themselves. This was a daringly modern book for the time. Rather than locate the Chukchi within a Marxist rubric of historical progression, Rytkheu's novel presents the virtues of a traditional Chukchi subsistence way of life, perfectly attuned to the demands of the arctic setting and resistant to modernizing influences. His deeply exotic descriptions of an arctic counter-reality within Soviet boundaries appealed immensely to the sentiments of his early readership.

Today, when settlers narrate their first encounters with Chukchi reindeer herders and whale hunters upon arriving in Soviet Chukotka, it is often in service of the assertion that their motives in the North were entirely romantic *(Ia byl sploshnym romantikom).* But, for many of them, the landscape itself was the first repository of their romantic aspirations. To them, it could seem entirely raw, untouched by humanity, an unmapped and fantastically rich tabula rasa upon which to inscribe their signature. The tundra wilderness offered an unparalleled opportunity for self-testing.

For this reason, the geologist became an emblematic romance figure in 1960s Chukotka. Geology was an ideologically safe profession, but it also demanded scientific creativity and offered liberation from the routines of the modern workplace. It perfectly suited the Brezhnev-era cult of single combat with nature; geologists spent much of the year on long expeditions, where success was measured by their own survival and the richness of the natural resources they uncovered. For young graduates depressed by their prospects in the Soviet city, a geological career in the Far North promised psychological and geographic liberation from the slow-motion society of late socialism. Chukotka, moreover, was the ultimate testing ground for the geologist: the final frontier, the last unmapped territory, and one of the most geologically complex regions in the Soviet Union. Interest in geology peaked in the mid-1960s, and when the popular bard Aleksandra Pakhmatova recorded the song "Derzhis' geolog, krepis' geolog" (Hold on, geologist, be strong, geologist), applications to institutes of geology soared. The publication of

Geologist on summer expedition carrying a stack of Russian-style wooden gold pans, 1970s
Unknown photographer, Archives of the Heritage of Chukotka Regional Museum

the hugely popular novel *Territorya,* written by the former geologist Oleg Kuvaev (1982), not only deified the geologist but indelibly located him in Chukotka, a suitably exotic and romantic territory in the mind of the Soviet reader.

Set in the 1970s, Kuvaev's *roman à clef* celebrates the iconoclastic individualism of a hardened band of geologists who, just as the riches of the Kolyma in Magadan Oblast are exhausted and in contravention to prevailing theories, prove the existence of huge gold deposits in Chukotka, thereby saving Soviet gold production from disaster. Fully within the spirit of the times, Kuvaev's work associated Chukotka with the literary cult of the self by presenting the territory not as a stage of state building and ideological evangelism but as a setting for the individual quest. This might have been too decadent an assertion for the censors of the Brezhnev era, were not Kuvaev's geologists in fact realizing themselves through a cult-like dedication to work. All the same, the state and its interests are virtually silent in Kuvaev's novel. Rather, he engages deeply with the inner world of his characters, who operate in the profoundly existential arena of the distant tundra, devoid of either support or constraint from the structures of the state. In this way, Kuvaev (1982, 8) manages to recast a prime truism of the socialist realist tradition ("Work – that's the main thing ... Everything else is just an accompanying phenomenon") as though loyalty and productivity on the job had nothing to do with the demands of Soviet citizenship.

Kuvaev's image of the geologist still pervades popular discourses on the geological profession in Chukotka, which advance a non-ideological and vaguely ascetic worldview. Indifference to money, altruistic self-sacrifice, loyalty to colleagues, and egalitarianism were the pillars of this late-Soviet romantic philosophy. Geologists appeared to be at once politically correct and indifferent to Soviet policy; adventure, comradeship, and the joy of work were, for them, the true rewards of northern life. They epitomized Vladimir Shlapentokh's (1989) notion of the "professional enthusiast," for whom work itself offered self-fulfillment, the last category of Soviet worker still productive in the stagnation period. But is it possible that life in the North could offer such nourishment to the soul that material inducements became unimportant? In my interviews with present-day settlers, and particularly in conversations with former geologists, anti-materialist assertions were constant. Yet, the generosity of their employer, the Chukotka branch of the geological survey authority (simply referred to as the Ekspeditsiia), their lifestyle of material privilege, long periods of leave, and early retirement also play a central role in their narratives of the past. Geologists, like many other types of expert settlers in Chukotka, could afford to cultivate attitudes of asceticism and dedication to their profession because they were so fully liberated from any real worries about their material well-being.

In the figure of the well-fed settler-romantic, we arrive at an important insight: not only did the discourse of romantika severa operate as a key index to the personalist obsessions of a generation of Soviets, it was also enlisted by the state and the individual alike as a valorizing logic of remarkable flexibility. From the perspective of the state, romantic images of the North encouraged northern settlement, and in the hands of approved novelists such as Kuvaev, they were used to promote labour discipline and self-sacrifice. But just as usefully, with the notion of romantika severa, settlers could encrypt the acquisitive desires that always remained a driver of settlement into a language that, on the face of it, dismissed the importance of material privilege without seriously endangering its perpetuation. The material benefits of life in Soviet Chukotka mattered little next to the beauty of the northern landscape, the freedom of the northern lifestyle, and the simple honesty (*prostota*) of human intercourse in northern communities – these are the main tenants of the northern romantic. But such a discourse could never have

Geologists playing chess in the field, 1970s
Unknown photographer, Archives of the Heritage of Chukotka Regional Museum

attained any kind of practical meaning if settlers had not actually lived in extraordinary conditions of privilege. By leaving shortages and cramped living conditions behind on the materik, they could devote themselves to various projects of self-realization without distraction, rendering the personalist quest more tangible in everyday life.

Spaces of Freedom, or Extreme Hobbyism

By Soviet standards, there was a remarkable amount of free time in the life of Chukotka's settlers. They rarely stood in queues, and in their compact settlements and towns, most lived only minutes by foot from their workplaces. Not only did northern workers receive two months a year in annual leave, geologists, miners, drivers, aviators, sailors, meteorologists, veterinary specialists, and many others worked in shift patterns, which usually resulted in regular, extended periods of paid leave.[10] As in other parts of the Soviet Union, a state-run system of cultural centres *(klub kul'tury)* and other social venues was intended to absorb and structure the leisure time of northern residents in directions deemed healthy and constructive (falling under the rubric "*kul'turnyi*"). But, as in the rest of the Soviet Union by this time, settlers were more likely to direct their energies to private and unofficial pursuits. What was significant about life in Soviet Chukotka was the extent to which they could do so, with approval and even assistance from the institutions of the state.

The wild popularity of hobby circles during this time wonderfully illustrates how amenable northern life was to the appetite for private life and social interaction in spaces outside state control. Hobbies were a fundamentally important part of late-Soviet life everywhere: Shlapentokh quotes sociological data suggesting that by the 1980s, 70 percent of Soviet people had a regular hobby, and time devoted to hobbies rose by five times between 1963 and 1977. In Chukotka, the patterns of working life, the absence of shortage, and the small size of settlements and towns facilitated a particularly intense flowering of special interests. In the district centre of Egvekinot, with a population of roughly five thousand before the Soviet collapse, sixty-seven independent hobby clubs were registered with the local department of culture. Unlike officially organized activities in the local cultural centre (dances, film screenings, talent shows), these were spontaneous initiatives, set up with official consent but entirely dependent on the energies of their enthusiast members. A former construction worker, who founded Egvekinot's karate club, was also a member of a documentary film-screening club, helped establish a bodybuilding studio, and regularly sang in a men's choir. A biology teacher who moved to Egvekinot at the end of the 1970s started a stamp-collecting group, wrote to teachers in Eastern Europe as a member of a pen-pal club, and helped to build a downhill and cross-country ski area near the town with a group of volunteers. A couple, both former geologists, were already members of an amateur photography club, a rock-collecting club, and a wilderness trekking and alpinism group when they founded the local history museum and began organizing expeditions to collect artefacts from abandoned prisoner-labour camps in the district.

The hobby culture in Chukotka was at once a reflection of the sense of commonality that settlers felt with one another and a product of the initiative and skill found in this population. After all, admission to this most privileged region of the North was controlled by a vetting process that, in most cases, selected the highest-achieving graduates of vocational colleges and universities for settlement. Maintaining forms of "cultured life" in no way inferior to those to which they were accustomed in large Soviet cities on the materik was immensely important. Settlers' exceptional mobility afforded them regular access to cultural life in the Soviet metropolis (Moscow and Leningrad), and they did their best to bring a facsimile of this lifestyle to their northern settlements. If a settler had played the guitar and occasionally read poetry on the materik, in Chukotka he joined an amateur jazz band and wrote radio plays. A teacher of foreign languages in a local school would start conversation clubs for settlers learning English and German. Indeed, settlers recall that northern life *forced* them into a process of self-realization, as though the leisure opportunities, combined with the conditions of life in northern isolation, demanded a commitment to the unofficial social life of the community.

The official rationale for high pay and long annual leave, considered by the regime (and by settlers themselves) necessary compensation for life in a far northern setting, perhaps also convinced local authorities of the need for as rich a range of leisure activities as possible. Authorities in Chukotka encouraged the growth of the hobby culture by providing space and financial support, as another former geologist from Egvekinot explained:[11] "There was something for everyone, but many of us just started up our own clubs – I was one of the founders of this club, Iskatel'. It was for adventurers – hiking, mountain climbing, expeditions in the district. I went to the local Party committee [Raispolkom], they welcomed it, assigned us a basement, and we redid the place – we had a storeroom, a meeting room, we met visitors to the district, explorers" [64].

Hobby circles were outside formal state supervision, and they were watched only at arm's length. Stamp collecting and photography were a better investment of private time than drinking, and in practice, Party officials were often avid amateur enthusiasts and club members themselves.

Particularly for a non-Russian audience, it is difficult to understand the importance well-educated northern settlers attached to their hobbies. The English term suggests a harmless diversion from daily routines, an informal pursuit, an amateur interest. The Soviet idea of the *kruzhok* (social circle) was altogether more potent. The kruzhok provided an unscripted entrepreneurial space, where action was authentic in a way that the official rituals of citizenship were not. Unlike Party meetings, official celebrations, and "voluntary" work days, hobbies were attractive precisely *because* of their non-ideological, non-political character. Because the hobby circle was itself the product of genuine spontaneous enthusiasm (for karate, collecting stamps, or painting tundra rhododendrons, for instance), sincerity also characterized the relationships within them. Obsessive interest in hobbies, which a non-Soviet might regard as pointlessly trivial, simply reflected the search for any opportunity to exercise personal initiative, opportunities that outside Soviet reality might be taken for granted. In Soviet life, the very novelty of independent action in a social context beyond the narrow world of intimate friendships was enough to afford almost any hobby a degree of appeal. Founding a business or a political movement was impossible (and unthinkable), but a Soviet could always start a photography club or a knitting circle. The marvellous thing about life in Chukotka was the time and the freedom at settlers' disposal to do just that.

The Benefits of Colonial Agency

The obsession with unofficial and private life, which so vividly manifested in the culture of the hobby and endowed settlement in Chukotka with such appeal, was not simply a hedonistic turn in stagnation-era society. Soviets were in search of purposeful lives, whose essence was the exercise of personal initiative within a project of some apparent value. Any decision as radical as settling in the Far North could not but reflect, in these circumstances, the widely felt desire for self-renovation. This quest, as I have already discussed, certainly had a material dimension, for northern settlement in the most immediate sense removed Soviets from material hardship. But it also had an existential aspect, for whether they consciously understood it at the time of their move north, migrants also found a degree of relief from the manifold features of Soviet life that had previously eviscerated their sense of agency and intentionality.

Throughout the Soviet era, non-stop policies of social engineering, some coercive, some admonitory, and some relatively benevolent, sought to transform a peasant nation into an industrial proletariat and construct a new Soviet individual. Under Stalin, the frenetic and violent character of the Soviet state-building project, interrupted only by the devastation of successive wars, tore Russians out of their families and communities, leaving them more urbanized and literate. Forging a new Soviet type – *homo sovieticus* – entailed an intensive program of persecution, surveillance, and "re-education," while the more stable, and usually rural, settings of life in the pre-revolutionary era, which formerly furnished habits of behaviour and standards of moral judgment, were left behind in the move to Soviet cities. This was a process already in motion for centuries in the industrial West, where, as Michel Foucault (1979, 198) reminds us, the basic goal of the modern state was to achieve the "parallel increase in the usefulness and docility" of its subjects. But if Foucault's "disciplinary power" has spread almost invisibly in Western European societies without supplanting the discourses of law, human rights, and justice, Soviet efforts to transform and discipline the citizen were overt and often violent. The psychological result was a sense of mass insecurity; the individual in Stalin's time lived in a culture of state-sponsored meetings, self-examination, and mutual condemnation. Even after Stalin's death, failures in discipline – in thought and action – were characterized as a lack of "culture," a mode of behaviour recommended by the state yet portrayed as always slightly beyond reach.[12] So anxious was the regime that levels of labour discipline match its radically modernizing industries that individuals were placed in continual doubt, unsure of the proper way to live but quite used to hearing that their attempts were falling short.[13] In the Brezhnev era, this was a state of mind still firmly in place and perpetuated by the rituals of official public life.

The settler experience in Chukotka presents an entirely contrasting picture. It illustrates how a deracinated population of migrant workers, once empowered with a colonial mandate, can rapidly assemble a recognizable sense of purpose and mission, and by extension a sense of common identity. Whereas earlier Stalin-era initiatives to instill "cultured behaviour" – *kul'turnost'* – in the peasant-worker signalled the insufficiency of the average citizen before the demands of the bureaucratic and cultural elite, in the North, the settler naturally now occupied the "cultured" position. By moving to the Soviet frontier, he or she found an entirely more primitive type in the native, over which any Slavic outsider was by definition superior. In contrast with indigenous nomads, newcomers inhabited the model urban space. Their richly proletarian titles – diesel-machine operator, underwater welder, specialist veterinarian, helicopter pilot – radiated the embodied skills of modernity they brought to northern territories. Like Party commissars of an earlier generation, settlers were even recruited as proselytizers of Soviet kul'turnost' in a literal sense, striking out from the *kul'tbaza* (literacy and propaganda bases) in groups of teachers and professional propagandists to establish *krasnye iarangy* (agitprop camps) as a foothold of modernity in the indigenous domain.[14]

Contact with the native in Soviet Chukotka furnished an invaluable reference point for newcomers in the construction of their own self-understandings. Out of this emerged a sense of settler agency, as newcomers assumed their role as members of a colonial master class. Official Soviet discourses conveniently reassured them that natives were entirely satisfied with this arrangement, thereby furnishing insulation from the corrosive effects of colonial guilt. This was powerfully communicated by literature on the North, which construed the colonization of indigenous territories as a happy meeting of the enlightened and well-meaning newcomer with the primitive but receptive native. Ethnographers from the 1920s onward described indigenous peoples as "without culture," a population as uncivilized and raw as the frontier landscape itself, and therefore an ideal site for the inscription of a new Soviet identity and lifestyle (Grant 1993, 231; Slezkine 1994; Diment and Slezkine 1993). The three most widely read and remembered writers of this genre were Vladimir Arsen'ev, Tikhon Semushkin, and Yuri Rytkheu, all of whom were in print by the 1950s and whose stories of the "small peoples of the North" contributed to the idea of the native as a primitive communist, a paradoxical figure at once technologically backward and morally advanced. Semushkin, who won the Lenin Prize for Literature in 1949 for his stories of life with the Chukchi, was widely read in the period coinciding with the first wave of mass "volunteer" or "enthusiast" labour to the region. Out of Semushkin's writing evolved enduring stereotypes of the Chukchi as a simple and pure people *(prostoi).* He (wrongly) reported that there were no curse-words in the Chukchi language and that the Chukchi were preternaturally incapable of stealing (Semushkin 1950). Yuri Rytkheu, who happened to be a coastal Chukchi himself, made his career as an apologist for the establishment of Soviet power in his native territory, and his early works explicitly credit the Soviets for saving the Chukchi people from the primitive way of life that, he claimed, was leading to their extinction (for example, Rytkheu 1967, 1981; Barker 1993). Rytkheu helped portray the telescoping of indigenous peoples into modernity, bypassing slave-holding, feudal, and capitalist modes of production, as a flagship achievement of the Soviet people. These writers collectively shaped the conviction among Soviet newcomers that the existence of indigenous peoples in the North represented not an obstacle to settlement and industrialization, but rather an urgent requirement for it.

Having constructed a colonial hierarchy in Chukotka and a place for themselves at the top, settlers then proceeded to engage in nativizing practices of cultural appropriation. Many in the post-war generation were actually dismissive of the Leninist (and Great Russian) orthodoxy of Soviet cultural superiority, a rejection that late-Soviet novels such as Rytkheu's *A Dream in Polar Fog* simply encouraged. The romantics of the Thaw came north not to deliver "culture," but rather, in search of cultural instruction, a phenomenon Yuri Slezkine (1994) dubbed "the return of Dersu Uzala."[15] This changing regard for the Oriental other resulted in a paradoxical intermingling of colonial arrogance with adulation, even mimicry, of the native identity. For newcomers out of contact with their former communities and families, the seemingly primordial and fixed cultures of Chukotka's indigenous peoples could be intoxicating.

Indeed, many migrants to Chukotka, although ostensibly the agents of cultural and technological osvoenie, found in its native population an attractive cultural solidity. To borrow the words of Donna Haraway (1989, 67), migrants in search of personal renovation in the land of the Chukchi engaged in "the construction of the self out of the raw material of the other." Of course, in the Soviet era, indigenous "tradition" was the very busiest site of cultural construction.[16] If one could close an eye to the institutionalization of indigenous children in residential schools and the destruction of traditional economies, here apparently was a remarkably intact cultural package. A little distance from the realities of life in the village was necessary, and it was convenient that the vast majority of settlers lived in "settlements of an urban type," with relatively few opportunities to interact with Chukchi herders and coastal hunters in their traditional domain. After all, although romantics could construct an idea of the Chukchi from a distance, in close contact, the reality of their common humanity endangered the ideal of the noble savage. It could be very discouraging to meet the Russified members of the indigenous intelligentsia, or worse, those native migrants to the towns who occupied the lowest rungs of the job ladder and drank in public. A Byelorussian seamstress, who left behind a devastated post-war landscape and settled in Chukotka, remembers: "The Chukchi I knew in Magadan who so enchanted me turned out to be completely different in the villages – I was wild with fear when I arrived. I saw them getting drunk continually and it was obvious that they were already a ruined people" [4].

In response, settlers duplicated in their new northern towns the urban lifestyles familiar to them, while examining the "rooted native" and his package of sanctioned cultural forms at a remove. This permitted a selective appropriation of the most attractive features, a process that appears to have been an important part of "settling in."

Chukotka's Soviet settlers embraced no aspect of indigenous tradition more enthusiastically than walrus-tusk and whalebone carving, a pursuit unique to the region, which they practised in hobby groups in every town and settlement. From a settler perspective, carving signified a deep immersion in the natural world of Chukotka and a concomitant sympathy with Chukotka as a Chukchi place. Particular skill in carving also signalled an investment of time in the North and therefore conferred the status of authentic northerner. But, as carving was acquired by settlers as a mark of local rootedness, it inevitably lost its identity as a strictly *indigenous* art form. This was certainly the case by the post-Soviet era. When (in 1999) the governor of Chukotka commissioned a millennium sculpture – a whalebone key to the city of Anadyr – he chose a local Russian artist. As the out-migration of former settlers has accelerated in the post-Soviet era, "traditional" Chukotkan carving is now also practised outside Chukotka. For some of those resettled in central Russia, carving serves not only as a way of passing the time, but also of maintaining their northern identity. I visited a former telephone engineer who left Chukotka in 1995 and resettled in St. Petersburg. The pride of his newly renovated flat was his tusk-carving studio.

For many settlers, the appropriation of native cultural forms played a central role in the construction of their own personal story and gave the most deracinated among them a sense, finally, of being rooted in a place. This was evident in the account of a retired geologist I encountered in Smolensk [15]. He had worked in the Egvekinot geological survey branch from the late 1950s, but he first arrived in the North as a political prisoner. Born in Smolensk in the 1920s, he was exiled with his mother to a labour colony in Kazakhstan when his father was arrested and shot by the NKVD, and at the age of fifteen he was himself sent to the Kolyma goldfields. Deprived of the right to return to central Russia after his release, he worked as a geologist's assistant in Chukotka (then part of Magadan Oblast) while studying for a degree in geology by correspondence. He carried on for four decades in Chukotka and became a respected leader of geological survey parties before retiring back to his central Russian birthplace. When I met him in his flat in 2003, every available space was covered with rare rock specimens found on expeditions in Chukotka, his own oil paintings of the Chukotka landscape, and tusk carvings in the Uelen tradition. Of furniture and the standard paraphernalia of an urban home in Russia – china and crystal in a cabinet, a book collection, Central Asian carpets, modern electronics – there was almost nothing. Art, he told me, was his life's passion, and even though he lived in a western Russian city, his idioms and subjects remained exclusively those of Chukotka. Adopted Chukotkan art forms, as well as his career in northern geology, had for this victim of state repression helped to efface the trauma that he initially carried to the North by providing the constituents of a new identity. The Kolyma and Chukotka were originally the sites of his persecution, where all ties to his former life on the materik were severed. But

Atomka (diminutive for "atomic power station"), depicting the Soviet-era slogan "from the oil lamp to atomic power." Traditional reindeer skin dwellings, called *yaranga,* are visible in the top left. The central Chukchi figure holds a portrait of Lenin. This print was executed to celebrate the construction of Chukotka's atomic power station in 1973.
Woodblock print, artist V. Istomen

over time, that austere landscape came to fascinate him, and with the help of the "native" artistic forms at hand, it became familiar and safe. The truth was, this "newcomer" became a native of the North during his lifetime, and his central Russian birthplace (his home again) seemed now a place of exile.

The gains settlers made in finding lives with purpose in the North, however, came at a cost to indigenous locals. No matter how they idealized and mimicked aspects of native life, settlers in Chukotka were fixed within a modernizing and civilizing project that supported a life of privilege relative to that of their indigenous counterparts. Settlers had assumed the missionary role; they were handed powers to manage and dictate the specific terms of a project aimed at changing locals and appropriating the landscape for industrial uses. Ironically, the assumption of colonial privilege disciplined the settler (in a Foucauldian sense) in a way that state practices of social control in mainstream Soviet life were failing to do, because settlers experienced power over natives as a liberation: their newfound agency was intoxicating and helped them believe in the official idea of northern osvoenie.

One of the most decisive aspects of their privilege within this project was the manner in which settlers gradually assumed mastery over powers of movement in Chukotka. Exceptional mobility was already a constitutive element of their sense of difference from mainland Soviets, but mobility *within* the northern domain soon became a key marker of settler distinction from the indigenous people they were recruited to educate and manage. As I explained in the Introduction to this book, the ability to move over the northern landscape had forever been a criterion of survival in Chukotka, and superior mobility supported the political and economic dominance of the Chukchi reindeer herder until the early years of the twentieth century. With successive waves of Soviet modernization, however, European newcomers introduced technologies of movement that made indigenous herders and hunters seem stationary in comparison, and these technologies enabled Soviets to reach, monitor, and with time subjugate the indigenous population, while simultaneously mapping the landscape and its natural resources. The late-Soviet geologist in Chukotka exemplified the fantastic mobility of the settler, for the regular movement of geologists between the field, the geological camp, the survey base in district centres, and the materik was supported by immense state investment in a system of airplane and helicopter transport, and the all-terrain tracked workhorse of tundra travel – the military-issue vezdekhod – which even today remains the only practical means of mechanized movement over the tundra.

Where settlers came into direct contact with Chukotka's indigenous people, as managers and specialists in the system of state farms established to modernize traditional production, the privileges of mobility were clearest. In the era of collectivization, which in Chukotka stretched from the mid-1930s until 1955, the nomadic way of life, and specifically the domestic environment of the *yaranga* (the reindeer-hide-covered portable dwelling of inland Chukchi), was condemned as primitive and unhygienic, helping to justify sedentarization in newly built villages, along with the institutionalization of native children in residential schools. The "rationalization" and modernization of the herding economy created a growing reliance on helicopters and the vezdekhod to move reindeer-herding brigades along their migration routes and to transport herders between herd and village as the shift-work system developed. Meanwhile, elements of the modern village lifestyle – postal and telephone communications, modern medical treatment, formal education, and the consumption of imported foodstuffs and consumer goods – made the newly sedentary native population reliant on settler aviators, drivers, communications engineers, doctors, and other experts. As a consequence, expert newcomers in the rural sphere assumed influential brokering roles, for they were empowered not only by the dependence of the local indigenous population on essential services and goods originating outside the village, but also by the reliance of state authorities, who looked to them to convey the development agenda into the village domain. In control of the technologies of movement, able to move back and forth between village and town, town and city, and further to the central Soviet metropolis, settlers were thus empowered from above and below, a fact immensely magnified by the conditions of extreme remoteness in which they operated.[17]

Discovering Community

> We came from all the nations of the Soviet Union. The North forged us as one people. [66]

If migrants moved to the Far North in search of a "life of purpose," driven by romantic and acquisitive motives to seek escape from the anomie of stagnation-era life on the materik, these factors do not alone account for the resilience and permanency of the communities that subsequently emerged in Chukotka. The conditions of privilege in settler life, the sense of common mission, the hazards of the arctic climate, and the light hand of the state permitting an exceptionally rich unofficial public life to flourish created ideal conditions for the growth of a strong sense of community. It was the presence of an embracing community life that ultimately kept long-term settlers in Chukotka.

We can understand a community in practical terms as a population whose members are integrated into a network of reciprocity and mutual reliance, and who possess the means to understand their commonalities as constituting a cultural whole.[18] Accounts of late-Soviet life often stress the degree to which state practices aimed at constructing the Soviet individual *(homo sovieticus)* and achieving rapid industrialization compromised Russian traditions of community life. During the first three decades of Soviet power, the disruptions of revolution, repression, and war removed people from rural networks, split extended families, and pulled people out of whatever homes they had. Between 1926 and 1939, 31 million peasants moved to the cities (Lewin 1985). Stephen Kotkin (1995) describes Magnitogorsk in the 1930s as a city almost entirely comprised of refugees from the persecuted rural sphere and industrial workers resettled from central Russia. Once the stable social life of old peasant Russia was upset, the experience of frequent dislocation, living in overcrowded communal flats and dormitories, and practices of state surveillance and social control cauterized the instincts of curiosity and trust upon which spontaneous horizontal engagement normally relies. And once damaged, community life did not easily re-emerge. This resulted in a crisis of "social atomization" (Jowitt 1992), in which individuals lived in isolation from each other because they lacked membership in unofficial forms of association, and for whom their most important relationships were within the immediate family. This was a corrosive shift in Russian culture, which transformed the neighbour from ally to enemy.[19]

Every Soviet-era migrant to the North was, to some degree, a product of these deracinating experiences. But were the habits of estrangement permanent and self-sustaining, or were there latent but enduring yearnings for a return to community life? The act of settling in the North, and in particular of crossing the threshold in self-perception between transient and rooted northerner, certainly indicated such a desire. Migrants carried with them family histories of dislocation from old communities, and knowing what they lost afforded an awareness of what they sought. Those migrating north in the 1960s and 1970s came of age in the freer and less austere era of the Thaw, but they nevertheless framed their personal experiences within a multi-generational chronology of struggle. A man who spent forty years driving garbage trucks in Anadyr related, in a series of interviews in 2003, the story of his family reaching back into the nineteenth century. His father had inherited the profession of Orthodox priest, like all first-born sons before him, the family having ministered to a Byelorussian town for as long as anyone there could remember, and he was arrested first in the 1920s and again in the 1930s. Consequently, this informant grew up a son of an "enemy of the people," and the resulting stigma left only the most menial careers open to him.[20] Coming to the North was the final act in a series of movements away from his primordial village, through cities in central Russia and eventually the Virgin Lands in northern Kazakhstan [9]. In my encounters, he was not the only settler with a family history combining some degree of hardship and repression, and many informants were deeply conscious of an ideal village past where community was once strong and stable, a place located generations back but still felt to be running in the veins.

Trust, Reciprocity, and Inclusion

In the last decades of the Soviet period, long-time settlers claim to have lived in a kind of northern idyll, a place of unique privilege filled with remarkable people. Present-day narratives of life in Soviet Chukotka celebrate the (purportedly since degenerated) qualities of honesty, generosity, and mutual trust, forming a kind of social glue to which a sense of settler solidarity adhered. One of the most pervasive discourses in this genre – "we never locked our doors" – both evokes a time of unconditional sharing and offers a striking contrast to the post-Soviet present, when, in most of Russia and now even in Anadyr, families live behind solid steel doors. Like the statement "snabzhenie bylo otlichnoe" (the supply of goods was excellent), the "open-door" narrative economically captures a number of social norms, which set off life in the region from both the mainstream Soviet reality of the time and the present day. First among these was the convention of mutual support, which, rather than operating in a highly selective way, as in Finn Sivert Nielsen's Leningrad, was inclusive and welcoming. One informant recalled, "No one would come in [to an open flat], just your own people *[vse svoi]*, if they needed something. No one ever stole anything. There was huge mutual reliance *[ogromnaia vzaimnopomoshch']* – people relied on each other" [7].

The most fundamental and sustaining feature of the northern community was the particular character of reciprocal giving. An open door facilitated intensive sharing, enabling people to borrow and replace food, tools, and even money. Within settlements and across the region, not only was sharing a pervasive social practice, but also, sharing without shrewd calculation followed an informal "code of the North," which specified a high degree of loyalty and self-sacrifice for one's fellow northerners.[21] Trust and sharing were critical elements in the development of community feeling, but I am not the first to observe this. Following earlier studies of gift-giving and barter (Mauss 1990; Taussig 1980; Sahlins 1972), Caroline Humphrey (2000) observed that activities she roughly characterized as "barter" in late-Soviet society had important socially animating properties. But, like Marshall Sahlins, who introduced the principle of "kinship distance" to distinguish between gift-giving and commodity exchange, Humphrey found that social proximity within a contained community was necessary for maintaining the aspect of non-specific reciprocity in acts of giving. The modes of reciprocity settlers describe in Soviet-era Chukotka indeed follow the patterns of generalized gift-giving – the kind of sharing felt to be non-transactional. In *The Gift* (first published in 1925), Marcell Mauss asserted that gift-giving was an enactment of community, and the gift was itself a symbol of the cherished relationships within its limits. Giving a gift, he wrote, was one form of reciprocity in which no monetary value or any expectation of immediate return were implicit. Pierre Bourdieu (1990) extended Sahlins' model of "generalized reciprocity" by observing that gifts in fact carry a strong obligation of payment in the form of a return gift. But the act of return requires a proper sense of timing in the party to an exchange. The transaction of gifts must be staggered to hide the reality of mutual debt and to forefront the illusion of unconditional generosity. The essence of non-specific reciprocity, therefore, is a constant and mutual condition of obligation between members of a community.

Studies of community and social capital have characterized the embracing entanglements of giving and receiving that take this non-immediate and non-transactional form as a critical underpinning of social cohesion. A functioning community contains a stock of unspecified obligation, in which gift circulation is made possible by identification with the group. Bonds of indebtedness must never be extinguished by immediate reciprocity – in the form of a monetized transaction, for instance – because their continuity attests to the strength of trust that community members invest in each other. Robert Putnam (2000), a theorist of social capital, identified trust as the lubricant of community life, enabling members to leverage their position within a community into a steady flow of material and emotional benefits. Trust erodes rapidly when the intensity of sharing and gift-giving drops, which can be the outcome of higher turnover and increasing heterogeneity within the group, a lack of social sanctions buttressing the norms of reciprocity, or conditions of general scarcity and hardship. Humphrey (2000, 73) contends that mutual trust and a high intensity of reciprocity are easiest to sustain when communities are comprised of actors "with more or less the same clout" – a condition of relative social, economic, and ethnic homogeneity. This helps to explain why, in Chukotka, where the egalitarian social fabric she identifies was present to an unusual (in Soviet terms) degree, community spirit was so strong.

There, habits of trust grew out of several circumstances particular to the region. First was a sense of common membership among migrant settlers. The settler population reached Chukotka via filtering processes that ostensibly rewarded only the best (graduates, skilled workers, and professionals) with a northern propiska. Through participation in a kind of initiation ritual winnowing the wheat from the chaff, late-Soviet settlers who gained admission to Chukotka enjoyed an elite corporate identity.[22] Many settlers proudly explain that they won a "work assignment" *(raspredelenie)* to the region by finishing as the top students in their graduating classes. Elitist self-perceptions were quite common among the settlers I met in the course of my research, and the following statement could stand for many I heard: "For Chukotka, they selected only the best and the most physically fit, those who could endure the extreme conditions. We had a reputation – there were no people with criminal records sent here and so people trusted each other" [17].[23]

The filtering process supported the perception, even in Chukotka's larger communities, where familiarity with everyone was unlikely, that the settler next door was a reliable and talented selectee like you. As another chosen member of the osvoenie project, any settler, even a newly arrived stranger, enjoyed the benefit of the doubt. If, in reality, the process admitted as many settlers via the back door *(po blatu),* the clubbish sense of membership pervaded settler communities nonetheless.[24] Although theorists of exchange and community have argued that norms of gift-giving are insupportable outside of stable, small groups of intimates, in Chukotka this general sense of common purpose and identity embraced the entire northern settler population and actually transcended the boundaries of acquaintance.

The prosperity of settler life also played a part. The conditions of relative abundance meant that settlers had a little to give away, unlike in the daily lives of average Soviets on the materik. The existing ethnographic accounts of life at that time in major Soviet cities emphasize the strict manner in which people protected their private domain, in order to maintain intensive sharing circles among intimates while repelling strangers. In conditions of shortage, the strength of the defences constructed around these islands was critical (F.S. Nielsen, 2007). Along with Nielsen, Alena Ledeneva (1998) describes life in the shortage society of late-Soviet Russia. In her analysis of reciprocity and social connection (blat), she argues that the grim and unmediated character of relations in the public domain (as opposed to the familiar and intimate) was reflected in vigorous and continual acts of group boundary marking.[25]

In Soviet Chukotka, by contrast, acts of sharing were often extended to strangers because new arrivals were easily inducted into the settler community. Indeed, another stable genre of recollection is the arrival narrative, the moment when migrants to Chukotka realized how different this community was from anything they had experienced before. Newly arrived in Anadyr from the materik, a former geologist recalled how surprised he was that whenever he was walking from one end of town to another, strangers would stop their cars and give him a lift. Another newcomer remembered, "It was a bright and sunny day in February when I first came to Anadyr, and we got in a little bus at the airport. I immediately noticed a different atmosphere. People talked to each other, asked each other questions. I jumped into the conversation and someone straightaway started explaining where everything was in town" [8].

Finally, localized sanctions on behaviour typical of closely knit communities maintained stability in social relations. Settler communities were often village-sized, and their populations were small and stable enough that people could literally "know everyone." The general familiarity extending to the boundaries of the community and the strong fabric of social sanction this made possible assured the giver in any act of giving that "you knew it would get back to you in the end."

Open-door sharing, which is presented in retrospect as an unconditional and unlimited gesture, also underlines the degree to which settlers felt they lived within an unstratified, classless milieu. Intense practices of sharing indeed acted to level whatever economic imbalances might have been possible within communities (although they nevertheless persisted, for example, in housing), since the code of the North stipulated an egalitarian approach to fellow northerners. Implicit in sharing narratives is a valorization of "northern types." According to workers at a forest-fire-fighting base in one isolated inland village, the northern breed of *muzhik* – a straightforward and reliable "man of the earth" – must be strong and a good drinker, must not value his own life above the lives of his mates, and must not care much about material wealth.[26] An expansiveness of spirit and a readiness to lay oneself on the line for one's comrades – irredeemably collectivist qualities – best describe this ideal. By valorizing such types as this, settlers were evoking a particular idea of northern community life, the quality of which they explicitly distinguished from the hostile social milieu found on the materik. A young woman born to settler parents in rural Chukotka recalled her first experience living outside the region: "Life in Chukotka was completely unlike life on the materik, and I realized when I went to the materik that I was naïve. People here were pure *[chistie]*, open-hearted, trusting" [7].

Paradoxically, though settlers remember their communities as stable, in-migration and departure nevertheless created a degree of fluidity and the need to continually interact with outsiders contending for membership in local social life. Equally paradoxically, it appears that a degree of transience in northern settlements actually reinforced a grounded identity in established settlers. This is because the presence of incoming migrants continually called attention to the comparative rootedness of those already there. In part because new and growing northern settlements were networks of community life in the process of construction, the rules of inclusion and exclusion were more flexible in the North than in mainstream Soviet society. Newcomer migrants to Chukotka had no choice but to project extraordinary expectations on the relationships they made with fellow northerners, in order to replace the more enduring bonds that on the materik they might have had with relatives and lifelong friends. The lack of filial bonds for migrants who came to the North in ones and twos was made up by "surrogate kin" – friends they made in their work collectives and apartment stairwells. A single mother who moved from Leningrad to the Bering Strait settlement of Lavrentiia in the 1980s recalled, "Of course I had my difficulties. I was alone, I had no parents, no nanny. But if I needed to slip out to the shop, I could just knock on my neighbours' door and ask them to keep an eye on my baby. They always agreed without hesitating – in the North, people were good to each other" [11].

Surrogate kin constituted the inner circle of mutual reliance, but as in any small community, most relations in Chukotka's settlements were nevertheless somehow personalized. The anonymity of bureaucratic roles was subverted by the simple fact that people knew each other; it was difficult to maintain the pretence of officially prescribed behaviour in contexts of continual familiarity. This situation continues today. In central Russia, joining the traffic police (GAI) is usually thought of as a route to self-enrichment because *gaishniki* have the power to stop and fine drivers for petty infractions. But, in Anadyr, although the traffic police maintained a visible presence, drivers tended to know gaishniki and their families by name, and so bribe extraction, never mind legitimate sanction, usually foundered in the domain of personal loyalties.

In Soviet Russia, public-sphere transactions were generally enacted most effectively if they could be personalized, but this was only sometimes possible. In Chukotka, the size and insularity of most communities permitted a personalization of almost all such transactions. Long-time residents spoke of the role of *vas-vas,* (referring to a way of obtaining something by resort to personal favours, by switching from a formal to an intimate mode when enacting a transaction).[27] Being on vas-vas with people allows one to circumvent normal channels: at the post office, your acquaintance will slip you a package around the back so you don't have to stand in the queue; in the shop, you can get a little of the freshest meat from the counter-woman. One informant explained the critical importance for incoming migrants of mastering the rules of personalized problem solving – within a window of a few months, a newcomer must penetrate to the level of vas-vas with locals and thereafter succeed in breaking down formal relationships with an injection of intimacy. As she put it, "The north pushes those people away who can't understand this, who can't get a feel for putting people onto vas-vas – they usually return to the materik" [20].

Among communities of acquaintance, norms of exchange (vas-vas) and the principle of surrogate kin pointed to high levels of mutual trust, an idea itself pivotal to the code of the North. This characteristic openness to all members of the settler community, stranger and friend alike, distinguished northern society. In Soviet urban life on the materik, familiarity was an essential precondition of trust. Networks of exchange and support were based on personal relationships. Only through these relationships could dwellers in the Soviet city confer the status "one of us" – *nash chelovek.* But, in Chukotka, any settler was potentially nash chelovek. Settler networks there were not strictly exclusive: they stretched beyond the limits of acquaintance and accommodated the inclusion of the settler newcomer. A sense of common purpose and destiny binding northern settlers together and bridging networks of familiarity was an unusual phenomenon in Russia, in striking contrast with the habits of mistrust in public life and the "island-like" atomization of social life *na materike.*

Although the formal, advertised benefits of northern life were vital for prompting talented young Soviets to attempt it, settlers in Chukotka today evoke the less tangible aspects of the northern experience as the cause of their long-term commitment. Material rewards may have been structured to incentivize staying on, but after a few years in the North, it was not prosperity itself that they valued so much as the quality of social interaction and the sense of purpose that conditions of prosperity helped to support. Settler life contained the precious "spaces of freedom" – that aspect of "statelessness" in which the individual could pursue personal projects, no matter how quixotic – that furnished the means for existential self-renovation. Settlers not only recovered control over their leisure time: as "experts" in a campaign of colonial development, they were also invested with power over their indigenous counterparts, of which the brokering role is a perfect illustration. Ultimately, a corporate sense of community emerged on the basis of a common sense of mission, one attended by norms of mutual aid and respect quite unlike any that settlers might have experienced before they migrated north. If these intangible rewards soon outweighed the importance of the long ruble, they were even less portable. On the first long visit back to former homes on the materik, this became abundantly clear. Settlers were a leisured colonial elite only as long as they remained in the colony; when they returned, they became ordinary Soviets once more.

The "settled North" inhabited by voluntary migrants was a deliberate creation of Soviet policy. There, the regime engineered a lifestyle of privilege that appeared highly anomalous beside the encroaching shortage and ideological anomie in stagnation-era society. The features of northern privilege incubated a sense of difference and community identity in settler life. Yet, the state program of severnoe osvoenie maintained the viability of this lifestyle only so long as the Soviet regime could direct a large share of national wealth northward. Its collapse revealed the fragility of this arrangement, for the annihilation of settler privilege after perestroika directly reflected the extent to which it had been a creature of distributive policy rather than sustainable economic enterprise. Furthermore, the myth of a classless settler society, built upon the idea (if not the manifest reality) of equal sacrifice and equally apportioned privilege, was thoroughly discredited by the deeply unequal fortunes of those caught in Chukotka during the ensuing crisis. The implications for the settler identity were profound, and the following chapters explore how the end of privilege – of subsidized and easy travel, of heightened consumption, and of colonial agency – transformed the settler sense of community and person in the North.

Part 2
Transition to Crisis, 1991-2000

4
Idyll Destroyed

To maintain the privileges of the settler and the appearance of state functionality in the Far North required a deliberate investment of resources that was in scale both massive and, as stagnation developed into perestroika-era crisis, unsustainable. If, in more central parts of the country, everyday hardship and the emergence of the second economy constituted a partial inoculation against the effects of the Soviet collapse, northerners had no preparation. In Chukotka, the perquisites of settler life evaporated abruptly, as practical and ideological support for northern osvoenie was withdrawn by the new Russian state. Although shortages of basic goods occurred sporadically in the region in the final years of perestroika, the era of crisis in Chukotka began only as the Soviet state dissolved, a point roughly coinciding with the arrival of Governor Aleksandr Nazarov (1991-2000). By the end of the 1980s, state support for resettlement of northern workers back to central regions was failing, and the subsequent hyperinflation commencing in January 1992 wiped out northerners' large ruble savings. Daily life rapidly became a struggle for survival, as the state system of northern transport failed and the burden of distance in arctic conditions returned for the first time in a generation. Suddenly, it seemed that hardly anything got up to the North and hardly anyone could afford to get out.

Triggered by the collapse of state subsidies, budget investment, transport, and supply, Chukotka's industrial input dropped by more than 60 percent between 1993 and 1995 alone, and the cost of living rose to the highest level in Russia (Goskomstat 1999). As prices were freed, the cost of air travel jumped drastically, rendering movement in the region and flights out extremely expensive. Meanwhile, state enterprises exposed for the first time to the unsubsidized costs of operation in northern conditions were rapidly pushed into insolvency, leading to layoffs and closures. These changes sparked mass out-migration: Chukotka's proportional rate of departure was the highest of any region in Russia, and from a peak of 160,000 in 1989, the population dropped to under 100,000 by 1996, falling to under 75,000 by the end of the decade (FSGS 2004). Since non-indigenous specialists were the first to leave, out-migration deepened the spiral of decline in living standards, devastating public services – health care, utilities, administration, education, and transport. As mines and factories closed, industrial settlements were abandoned.

The rural indigenous economy, by now reliant on mechanized transport and settler-managed state farms, followed a similar path, although herders possessed in their reindeer an invaluable and immediate source of food, without which conditions in the rural sphere would have been even graver. Over the 1990s, Chukotka's total reindeer herd shrank from half a million head to under ninety thousand (Abramovich 2001). This decline alone amounts to as meaningful a single measure of the cost of human survival through the crisis decade as can be found. The missing deer did not simply wander off – rather, they filled a yawning deficit in food supply left by the collapse of northern transport and the end of paid employment. By the end of Governor Nazarov's tenure in 2000, Chukotka's public debt exceeded the annual budget by three times, fixed assets had dropped in value by over 90 percent, and reindeer herders had gone unpaid for six years (Gray 2000). Trauma and suicide were the principal causes of death. Much of the indigenous population and many rural settlers were dependent on international food aid from the Red Cross and charities based in Alaska. An all-Russian survey of quality of life in 2000 rated Chukotka second to last of Russia's eighty-nine regions; only in the battleground Republic of Chechnya was life more precarious ("Annual Ranking" 2000).

Despite its severity, the world knew little about Chukotka's humanitarian crisis. This was partly because Nazarov's administration erected bureaucratic walls to entry to intensify Chukotka's extreme natural isolation. Information leaked out regardless. In October 1998, a letter describing life in the remote inland village of Vaegi reached the anthropologist Patty Gray in Germany. Her Chukchi friend Tamara Korav'e reported that

> Life in Vaegi has gotten really bad. I've gotten to understand what famine means! Can you guess what the most precious and valuable food we have in the house is? Bread. If we have bread, it's a real celebration. Even if we don't have anything else in the house but bread and tea, it's a celebration ... Recently the husband of a girlfriend, Tolya, said to me, "My God, it's gotten to the point that the children don't even ask for sweets, they just want bread." They have an eighteen-month-old son and a three-year-old daughter, and they go for days on end on boiled water alone. And the mom is trying to breastfeed! ... Other than food, there are shortages of clothing. There aren't even socks. Children have nothing to wear to school. There aren't any pens, pencils, or writing pads either.[1]

The cataclysmic rupture of settler privilege, the return of isolation, the nostalgia for a sense of confidence in the future – this is hardly conveyed in the statistics of collapse. The crisis was experienced, as this letter from Vaegi shows, on a human scale. Let us consider another example. Few organizations had been so emblematic of Soviet power and industry in Chukotka as its geological survey. In the

Soviet era, just as dimensions of the settler identity and lifestyle seemed to converge in the professional geologist in a concentrated form, the subsequent collapse of the geological survey provided an effective allegory on the crisis and its impact on post-Soviet Chukotka. Referred to by locals simply as the Ekspeditsiia, this organization was formed in 1955 to succeed the prospecting branch of the Far East Construction Trust (Dalstroi) and map the okrug's resource wealth. As one of the most geologically complex regions of the Soviet Union, and the last territory to be surveyed to the detailed scale of 1:200,000, Chukotka was a final frontier for geologists [5] [32]. The Soviet regime set great store on the prospect of natural wealth hidden in its least-surveyed resource province. Thus, as oil revenues and gold production slumped in the 1980s, geological research and exploration boomed in Chukotka, and investment poured into the Ekspeditsiia. The main facilities in Anadyr employed over 800 specialists, with 180 more in an aligned research institute. Branches were also built in Egvekinot (where roughly 700 survey staff comprised one-fifth of the town's population) as well as in Pevek, Bilibino, Lavrentiia, and Provideniia. Added to these was a rapidly growing oil and gas survey, which at its peak employed another 500 specialists in the Anadyr district.

Even as the perestroika-era economy collapsed and chronic distribution problems created acute scarcities in the 1980s, the Soviet authorities protected the Ekspeditsiia, hoping Chukotka might produce a golden egg to soften the nationwide crisis. But finally in 1993, the Russian government abruptly cut all funding and the profession of geology in Chukotka was left, in the words of its then senior geologist, to "the whims of fate" *(na proizvol' sudby)*. Thousands of geologists abandoned the North, joining an exodus of other highly qualified specialists from the okrug. Those who remained in Chukotka migrated to other professions, some taking a second education, some going into small-scale business, others cashing in on connections to secure a government post. A small number sold their skills to gold-mining concerns, but nowhere did the former belief in geology as a key northern endeavour survive intact. Ekspeditsiia managers attempted to make of the organization a set of self-sufficient enterprises, using the considerable assets still at their disposal. Divisions were spun off the mother enterprise and their directors became shareholders.[2] The most valuable assets – heavy vehicles and mining equipment, newer buildings, fuel supplies, and even cash reserves – were transferred out of the Ekspeditsiia into these new ventures, leaving the hollowed-out shell of the state company with debt and liabilities (for example, the obligation to resettle all former employees to the materik). But most attempts at reform failed – the predominant pattern of "business activity" turned out to be asset stripping. Only two businesses that emerged as spinoffs still survived a decade later.[3] By 1997, a successor organization to the Ekspeditsiia was assembled in Anadyr by a few committed geologists: in 2002, it had a staff of just thirty-five and a single working vezdekhod.

In the disappearance of the Ekspeditsiia, and the loss of the Soviet-era faith in geology, we find many of the most important characteristics of Chukotka's "transition": the withering of central powers of command, the departure of expertise from the North, and the carving out of valuable assets in a process of transferring ("privatizing") public resources. Geologists, like other specialist settlers in the region, were very rapidly unmoored and disoriented by the loss of their professional roles. The settler mentality of the Soviet halcyon (1960-90), characterized by a sense of mission, of membership in a chosen elite, and of easy cosmopolitan kultur'nost', suffered the collapse of its old props: northern abundance, good transport, and ideologically endorsed colonial agency. At the same time, the fiction of a classless settler society was exposed, as many of the most privileged exercised their residual powers of mobility to depart, leaving the remaining settlers and natives immobilized by their poverty, a lack of contacts on the materik, or simply an enervating paralysis brought on by the speed of change. Settlers were witnessing, they believed, the end of a system of living and a structure of knowledge, as all the attending points of reference and reassuring routines evaporated. What is more, coming north was originally an act of escape. Now, the crisis they thought they had left behind had somehow discovered them in their northern oasis. At first, the uncertainty seemed far away. As Soviet power buckled, people in Chukotka's settlements watched the televised debates of the Russian Congress of Peoples' Deputies in Moscow with detached bemusement, believing as always that developments on the materik did not apply to the North. In a very short time, however, the collapse of Soviet power was destroying their own world, removing their sources of self-understanding layer by layer – professional status, colonial rightness, egalitarian regard for fellow northerners, their cherished standard of life, and, finally, the power of movement itself. The speed of change was merciless, leaving little time to determine a correct response, because how could they prepare for a future that was unknown – would there be life in the North, would a profession count for anything, where would children be best protected from it all? All courses of action seemed equally fraught with danger – leaving the North with nothing seemed rash, but staying could be suicidal.

This left many settlers floating in an ideational void, a kind of acid bath in which the moral certainties of the Soviet era were dissolved, and in the aftermath, only the most "personalistic" behaviours seemed appropriate. Patty Gray (2005, 185), an anthropologist who followed the struggles of indigenous-rights advocates in Anadyr from the mid-1990s, remembers the prevailing sense among locals at that time of "*vse sami po sebe*": 'It's everyone for himself.'" The end of settler privilege, which in its various aspects had underwritten in-migration and long-term commitment, exposed a latent but powerful belief in the North as a temporary home, a mentality of transience, among much of Chukotka's non-indigenous population.

The crisis fuelled an atmosphere of evacuation, and with the disappearance of savings and livelihoods, this generated the sensation of suddenly being trapped in the North. Settlers also felt betrayed by the state, and they viewed their suffering within the terms of a moral economy of sacrifice and entitlement. Despite the manner in which Soviet policy had cushioned them from so many of the depredations of stagnation-era life, the rhetoric of northern sacrifice, which constructed a settler's residence in Chukotka as service to the Motherland, contributed to the notion of a moral contract between the settler and the state. The collapse of state-sponsored osvoenie policies was, by extension, experienced as the abrogation of this contract.[4] If the state had abandoned the settler, many settlers decided they in turn were freed of the moral imperatives of citizenship, and the only realistic moral code became loyalty to the needs of self-preservation. Behaviour that in Soviet times would have been considered destructive and anti-social, and had once met sanction within the settler community, now appeared justified by the circumstances. After all, life for most settlers had become a struggle to survive, to regain some measure of material security, and to leave for the materik on the best terms possible. Post-Soviet arrangements of power and wealth in the region naturally created very steep hierarchies of opportunity within which these strategies of departure played out; certain locals, almost exclusively settlers, were positioned much more fortuitously than most.

Evidence of this mentality emerged most visibly in the record of public service and reached an apotheosis in the decade-long administration of Governor Nazarov. Benefiting from the impunity granted by the evaporation of centralist powers and Yeltsin's policies of extreme federalism, Nazarov's regime completed a total shift from the nominally statist political rationality of the Soviet era to a kind of neo-Machiavellian opportunism.[5] Governor Nazarov and members of his circle used the regional administration to instrumentalize a strategy of departure; indeed, the behaviours of transience that so corroded the prestige of the administration and the economic prospects of the region were possible only for members of the regional elite. Those at this level included members of the okrug and district Communist Party Executive Committees and other Party organs such as the Komsomol, senior members of the regional security establishment (KGB, the Interior Ministry, Border Guards, and the military), and directors of industrial enterprises. In contrast, for settlers without access to state resources, the only sustainable strategies of survival relied on fostering rooted networks within local communities and cultivating grounded skills of subsistence on the landscape. This is the subject of the next chapter, but here I focus on *elite* strategies of coping with the post-Soviet crisis, for though they were open to only a very few, the consequences of what we might term "Nazarovism" shaped for a decade the lives of all those in Chukotka.

Devolution and Capture

Chukotka played a leading role in the "parade of sovereignties" that, beginning in 1990, devolved decision making from Moscow to the regions and contributed to the rise of the Russian Federation out of the ruins of the Soviet state. On 28 September 1990, only one day after the Sakha Republic announced its independence, Chukotka's Supreme Soviet declared its secession from Magadan Oblast, to which the okrug had been subordinate since 1953. Three years later, the federal government recognized the Chukchi Autonomous Okrug as a sovereign unit of the Russian Federation.[6] Over this period, the distribution of administrative power within the region was just as uncertain as its status within the federation. The head of Chukotka's Soviet of Workers' Deputies was an indigenous Chukchi, Vladimir Etylin. Because he was the nominal leader of the okrug government, Chukotka's declaration of sovereignty was issued in his name; indeed, rights of indigenous self-determination were central to its original intent.[7] Etylin, however, was locked in an increasingly unequal struggle for authority with Aleksandr Nazarov, the ethnic-Russian chair of the Soviet's Executive Committee, who from 1990 publicly aligned himself with Yeltsin's aims of democratization and market-oriented reform. It was thus Nazarov whom Yeltsin appointed in 1991 as head of administration *(glava administratsii),* a position created to counteract the anti-reformist interests embedded in the Party ranks of regional Soviets throughout the Russian Federation.[8] From August 1991 to September 1993, Etylin (representing the regional and national Soviets) and Nazarov (representing the executive wing of power and ultimately President Yeltsin) administered Chukotka's affairs in concert under the ambiguous terms of "dual power" *(dvoevlastie)* then prevailing in every region of Russia. However, dvoevlastie was a local manifestation of an undecided conflict of authority in Moscow, a struggle in which Yeltsin ultimately triumphed, culminating with the violent dissolution of the Russian Supreme Soviet, along with all the regional Soviets, in autumn 1993. This development removed Etylin from office and handed Nazarov, still nominally only glava administratsii, effective control over Chukotka's newly sovereign administration.

Chukotka's secession from Magadan was not the outcome of a popular campaign for independence; nor were its original architects the ultimate beneficiaries. Patty Gray (2005, 185, 187) describes how "the weight of administrative authority in Chukotka gradually shifted from an indigenous Chairman of the Soviet to a Russian Head of Administration," leaving "the interpretation of Chukotka's newly independent status ... in the hands of Aleksandr Nazarov." Despite its rather accidental character as a by-product of federal power struggles, Chukotka's secession resulted in a personal victory for Nazarov and his close associates. By gambling his political fortunes on the ascendance of Yeltsin's reformist agenda, Nazarov was by 1993 in position to assume control over a process of devolution that was until then at least partly intended to advance *indigenous* interests. Moreover, the dissolution

Governor Aleksandr Nazarov (centre), with school graduates, mid-1990s
Unknown photographer, archives of Krainyi Sever *(a regional weekly newspaper)*

of Chukotka's only elected body (the okrug Soviet) tore the ground from under Etylin's feet and left the federally appointed Nazarov in an unassailable position of power.[9] Secession from Magadan necessitated the creation of a new layer of local bureaucratic agencies, duplicating the services formerly provided from the capital of the former parent oblast. This arrangement enhanced the powers of local government in Anadyr, and in particular the newly established office of the glava administratsii. Describing the situation in 1995, Igor Krupnik and Nikolai Vakhtin (2002, 10), two Russian anthropologists long familiar with the okrug, wrote, "the regional government quickly filled the short-lived power vacuum, at the expense of clumsy and now cash-stripped federal agencies. Regional government agencies, first and foremost the Governor's office seated in Anadyr, have become the source of an almost unlimited bureaucratic authority – just as the old Soviet federal agencies had been before."

The manner in which administrative and distributive powers were concentrated in the hands of the unrepresentative office of the head of administration (officially the "governor" from 1996) suggests a process of "capture" rather than democratization and devolution to a locally accountable leadership. The ten years during which Nazarov was (de facto) governor of Chukotka (1991-2000) offer a vivid illustration of what anthropologist Katherine Verdery (1996, 216) has termed the "parcellisation of sovereignty," a tendency evident throughout the post-socialist space in which "local bosses arrogate[d] central coercion and evade[d] the centre's sanctions, often to protect their new entrepreneurial activities." For her part, Caroline Humphrey (2002) employs the model of *feudalism* to describe the process by which forms of local power filled the vacuum created by the failure of centralized power in Moscow (exemplified by legislative confusion and the loss of a monopoly over the use of force). Enterprises and local administrations in the regions took the form of "suzerainties," as local bosses assumed an ever-increasing range of powers as a means of defence within the economic and legal uncertainty pervading the post-Soviet domain. Yet, the devolution of power was in progress long before, according to Gerald Easter (2000), who views the rise of Brezhnev as the triumph of regionally based elites over the unchecked power of the centre. From the point of Krushchev's ouster, power was increasingly exercised through informal local and regional networks, rather than via a bureaucratic chain of command, and administrative authority thereafter diffused out of Moscow, making possible the Soviet Union's "collapse from within." Nazarov's capture of Chukotka and its subsequent transformation into a kind of feudal demesne – a sovereign administrative parcel – might therefore be understood as a natural culmination of a process of regional ascent initiated not at the time of the post-Soviet parade of sovereignties, but instead in the early years of Soviet stagnation.[10]

Having achieved Chukotka's sovereignty in principle, the okrug administration still required the achievement of regional authority in practice. In a pattern followed by local bosses throughout the former socialist space, Governor Nazarov consolidated power through either the calculated destruction or the co-option of the old Soviet relationships of vertical subordination, arrangements that previously linked local enterprises and political activity to higher authorities based in Magadan and Moscow.[11] As vertical relationships of authority withered, local power figures reoriented their loyalties *horizontally* within Chukotka's regional networks.[12] For Nazarov, the economic crisis, and the resulting failure of large industrial enterprises previously subject to federal control, was critical for the accumulation of power, since these vedomstva (the conglomerate institutions that comprised the basic cell-structure of the old Soviet economy) were in potential competition with the okrug administration. During the years 1993-95, most of the biggest industrial enterprises of the Soviet-era economy were slated for closure and abandonment, including the Iul'tin tin mining and concentration plant (and its settlement of 5,300), and the gold-mining settlements of Poliarnyi, Otrozhnyi, and Vostochnyi. The demobilization and dismantling of Chukotka's vast military bases also commenced, leading to the removal from the region of probably the most influential set of federally controlled institutions.

Simultaneously, the emergence of bureaucracies in Anadyr that reflected Chukotka's new status as an independent administrative unit of the Russian Federation rechannelled the flow of budget revenue through the organs of Nazarov's administration. The subsequent growth of bureaucracy in Anadyr provided a landing pad for many well-connected settlers – refugees from the dismantled enterprises of the old productive economy.[13] As industrial settlements were closed, former geologists, drivers, miners, and bookkeepers migrated to Anadyr and into newly established or expanded government offices.

A new equilibrium soon established itself under Nazarov. As Moscow's influence drained away, a system of patronage, focused on the office of the governor, rose in its place. Patron-client rule was no innovation of the post-Soviet era, for it followed norms of administration perennially alive in Russian society. As the historian Geoffrey Hosking (2000, 301) has observed, the enduring stability of autocratic government (in whatever guise) results from the exercise of personal power at the grassroots. Beneath the impressive emblems of the rational bureaucratic state, a potent tradition of patrimonial problem solving has always operated.[14] But the trappings of the bureaucratic state have often disguised, and even modified, the importance of personalized relationships to administration. Only at certain junctures does the logic of patron-client rule become overtly apparent. Such a time was Nazarov's Chukotka, when Soviet-era cliental relationships were reactivated as the sinews of governance in a completely unapologetic and overt fashion. Indeed, to drum home the message, the rules of patronage were advertised. And at the centre of this new domain of his own making sat the governor, Chukotka's ultimate and final patron.[15]

The Operation of Patronage Rule

Almost as if by magic, unaccountable patronage-based rule afforded Chukotka's mostly settler elite the power to demand loyalty and maintain administrative control while simultaneously implementing a strategy of departure. The efficiency of the system Nazarov erected helps to explain the remarkable survival of his regime over a ten-year period, despite the human tragedy of the crisis years for which it was largely responsible. Indeed, the durability of such a parasitic and venal administration as this is difficult to comprehend until we consider how enveloping, intoxicating, and coercive a fully articulated culture of patronage can become.

To employ the patronage model of power as a prism for understanding the Nazarov phenomenon requires some preliminary theorization. Although Humphrey's metaphors of feudalism do suggest how, in post-Soviet conditions, local elites arrogated central administrative power to establish a measure of sovereign authority in their regions, historians typically interpret feudalism as a system governed by clear rules of reciprocal obligation.[16] Patronage, in contrast, is an *informal* relationship of exchange, in which there is an imbalance of power between patron and client, but in which each requires the other for survival.[17] Reciprocity is at the heart of any patron-client relationship, but as Marshall Sahlins argued, acts of reciprocal exchange do not necessarily connote a parity of power. Exchange is also an opportunity to reinforce asymmetry in a relationship. The generosity manifest in an exchange, Sahlins (1972, 162) observed, can be "enlisted as the starting mechanism of leadership [or patronage] *because it creates followership*" (my emphasis). Robert Paine (1971) employed the approach of both Sahlins and Marcel Mauss to illustrate how patrons establish and sustain their authority through a continual dispersal of assets over which they have control, promoting the dependence of their clients on this relationship. But Paine does not offer a working explanation for the imbalance of power in a patron-client relationship, whereby, despite the reciprocal flow of resources upon which each is reliant for survival, the roles remain fixed within a stable hierarchy. Paine in fact argues in the other direction by suggesting that the respective identities of patron and client are made *ambiguous* by acts of exchange.[18]

If we consider the case of Chukotka under the Nazarov administration, we must return to Sahlins' model of "asymmetrical reciprocity" to understand why the identities of patron and client remained both stable and relatively far apart. After all, the governor wielded considerable power over even those clients and constituencies whose services and loyalty he very much required for survival. Indeed, the manner in which Nazarov exercised patronage power illustrates that deep inequality can in fact reside and be sustained within patron-client relationships. Inequalities of power, in turn, help us understand that though many within Chukotka's post-Soviet settler population may have wished to leave, it was only a particularly powerful minority who could translate the transient mentality into action. The manner in which Nazarov's system of patronage rule functioned, for its part, was vital in forming new arrangements of power and setting the trajectory of development (and decline) that Chukotka took in its particular experience of post-Soviet "transition." His administration relied on three principal strategies to erect and perpetuate its authority, which we will now explore in some detail.

Sealing Off the Patronage Domain

By definition, a patron possesses privileged or monopoly access to resources that are required by a client. Whether these originate externally or are internal resources whose redistribution the patron controls, any patron who hopes to maintain superiority in the exchange must command their flow and will naturally abhor the presence of alternatives to which clients might turn. A free market, open to entry, corrodes strong patron-client relations because diversity affords the client a range of options and forces patrons into competition with one another. Choice, in either political or economic terms, inverts the balance of power in favour of the modest citizen – the voter, the customer, the client. For this reason, it is particularly relevant to speak of "capturing" or "sealing off" various kinds of space when describing the operations of a patronage system.[19]

Certain students of Russia's post-Soviet transition interpreted the ascendance of strong local power bases at the expense of centralized state control as the emergence of crypto-capitalist organizations and the early signals of a nascent free market.[20] In fact, this process reflected strategies to monopolize control over markets more than attempts to free them. The "privatization of power" by local bosses in the post-Soviet space was a means of creating sealed defensive domains (the feudal demesne), within which it was possible to maintain monopoly positions as patrons and brokers. Governor Nazarov adopted this strategy in Chukotka, a naturally isolated territory well suited to the kind of total administrative capture he engineered.

The instinct to monopolize control and exclude competition from alternative patrons helps to explain why Nazarov's administration adopted measures that actually deepened Chukotka's crisis, including bureaucratically strangling relations with outside partners, particularly in Alaska. After a brief period of liberalization in the late perestroika period and the early 1990s, Chukotka diverged from the pattern set in other Far East regions (Magadan, Kamchatka, Sakhalin), which were then building relationships and collaborating with partners from abroad. Rather than dismantling the bureaucratic infrastructure that in the Soviet era strictly regulated access to the okrug, the administration petitioned Moscow to maintain traditional border restrictions.[21] Alaskans, who had initiated a range of partnerships with nascent Chukotkan native-rights and community-development organizations, spoke of an ice curtain falling across the Bering Strait once again.[22] Foreign and Russian researchers met with growing difficulties as they attempted to arrange community-based fieldwork.[23] From the mid-1990s, even members of the Russian press faced serious obstacles in obtaining the necessary *propusk* (the special pass required of visitors) to report on Chukotka's socio-economic crisis.[24] The border regime, enforced by locally based Border Guards and the FSB (Federal Security Service), was apparently manipulated to the administration's benefit, despite the fact that okrug authorities held no formal jurisdiction over this system.[25]

The fate of Beringovskii illustrates the aggressive role the governor's office played in erecting bureaucratic barriers to movement. Living conditions in this mainly settler community of five thousand (in 1989), both a district centre and the site of Chukotka's premier coal mine, were atrocious in the second half of the 1990s, when public utilities – water and heating, electricity, and sewage drainage – collapsed. Beringovskii's coal fuelled the heating and power plants of many of Chukotka's settlements, but its population was effectively erased from public consciousness. To conceal the growing crisis, no visitors from outside Chukotka were permitted to come to the settlement between 1997 and 2000, and Nazarov's office directed the local security organs to censor any descriptions of living conditions from outgoing post and telegrams.[26] Long-distance telephone calls were impossible to place. Desperate residents resorted to making the difficult journey to

Anadyr, in order to post word of their plight to relatives in central Russia (and to the national press).[27]

The bureaucratic sealing of Chukotka's territory enabled Nazarov's administration to suffocate the development of its independent civil society organizations, for whom collaboration with foreign partners was critical. After an initial outburst of grassroots activism, the post-Soviet political "thaw" receded as Nazarov's office took action against any initiatives it viewed as a threat to its monopoly position. Igor Krupnik and Nikolai Vakhtin (2002, 10), who produced one of the only comprehensive studies of life in Chukotka under Nazarov, reported that, "By the time of our survey in 1995-96, former debates about self-government, public control and local sustainability were becoming less and less audible." Patty Gray (2005), also a witness to this crisis, described a series of repressive measures, including the appropriation of the printing press with which Chukotka's only native-language newspaper was published. The okrug's most prominent indigenous activist, Vladimir Etylin, fought with little success to achieve an independent voice for native people, unsuccessfully running for governor in 1996 and 2000.[28] In an interview I conducted with Etylin in August 2002, he remarked that patronage politics under Nazarov reduced native elites to a position of passive subservience before the okrug administration, a habit that survives into the present. A long-time local ally of his observed that, by about 1996, the formerly activist Association of Indigenous Peoples had reverted to an "arm of Nazarov's administration" whose delegates and leadership were "always fixed by the okrug and city [Anadyr] administrations" [26]. Only two organizations managed to sustain an active collaboration with foreign partners over this period, the native NGOs Yup'ik (The Society of Eskimos) and Naukan. Is it significant that both are based in communities along the Bering Strait, in proximity to Alaska but distant from Anadyr, and that their members benefited from the right of visa-free travel to the American shore throughout the 1990s? Their achievements continue to set them apart in the post-Nazarov era, and their organizational maturity and political independence are obviously greater than those of other civil society initiatives in the okrug.[29]

Distributing Patronage

Having monopolized access to critical resources, the aspiring patron must then assemble the capacity to distribute them. This is the function of the patronage networks that so many commentators on Soviet and post-Soviet Russia identify as defining structures of this society. In the case of patronage-based administration, formal mechanisms of distribution – bureaucracies and their payrolls, budget transfers, revenue collection – are wasted if allowed to operate beyond the personal control of the patron. The formal agencies of state power, therefore, are colonized by personalized principles of reciprocity, which permit patron figures to direct resources for the benefit of their own position.

Chukotka's severe economic crisis opened the way for a greater level of capture than a diverse and growing economy would have permitted. The closure of the industrial drivers of Chukotka's resource economy narrowed the range of economic possibilities in the okrug to those controlled by Nazarov's administrative networks alone. By assuming budget control over Chukotka's new post-secession bureaucracies, the administration subsequently entrenched its near total distributive powers, and the migration of formerly productive labour into these newly minted administrative vedomstva created a large pool of clients owing their security to the patronage of the governor's office. As the okrug ceased to produce any export products of significance, a parallel economy blossomed within this elaborate bureaucratic apparatus, fed by subsidy and transfer payments from Moscow. By implication, an ever-growing population of local residents was "polluted" by their involvement in the patronage embrace, an important factor in the decision of Chukotka's subsequent governor, Roman Abramovich, to exclude locals from administrative positions and import his own loyal agents when he took office in 2001.

Between 1992 and 1995, administrative jurisdiction was devolved to Russia's regions without a corresponding devolution of tax-collection responsibilities. In effect, Nazarov was administering okrug affairs while remaining free of the burden to finance them. The federal government simply transferred funds to the okrug administration, entrusting it with the responsibility for their distribution to the respective state agencies and departments.[30] As a consequence, until federal authority was re-established over the disbursement of funding in 1997, Nazarov held almost unchallenged control over the money designated by Moscow for the running of Chukotka's bureaucratic apparatus. This proved to be an invaluable arrangement for distributing patronage and one of the most tangible rewards for Chukotka's capture from Magadan. The governor's office, in the absence of scrutiny by any federal body, could disperse funding as it wished, rewarding the loyal and punishing the rebellious.

But, in the accumulation of patronage power, the governor was not content with control over the disbursement of transfers from Moscow. In 1994, the administration began to withhold actual ruble funding altogether and introduced a system of "mutual credits," a kind of autonomous okrug-level currency system. Government departments received, instead of liquid funds, assurances that they would be paid in services via transactions arranged by the governor's office on their behalf. The former director of one agency recalled, "If I needed to pay ChukotAvia [Chukotka's monopoly air-services company] for flights, I would call the governor's office, they would ask how much I needed, and I'd send them a letter stating how much. Then some deputy governor would call the director of ChukotAvia and tell him to grant [us] a certain amount of service. In exchange, they would have an amount knocked off their tax bill. So I never touched 'living money' – there was no actual money in the system, just mutual debts" [25].

The lack of actual currency in the local economy was deliberate – throughout this period, the okrug administration itself continued to receive budgetary transfers from Moscow in "living rubles." By withdrawing money from the functioning of government departments, Nazarov inflated the role of his office as a broker of transactions between the major economic and administrative players in the region. Mary Douglas' (1967, 7) comments on the use of surrogate currencies in tribal economies of New Guinea could hardly be more relevant: "The object of coupons or licensing is protective: to limit access to particular goods to certain groups of people. An important side effect of coupons is to create advantages, even sometimes monopolies, for those who issue them." Deprived of living money, Chukotka's lesser bureaucratic authorities could no longer deal directly with their clients or collaborate horizontally with other departments. If the director of the okrug hospital required fuel for his ambulances, he could no longer pay the Anadyr fuel depot directly; he waited on the governor's office to effect the transaction. This system penetrated to the level of everyday life, as government departments were deprived of funds to pay their employees. State employees reverted to a coupon system in local shops, and shop owners were promised compensation from the authorities in the form of "services" (transport, heating, power). At every level, the economy was becoming demonetized. Nazarov often justified the withdrawal of funding in living money with the rhetoric of fighting corruption in the government departments that answered to him. Ironically, the measure simply concentrated these abuses within the okrug administration.

The Performance of Patronage

The importance of patrons in an economy of favours leads to the association of power with the individual leader rather than the agency of administration. Just as the structures of rational bureaucracy conceal personalized relations of exchange in a system of patronage, the focus of authority in such a system is the person, not a codified body of rules. Attention is thus continually drawn to the manner in which patrons *personally* dispense resources and collect forms of tribute, as if ritually reconfirming their identity. In this way, acts of patronage distribution – of giving gifts, favours, help – take on a performative aspect. This performativity is critical to patrons' charismatic power (see Weber 1968), which, within a system where informal relationships have supplanted formal regulation, alone guarantees the continual rehearsal of patron-client exchange.

In Chukotka, the authority of the governor's office as a source of patronage and its capacity to extract reciprocal benefits from its clients required that acts of distribution never became routinized. The governor, and his deputies *(zamestiteli* or *zam-gubernatory),* encouraged the directors of various departments and agencies to appeal for funding to their person, rather than their office. This in turn permitted a continual performance of the act of giving, which lent such transactions the flavour of generosity rather than legal obligation. A deputy of the okrug Duma under Nazarov recalled that "everything was done on a personal basis. You had to fight [with the administration] to get ordinary things done" [27]. Another senior official from that time remembered "the crowds in the reception rooms of the governor during his visits [to Chukotka], in contrast with the empty reception rooms of his deputies. When the governor was absent from the okrug, life in the administration building died away" [28].

Nazarov's office operated much like the court of a feudal lord. Lesser government figures would play the part of vassals, attending in person to pledge loyalty in exchange for the resources their own offices required to function. Nazarov frequently travelled to Moscow, where he cultivated a network of powerful allies including Mayor Yuri Luzhkov. So successful did he prove that, in 1994-95 alone, Chukotka received federal credit worth US$190 million ("Another Oligarch" 2004). However, though these relationships afforded Nazarov access to federal resources vital for "feeding" his own domestic constituencies, it was equally crucial for him to personally "perform" their distribution back in the okrug. A senior administration figure of the early 1990s related to me that whenever Nazarov travelled out of the North, he called his deputies continually to ensure that no major decisions were taken without his knowledge; it appeared he sensed a danger in withdrawing from the patron's throne, if only momentarily. In this regard, it is helpful to view the performance of distribution as "cooked" in the Lévi-Straussian sense: each performance is an act that in its cultural context carries a recognizable symbolic meaning. For Nazarov, to perform the act of giving was to ritually confirm his ability to secure resources (from Moscow) and to personally decide where they would eventually come to rest within his administrative domains.

Just as budget distribution was converted into personalized transactions, so was it vital to maintain uncertainty, to avoid the formation of set transactional patterns. Thus, the flow of patronage from Nazarov's office was inconstant, and certainly the amount and the timing of transfers were difficult to predict in advance. Those who engaged in the budget-funding dance with the governor's office remember a kind of deliberate psychological terrorism, which kept the client in perpetual fear that what was nominally owed might be arbitrarily withheld. The director of an Anadyr-based government agency throughout Nazarov's tenure described his own experiences in the governor's "court": "We knew when Nazarov got our funds from the federal level, but we never knew when they would get to us. So every year I went through the same ritual" [25].

Of course, the fact that these performances took the shape of a ritual did not guarantee an identical outcome every time:

> For weeks, I started each day at the office of the deputy governor responsible. If I missed a day, the next time I came in he would joke that I'd gone AWOL. He was so

> accustomed to my presence that he'd begun to look at me like a mosquito – you know, you walk on the tundra and you are surrounded by mosquitoes, but you can never escape them. Wave your arms all you want, they're still buzzing in your ear. He would scream and kick me out, curse my name, but I didn't have to make excuses for myself. And then maybe I'd get a little money. Or maybe I wouldn't. [25]

The distribution of funding for the indigenous economy (reindeer herding and marine-mammal hunting) was similarly personalized and performed. The okrug administration subjected indigenous settlements and their state farms *(sovkhozy)* to a series of poorly funded and badly organized programs of privatization and renationalization throughout the 1990s (see Gray 2000, 2003), and this was an area of severe social and economic crisis. In fact, Nazarov viewed indigenous communities as never fully captured within his sphere of patronage influence and therefore as a potential threat to his administration. The limited success of some native organizations in cultivating foreign collaborations (in effect, finding patrons alternative to the governor) simply reinforced these suspicions. Under policies enacted by the governor's office, workers in the state farms (and their successor organizations) were the worst-paid employees in Chukotka's public sector. This magnified the socio-economic crisis in the rural sphere, to which the governor then attended with highly visible performances of giving. Nazarov made carefully staged visits to destitute natives in their villages, occasions when the okrug media filmed and photographed him personally distributing aid.[31] An examination of agricultural funding leading up to the Abramovich era revealed the extent of patronage giving in the rural sphere: the 2000 agricultural budget of roughly 5 million rubles (approximately US$200,000) was delivered to the Department of Agriculture entirely in the form of "gifts."[32] One staple of Nazarov's rural tours was the annual reindeer sled-race in the remote Chukchi community of Chuvanskoe, when he would deliver crates of food and alcohol by helicopter. Toward the end of his second term, he distributed aluminium whaleboats and outboard engines to coastal villages under the banner of the "Governor's Program." To this day, in the village of Vaegi, located seven hundred kilometres upriver from Anadyr, a once-luxurious motor yacht lies abandoned on the bank, a gift to the village with the faded words "Programa Gubernatora" still visible on its bow.

Corruption and the Mentality of Transience

Kormlenie – literally "feeding off" – is an ancient practice of Russian governance, employed to best effect on the periphery of empire. During the fifteenth and sixteenth centuries, governors of Russian provinces received no state salary and were instructed to live off the souls under their jurisdiction by levying unregulated taxes. This system enabled the Russian imperial state to hold vast territories at little cost to itself, a pattern simply perpetuated by the conquest of Siberia and the Far East

Governor Aleksandr Nazarov visiting a native village, mid-1990s
Unknown photographer, archives of Krainyi Sever *(a regional weekly newspaper)*

in the seventeenth century. The tsar's representatives across the Urals were given rights to entrepreneurially tax indigenous locals and Slavic settlers, with the caveat that some portion was passed back to the Russian Crown. This practice generated the revenue necessary to fund the operations of remote outposts and further campaigns of expansion into new fur-rich lands. Local officials naturally treated their office as a means of rapid self-enrichment, and the only practice introduced to limit such behaviour was the rotation of administrators out of their posts every two years. Even with Count Speranski's Petrine reforms of Siberian administration, extreme distances prevented authorities in St. Petersburg from scrutinizing the operations of their representatives across the Urals.[33]

In a modern-day adaptation of the kormlenie principle, Governor Nazarov's inner circle fed itself on Chukotka's eviscerated post-Soviet carcass. In its outer form, Nazarov's bureaucratic capture of Chukotka followed a pattern proposed by Verdery, Humphrey, and Easter, one common throughout the post-Soviet domain: the "parcellization of sovereignty." Verdery (1996) characterized this as a defensive posture, a strategy that many post-Soviet bosses employed to reinforce the security of their vedomstva, partly in an effort to protect their workers from the vagaries of post-Soviet uncertainty. Regional leaders duplicated this process within their administrative territories, often in an attempt to keep alive Soviet-era systems of social support and economic production (as, for example, in the Sakha Republic). Mixed with self-interest, therefore, an ethic of personal responsibility guided the actions of the post-Soviet boss. Indeed, the two were mutually reinforcing, for the long-term survival of any enterprise or regional administration depended on the well-being of those within its embrace.

But this is where Nazarov's approach to power differed. Although Chukotka's secession from Magadan followed a national process of devolution, the manner in which its regional elite thereafter used their devolved powers had little to do with protecting local living standards and keeping the local economy alive. Rather, Nazarov and the members of his administrative circles captured the okrug and its resources in an effort to effect their own exit from the region on the best material terms possible. In retrospect, little regard appears to have been paid to the long-term prospects of Chukotka's economic and human potential, or to the esteem in which locals held the Nazarov administration. Rather, Nazarovism was a highly unsustainable mode of rule, engaged on one hand in patronage distribution, but, on the other, quite plainly cycling the harvest of power into investments outside the North. Not only were Brezhnevite habits of overt self-interest – a sociocultural cancer that Ken Jowitt (1992) terms "personalism"[34] – ingrained among Chukotka's former Party elite, these figures operated on the assumption that they, and most of their clients in the local political economy, were playing for the short term. Nazarovism was the privatization of power in a northern variant. It was a paradoxical combination of, on one hand, the capture of administration by a local elite and, on the other, a dream of departure, a toxic outcome of the failure of the old settler identity amid a general atmosphere of evacuation.

It is difficult to determine the extent to which Governor Nazarov sought control over budget funds in order to oil his patronage machine and thus enhance his political invulnerability, or conversely, to enrich himself and his inner circle. In any case, spending power and political power are interdependent features of any patronage system of rule. According to informants who ran government department budgets in the 1990s, the administration routinely "diverted" a portion of the funds it received for disbursal to accounts controlled by Nazarov and his associates. The introduction of the mutual credits system in the mid-1990s vastly increased the administration's ability to manipulate public resources. This system enabled it to withhold the budgets of entire departments, living money that could be redirected for other uses. A portion of these payments was deposited in a series of pocket banks in Moscow, including Presnya-Bank and Intermed-Bank, allegedly owned by associates of the governor and used for currency trading and investments. These two banks were declared bankrupt in 1998, and the okrug funds they contained were written off as a loss. Many residents of Chukotka who witnessed these developments report that Nazarov conspired in the banks' collapse and received a personal payoff as a result [28] [25] [17] [3].[35]

Another example of apparent administrative corruption was the affair of the "gold credits." After 1991, Chukotka's gold production suffered a dramatic slump, as the departure of skilled labour and the fall in state investments early in Nazarov's tenure devastated Soviet-era enterprises. Yet, as he contemplated the virtues of Chukotka's secession from Magadan Oblast, Nazarov still harboured hopes of a renewed boom in gold mining, from which rent could be captured to support the sovereign okrug.[36] In order to stimulate mining operations in Chukotka, the governor approached the Russian Ministry of Finance in 1995, requesting large-scale credits secured on the basis of projected production from two major deposits in the area of Pevek and Bilibino.[37] Low-interest loans were subsequently advanced, leading to the creation of new mining enterprises. However, specialist geologists and engineers were not placed at the helm: instead, management was turned over to former Party officials drawn from within administration networks. Chukotka's first deputy governor was appointed the president of Chukotkan Gold (Chukotskoe zoloto), and a parallel company, Gold of Chukotka (Zoloto Chukotskoe),[38] was controlled by senior officials in the governor's office and associates of Nazarov's from Bilibino, his home town and original power base. Over several years of operation, neither company produced any gold on an industrial scale, although senior managers bought flats and suburban homes in Moscow, where they worked from a suite of offices and travelled in chauffeured luxury cars, occasionally visiting South Africa, northern Canada, and Alaska on "fact-finding missions." The gold credits themselves were held in Presnya-Bank before its 1998 bankruptcy [28] [25].[39] Federal government auditors, attempting to track the lost money, continued their search into 2003 without success.

These episodes of apparent large-scale budgetary embezzlement concerned only a very small number within Governor Nazarov's inner circle. A more general practice observed throughout Chukotka's bureaucratic structures was the abuse of fixed state assets for personal enrichment. The regional elite adapted to post-Soviet conditions by capitalizing on the resources it possessed: well-developed personal networks and administrative control over state property. Asset stripping – selling off any state assets you could lay your hands on – became the prevailing mode of business activity. Military commanders "privatized" their fleets of heavy trucks and vezdekhody, selling them into the private market at cut-rate prices. State farm directors drove herds of reindeer to Anadyr and other large centres for wholesale slaughter. The Ekspeditsiia fleet of imported bulldozers was sold to buyers on the materik for a fraction of its value, by directors who then disappeared from Chukotka with the proceeds [5]. One witness of the great sell-off remarked, "The thing is, everything was legal. The authorities just said 'the more private property the better, we have to sell everything off!' So what happened is that anyone with connections appropriated anything of value and sold it off before leaving the okrug. Farewell! And nothing was created here, nothing was left behind that could make a profit – it was out-and-out robbery from the state by the people. It was like 1917 in reverse" [26].

Unsure of Chukotka's future, local entrepreneurs made short-term investments calculated to reap immediate profits rather than to ensure long-term productivity. This approach to business usually involved wringing maximum profit from existing enterprises and assets without reinvesting the profits locally. The former director of Chukotka's largest fish-processing plant, which in the Soviet era was second only to the Otrozhnyi gold mine in "profitability" (measured by local tax contributions), described how in 1993 members of the governor's circle privatized the operation and became its directors. This gave them control over the lucrative export of salmon roe *(ikra)* to Moscow, but despite the large revenues they secured, the new managers over-fished local stocks in contravention of state regulations and neither invested in plant and equipment nor paid their workforce regularly. By 1998, the operation had collapsed and the owners had left Chukotka [33].

But perhaps their choices were entirely sensible. The conditions of economic uncertainty in Russia over this period naturally made any kind of long-term investment exceedingly risky. This was particularly true in the North, where the complexity and delay arising from the climate and the okrug's remoteness made it necessary to borrow credit over longer periods than in the compact markets of central Russia. This particularly exposed Chukotka's businesses to the periodic currency devaluations that plagued the Russian economy (big crashes occurred in 1992, 1994, and 1998). So even those local entrepreneurs who did engage in productive business activity worked on very short timelines, hoping to convert profits into more stable enterprises and investments *outside* the North. One former Party official in Anadyr obtained a low-interest loan from Nazarov's administration to found a telecommunications firm. He subsequently won contracts to install phone systems in most of Anadyr's new government offices. But although he ran a small local office for a few years, he invested all his profits in property in St. Petersburg. In 1998, he wound up his Anadyr operation and left Chukotka permanently. In retrospect, his transient approach to business was entirely justified: had he remained in Anadyr another year, the default of September 1998 would have bankrupted him.

There are many stories in circulation following similar patterns: embezzling budget funds, selling off state assets, running down productive enterprises.[40] Two themes unite them: they involved members of the former Party and managerial elite, and they were strategies of departure from the okrug. By activating patronage networks to maintain the effectiveness and authority of his administration, Governor Nazarov might have acted to preserve the few viable sectors of Chukotka's post-Soviet economy and cushion the region in its inevitable decline. But stories of pocket banks, corruption in the gold-mining industry, and asset stripping illustrate that self-preservation was the first principle within the administration's inner circles.

To return to this chapter's main argument, Chukotka's devastating decline was closely linked to the transient mentality prevailing among its local elite and characterizing the style of administration distinguishing this okrug from regions of central Russia in the post-Soviet period. The objective factors driving the economic crisis were common throughout the Russian space – macro-economic instability, immature legislation and markets, an anaemic business culture, and fragmented and disconnected populations and enterprises. As in other parts of the country, Chukotka's productive assets, including its administration and budget, were captured by what Verdery (1996) terms a "rising class of entrepratchiks." But in other regions of Russia, new forms of productive enterprise emerged from the era of asset stripping and abuse of state resources. Chukotka, in contrast, was stripped bare in a remarkable process of de-industrialization that was blind to the region's actual economic potential. Wealth wrung from the remains of the old Soviet economy was converted into portable forms of capital and taken elsewhere.

When we consider Chukotka's experience of post-Soviet transition, the corruption and arrogance of its mostly settler bureaucratic-administrative class emerges as its leitmotif. As I spoke with a broad range of people in Chukotka and central Russia who had knowledge and experience of these practices – mostly settlers who had worked with Nazarov and his deputies – a detailed and quite compromising picture formed of a mode of settler response to the Soviet collapse. Why these people were willing to talk says something about the nature of Nazarov's authority, and indeed offers a comment on the transient mentality itself. It is in the nature of a patronage system to implicate all those within its distributive embrace – to effectively "pollute" an entire community with the identity of vassalage. Indeed, my best informants on the Nazarov era were all by definition participants in the transactions of patronage; in telling me their stories, they incriminated themselves. Although this might cast doubt on the veracity of my material, I believed their accounts could be trusted.

There are three compelling explanations for this. First, in a patronage system such as Nazarov's, loyalty derives from the distribution of material rewards. There is no loyalty transcending this expectation, and so Nazarov was compelled to continually feed his constituents while combating the intrusions of alternative patrons. As soon as a better patron emerges, loyalties shift quite effortlessly, and this occurred with the arrival of Roman Abramovich, Nazarov's successor, in 2000. Second, as I gained the confidence of key informants, they became eager to tell their stories because, despite their own implication in former patronage networks, they had all personally suffered the consequences of corrupt administration.[41] In post-Nazarov Chukotka, there was no public forum for ventilating pent-up feelings of anger, guilt, and shame, no Truth and Reconciliation Commission, no regular columns in the newspaper dedicated to revelations of Nazarov-era abuses of power. It simply compounded informants' frustration that just as Nazarov was unaccountable for his actions while in power, so he remained after his removal from office.[42] By relating their experiences of living with Nazarov, informants with a personal history of clientalist behaviour may have found a kind of expurgatory therapy in helping to create a permanent record.

Finally, it is usually the case that what people say about the past is a reflection on the present. By vituperating Nazarov and his administrative circle for their "strategies of departure," present-day settlers were pointing to an alternative way of living in the North. Narrating Nazarovism became a self-constituting act, which, through a process of externalizing and distancing those settlers who left Chukotka in the 1990s, made sense of the decision to remain behind. In my presence, settlers vilified the transient mentality at the heart of Nazarovism and thereby constructed a moral framework for a new post-Soviet conception of rootedness in the North. They attached a virtue to practices of belonging in a local, northern community. In the final chapters of this book, I examine how these enriched senses of local rootedness – in a community and a landscape – framed the modes of settler response to outsider-led challenges in a more recent era. But in the coming pages, we remain in the 1990s to explore an alternative experience of settler life in Chukotka's crisis decade, one very distant indeed from the lives of Nazarov's elite associates. Just as the Soviet collapse revealed vast differences in power within the settler population, so did it trigger a radical divergence within what previously seemed to be a homogeneous community of settlers. Far from dreaming of departure, many of them responded to the Soviet collapse by deepening their commitment to the North.

5
Surviving without the State

The collapse of the Soviet state stripped the settler of practically all those features of privilege that previously defined this population, and it did so with remarkable speed and thoroughness. Northern osvoenie had been one of the Soviet regime's most cherished projects, but the suddenness of its end showed, finally, how little rationale it possessed beyond Moscow's fiat. Settlers once lived within a zone of remarkable abundance and earned far more than workers on the materik. Now Chukotka suffered acute shortages of everyday goods and food, and by the mid-1990s prices rose to the highest level in Russia (Shmyganovski 1997, 158). Meanwhile, savings were destroyed by inflation, industry collapsed, and unemployment exploded; for those who were able to keep their jobs, pay was sporadic and insufficient. Settlers once inhabited a space of benevolent statelessness, a paradoxical condition of relative freedom from the rituals of official public life, of unscripted leisure time, made possible by a state presence in the Far North that was, at its height, effective and charismatic. The accomplishments of northern mastery and industrialization reinforced to northern migrants the power and rightness of the Soviet socialist system. Their sense of participation in this process was likewise interwoven with their involvement in the project of civilizing Chukotka's indigenous population, as the agents and embodiment of Soviet modernity.

Now, this sense of mission and colonial agency was abruptly undermined by the failure of Soviet ideology. A nationwide re-examination of the past had produced a sustained critique of Soviet efforts to "lift up" northern peoples, and the northern settler was frequently recast as an agent of cultural destruction.[1] The idea of Soviet technical mastery in the North was likewise overturned, as liberalization revealed the wildly unsustainable costs of the industry and infrastructure settlers had come north to build. Finally, settlers were abruptly thrust into an entirely more malevolent experience of statelessness, as the North (and particularly its most distant regions) was dramatically cut off from the surviving Russian economy. Settlers were once supremely mobile, moving between the northern periphery and the Soviet metropolis as the agents of cultural and technical modernity. Now, the centralized state withdrew from northern life and left Chukotka's settlements extremely isolated, forcing settlers to cope with the exotic new reality of immobility. As aviation failed, settlers faced not only the end of frequent travel to the materik, but, indeed, the prospect of never leaving the North at all. In 1990, a ticket from Anadyr to Moscow cost 230 rubles [64]. By mid-1992, the price had risen to 6,390 rubles, and by 1995, it had reached 2,150,000 rubles, a rise of almost 10,000 percent (Goskomstat 1998).

These radical changes in northern life naturally had an impact on the ways in which settlers saw themselves, as individuals and as members of a community, and on their modes of social interaction. Most importantly for this study of migrant identities, by exposing radical differences in opportunity and power within settler society, the post-Soviet collapse fractured the sense of commonality that once encompassed the entire settler population. With shared ideals of mission and purpose disappearing alongside the Soviet way of life, the perception of "community," as a notion of solidarity with practically any settler, whether friend or stranger, was discarded in favour of a much more limited and literal idea. The non-transactional spirit of the Soviet-era settler "sharing society" foundered on post-Soviet shortage. As we have seen, the asset-stripping mode of administration that defined crisis-era Nazarovism was practised only by Chukotka's elite industrial managers, bureaucrats, and political leaders, and it rested upon a machinery of patronage inaccessible to most of the settlers (and almost all of the natives) remaining in the region in the 1990s. For those without access to state resources and capital, the notion of common cause with those who did was nakedly absurd. Most settlers, particularly those in rural villages and industrial towns distant from Anadyr, joined their indigenous counterparts in a daily struggle for survival that lasted, more or less, for a decade.

Just as mobility served as one of the clearest indexes of power in Soviet times, so did the power of movement offer the best barometer of privilege and disempowerment in conditions of post-Soviet crisis. Once defining the divide between in-migrant specialists and indigenous locals, extremes of mobility and fixedness now appeared *within* the settler population. As the Soviet system collapsed, shortage, poverty, and the fragmentation of the old notion of settler community set in motion myriad strategies to regain mobility and security. Many of the most privileged settlers – the highly skilled or the well connected – exercised their powers of mobility to leave the North soon after the collapse. These comprised the wave of sixty-four thousand residents (41 percent of the population) who left Chukotka between 1992 and 1995 alone (Goskomstat 1998). The rapidly dwindling population that remained contained a growing proportion of settlers trapped in the region by material difficulty, but there were also many who chose to stay and who adapted to the times by accumulating new forms of mobility in more immediate settings.

At the same time, many settlers were struggling to redefine positions of dominance over their indigenous counterparts. The old hierarchy of settler privilege in relation to natives lost its monolithic aspect, for survival and success in post-Soviet conditions of statelessness became in many ways a more meritocratic and less ethnically determined affair. Whereas travel was previously a more or less neutral and affordable state service, now the resources of movement were privatized, and mobility became a commodity of trade, a means of survival, and a reflection of power. In Chukotka's newly isolated villages, those with access to transport could thus dominate local networks; they brought in essential goods and moved people to and from larger towns. In theory, anyone with knowledge and energy could grasp the opportunity and become a transport entrepreneur. But in practice, powers of mobility were largely inherited from Soviet-era status arrangements. Thus, certain individual settlers – sovkhoz managers and technical specialists (mechanics, engineers, drivers) – found themselves in a position to privatize transport resources. But most – the less fortunate, less skilled, or simply less mercenary – became as fixed in place, and thus as vulnerable, as rural natives.

Whether ordinary settlers stayed in the North by choice or because they lacked the resources and connections to leave, their only viable means of survival entailed a close attention to those resources they still possessed: local knowledge, specialist skills, and membership in local circles of friends and family. At the same time, hardship and its corrosive effects created a radically different setting in which those means of survival could be applied. Limits of mutual trust and forms of sharing realigned themselves as settler networks narrowed, and more locally rooted criteria emerged as the marks of reliability and group membership. The old sense of embracing commonality among settlers changed, and forms of community concentrated down onto smaller geographical and social domains, which themselves came to be more fiercely valued and defended. To a large degree, survival came to rest on membership in collectives – both formal and informal – which now limited the boundaries of reciprocal giving but also ensured an intensity of exchange sufficient to support each member in uncertain times. Social life in Chukotka's settlements became more antagonistic, as competing circles and networks assumed new positions within an ever more stratified hierarchy of privilege and poverty. Strategies of survival were often predatory, earning their proponents a measure of security and social footing at the expense of indignation from other quarters; the settler *kommersant* (private trader) bootlegging alcohol in the villages epitomized this phenomenon.

Just as the constituents of the old settler identity were annulled by crisis and collapse, the experience of surviving subsequently generated new senses of belonging among settlers. To get by, they responded to unfamiliar circumstances in innovative and entrepreneurial ways that entailed the assumption of new roles, often to fill the vacuum left by retreating state services. In this way, non-elite strategies of survival were *localizing* practices; the erstwhile transient migrant was compelled to invest in immediate relationships and to deepen knowledge of local needs or of the immediate natural environment. Experience in the North, and the forms of local knowledge this produced, shifted from its totemic role as a marker of status to become a practical condition of survival. Local knowledge was critical to movement between settlements, and thus to the transport of people and goods; navigating up the Anadyr River, for example, requires an exquisite knowledge of its ever-shifting water levels and its labyrinthine channels and braids. Even when settlers were mobile, moving into and out of their home settlements, and even into and out of the North, they tended to remain tightly woven into the social fabric of their home settlements and districts through arrangements of mutual reliance. These entanglements renewed a sense of practical and emotional belonging in specific places (which could co-exist with attachments to former homes outside the North and which were usually in ever-fluctuating competition with them). Consequently, as settlers reoriented their loyalties to more immediate settings, they abandoned faith in the wider civic project of building a pan-Chukotkan society for the post-Soviet era (which had been the notional intent of Nazarov's initiative to secede from Magadan). Indeed, the point at which practices of localist survival emerged to replace a disappearing state presence marked a vital turning point in Chukotka, after which it became possible to speak of a truly "post-Soviet settler." The features of privilege and distinction were gone, as was the old sense of easy mobility and multi-sited cosmopolitanism. Now, those migrants remaining, and in particular those choosing to remain, began to render the notion of "settling" palpable through their investments in very localized, one might even argue "native," ways of life.

Shrinking Networks and the Costs of Exclusion

Chukotka's late-Soviet communities were remarkably more open and inclusive, and more animated by norms of trust and sharing, than the social environment settlers left behind on the materik. In conditions of abundance and full employment, everyone to some degree controlled resources of tradable value – access to transport, fresh vegetables, or fresh reindeer meat, the skills to tutor schoolchildren, or a little knowledge of plumbing. By cultivating a set of networks and contributing to them with inputs of those valuable resources over which they had direct control, settlers enjoyed reciprocal access to a wide range of goods. Informants do not recall this behaviour as transactional – they remember a culture of generosity. On one level, the conditions of abundance sustained the flow of goods and services, within a theoretical rubric based on the anthropological principles of "generalized reciprocity." The obligations of reciprocity remained unspecified; exchange operated under the putative terms of unconditional sharing (the "gift," see Mauss 1990). After all, in Soviet Chukotka, when everyone was materially secure, giving more than you got back hardly carried a penalty. On another level, the culture of generosity was intrinsic to a specifically Chukotkan identity, playing a key role in the ideology of its settlers. One very important ingredient in the sense of difference, indeed, superiority, that settlers felt vis-à-vis the average Soviet was membership in an enveloping, benevolent, and robust community, which, through practices of sharing, generated a constant sense of social belonging.

However, the venal practices of Nazarov's patronage polity, combined with desperate hardship and the fear of worse to come, denatured the old Soviet sense of community, which was already under attack as the props of the settler identity were withdrawn. As economic collapse compromised a way of life, stranding settlers in positions outside the remaining channels of access to food, pay, and influence, the broad and inclusive networks of the Soviet period shrank back to enclose and protect those precious resources that still existed. Conditions of shortage acted to stratify power in Chukotka's society and make the venality of network exchange more overt. People in control of key resources became more powerful in relation to those abandoned on the periphery of shrinking networks. In an impoverished socio-economic milieu, patrons were forced to limit their relations of exchange to those who likewise possessed a tradable asset.

For Chukotka's settlers, once refugees from the atomized society of the late-Soviet era who found relief in the North's broad and embracing communities, the consequences were perverse: as the crisis unfolded, the fragmented social texture they had left behind finally caught up with them again. In his examination of late-Soviet Leningrad, Finn Sivert Nielsen (2007) argued that in order to survive in conditions of low-level political repression and chronic shortage, individuals inhabited island-like networks among narrow circles of intimates.[2] In the 1990s, settler society came to resemble Nielsen's model of the social archipelago, as mistrust of the outsider came to delimit the boundaries of the network in a way foreign to the expansive and welcoming Soviet-era settler spirit. As the former confidence in a common (colonial) purpose and a common identity was eroded, exchange outside of the familiar domain became fraught with risk. Networks became more insular and competitive, and zones within which sharing was possible shrank back into themselves as the distinction between svoi and *postoronnyi* ("our own people" and "from outside/elsewhere") became more often and more passionately expressed.

At the centre of the shrunken, outwardly defensive post-Soviet network typically stood some font of patronage and security, usually in the form of a surviving work collective or institution. Long-time settlers recalled how in the Soviet halcyon they moved between jobs and professions, often with extraordinary frequency. A typical explanation – "I wanted something new and more interesting" – points to a variety of actual motives, from touristic to rational choice. But movement was possible only because the penalties were low – pay was relatively even across the professions and labour was always in demand in the North.[3] These conditions had disappeared by the post-Soviet era, when, if people changed jobs, it was to survive. Once located within a stable organization, where either pay was regular or some other access to resources was open (examples of such institutions were banks, food shops, district administrations, and the more influential government departments), people tended to stay through thick and thin. As the sharing society fragmented, the work collective became a fortress, an island of safety.

The closing of Iul'tin, an industrial town based on a massive Soviet tin- and tungsten-mining complex in northeastern Chukotka (in Iul'tinskii District), generated some vivid examples of networks on the defensive. This enterprise had been a critical prop for the regional economy in Soviet times. It was also the raison d'être for the port town and district centre of Egvekinot, the large sovkhoz in Amguema to the north, and the all-season road linking the three (see Figure 1.1). Built by forced prison labourers after the Second World War, Iul'tin sat on a special list of the Soviet Union's 100 most strategic and valuable enterprises. But its tin was ultimately too expensive to compete on world markets after market liberalization, and, in 1995, on the orders of then prime minister Viktor Chernomyrdin, the mines were closed and Iul'tin was abandoned. With its elimination, the district administration further south in Egvekinot, whose chief enjoyed good relations with Governor Nazarov in Anadyr, became the undisputed arbiter of funding and policy in Iul'tinskii District. As out-migration reduced the district's settler population from over ten thousand at the time of closure to under four thousand by 2002, an intense struggle ensued for protection within the departments that still survived, almost all based in Egvekinot and subordinated to the district chief (FSGS 2004). The liquidation of the mining enterprise at a time when social security and employment prospects were at a general nadir hit its victims particularly hard; formerly the labour elite of the district economy, Iul'tin's miners and plant workers were abandoned with little compensation and few provisions for resettlement. This was likewise the fate of those who worked within its satellite enterprises: the livestock farm and greenhouses, the power plant, the bakeries and food shops, and the trucking transport fleet. Thus, a population of several thousand industrial workers was in the span of half a year reduced to poverty and made homeless.[4] A large proportion of the industrial workforce was Ukrainian, and the collapse of the Soviet Union rendered their citizenship (and therefore their entitlement to state assistance) uncertain.

In contrast with the mine and plant, certain other institutions in Iul'tin coped with the closure more effectively. From its base in Egvekinot, the district education department organized a fairly orderly retreat, evacuating its assets and its staff to enrich a few surviving schools farther south. The public works department implemented a similar amalgamation of resources, provisioning its Egvekinot garage with Iul'tin's now surplus buses, bulldozers, and heavy trucks. Party and administrative networks likewise absorbed their colleagues from Iul'tin into administrative structures in Egvekinot, which thereafter created a rough parity of original locals and Iul'tin refugees in the district's bureaucratic "warm seats" *(teplie*

The abandoned mining town of Iul'tin, 2003
Photographed by author

kresla). Seven years after the closure, the district chief was a local from Egvekinot, and his deputy was Iul'tin's former mayor and one-time head of the municipal office of the KGB. The heads of education, agriculture, and social welfare were also all former Iul'tin residents.

The removal of Iul'tin-based enterprises from the political economy of the district elevated the state (in the form of the district administration and its departments) as the chief employer, an apparatus over which the district head of administration thereafter possessed complete control.[5] In this process, which might be viewed as an abrupt narrowing of access to resources and the ascent of a single local (administrative) boss to the position of ultimate patron, certain former networks and institutions were suddenly drained of security value for their inhabitants. At the same time, other institutions increased their powers: Egvekinot's public works, for example, inherited an array of responsibilities, from power generation to running the port. In Soviet times, geologists and other high-status professionals had derided public works as a collective of "shit-shovellers" *(govnochisti'e),* but in the new era, it became a highly desirable employer. As the crisis unfolded in the district, there was less and less work to go around – Egvekinot's post office, hospital, and schools could not absorb all the labour refugees flooding the town. Networks pulled back, and the old norms of an inclusive community failed. The remaining institutions took care of their own, but those that failed completely left many settlers entirely without protection.

As in post-Soviet Russia generally, in Egvekinot and Iul'tin, the crisis took a highly gendered form. In the late-Soviet era, the productive-industrial sectors where

Former underground miner from Iul'tin, living alone on the Amguema River, 2003
Photographed by Linda Rosenstrom Chang

pay was highest became a masculine domain, and it was precisely here that post-Soviet economic failure bit most deeply. Along with the Iul'tin mining complex, the district's geological Ekspeditsiia branch also collapsed, leaving a mostly male workforce of seven hundred without work. Indeed, almost all industrial employment evaporated, as a constellation of gold-mining enterprises in the district followed the fate of the tin mines. The result was acute *male* unemployment. In the event, the position of women in the northern labour force actually saved many out-of-work men from destitution. This was because, after playing a part on the shop floor in the Stalin era, women had migrated in large numbers to the less prestigious and worse-paid white-collar professions (medicine and teaching in particular). These domains were the direct responsibility of the state, and their workers (known as *budzhetniki*) – doctors, postal workers, teachers, secretaries, and bank clerks – were thus cushioned by the relative stability of work in the core state services. These women, in turn, were typically married to former industrial workers, and they assumed the role of sole provider as their men lost their jobs.

Not all unemployed men had the security of a budzhetnik wife, however, particularly because highly paid jobs such as those in Iul'tin's mines had attracted many bachelors and divorcés in the Soviet era. This segment of the population was more or less defenceless after the collapse – its industrial employers were a sinking ship, and in contrast to their married colleagues, bachelors were not bridged to more secure institutions within the state sector. Egvekinot in the late 1990s became a home for broken men – former miners, road workers, builders, geologists – many living together in the ruined apartment buildings recently abandoned by out-migrants, drawing their irregular pensions and drinking them away. As one refugee from Iul'tin, a former hard-rock miner, explained, "[When the mine closed] we all came to Egvekinot and set up in empty flats, but [seven years later] a lot of us have died from drinking and accidents. [When Iul'tin was abandoned] ... jobs were already scarce in Egvekinot, but for outsiders it was impossible. What was there here? The port – twenty-five people or so, all their own people *[vse svoi]*. Public works – all their own people. Administration – forget it – all their own people. You couldn't get work without knowing someone, and we were all from outside" [34].

The phenomenon of narrowing networks also impacted the frantic struggle among settlers to leave Chukotka, determining to whom the vastly inadequate state support for resettlement out of the North would be channelled. According to Russian state law, all "veterans of the North" – residents with a fifteen-year work history in a far northern region – were eligible for resettlement to temperate zones of the country.[6] But as the crisis deepened in the 1990s, state support for moving to the materik was awarded on increasingly nepotistic lines. The institution for which the employee worked was liable to share the cost of resettlement with municipal and regional governments. The okrug administration made attempts to acquire or build housing for resettlers in southern regions, the municipality took possession of the relinquished flats, and the former employer paid the costs of travel and containerized shipping out of the North.

In practice, only the best-connected settlers could expect this level of support. Afflicted as the okrug was by an atmosphere of evacuation, the chief problem was an acute lack of funding to meet the huge demand for resettlement. The nominal rules, whereby residents would take a place in a resettlement queue lodged with their municipal administration, were frequently subverted. Anadyr's municipal administration, which controlled the lists, employed its powers to reward its clients. The handful of resettlement opportunities each year went to families with connections in the city or okrug administrations, whereas pensioners outside key networks were passed over, regardless of how long they had been in the resettlement queue. Indeed, "resettlement through connections" *(blatnoe pereselenie)* was the norm in most institutions with the power and resources to implement such programs. The geological Ekspeditsiia, for example, managed the resettlement of far fewer employees than were eligible under the rules. In 1997, when hundreds of former geologists in Anadyr were on its resettlement lists, funds were sufficient to resettle only fifteen families. Still, if Anadyr residents lacked sufficient pull, they could hope for resettlement if they owned a particularly desirable flat in the city. This was because geologists, along with many other formerly privileged categories of worker, were often in a position to turn over the best flats in the city in exchange for resettlement [5] [35].[7]

As networks narrowed and norms of reciprocity became more delimited, security and privilege – via business success, resettlement, or obtaining a bureaucratic sinecure – hinged on proximity to the circles the governor's office sought to cultivate. The former Party elite to which Nazarov belonged were at a clear advantage. From the ranks of the former town- and okrug-level Party committees and the Komsomol emerged Chukotka's successful businessmen and administrative officials. As the economy lapsed into state-supported parasitism, almost the only profitable business was retail – shipping and selling food and durable goods into the region. Chukotka's leading entrepreneurs all obtained, in some combination, monopoly import licences, interest-free loans from the administration or some other large institution, and the use of state-owned buildings. The most successful among them was a former Komsomol leader who obtained the licence to import and wholesale alcohol in Chukotka throughout Nazarov's tenure. Another former Party associate based in Egvekinot controlled the supply of food to rural communities in northeast Chukotka. Yet another figure received large loans (effectively grants in the prevailing conditions of hyperinflation) and the use of state warehouses to set up a successful greenhouse operation in Anadyr. Unless they could win some degree of patronage support from city or okrug authorities, small-scale business initiatives attempting to compete in these conditions were at a serious disadvantage. For example, a number of entrepreneurs in Anadyr set up greenhouse operations and brought their produce onto the market in competition with the administration's chosen man, but their property licences were subsequently disputed and withdrawn by the city administration [37]. Retailers attempting to compete with the established circle of well-connected shop owners often suffered the confiscation of their shipping containers by posses of policemen and customs officers [26] [25]. One failed Anadyr entrepreneur remarked that his competitor prevailed because "He had friends in the right places, and so he got start-up capital.[8] I never got a thing. I had to create everything with my own hands, and I was spinning my wheels all the same. You have to have pull in this city, because there are very tight and very small circles" [37].

However, okrug administration circles were never the sole source of patronage and protection, and several successful businesses in Anadyr sheltered under alternative institutional *kryshi* (roof, or protection). Anadyr's largest retailer of electric appliances was founded by two geologists, who used the state geological survey's cash accounts as a source of credit, enabling them to buy and ship goods from the materik. Only once they had firmly established their business did they cut their ties with their former patron. Another well-established food retailer in Anadyr, a former senior military officer from a local base, accumulated his starting capital by using military aircraft and tracked all-terrain vehicles to ship alcohol to remote settlements. The military has since withdrawn from Chukotka, but his shops remain.

The settler community in the Nazarov era thus resembled a fragmented Balkans of internally loyal mafia-like networks, with clusters of relative security centred on powerful institutions and the patron figures who controlled them, set amid conditions of general insecurity and demoralization. The governor was the indisputable "godfather," the biggest *vor v zakone* (the traditional Russian equivalent of a mafia boss), as locals remember him. Patronage networks emanated out from his office and bridged to the okrug's lesser patrons and their own institutional fiefs. But personal influence and the flow of resources never assumed a unified pyramidal structure under the governor's office. His ability to personally arbitrate in the transactions of administration – to animate bureaucratic functions with the performance of patronage acts – was finite, and so he cultivated relationships only with institutions whose loyalty or resources he required. This consequently "de-animated" large areas of local life for which his administration held nominal responsibility, with the result that, for example, the district centre of Beringovskii was left without heat and water, and reindeer herders were left without pay. These were simply constituencies with which the governor's office found little reason to engage – they had little to offer him, just as they were powerless to threaten him.

Case Studies of Survival, or Subsistence Entrepreneurialism

Within the many domains of life outside Nazarov's inner circles of patronage, norms of community were already adapting to post-Soviet conditions and beginning to achieve new forms of equilibrium. Strategies of survival took shape, based on established traditions of reciprocity but also exhibiting the atomization of formerly broad and open communities and the retreat of the individual into intimate and defensive networks. Hardship and shortage were partly to blame, but the more cellular structure of Chukotka's post-Soviet society was also very much the outcome of northern geography – the collapse of transport in such a sparsely populated vastness pushed people into social clusters of local proximity while cutting them off from the outside world. Whereas those in a position to capture state assets often proceeded to liquidate them in spectacular demonstrations of self-interest, ordinary settlers and natives had no choice but to build the means to survive out of the wreckage left behind. Asset stripping (a particular mode of post-Soviet survival) was by definition a strategy of departure, because in the process of creating portable capital it destroyed local resources and consequently the perpetrator's standing in the local community. This was a kind of scorched-earth method of retreat. But, as the following case studies reveal, settlers who might once have harboured aspirations of departure, but whom northern collapse had stranded in place, found that putting down roots became the only effective means of survival. To get a yield, they made investments, and so their efforts tended to create things of value and deepen key relationships in local settings.[9] Unlike members of the elite, ordinary settlers who wished to build new ventures could hope for only one form of capital – trust.

Grisha

Most settlers in crisis-era Chukotka were, in the loosest sense of the word, entrepreneurs. Getting by and supporting children demanded creativity, resilience, the support of friends, and local knowledge. This is evident in the story of Grisha, born in Anadyr in 1965 to working-class parents, raised in Chukotka, and in 1989 forced to abandon his studies in Vladivostok when he could no longer afford tuition.[10] Already with a young family, he returned to his native Anadyr to find work as a music teacher. This soon proved inadequate, and in 1990 he launched into what he wryly termed "the world of business." At first, he employed a skill learned from his father: "When they stopped paying us altogether I became totally reliant on the moonshine business to survive – I had no other option." But he was soon forced to combine a number of "jobs" to keep his household afloat. By taking a position as night watchman at the geologists' vezdekhod garage, where he was paid with access to transport, he was able to travel out on the tundra to pick mushrooms and berries through the summer months (a vezdekhod is the only vehicle able to travel on the tundra in summer conditions). The following year, the city administration began cracking down on unlicensed distillers (to protect the business of the monopoly alcohol importer, a former Party official). By this point, Grisha had assembled a snowmobile from scrap parts lying about the geologists' garage. This was particularly timely, since that year the Ekspeditsiia sold off all its vezdekhody, depriving him of summer transport. He then joined with an experienced Chukchi hunter (an old schoolmate) and spent several winter seasons hunting and fishing on the tundra, bringing a portion of the catch home and selling the remainder through his local networks. Grisha and his Chukchi friend also took jobs as boiler stokers in a local heating plant. Here, they got access to the plant's sole vezdekhod in lieu of pay, and once more Grisha was mobile in the summer hunting season.

In 1994, after Grisha's hunting partner succumbed to the bottle, a new law on agricultural enterprises was introduced, and he responded by setting up a greenhouse operation in Anadyr. Using an abandoned warehouse on the outskirts as his base, and with enough money to buy only three rolls of polystyrene sheeting, he created a functional growing space and began supplying dill and parsley to local shops. With the profits, he invested in five hundred laying hens, which he flew in from central Russia. Due to the poor state of his buildings, however, an autumn storm destroyed the roof and the chicks died, leaving him in debt to another Anadyr shop owner. It was at this point that the city disputed the title to the land he was using and effectively confiscated his greenhouse. Yet, within a year, he had built another operation on land he managed to buy from a departing settler and struggled on until he was finally driven out of business by the 1998 ruble devaluation. At this point, Grisha returned to subsistence fishing and hunting but also began teaching music in the Anadyr children's centre. This led to a job producing radio programs for a regional station and subsequently to a position as freelance composer for a native dance ensemble. Eventually, with the arrival of Governor Abramovich in 2001, he secured a full-time job for one of the new administration's charities. He earned US$400 a month, his first regular and substantial income since the Soviet collapse.

Grisha's account of survival over the crisis years reveals that his flexibility – a remarkable capacity to grasp momentary opportunities – was decisive. But even Grisha's opportunistic flexibility would have been too little had he lacked a fluent familiarity with the local landscape.[11] Excluded from elite circles and access to state property and credit, Grisha nevertheless embarked on a series of entrepreneurial ventures, trading on his initiative and skills, fulfilling a local demand for music, dill, fish, and berries, and exploiting his network of friends built over a lifetime in Anadyr. Literally on the rubble left behind by dissolved enterprises – one an experimental agricultural farm whose director had "privatized" the machinery – he built two greenhouses, which for a time supported his family and enriched the local supply of fresh produce. Grisha never had the opportunity to strip assets and pocket the proceeds; only by creating assets could he and his family survive. In this way, through various localizing practices of survival, Grisha continuously exercised and renovated a rooted and locally specific identity.

Sveta

Despite economic collapse, the residual cash economy and the demands of a larger population in Chukotka's capital enabled Grisha to surf opportunistically through a series of roles. The degree of institutional collapse in Chukotka's more remote settlements, however, forced settlers to compensate for disappearing administrative and social services in order to maintain even a basic standard of living. Extreme isolation exacerbated the desperate conditions of life in the settlements, and so any form of transport became an invaluable resource.

The predominantly Chukchi village of Meinypil'gyno is located on Chukotka's southern coast, roughly two hundred kilometres from Anadyr across a range of mountains, and is accessible only by helicopter or ship. In 2000, there were eleven mixed and settler families living among approximately five hundred coastal Chukchi. Under Nazarov's administration, as a result of extreme isolation and a near-total failure of transport, a particularly harsh climate, and the collapse of the state farm along with its reindeer herd, living standards in Meinypil'gyno were dire even for Chukotka. Constantly poor flying weather cuts the area off for much of the year, and after 1992, barge and ship traffic practically ceased. Meinypil'gyno even lost the support of its district administration in Beringovskii to the east, where basic services collapsed (to the extent that it was finally evacuated and closed in 2002).

Sveta, a Russian, came to Meinypil'gyno in the early 1980s with her schoolteacher mother. During the perestroika era, she married another Russian living in the village and gave birth to the first of three children. Problems at the settlement's school began to mount in the mid-1990s as non-native teachers departed for the materik, and by 1996, Sveta faced the prospect of sending her two eldest away to a residential school in Beringovskii. In the prevailing transport crisis, this meant placing her children beyond contact for most of each year. In response, and despite the difficulty and cost involved in leaving the okrug, she flew to Moscow to trawl teacher-training colleges in central Russia for graduates willing to fill positions in her settlement. She managed to recruit two teachers, with whom she returned to the settlement for the beginning of the 1996 teaching year. Because of an acute shortage of habitable accommodation, her family lodged them in one room of their two-room house for their first six months. Although Meinypil'gyno's school eventually closed, Sveta's initiative postponed its closure. When I asked her why she shouldered a responsibility that lay with the education authorities in Beringovskii, she answered without acrimony: "I did it because without me it wouldn't have gotten done." Sveta recognized that, in Meinypil'gyno, the state had effectively evaporated, and its retreat created an administrative vacuum that individuals like herself, with a stake in the life of the settlement, had to fill.

This is only one illustration of the pivotal role Sveta's family played in the survival of community in Meinypil'gyno. In 1992, when their youngest boy was only six months old, she and her husband lost their jobs with the village public works department, and their apartment building became uninhabitable. Instead of leaving to join relatives in central Russia, they built a house using materials scavenged from abandoned buildings. Poor transport was becoming a critical problem at this time, and here they spotted an opportunity. A mechanic and welder, Sveta's husband knew of a vezdekhod that had gone through the ice of a nearby river several years before, and that no one had yet succeeded in recovering. Over the course of a winter, he devised a system to extract it from the riverbed using piles drilled into the river bottom through holes in the ice. He then spent a further two years cannibalizing the carcasses of abandoned vehicles in the settlement to rebuild this machine. Although, by 1994, diesel was no longer being delivered to the settlement, the tundra was littered with thousands of fuel barrels, still sealed, left behind by the armed forces, cached by the defunct geological Ekspeditsiia, or abandoned by Meinypil'gyno's state farm. In light of the total collapse of state transport, Sveta's family now possessed an invaluable resource. In 1995, they began to ferry villagers and food between the settlement and Beringovskii, twenty hours distant by land. Because the old state-run village shop had closed, Sveta's family became the sole supplier of essential goods – flour, salt, matches, oil, soap. In order to secure suppliers, they cultivated relationships with merchants in Beringovskii, and eventually in Anadyr. Within Meinypil'gyno they traded the use of their vehicle and the items they brought in for locally available reindeer meat, building supplies, and tutoring for their children, none of whom left for distant residential schools. Finally, after the election of Governor Abramovich in 2000, conditions improved: regular helicopter flights to Anadyr resumed and a range of subsidized products appeared in the re-opened village shop. Meanwhile, Sveta opened Meinypil'gyno's first hairdressing salon with her oldest daughter, and her husband rebuilt a second vezdekhod.

The stories of Grisha and Sveta indicate how the system of patronage emanating from the governor's office in the 1990s excluded a large proportion of Chukotka's settler population from once routine forms of contact with the state. Both Grisha and Sveta inhabited networks that were socially distant from elite circles, and within their given milieu, they were compelled to invest in long-term strategies of survival that entangled them in local webs of mutual reliance. Individuals on the geographic periphery in settlements like Meinypil'gyno were particularly threatened by the "retreat of the state" – Grisha in Anadyr could at least sell his dill and smelt within the capital's more secure and numerous settler circles. Sveta and her husband, on the other hand, filled the vacuum left by a failing school, a crumbling transport system, and an empty village shop with their own initiatives, displaying a pragmatic form of subsistence entrepreneurialism that ultimately served their interests by serving the interests of the settlement.

Throughout post-Soviet Chukotka, settlers who stayed in their communities were similarly challenged to find local resources and exploit local networks, in pursuit of various means of survival less tied to the vagaries of the pan-Russian economy. In Anadyr, unpaid bureaucratic employees routinely left their offices to fish for smelt and salmon. They traded whatever services they could render for reindeer from state farms in the interior. In other places, the retreat of the state stranded the individual outside the official economy in a more extreme and complete fashion. In the abandoned mining town of Iul'tin, a handful of residents refused to leave and soldiered on for years in a post-apocalyptic urban landscape, subsisting on a diet of fish and berries, and warmed by improvised barrel stoves

Long-time settler and tundra driver leaning on his vehicle, a Soviet-era *vezdekhod*, Amguema tundra, 2003
Photographed by author

burning floorboards ripped from empty flats.[12] One hermit-like figure brewed moonshine for the odd gold prospector who travelled through; another drove over the nearby tundra in a six-wheeled vehicle powered by an old generator engine and constructed entirely of scavenged metal. These settlers had come full circle: they once migrated north to earn a Soviet fortune and now they had exited the monetary economy altogether. But they were an exception. Chukotka's rural settlers typically survived by virtue of their social embeddedness in existing communities, and they often simultaneously maintained networks reaching to Anadyr and the materik beyond. Engaging in this way to protect the integrity of local services was a precondition of getting by, an exemplary strategy of survival.

Predatory Survival

The preceding illustrations of local initiative on the social and geographic periphery of Nazarov's patronage state are not intended to suggest that Chukotka's political economy was stratified into steep hierarchies of opportunity and exclusion at its core but devoid of power differences at its edge. The struggle for influence and domination was fought just as fiercely in those domains neglected by the governor's intervention. The extreme post-Soviet isolation of the northern village provided perfect conditions for the rise of new and highly unequal arrangements of power. In fact, where the retreat of the state was most complete – in the remote northern village – there was most to gain by replacing it and, indeed, the weakest official restraints on the means one might adopt to achieve this. This was at least partly because the collapse of transport not only cut off people in the settlements from larger centres, it also cut off the structures of administration in the okrug capital from their rural areas of responsibility. The result often resembled a near-Hobbesian State of Nature, in which the least scrupulous, particularly those with their hands on key resources, could quickly rise to dominant positions within each settlement. These tended to be individual settlers (not settlers as a class), people who translated their Soviet-era authority as managers and specialists in village administrations and state farms into new forms of power, usually combining official bureaucratic position with entrepreneurial interests. Those few who could provide a bridge to the outside became vitally important brokers, and however they chose to use this power, they usually faced little threat from police and other representatives of the distant state. So, though the stories of Grisha and Sveta suggest the locally enriching potential of survival practices, the challenges of life in the crisis-era village very often placed individuals in insoluble moral dilemmas. The exigencies of life in conditions of total collapse always required some degree of flexibility and subjectivity in the approach to morality. By necessity, strategies of survival in northern life assumed at times *predatory* forms. But, as we will see, survival is itself a transformative process, producing with time the most surprising moral realignments.

The Bogorev Brothers of Vaegi

The remotest of Chukotka's villages are not those, like Meinypil'gyno, dotting the shores of the Chukchi and Bering Seas, but are, rather, a handful located deep in the interior beyond the reach of ocean-going vessels. One of these is Vaegi, a mixed village of Chukchi, Koryak, and Russian settlers set on the bank of the Main River, a shallow and swift-flowing tributary of the Anadyr, about seven hundred kilometres upstream from the okrug capital (see Figure 1.1). The present village was founded in 1951 to accommodate sedentarized reindeer herders from the upper reaches of the Main and Velikaia Rivers (territories bordering on Kamchatka Krai to the south), and indeed its native population was one of the last in the Soviet Union to be collectivized. Only in 1955, after several years of violent resistance and finally the intervention of MVD troops, were the region's large herds fully subjected to the authority of Vaegi's collective farm (kolkhoz), the Path to Communism. Despite the slaughter of a large number of privately owned reindeer by Chukchi hostile to their appropriation (many of whom were subsequently shot or exiled to gulag camps), the Vaegi kolkhoz soon became one of Chukotka's most productive, and its annual slaughter reached seven thousand head in the 1960s. For three decades, the village grew rapidly, and by 1985, almost half of its population of 813 consisted of newcomers and their locally born children. Many of the agronomists, mechanics, teachers, and other incoming specialists had married

Two generations of settlers, Vaegi, 2002
Photographed by Linda Rosenstrom Chang

local native women and raised their families in Vaegi, radically altering the ethnic complexion of the population. Living standards were generally high, with two well-stocked state shops, regular flights to Anadyr and Magadan, and a wealthy collective farm that not only produced reindeer meat, but also ran its own dairy and vegetable-growing operations. Situated in a transitional taiga ecosystem and sheltered from the harsher climate along the Bering Sea coast, Vaegi was virtually the only settlement in Chukotka where locals could grow fresh produce in open soil.

When the Soviet era ended, Vaegi's extreme remoteness even by northern standards created a state of near-total isolation and resulted in a particularly complete degree of self-sufficiency. Although it had a gravel airstrip, scheduled aviation failed entirely, with the sole exception of the odd emergency medical flight *(sanreis)*. To reach Anadyr, villagers had to travel by boat or overland to the larger settlement of Markovo, a hundred kilometres downriver, and catch the occasional flight to the capital, or go by vezdekhod or riverboat directly, a three- to four-day journey. But not only were outboard engines, snowmobiles, and vezdekhody far beyond the means of the average villager, there was practically no fuel to be had in the deepening crisis. The settlement's economy remained, at least in theory, based on its reindeer-herding operation, but herd numbers fell so precipitously over the 1990s that by the end of the decade, regional agricultural authorities were proposing to move the remaining reindeer to Markovo and liquidate Vaegi's kolkhoz altogether.[13] Meanwhile, from a peak of over 800, Vaegi's population dropped below 450, as settler specialists and indigenous villagers alike left the settlement. Indeed, but for Vaegi's fortunate growing conditions, its isolation might have necessitated its abandonment, as was the case with several other remote inland settlements in the district. Villagers turned to intensive vegetable cultivation when food supply from the outside collapsed. Using manure from the small herd of kolkhoz dairy cows, they converted every available patch of land in the settlement territory to gardens, and many locals, particularly settlers and mixed families, built large and elaborate heated greenhouses using wood from local forests. (Potatoes, beets, cabbages, and leeks grow in the open air, and the greenhouses produce tomatoes, cucumbers, and even watermelons. Fishing, hunting, and mushroom gathering are superb along the Main River watershed.) As a result, locals in Vaegi created an almost entirely self-sustaining food economy over the decade of crisis.

This small village, as remote from the thoughts of Anadyr's bureaucratic elite as it was physically isolated, offered as perfect an illustration of the "predatory mode of survival" as I have found in post-Soviet Chukotka. At the time of my first visit, in the summer of 2002, two brothers – Viktor and Sergei Bogorev – commanded complete control of every position and office of any significance in Vaegi. With the help of a third brother – Nikolai – living downriver in Markovo, they operated with effective impunity by insulating their village demesne from any kind of outside challenge. Yet, when they arrived in the 1980s, fresh from army service, without much education, and completely lacking contacts in the region, such fortunes hardly seemed likely.

Sergei, the eldest, was the first to come north. The only one of the three with any formal education, he was a professional *parashiutist*, trained to parachute into remote areas in small teams, live off the land for weeks at a time, and extinguish tundra and bush fires with a combination of hand pumps, pickaxes, and dynamite.[14] By 1990, Viktor and Nikolai had joined him, and Sergei had risen to command the Chukotka branch of Avialesokhrana – the regional firefighting service – from its base in Markovo.[15] Shortly thereafter, he established an additional firebase in Vaegi, sixty kilometres by air from Markovo, apparently in order to better cover the southern reaches of the okrug. Whatever his intentions, the Soviet collapse and Chukotka's subsequent secession soon threw the forest-fire-fighting service into chaotic decline, as hundreds of parashiutisty left the North, and Sergei faced the prospect of building an entirely new Avialesokhrana for the now independent Chukotka. But rather than move to Anadyr to tackle this challenge, or leave the North altogether, the Bogorev brothers stayed in the interior. In fact, they chose to move from the mid-sized town of Markovo to Vaegi, a village whose prospects must have seemed very dim indeed. All three remained on the Avialesokhrana payroll, and Vaegi became a key inland base for what remained of the fire service. I developed the impression that their motives in this had less to do with fighting fires than with using Avialesokhrana as a foundation from which to navigate their own entrepreneurial course through the post-Soviet crisis. As it turned out, Vaegi's deepening conditions of extreme isolation and poverty created the perfect setting in which to enact this strategy, and for the Bogorevs to prosper.

To understand their eventual success requires some knowledge of Avialesokhrana itself, for this was their font of patronage, their institutional island of security (see F.S. Nielsen 2007), and the source of their power. In Chukotka, wildfire protection provides a vital service to reindeer herding, which is perpetually vulnerable to tundra fires that consume pasturelands. In Soviet times, Chukotka was served by an Avialesokhrana service based in Magadan, but with the post-Soviet secession, it lost this connection. The likelihood of building a new independent Avialesokhrana for a newly independent Chukotka was slim: the okrug was beset by fiscal and administrative chaos, and fighting forest fires is an immensely expensive activity involving large outlays on helicopter and fixed-wing aviation. Many equivalent services disappeared in other remote regions during the post-Soviet crisis, as happened in the neighbouring Koryak Autonomous Okrug. But, against the odds, it happened. Just as Sergei Bogorev resigned and moved to Vaegi in 1992, another young parashiutist, an energetic Tatar from the southern Urals named Al'bert Klimentiev, set himself the task of building a firefighting service for Chukotka and becoming its director. In 1993, he flew to Magadan and returned with an Antonov biplane full of documentation and equipment. Late that year, he won direct funding from the Russian Ministry of Natural Resources. Thereafter, as he slowly built the organization from a base in Anadyr, he fought to maintain Avialesokhrana's independence from Governor Nazarov's office, which coveted the service's federal budget transfers. By cultivating his relationship with the ministry in Moscow, Klimentiev survived the worst years. By 2000, he managed thirty-three full-time employees, up from a much smaller core of staff who weathered the 1990s and stayed with the service despite payless periods lasting as long as nine months.[16]

Even by the standards of Chukotka's typically close-knit work collectives, Avialesokhrana benefited from an exceptionally strong culture of internal solidarity. In my experience (2002-5), divisions between working life at the office and the private, domestic sphere were so blurred as to be indefinable. At the Anadyr headquarters, staff stayed most Fridays after work for long meals, with singing and dancing. They constituted a kind of extended kin network, and rather than cultivating networks exterior to the Avialesokhrana collective, they made the base the focus of social life. Multiple family members worked within the service, some spanning two generations. Because the staff was continually travelling between the headquarters and one of the three remote bases in the interior, they would often spend time living in the homes of their colleagues while seconded *(na*

Avialesokhrana riverboat unloading supplies in Vaegi, 2005
Photographed by author

komandirovke). Highly valued attributes in Chukotka's workplaces – loyalty, congeniality, and habits of mutual aid – were clearly evident within Avialesokhrana's collective. When one spent time with Avialesokhrana staff, it was not unusual to hear bitter denunciations aimed at other departments and offices in town, focusing on a perceived weakness of collective spirit (using terms such as *neteplie,* "cold," or even *vrazhdebnie vzaimnootnosheniia,* "internecine spirit of relations").

Girding the Avialesokhrana community, and a feature setting the organization apart from larger and better-resourced bureaucracies, was its unusually rich array of transport resources. Well-maintained vezdekhody, a 150-ton riverboat, a few lighter vehicles, and, in the summer fire season, chartered helicopters and An-2 biplanes ensured that Avialesokhrana could operate over Chukotka's vast territory, moving equipment and firefighters and maintaining bases in the distant inland settlements of Bilibino, Markovo, and Vaegi. Because movement between Chukotka's settlements is so difficult, villagers are forever calling in favours to hitch rides across the tundra, over the sea, or along rivers. But Avialesokhrana's employees had the extraordinary advantage of transport resources located within their own institutional network, and so they travelled often and together, a practice that naturally knit the collective yet more tightly. Unusually, for a bureaucratic office in Anadyr, quite a few of the staff were from small rural settlements in the Anadyr district, in particular, Vaegi. Even more unusual, some of them were métis and Chuvantsy; others were newer settlers in mixed marriages with natives.[17] (In terms of its ethnic makeup, Avialesokhrana contrasted with most of Anadyr's other departments and agencies, which tended to be exclusive settler domains, reflecting the ethnic division of expertise and the settler-dominated patronage apparatus that Nazarov erected over the 1990s.)[18] Most firefighters and mid-level office staff were born in the okrug, and they enjoyed large local kin networks. For them, movement by land, river, and air between the Anadyr headquarters and the forward bases in Vaegi, Markovo, and Bilibino was vital to cultivating these relationships. Maintaining a dual presence in the settlements and Anadyr was a survival strategy: for example, bookkeepers, dispatchers, warehouse managers, and legal assistants used Avialesokhrana's transport to bring their children to Anadyr's schools for the winter and then send them back to relatives upriver in the summer months, when local sources of food were plentiful in the hinterland. Firefighters and technicians worked from the villages through the summer fire season, away from their families in Anadyr. But wives and older children often followed them, moving between village and city when an Avialesokhrana helicopter or riverboat presented the opportunity. In the winter, when the work of the service slowed, the vezdekhody were in constant motion, taking the Anadyr collective out for ice-fishing trips and ferrying supplies and people between Markovo, Vaegi, and Anadyr.

Based in the interior, the Bogorev brothers were key members of the Avialesokhrana collective, and they drew on the fraternal bonds of the parashiutisty and their close relationship with Director Klimentiev in order to enact their own strategies of survival. From a firefighting perspective, there never had been a compelling reason to build an additional firebase in Vaegi, as Markovo was already positioned to protect the southcentral forest and tundra zone. But Sergei understood that whereas the larger and less remote town of Markovo contained many competing institutions and was more intensively scrutinized by authorities in Anadyr, the remote village of Vaegi could be easily dominated by a single institution, particularly one with transport resources. As Sergei and his brothers witnessed the mass spontaneous settler evacuation around them amid the collapse of employment, transport, and supply, this opportunity became their lifeline. Their common dream of saving their earnings, returning to their home village in Smolensk Oblast, caring for their ailing parents, and starting their own families was evaporating. As new arrivals to the North, they knew only firefighting. Hyperinflation destroyed in weeks what they had spent years building. The acute sense of betrayal in the village – a realization of wasted effort, vain aspirations – was eating away at the people around them. Alongside the departures were many less dramatic disappearances, as drinking and suicide took a rising toll, especially among unemployed men. In this climate, it was an act of courage not to succumb to hopelessness. But to recover the losses and regain a measure of security also inevitably involved moral ambiguities. Avoiding victimization could require making victims of others. As Sergei put it, "Then there were no rules. Everything was gone, everything we had and everything around us. So we thought, 'We'll get it back – no matter what it takes, we'll get out of this rut, we'll get our money back!' ... We knew we would, you see, because there were no rules any more."

There were few ways of making money amongst the economic ruins of post-Soviet Vaegi, but the Bogorev brothers found them. As the professional identities of so many villagers eroded away with their jobs, and the crisis resulted in a kind of mass nihilism among natives and settlers alike, bootlegging became a lucrative business. In the early 1990s, using Avialesokhrana's helicopters, vezdekhody, and in particular its riverboat, they began to ship vodka from Anadyr. Viktor sold bottles out of his back door, for a high price during the day and an even higher one at night. Sergei brewed his own spirit, which he sold for only slightly less. The brothers also filled Avialesokhrana transport with cargo for the return trip to Anadyr. They travelled out to Vaegi's six reindeer-herding brigades by snowmobile and vezdekhod to trade their vodka for reindeer meat and antler velvet, both of which commanded a high price in the capital. In fact, much of the village herds' decline (from thirty-three thousand head in 1990 to under five thousand at the end of the decade) was the work of the brothers alone. Sergei, Viktor, and Nikolai also took over an abandoned fishing camp downriver from the settlement, where they net-fished salmon during the prodigious annual run. In a good year, they could bottle over nine hundred litres of salmon roe, which they sold to middlemen at Anadyr's airport for shipping to Moscow. Viktor even started a cable television service for the village, spooling out wire from his house to subscribers and playing a nightly program of American action movies followed by Russian pornography.

Avialesokhrana's director Klimentiev was a partner in most of these ventures. When in Anadyr, he was mindful of his official persona as a public servant and strove to preserve the formal identity of the fire service; when inland, however, he was an entrepreneur. He was in business with the Bogorevs, and each load of reindeer meat and salmon roe was a venture they took jointly. From Klimentiev's perspective, this arrangement provided the means to build up his still-fragile fire service as much as it suited his personal interests. If it was true that he diverted state resources into a kind of privatized transport operation for Vaegi, the proceeds were mostly recycled back as a vital ingredient in Avialesokhrana's survival. The profiteering dimension of its operations sustained its staff, gave Klimentiev the resources to build up the headquarters and maintain a fleet of vehicles and boats, and justified the presence of a firebase in Vaegi.[19]

A kind of imbalanced symbiosis developed between the fire service and the village population, for Vaegi could never have survived in complete isolation. In fact, the Bogorev brothers' entrepreneurial activity enabled Avialesokhrana to fill the vacuum left by the evaporation of state services: local men worked as temporary firefighters, a network of housewives cooked food for fire operations in the summer months, and a few villagers migrated to positions in Anadyr's central firebase. Moreover, Avialesokhrana's transport resources became the sole means of travel to the outside. For parents sending children to residential schools in Markovo or relatives in Anadyr, for villagers requiring hospital treatment, or for settlers travelling to the materik, an Avialesokhrana vezdekhod or riverboat was often the only means of getting out. As in Meinypil'gyno, the state shop was empty throughout the 1990s. Spotting an opportunity, Avialesokhrana staff became monopoly suppliers of food and durable goods. When the kolkhoz and the village administration could no longer obtain diesel, the fire service shipped in fuel for the village generator. Avialesokhrana moved postbags between Anadyr and Vaegi. On those rare occasions when the okrug administration paid the salaries and pensions of teachers, nurses, and kolkhoz employees, Avialesokhrana staff flew in the funds.

As the senior representatives of the fire service in the village, the Bogorev brothers were key figures in all these transactions, and the influence and profits that resulted enabled them to erect locally unassailable positions of power. Viktor, the middle brother, was the most successful; by the time I arrived, people called him the Prince of Vaegi. In the mid-1990s, Klimentiev made him Vaegi's firebase manager, and thereafter he personally piloted the riverboat and drove the vezdekhody between Vaegi and Anadyr, establishing himself as the most important local kommersant. All this travel had important secondary effects as well. The Bogorevs' power of movement in the local domain was underwritten by more than simple access to Avialesokhrana transport: over time, they also became among the most skilled and knowledgeable on the land. Of course, this was an ability they developed gradually, for they were relatively new arrivals in Vaegi (compared to Russian men who had settled as early as the 1960s). Nevertheless, during the worst years of crisis, they owned the only reliable and high-powered outboard motors and snowmobiles in Vaegi. Thus, the voyage to Markovo, difficult and uncertain for most villagers, was a matter of half a day for them, whether in winter or summer. Downstream from Vaegi, where the Anadyr and the Main meet, the river route crosses a labyrinthine territory of channels, in which not a few locals have lost their way (and sometimes perished); in their fast boats, the Bogorevs learned to navigate the distance with ease. And whereas Vaegi's villagers hunted and fished only in the immediate vicinity of their homes, the brothers could fish the length of the river and hunt far into the surrounding mountains.

Because their survival depended on unlicensed commerce, bootlegging, poaching, and other more or less predatory activities, it was vitally important to the brothers that Vaegi became their own sealed domain of operations, insulated from prying by anyone who might threaten or constrain them. This was best achieved by colonizing all Vaegi's remaining institutions of any influence, a strategy they adopted toward the end of the crisis decade. Through a combination of intimidation and selective patronage, Viktor was elected the first non-indigenous mayor since the founding of the village.[20] Shortly thereafter, when the village kolkhoz lost its director, he tapped a Russian friend in Anadyr to fill the post. A new policeman arrived, and Viktor arranged a job for his wife as Avialesokhrana's bookkeeper. As for Sergei Bogorev, whose wife was already the village postmistress, he also pulled strings in the capital to become the local fishing and hunting inspector, as well as the inspector of small boat safety, giving him control over licences and thus protecting his extensive poaching operations. Meanwhile, the youngest brother, Nikolai, moved to neighbouring Markovo to become the head of its own firebase, as well as hunting and fishing inspector for that area. With this accumulation of offices, the brothers between them could not only deflect most unwanted intrusions into Vaegi, but also, they themselves became the vested representatives of most of the bureaucratic agencies that might have had business there.[21]

But then a very interesting transformation occurred. Although Sergei was the first to come north, his younger brother Viktor had with time become Vaegi's most successful kommersant and, as mayor, its most influential citizen. It would seem, given his various activities and needs during the 1990s, that he coveted political power only as a subsidiary to his business plans – a game of oligarchy at the village level. But it would also seem that at the same time he was passing over a certain threshold, beyond which lay a new consciousness of his rootedness in the village and of the many ways in which his own fate was now bound to that of his neighbours. The very year he became mayor, a young native woman bore him the first of three children, an event that brought him into the largest and most influential Chukchi clan in the village. As a result, he began to see Vaegi as not only the site of his operations, but as the future home of these children. The state of its school, its profound isolation, and the demoralized and addicted condition of its population now awakened in Viktor a sense of foreboding. This, by his own confession, triggered a moral realignment, and Viktor abandoned the most mercenary of his ways. He in no way curtailed his trading (in fact, he expanded it by opening a new general store), but now he ceased shipping hard liquor and sold only beer – in his reckoning a kind of public health measure. He also began persecuting moonshine brewers in the village, his brother Sergei among them.

Viktor's timing was serendipitous, for his election came on the cusp of the Abramovich era, when, to every villager's surprise, reconstruction in the villages became a reality. The changes Abramovich brought to the region are the subject of later chapters, but it is significant for Vaegi's own story that Viktor energetically grasped the opportunity to attract an extraordinary amount of investment in new housing, public works, and schools to his village. This money would not have reached so far into the interior, nor in such volume, had Viktor not devoted all his energies to the task. On several occasions, he personally ensured that materials and workers reached Vaegi by piloting river barges up the treacherous currents of the Anadyr and Main Rivers himself. He visited other villages in the district, trawling for teachers, nurses, and agronomists to fill long-vacant positions in Vaegi. And he made it his (and Avialesokhrana's) business to ensure that the struggling kolkhoz begin to show promise, shipping in an industrial freezer to store reindeer meat and restarting the abandoned village vegetable-growing operation. This was a remarkable transformation. Only a few years before, Viktor and his brothers were filling the hole left by the retreating state in an entirely different fashion, bootlegging vodka, poaching the salmon run, and selling alcohol to the herding brigades in exchange for their reindeer.

In contrast to those of Grisha in Anadyr and Sveta in Meinypil'gyno, the strategies of survival with which the Bogorev brothers piloted their way through the post-Soviet crisis were predatory, reassembling in a harshly neo-Darwinian fashion a new post-Soviet arrangement of power in the village. But, in the amelioration of Viktor Bogorev, we also see a story of personal redemption. When the crisis erupted and they lost their livelihood, the Bogorevs were still fresh arrivals in Chukotka, and nothing lasting anchored them in the North. They stayed on in Vaegi for an opportunity, which they exploited as a strategy of departure in much the same way as did, at the same time, the governor in Anadyr. But, by remaining, they paid a price they did not foresee. As much as they originally intended to stay for a time and leave, the price of survival was ultimately a deeper condition of rootedness. After years of living in the village, both Viktor and his younger brother, Nikolai, were raising families with Chukchi women, and they were already seeing the future through the eyes of their children. As mayor, Viktor was fighting to build up Vaegi's school and clinic, travelling to Anadyr to lobby the okrug administration for investment and shipping in beer as part of his sobriety campaign. The oldest brother, Sergei, and his Russian wife fervently desired that their children would have a university education outside the North, but in the service of this dream, they also seemed to "go native." The cost of launching their children (Sergei reported that getting his son admitted to a military medical academy in St. Petersburg cost almost US$7,000 in travel, cash "fees," and carefully aimed "presents") forced them ever more deeply into the localized life they led in Vaegi, poaching and selling salmon roe while living off what they could grow in their greenhouse and vegetable plots. When I got to know him, Sergei was no longer young, and the only things he knew in life, as he said himself, were hunting, fishing, and travelling over the land he lived in. In a bemused recognition of his own condition, he admitted that all his frantic efforts to stay afloat, to claw back something of the security he had before the Soviet collapse, and to regain the dream of returning to Smolensk had resulted only in an ineradicable desire to stay.

Sergei now lived with the paradox of his own belonging: his vigorous efforts to ensure that his children could leave had so accustomed him to the land that leaving it had become a frightful prospect. He could sense this on his infrequent trips to the materik, where, "after one month in the city, my eyes are bleeding for the lack of northern vistas – the headaches go on until I breathe this northern air again."

Charting the Settler Identity

The experience of life in the first post-Soviet decade acted upon the "original settler identity" of the Soviet years, stripping away some aspects while reinforcing others. What therefore can be said of the sense this population had of itself by the end of the Nazarov-era crisis in 2000? How did the particular circumstances described in the preceding pages alter senses of settler belonging and the nature of settler communities? In the broadest terms, settler responses to the "transition to crisis" followed two trajectories.

The first developed out of a very common perception of northern life as a transient condition. To this category belonged the roughly 60 percent of the population that departed Chukotka between 1989 and 2000. As it became clear that the northern economy was a house built on sand, they saw more rewarding prospects in more temperate zones of Russia and the "near abroad." Departure was in fact a key signal of non-indigenous identity and of the relatively powerful position the so-called newcomer inherited from the Soviet period. Whereas natives and long-time settlers held rich stores of local knowledge, it was the recently arrived who possessed formal and professional expertise, management experience, and networks of contacts spanning North and materik. These resources made leaving possible, and the conditions of life in crisis-era Chukotka naturally recommended departure quite forcefully; for such settlers, this was the ultimate strategy of survival.

In these years, simply leaving Chukotka was not the only indication of a transient mentality; for a small number of settlers, a "hit and run" strategy of stripping it bare was another. Liquidating enterprise assets, abusing budget funds, poaching fish and reindeer, and bootlegging to the settlements were all variously employed as strategies of departure, calculated to earn their perpetrators moveable forms of security. Asset stripping was, for the most part, an elite-level practice, simply encouraged by the precedent set by Governor Nazarov. The manner in which this type cannibalized Soviet Chukotka's remains, and fed off whatever meagre resources the new Russian state provided to enable some kind of transition, amounted to a kind of elite-driven "tragedy of the commons" that beggared Chukotka's remaining population. When the era of shutting down, selling off, and embezzling new state investment came to an end, many of those involved had left for central Russia. Former governor Nazarov and most of his old deputies (former deputy governors) now reside in Moscow and St. Petersburg.

Although emblematic of a style of rule, this feeding frenzy concealed a second, and much more common, response to the post-Soviet experience in Chukotka: localized practices of survival. The vast majority of settlers, who were rendered desperately poor and physically isolated by the crisis, could survive only by adopting strategies of productive creativity. Governor Nazarov mouthed the language of independence and self-reliance in a cynical attempt to cloak Chukotka's secession and subsequent economic collapse in some kind of political narrative. But self-sufficiency did in fact become the paradigm of northern life on the level of family, work collective, and village. People became more fixed in place as movement became more expensive, less reliable, or just as often, simply impossible. In a series of remote settlements like Beringovskii, Meinypil'gyno, and Vaegi, settlers were cut off from the networks of family and friends outside the North that they had once cultivated. Even in Anadyr, many long-time residents formerly accustomed to travelling out were trapped in the North throughout the crisis years.[22] The mobile settler, with one foot in the northern village and another in the Soviet metropolis, envied for his wealth and privileges, and admired (in official discourse at least) for his role in a civilizing frontier campaign, was finally buried.

In his place emerged a settler type more palpably tied to Chukotka's landscape, whose networks were singularly embedded in a local community. Personal security became more tied to local resources and less to state investments and material supplies from outside the North. In the settlements, settlers hunted, fished, grew vegetables, and even joined natives in the traditional herding and marine-mammal hunting economy. In the larger centres, settler entrepreneurs built their own small businesses, installing phones, selling Chinese-made clothing, driving taxis, repairing machinery, developing film. Even rank-and-file bureaucrats inhabited the northern setting in a much more rooted fashion than they had in the Soviet era, of necessity harvesting the sea and tundra, and cultivating local friendships.

Because they were entrepreneurial, the practices of survival generated new, and often very steep, hierarchies in their local settings. As the state retreated, including not only the edifice of transport but also the old "vertical of power" extending from Soviet Moscow, a new landscape of domination and powerlessness took form. With the removal of Party control and the strict subordination of Chukotka's economic and political life to central authorities (and notwithstanding the monopolistic tendencies of Nazarov's patronage machine), space opened up for local actors to expand and innovate in their roles. Certain stronger institutions derived their strength from symbiotic interactions with communities distant from the capital, Anadyr, as the example of Avialesokhrana illustrates. In other cases, individuals stepped into the vacuum of state services to address the basic needs of their communities. Regardless of the motives they may have harboured at the outset, the experience of entrepreneurial survival usually had a localizing effect and eventually attenuated its most predatory forms. The contacts and skills settlers cultivated to fill the gap left by the state amounted to highly non-portable bodies of knowledge. Mere presence, with time, tied many of them down in the most predictable fashion: they fell in love with locals, often natives, and had children. This was a process that, as in the case of the Bogorev brothers, radically reoriented many intentions: gradually, plans to leave became a desire to stay.

Igor Krupnik and Nikolai Vakhtin (2002) observed that the post-collapse recasting of official political discourses effectively discarded the notion of homeland

A Russian-Chukchi couple in Vaegi, 2005
Photographed by author

(rodina) as constituting the entire Soviet space, in favour of regional definitions of home, a kind of localist rhetoric aiding the process of federal devolution. The case of Chukotka shows that the actual experiences of survival could render tangible the rhetoric of local belonging. Just as the constituents of the old settler identity were annulled by material and ideological collapse, strategies of getting by afforded new sources. Indeed, settlers who stayed, whether by choice or necessity, frequently employed "the local" in ideational terms to reconstruct a post-Soviet sense of their own selves. Certain aspects of their old Soviet identity were available for reheating – the idea of membership in a state-vetted elite (among first-generation settlers), the notion of a more generous and honest northern type, and even the romance attached to life in the extreme northern environment. But the idea of what it meant to be a settler was also radically renovated. The authority of colonial agency eroded away in parallel with the ideological basis for the Soviet-era project of northern mastery and the enlightenment of natives. It became untenable in the post-Soviet era to point to newcomer or outsider status as a source of prestige. What was lost among settlers – the sense of common purpose that characterized the Soviet era – was compensated in the emergence of localist terms in the discourses and behaviours of belonging.

From this moral realignment in the 1990s arose a valorization of belonging in the North, as people began to point to their long-term roots in Chukotka as a source of authority. Within post-Soviet ethnography, survival strategies have emerged as a recurring and sometimes central theme, whose meaning some have explicitly linked to practices of resistance, the subaltern exercise of agency and voice, and the eventuality of political change. Rehabilitative attempts to identify political agency in the condition of marginalized post-Soviet citizens suggest, perhaps, a degree of frustration at its absence. The case of the settler in post-Soviet Chukotka, however, suggests that strategies of everyday survival are in fact incipiently political, because it is in their nature to localize practice. As I will discuss in the final chapters, the more intimately settlers were tied to the local setting, the more protective of their status as people of a particular place they were likely to be. In this discourse, natives were not the only true Chukotkans, and ethnicity was not the only criterion of belonging.

Part 3
Reconstruction, 2001-5

6
Modernization Again: The State Returns

By the end of Nazarov's decade of crisis, living standards in Chukotka had reached such a perilous state that descriptions seem to descend into hyperbole. Trauma and suicide were the principal causes of death (Goskomstat 1999). Reindeer herders' wages had been unpaid for six years, and the region's herds were 15 percent of their Soviet peak, dropping from half a million in 1990 to ninety thousand in 2000. The regional debt was three times the annual budget, several mid-sized industrial towns and settlements had been without heat, water, and electricity for years, and during the lean seasons, outright starvation threatened much of the rural population (Abramovich 2001). Despite considerable obstacles to departure, Chukotka's rate of out-migration throughout the 1990s was the highest of any region in the Russian Federation.[1] In 2000, residents of the capital, Anadyr, were trading their two-room flats for one-way air tickets to Moscow. As teachers, doctors, veterinarians, and engineers joined the exodus of specialists out of the region, public services crumbled and many smaller communities were simply abandoned.

Nevertheless, after a decade of uncertainty and hardship, the everyday experience of getting by had created a multitude of local equilibria. A virtual economy of barter had emerged beneath the collapse of the formal economy. Particularly in the villages, many people, most of them settlers, had in the relative terms of the post-Soviet North created comfortable lives. Certain of them, like Sveta and her family in Meinypil'gyno and the Bogorev brothers in Vaegi, had assumed key brokering roles within their communities, positions founded on their control of transport resources. In this rural domain, a new elite of *kommersanty* and *vezdekhodshiki* vied for power with (and sometimes entirely subsumed) more traditional brokers – the *glava administratsii* and the director of the kolkhoz. Everywhere in the okrug, mobility in some form – the ability to move goods, to travel periodically to the materik, or simply to alternate between village and capital – was intimately linked to security and privilege.

In the closing months of 2000, however, the sudden and completely unanticipated arrival in the okrug of a new population promised to quite radically upset the existing relations of power. In December, Roman Abramovich,[2] a thirty-five-year-old resource "oligarch" of Jewish descent, soon to be the richest person in the country, was elected governor of Chukotka in a landslide victory.[3] If mobility had been the touchstone of power and privilege in post-Soviet Chukotka, the new

Governor Roman Abramovich, 2002
Press Relations Branch of the Administration of the Chukchi Autonomous Okrug

governor imported to the region a population of experts and a form of administration that made natives and settlers alike appear highly immobile in comparison. Governor Abramovich brought with him a cadre of specialists eventually numbering in the hundreds. Their hypermobile lifestyle now effectively recast local people as out-of-date and marginalized hold-overs from the Soviet era. A new era of modernization had begun, and just as in the previous (late-Soviet) version, the distinctions between the identities of modernizer and the modernized became vividly clear. Once again, the outsider both embodied the techniques and prejudices of a modernity rooted in the nation's metropolis, and possessed the power to move between this centre and the local, northern sites of the modernization project. Quite remarkably, however, as Abramovich brought to Chukotka a new generation of modernizing experts, among the local targets of their campaign were the very people who had "opened the North" and "lifted up" its native peoples during the Soviet modernization.

The euphoria with which Chukotkans initially greeted Abramovich contrasts strikingly with the cynicism Russians have typically directed toward "New Russians" (it also departed from traditions of Russian anti-Semitism). By his own estimation, the oligarch governor spent US$80 million on his campaign, providing summer holidays on the Black Sea for four thousand children and chartering shiploads of food and fuel for Chukotka's settlements. It might be argued that he simply bought the vote and that his powers of patronage thus outstripped those of his opponents. But, in fact, local voters tempered their ambivalence toward an outsider from the tainted world of Russian business with the hope that, after a decade of Nazarov, he alone could radically repair the crisis of administrative integrity. Ultimately, they perceived in Abramovich a completely new political entity, one offering a break with neo-Soviet governance in its devalued transition-era forms and heralding the arrival of corporate efficiency as a new model of administration. In this sense, his election might be understood as a kind of neo-Leninist arrival, embodying an ideology of Western innovation, promising relief to a suffering population, and offering a mystical formula for providing it.[4] Sibneft, at that time Abramovich's oil company and the flagship enterprise in his corporate fleet, had emerged after the 1998 ruble default as a defiantly new type of organization, apparently rising above the opaque operations of Russian capitalism as a model of Western management techniques. Lenin offered the teleology of salvation, whereas Abramovich offered the Sibneft formula: the achievement of wealth through efficient administration and serious capital investment. He openly promised to import his business model to Chukotka, as though his election to governor were another in a series of corporate takeovers and the okrug administration another division of his business empire. The claim that Sibneft represented a new culture of management, suitable for private and public life alike, and that all previous forms were merely derivative and neo-Soviet, animated Abramovich's election victory with an air of revolution. Tired of the indifference and venality of the local elite, voters elected Abramovich *because* his outsider status and wealth insulated him from the influence of local patronage networks.

In the 1990s, the crisis that gripped Chukotka could be understood as a process of disconnection, an unravelling of the modernizing trajectory that had previously drawn such a remote territory into the Soviet space, and indeed the global economy. Disconnection bred a sense of life at the margins of whatever the new Russia was becoming. Certainly, the "retreat of the state" and the departure of so many former settler-modernizers signalled a much lower status for the North in mainland-Russian preoccupations. But this simply heightened the effect of Abramovich's arrival. He suddenly and unexpectedly *demarginalized* Chukotka, relocating the region to a position of massive interest, both national and global. Whatever may have prompted it, the attention paid by Roman Abramovich to this distant and poor corner of the North seemed to place Chukotka at the leading edge of Russia's post-Soviet revival. From 2000 on, this became one of the most fertile sites in the country for the production of senses of Russian modernity, a place where money, youth, and managerial ideas achieved a remarkable concentration. Chukotka was in this sense unique; nowhere outside the capital had oligarchic wealth yet impacted on the everyday lives of Russian citizens in such a forceful and deliberate way.

Abramovich's project was indeed without precedent in its technologies, and also in the hypermobility of its modernizing agents, but although these young experts could not see it, his program was also deeply traditional in content and intention. Very few years had passed since Chukotka was standing at the leading edge of another wave of modernization, when its privileged Soviet settlers embodied a potent vision of modernity for that time. The post-Soviet collapse, and Nazarov's decade of crisis, amounted merely to an ebb in the perennial pattern of frontier transformations, whose form the Russian cultural and economic metropolis always defines. The oligarch-led "modernization" of Chukotka was thus only the most recent chapter in an uneven but relentless process of northern development (osvoenie), and as in the past, the work of "lifting up" local people was once again assigned to an imported population.

This chapter is partly an ethnography of this group, for Abramovich's campaign was manifest in the character of his imported avant-garde. What were their objectives, prejudices, and techniques, and how did they view the people they were sent to modernize? And how did this newest campaign of modernization differ from those of the past, particularly those of the Soviet era? To write about this phenomenon is naturally to risk adopting some of its missionary vocabulary. Of course "modernization" itself suggests, in James Ferguson's (1999) words, an optimistic "teleology of progress" really apparent only to those with an idea of the proposed end state, that of "development." Along with development, modernization presumes a hierarchy of material and cultural modes whose relative merit depends entirely on one's socio-economic and geographic perspective. In Chukotka, the reformist disciples of the Abramovich modernization held particular views on the nature of modernity from which local settler opinion often diverged. The term "modernization" must therefore signify not only the program of reforming and building that Abramovich funded, but also the particular point of view his imported cadre carried.

Contrary to the prevailing discourse of modernity in Chukotka, which claims for Abramovich's project the status of an *a novo* departure without precedent, this was a modernization very much like those that came before. So this chapter is also partly a discussion of modernization as an entirely intrinsic pattern of Russian life, a quickening of pace as much a part of the cycle as periods of stability and stagnation, and of entropy and collapse. Those domains of life most peripheral to the sites of cultural and economic production – the geographic and social frontiers – simply experience programs of reformation in their most aggressive and momentary forms, and their people inevitably have the least say in the process. Campaigns of modernization are also notorious for their unsustainability; they come and go, washing back and forth over the land like tides. For this reason, the matter of their content – their technologies, their fashions, their self-perpetuating discourses – is ultimately less interesting than that *which is sustainable* in the modernizing phenomenon: the structure of the cycle itself, which appears to have a socially regenerative power in Russian society. Chukotka, the site of successive waves of modernizing energy, both Soviet and post-Soviet, can show us in particularly vivid terms how modernizers make themselves. Here we can see how projects of modernizing reform are ultimately far more transformative for their missionary agents than they are for the place, and the people, they briefly seek to change.

The Projects of Modernization

Upon Roman Abramovich's inauguration in January 2001, a large number of specialists, most in their twenties, were recruited from within Sibneft's corporate networks to begin the task of restoring, in Abramovich's (2002, 3) own words, "an acceptable way of life to Chukotka." This was a two-pronged campaign of technological and cultural transformation, relying on an almost completely new administrative staff and the injection of massive capital investment; both the "experts" and the money came from Abramovich's businesses. After spending millions on humanitarian aid during the 2000 election, he transferred new investments and budget funding so great that by the end of 2005, they totalled approximately US$2.2 billion or almost $41,000 per resident.[5] These funds were used to erase wage and pension arrears accumulated under Nazarov, to ensure the full implementation of the exploding okrug budget, to fund a raft of social initiatives, and to build new infrastructure on a scale unmatched even during the late-Soviet period. His administration restored the Soviet-era system of reindeer-herding and sea-mammal-hunting state farms (sovkhozy) in native villages. Large investments improved and restructured school and higher education, and special youth-oriented initiatives sought to improve opportunities for the okrug's young. Finally, in what remained a highly subsidized region, a major set of initiatives sought to depopulate the okrug and consolidate the remaining population.

Building a Modern Infrastructure

Because the improvements in infrastructure were most immediately evident, new construction projects acted as a yardstick of modernizing transformation.[6] This was an area in which the new administration could make rapid progress, although to undertake the wholesale rebuilding of the okrug's towns and villages, foreign and Moscow-based companies and an imported workforce were required. Anadyr,

Post-Soviet Anadyr before modernization, 2002
Photographed by author

Anadyr after modernization, showing the new cultural centre at left and the new Holy Trinity Cathedral, the largest functioning wooden cathedral in Russia, 2005
Photographed by V. Sirtun

the working base for Abramovich's imported administration, was radically transformed. A Turkish company with over twelve hundred flown-in workers renovated public buildings and apartments, erecting an impressive new cultural centre and museum, and paving and landscaping the city's streets and sidewalks. By 2003, the town had a modern cinema complex, luxurious brew pubs, restaurants and a casino, an ice hockey rink and fitness centre, an internet café, a shopping complex, and a fully serviced branch of MDM Bank. Alongside the Turks, Canadian, Ukrainian, and other imported workers reconstructed public buildings, including the okrug Duma, and Anadyr's schools and kindergartens. In 2005, a new Serbian-built international airport opened across the Gulf of Anadyr. By 2006, an entire natural-gas field and pipeline network was completed to fuel a new gas-fired generating station for the capital, its output augmented by the world's northernmost windfarm. What wasn't knocked down and replaced was refurbished, and Anadyr's ubiquitous concrete apartment blocks were repainted in garish colours to relieve the city's weathered appearance.

Life changed just as radically in the rural sphere. The post-Soviet economic crisis and the failure of transport had created near-subsistence conditions in villages such as Vaegi and Meinypil'gyno, and already poor and over-crowded housing and public facilities had reached a state of terminal crisis. Under Abramovich, the burden of distance was rapidly lifted, with investments in the network of rural fixed-wing and helicopter routes, and heavy subsidies on flights between villages and their district centres. But, most remarkably, the new administration set about rebuilding the villages themselves, in some cases resettling almost the entire population into Canadian-style detached houses. Two Mi-26 heavy-lift helicopters (the world's biggest) flew year-round at the administration's expense, moving construction materials, retail goods, food, and even (in my company) a load of fifty-six adult pigs. Inspired by a visit to remote native communities in the Canadian North, Abramovich personally commissioned new Canadian-built schools, kindergartens, and sports facilities for many of Chukotka's settlements.

Securing the Native: Modernization in the Villages

At a 2004 meeting of Russia's northern governors, with President Putin attending, Abramovich stated: "the traditional subsistence way of life, which is the preserve of the indigenous peoples of the north, cannot be financially self-supporting. It follows that [natives] require state subsidies."[7] In early 2001, large investments began to flow into the traditional native economy, funding the resurrection of neo-Soviet state farms and, as already noted, rebuilding part or all of every native settlement in the region. Air travel from district centres to native settlements returned to the Soviet model, with frequent scheduled helicopter flights costing the ruble equivalent of fifteen dollars – less than the weekly income of even the poorest-paid kolkhoz employees. After reabsorbing all herding and hunting enterprises,

Coastal village of Vankarem before reconstruction, 2003
Photographed by author

ending a decade of (admittedly disastrous) flirtation with private and clan-based models such as the *rodovaia obshchina* (clan-based labour collective) and the "shareholders' cooperative" (ZAO), the administration made unprecedented investments in the rural economy via reconstituted state farms. These institutions not only received the money to pay their herders, hunters, and other mostly native workers, but also, a great deal of investment went toward restoring their facilities and stock of transport. They received vezdekhody, tractors, whaleboats, generators, and industrial freezers. In an effort to arrest the decline in herd numbers, veterinary specialists revived reindeer inoculation campaigns for the first time since the Soviet period. In 2002-3, the Department of Agriculture even bought reindeer herds from neighbouring Kamchatka and Sakha.

In September 2003, a new vocational college in Anadyr opened its doors. This facility, one of the most expensive and ambitious of Abramovich's gifts to the okrug, vastly improved the range and quality of teaching available to post-secondary students choosing to stay in the region.[8] Anadyr's college offered free full-time study to 650 students, 420 of them from outside the capital, all living in full-board facilities on the campus at no cost. With 70 percent of the student body coming from Chukotka's native population, this project was implicitly aimed at addressing the needs of indigenous students from the settlements, providing the practical skills in demand in their home communities, namely, teaching, nursing, veterinary science, engine maintenance, and heavy equipment operating. Settler students, particularly those from the capital, were generally expected to leave the okrug for

Village of Vaegi rebuilt, 2005
Photographed by author

higher studies in central Russia, a shift of setting they were at any rate better prepared for than their rural indigenous counterparts.[9]

Modernization through Cost Economies

Economic renewal and the return of paternalist forms of state funding in Chukotka came with an important caveat: modernization would be linked to the achievement of cost economies. In late 2002, I interviewed the director of the Department of Economic Planning, a polished, well-educated Muscovite in his mid-twenties. Trained in finance and with experience in the private sector, he brought the habit of cost-benefit analysis to this new posting in public administration. He assessed Chukotka as though it were a loss-making division in Abramovich's larger corporate apparatus, an enterprise that might be supportable through cross-subsidy today but that would ultimately have to be whipped into shape or sloughed off. In his view, Chukotka's population, wherever possible, should be amalgamated, remote settler communities should be closed, and even some indigenous settlements should be encouraged to relocate to more accessible locations.[10] Settlers lacking relevant skills should be resettled out of the North. He reminded me that with the collapse of industry and the growth of bureaucracy over the Nazarov era, Chukotka had become, despite its small population, a serious drain on the federal treasury. Now that Abramovich had taken responsibility for these costs, the young director explained, he was entitled to do everything possible to lower them: "the principal task of modernization is to remove inefficiencies in the northern economy, cut costs, and make money that is available to support life in the far north go further" [38]. If there might be resistance to mass resettlement from some quarters, it would come as a surprise to him. This young manager, like almost every other member of Abramovich's team, assumed that no non-native in Chukotka would choose to permanently settle there: "I'm convinced you can't have a decent life in Chukotka; all you can do is exist" [38].

Abramovich's approach to northern administration followed a line lately espoused by the Brookings Institute economists Fiona Hill and Clifford Gaddy, who contend in their book *The Siberian Curse* (2003) that over-settlement in Soviet Russia's northern regions created long-term and costly distortions in the country's economic geography. They assert that settlement and production should have been concentrated in the country's most temperate zones, as they have been in Canada, but that Soviet planning was blind to the cost implications of settling the North. This view also has its adherents in Putin's federal administration, who argue for a controlled but ambitious restructuring of Russia's entire northern population and the adoption of shift labour systems to exploit natural resources in the North.[11] Regional locally elected administrations in the North might have offered some resistance to cost-efficiency-related reform pressures, but the dispositions of Abramovich and his imported administration were clearly *not* informed by local experience. As the director of economic planning told me, in their view, every local in Chukotka represented a financial loss to Russia [38].

Following this line, the administration sought to concentrate Chukotka's remaining settler population, consolidating resources in selected centres while abandoning a series of "settlements without prospect" (besperspektivnye poselki), mostly former mining towns. A policy of selective infrastructural investments was used to signal which settler-dominated towns would remain inhabitable by the point of Abramovich's anticipated departure. During my first year in Chukotka, this process was clearly evident even in the Anadyr area. Not far north of Anadyr lay the airport, the coal-mining town of Ugol'nye Kopi, a formerly secret military base called Gudym, and Shakhterskii, once the home of Chukotka's largest fish-processing plant. As an army of imported workers paved the streets and erected new buildings on every corner in Anadyr, the sky across the water was black with smoke as Shakhterskii was abandoned and burned. The last remaining soldiers were likewise departing from Gudym, and the former airforce barracks in Ugol'nye Kopi were closed. Just as certain settlements were closing, others had been designated sustainable and were expanding. Anadyr and the remaining micro-regions of Ugol'nye Kopi were receiving a steady stream of migrants from industrial towns elsewhere in the process of closure.

The most radical means of cutting administrative costs in Chukotka was the resettlement of thousands of non-indigenous residents to temperate regions of Russia, which Abramovich's officials described as "getting rid of human ballast."

As demographers of the Russian North have noted, the economic crisis of the 1990s trapped a large pool of potential out-migrants in the remotest regions (Heleniak 1999; Kontorovich 2000). Two federal resettlement programs were already in existence before 2001, one providing northerners with lump-sum payments according to the length of stay in the northern zone and the other building resettlement accommodation in selected destinations. Yet, neither program was properly funded or efficiently administered. Abramovich's administration consequently announced a new resettlement program in 2001. This initiative ostensibly re-animated the pre-existing federal resettlement program with Abramovich's own practically unlimited funds, but in fact it bypassed the federal bureaucracy. His aim was to quickly resettle sufficiently large numbers of settlers from Chukotka, so as to noticeably decrease subsidy costs and create a smaller but more "economically active" population.[12] The administration thus created a high-capacity conveyor belt to shift large numbers out of the region, and no settler was "trapped" any longer. Regionstroy, a private company, was formed to manage the program, and in its first year of operation, roughly thirteen hundred residents were resettled. In 2002, another sixteen hundred departed, followed by nine hundred in 2003 and five hundred in 2004.[13] Administration officials hoped to halve the 2001 population of seventy-five thousand by the end of Abramovich's first five-year term, although in the event, the population stabilized at roughly fifty-five thousand.[14]

While "unpromising" industrial communities closed and their settler residents were relocated to central Russia, the huge volume of new construction work in the region was undertaken by Turkish, Canadian, Ukrainian, and Russian labourers flown in on short-term contracts. Presiding over a massive order book of projects, the administration had no recourse but to rely on imported labour under the direction of mostly foreign construction and engineering companies. After a decade of out-migration and asset stripping in Chukotka, there was little local expertise and equipment to tackle construction on this scale. Moreover, the companies contracted to rebuild Chukotka preferred to bypass the skilled workers who still lived in the okrug, opting to recruit labour from outside the North. Imported shift labourers enjoyed a distinct advantage over local workers, who still fell under the generous labour benefits legislation inherited from the Soviet era, including extended annual leave and the right of employer-funded resettlement to central Russia upon retirement.[15]

Abramovich in Chukotka

What were Roman Abramovich's motivations? With control over a large swathe of the Russian economy, managing what was Russia's fastest-growing oil company (Sibneft), and in the process of constructing a multinational business empire (Millhouse Capital), why would this young oligarch distract himself with the affairs of a remote and sparsely populated region of the Far North? In his own words, coming to Chukotka was an act of altruism, a panacea to the moral depredations of modern business life. On 2 March 2001, soon after the 2000 gubernatorial campaign, Abramovich told a *Washington Post* reporter that "Business is sport, and somehow it became not very interesting to participate in it. We achieved a certain success, but it is not interesting to develop it limitlessly." He continued, "I do it for pleasure. If I didn't like it, I wouldn't be doing it."

Rather mysteriously, Abramovich's stated justifications fell outside the terms of profit, power, and protection (*krysha*) central to the oligarchic enterprise of which he was a paragon in Putin's Russia. As one of the most successful survivors of the Yeltsin-era scramble for state assets, Abramovich sought to portray his appearance in Chukotka as evidence that, like a lotus flower rising from night-soil, he had now transcended that past. At first, this almost seemed likely, as indeed it proved difficult to understand how the governorship could possibly serve his oligarchic interests. The region held few easily exploitable natural resources, and Abramovich's oil and metals companies could operate far more profitably in other regions of Russia. Some postulated that the governor's post would protect him from criminal prosecution, thus insulating his business interests from state persecution just when Putin was eliminating other oligarchs (Boris Berezovsky, Vladimir Gusinsky, the Chernyi brothers, Rem Viakhirev, and later Mikhail Khodorkovsky). But in fact, Abramovich had *previously* enjoyed prosecutorial immunity, when he served as a deputy for Chukotka to the federal Duma (1998-2000). Russian governors, in contrast, did not enjoy this protection.

Abramovich also seemed committed to his role in a personal way. After his inauguration, rather than relying on a plenipotentiary, he was directly involved in steering reforms and investments in Chukotka. He made special efforts to visit remote settlements and speak with ordinary villagers, and he travelled the globe in search of the expertise and technology needed to modernize the okrug. Abramovich even seemed to enjoy himself; visits to the North were an escape from the high-pressure environment of Sibneft and Millhouse headquarters. In fact, Chukotka was play, on a vast scale. Apart from ordering all the building projects and charity initiatives, Abramovich presided over a series of gala events in Anadyr, flying in his favourite Russian pop groups and paying for impressive fireworks displays. The official explanation for all of this – that, for him, Chukotka was an affair of the heart – was difficult to deny.

I would not contest that Abramovich was emotionally invested in Chukotka's modernization. With the passage of time, however, it became increasingly clear that control over Chukotka's affairs also served his oligarchic interests: it protected him from political harassment and it offered his companies enormous tax advantages. Between 1996 and 1998, Abramovich and a few other oligarchs benefited from the controversial loans-for-shares deals, whereby the country's wealthiest industrialists helped President Yeltsin maintain his fragile grip on power in return for a virtual giveaway of the state's most valuable enterprises. The term "oligarchy" itself reflected the manner in which, during the 1990s, business and politics were conflated to the point of a virtual union. In the absence of the rule of law, and in particular, without clear laws on property ownership, political connections were the only means of securing control over former state assets and protecting these new private holdings. The most powerful business figures exercised vast influence through their media holdings and their links with the Office of the President and government ministers.

Even as President Putin inaugurated a new era of economic stability after 2000, oligarchic structures and various state interests remained locked in battle for control over profitable assets – resource concessions, land, state enterprises – in conditions no more predictable or secure than those of the 1990s. His election did, however, signal a change of rules for the oligarchy (a shift not all of them detected in time). Putin came to power vowing to eliminate the oligarchs "as a class," a populist approach engineered to appeal to an electorate that viewed these figures as the bastard children of the new capitalist economy, men with no legitimate claim over their wealth. Not surprisingly, Putin's presidential executive proved far harder for the oligarchs to co-opt than Yeltsin's, and after eliminating some of the particularly prominent among them (Berezovsky, Gusinsky) and securing state control over the print and broadcast media, he adopted a policy of holding those still standing "distant from power." Indeed, the term "oligarch" passed at this point from a realistic description (although it persists as shorthand for Russia's super-wealthy). It was at this juncture, deprived of many of the levers of political power they previously controlled in Moscow, that the richest industrialists of the oligarchic era began a rush to the provinces. Between 2000 and 2002, eight of Russia's eighty-nine regions were "captured" by national oligarchic structures. Abramovich's election in Chukotka in late 2000 was among the first – a signal, but not exceptional, event.[16]

Since 2000, oligarchic business interests have derived various advantages from their new regional power bases, not least of which has been undisputed control over their respective natural resources. Abramovich's aims in Chukotka were subtler, although from the perspective of developments in 2004 and 2005, his game turns out to have been masterfully executed. First, while it was still possible, he made a fortune in Chukotka. Although the region contained few resources of interest, Abramovich understood the potential of its status as a tax haven with special natural-resource export quotas, an arrangement he subsequently used to elevate the profitability of his oil and aluminium businesses, Sibneft and Rusal. Subsidiary trading companies based in Anadyr were structured to capture profit via transfer-pricing systems, as they were not subject to the same levels of taxation as their mother companies based elsewhere. These schemes lowered the effective tax rate of Sibneft, by far Abramovich's most important asset, from roughly 24 to 9 percent between 2000 and 2004, and the Russian Audit Chamber estimated that this arrangement generated over $470 million in tax breaks in that time. But of course Sibneft's "tax efficiency" was also a central cause of the company's spectacular share performance over that period, during which the principal shareholders approved several multi-billion-dollar exceptional dividend payments.[17]

Abramovich not only used Chukotka to make his fortune, he also used it to protect his fortune. He expertly harnessed the Russian and international media to broadcast his projects of charity, flying journalists to Anadyr to witness the reconstruction of Russia's most impecunious northern region. He did this while the only Russian wealthier than he, Mikhail Khodorkovsky, funded "civil society" initiatives, sought to buy influence through the recruitment of deputies in the federal Duma, and publicly denounced Putin's *dirigiste* tendencies. As the rules changed under Putin, both their oligarchic empires became increasingly vulnerable to de facto nationalization; Khodorkovsky tried to alter this reality, whereas Abramovich chose to accept it, all the while staying conspicuously out of national politics and attending to problems in Chukotka. His proved a sage policy, for in autumn 2003, Khodorkovsky was arrested and charged with tax evasion as well as other crimes. Sibneft was if anything even more successful at identifying loopholes in the existing tax legislation than Khodorkovsky's oil company Yukos, and Abramovich was certainly just as vulnerable to charges of fraud arising from his efforts to accumulate state assets in the 1990s. But it was Khodorkovsky who fell, receiving a sentence of nine years in a Siberian jail while Yukos' assets were nationalized (mostly acquired by state-owned Rosneft). In contrast, Abramovich amicably sold his 72 percent stake in Sibneft to state-owned Gazprom in 2005 for roughly US$13 billion, a company he had bought for under US$200 million less than a decade earlier. He is now the wealthiest man in Russia, ironically because of his success in helping the government regain control over national energy assets whose scandalous privatization made his fortune. Abramovich's career as the apolitical, altruistic governor of Chukotka netted him a king's ransom.

The Governor's People

One of the truly remarkable aspects of Abramovich's campaign was the extreme youth of those empowered to push it forward. Having no experience of life in Soviet times, and no meaningful exposure to the cultural chauvinisms and ideologies of progress saturating the official discourse of that era, these modernizers were incapable of judging how different their own vision of progress really was. In any revolutionary campaign, an arrogant belief in the particular novelty of one's own vision of modernity is a typical ingredient of the will to transform, a desire greatly aided by inexperience. But, for settlers who were once the appointed standard-bearers of Soviet modernization in the Far North and who latterly found themselves targeted for modernizing by a new force of experts not much older than their own children, the parallels with the past were altogether clearer. In fact, the modernizers of today carried with them many of the same obsessions as did the Soviets sent to civilize the North a generation earlier: hygiene, literacy, technical competence, and sobriety. As in the past, the most recent arrivals claimed a monopoly on these techniques of the "modern" lifestyle (now dressed up in a new language so as to appear unprecedented). And, as in the past, these "modern" techniques and customs not only stood at the core of their programs of re-education, they also operated as practices of differentiation from local people: new arrivals embodied modernity, locals embodied its opposite. And finally, the *urgency* of this newest campaign of modernization likewise betrayed its similarity to traditional Russian and Soviet projects of "catching up," with which any veteran of Soviet life would have intimate experience.

Yet, in certain ways, Abramovich's young modernizers were quite unlike the settlers of the Soviet era. They were not animated by a sense of northern romance or the desire to find a better way of life in the North. Mostly, they were intoxicated by the promise of upward mobility within both Abramovich's corporations and their urban networks in the capital, a posture that blinded them to Chukotka as anything more than an assignment. Their incredible mobility – shuttling between Moscow and Anadyr on chartered jets – was likewise unprecedented. Soviet settlers' notion of transience, in contrast, had been a three-year commitment to living in the North. Many of Abramovich's experts lived with their families in central Russia and commuted to Chukotka for a few weeks at a time. Settlers had viewed the project of severnoe osvoenie as infinite in duration, even if they themselves planned to limit their own participation in its execution. But this new modernization was as delimited as the personal plans of its architects. Once, Soviets could always look forward to another Five-Year Plan to succeed the current one; Abramovich's own Five-Year Plan had no successor. All this signalled a new and more extreme degree of ephemerality, and promised more explicitly a coming lapse in the modernizing cycle; this was a mode of development Chukotka's settlers had never witnessed before.

In a neo-Leninist fashion, Abramovich's modernization sought to transform the material and cultural fabric of life with revolutionary speed, and the instrument of change was a technocratic vanguard of cadres steeped in the ideology of the oligarchic corporate domain. It was not enough to teach the techniques and doctrines of post-Soviet modernity to local people: business-culture commissars who embodied these principles were required to penetrate and manage all aspects of the revolution. I was never able to properly count the numbers of seconded specialists in Chukotka, partly because they were constantly moving in and out of the okrug and partly because this population was so diverse in specialization and authority. They ranged from key figures of the innermost circle, some of them shareholders in Abramovich's companies, to an amorphous and transient mass of *kontrakshiki* imported for specific tasks but with little connection to the lofty world of the "New Russians" at the top. The differences between them were less clear to locals, who lumped them together under one catch-all term: "the governor's team" *(komanda gubernatora).*

The diversity within the modernizing population was obscured to locals not only because of the modernizers' relative wealth, but also because internal variation was intentionally disguised. Those whom Abramovich sent to Chukotka belonged to an emerging class of affluent Russians deeply engaged in an exercise of defining its separate identity in post-Soviet society.[18] Their manner of consumption, their tastes in food and clothing, and their favoured modes of leisure were, in the mould of parvenu social formations everywhere, intended to suggest their class affiliations, as well as to mask quite large differences in actual wealth within the group. With these practices, they were striving to create an inhabitable social category clearly removed from the grey monotypes of the previously available Soviet lifestyles. (Indeed, a taste for foreign luxuries and, as time has passed, for foreign lifestyles and technologies has been a principal mechanism for establishing social separation from ordinary Russians.) From the perspective of "below," the rich culture of popular jokes and caricatures on the New Russian reflects a vigorous process of "othering" the emerging master class by those unlikely to join it. Just as the stereotypes have materialized, however, the affluent have been even more rapidly reconstructing themselves, searching for more acceptable ways of living with wealth and converting financial capital into social capital. Indeed, as a middle class has emerged in the biggest cities, a much larger (mostly young) population has joined in this quest, one in which the incoming specialists brought to Chukotka by the modernization project were active participants.

The culture of this community was clearly influenced by perceptions of Roman Abramovich himself, who served as an exemplary cue for the proper comportment of wealth and power. The father of four (now five) children, the manager of a stable of companies admired as the epitome of modern, maturing Russian corporate sophistication, and a survivor of the economic and political instability that winnowed the field of original oligarchs, he became governor of Chukotka at thirty-six. Unlike the stereotypical New Russian, Abramovich eschewed conspicuous display, cultivating the image of a temperate, hard-working man of action. To distract from a natural shyness before the media, he insisted that the results of his efforts in Chukotka, and not anything he could say, would best serve for the record. Dressing in casual sweaters and jeans, always with a few days of growth on his chin, he consciously sidestepped the visual clichés attached to Russia's newly wealthy. But because he was the leading figure of this class, these signals in fact transformed the image of the New Russian – the *homo economicus* – at least within his own circles. Abramovich's youth was an equally powerful signal. He belonged to a generation of entrepreneurs too young to have occupied nomenclatura positions during the late-Soviet era. Aged twenty-five to forty, they "value success, individualism, efficiency. They are professional, decisive, business-like, practical, persistent, even aggressive, and able to handle difficulties" (Vladimir Kramnik, quoted in Ledeneva 1998, 204). They attached a stigma to idleness – time is money. Drinking, particularly debilitating oneself with vodka, was incompatible with personal efficiency, and in others it was suspect. It should not seem remarkable, then, that Abramovich's deputies made a study of dressing casually, worked late into the night, discarded grammatical formality, drank only light beer or water, and could often be found gasping on a treadmill in one of the administration's private fitness gyms.

Chukotka's modernizing elite originated in a few large Russian cities, and mostly from within a set of elite universities and modern, successful business environments.[19] The architects of the modernization within the inner circle of administrative authority were Abramovich's personal acquaintances, young professionals, some of them multi-millionaire shareholders in Sibneft and associated companies.[20] Sergei Kapkov, who became at twenty-four a deputy governor and the head of Chukotka's Department of Culture, Youth, Sport, Tourism, and Public Relations, was typical in many respects of the modernizing incomer. A native of Nizhni Novgorod, he won a scholarship in the 1990s to study within the elite Presidential Program set up to train a new generation of Russian leaders with skills such as foreign languages, management, auditing, and communications. He began working as an image consultant for politicians while still in studies, and after meeting Abramovich, he was hired to manage his 2000 gubernatorial campaign. When I knew him as a deputy minister in Chukotka, he lived in one room of the governor's Anadyr residence; much of the time, however, he worked in Moscow from a parallel set of offices. While in Anadyr, he dressed in casual corduroy trousers and a sweater, travelling in a chauffeured late-model black Land Cruiser. Although he was a government officer, his business card still bore the Sibneft logo eighteen months after the election, and his e-mail came to a Sibneft account. Indeed, he moved between various roles within Abramovich's political and business domains. After mobilizing support for the United Russia Party in Chukotka, and thereby engineering the election of a close Sibneft ally – Irina Panchenko – to the position of deputy to the federal Duma, he managed the campaign of Abramovich's friend, Omsk Oblast governor Leonid Polezhaev, before himself winning a seat in the Duma in the December 2003 elections. During his rapid political ascent, Kapkov lived within Abramovich's private and trusted circle. He celebrated his birthday in the

Caribbean and occasionally took holidays on the Cote d'Azur and the Swiss Alps.

A step down, yet still bound by acquaintance to the governor, were those appointed as district heads and the directors of key modernizing departments such as Finance, Economic Planning, Education, and Public Relations. One example of this type was Dora Poluksht, a native of Syktyvkar, the capital of the Komi Republic, where Abramovich was raised by his grandparents. Acquainted with Abramovich through family connections, Poluksht was appointed the director of the Department of Education, responsible for a wide-ranging reform program intended to revolutionize the quality of teaching up to the post-secondary level. She was empowered to hire a large team of education consultants (all themselves from Syktyvkar circles) and given responsibility for a huge program of building schools in the settlements and a vocational college in Anadyr. Also situated within the administration were a number of equally influential "personal assistants to the governor." Powerful and closely connected figures playing key roles in the modernizing project also ran institutions nominally outside the administrative hierarchy. Among these were the directors of Regionstroy (responsible for resettlement and community closures) and of the governor's personal charities in the region, Krasnyi Krest Chukotki (Red Cross) and Polius Nadezhdy (Pole of Hope).

The next circle of authority within the modernizing cohort was recruited at one degree of separation from the governor, and this level was fractured into cliques surrounding particular patrons within the inner circle and usually distinguished by place or institution of origin. In contrast to the political elite, they were ostensibly hired on the basis of their specialist skills, instead of proximity to the right circles. Not a friend of Abramovich but still very much within the governor's komanda, Pavel Apletin managed the okrug newspaper *Krainyi Sever* (Far North), which, under the new administration, expanded from four to twenty-four, often thirty, pages and revived editorial offices throughout Chukotka. Recruited six months after Abramovich's election via Deputy Governor Kapkov's networks, thirty-four-year old Apletin had been the advertising editor for a large newspaper in Nizhni Novgorod, earning a middle-class monthly salary of roughly US$1,000. When he and his wife relocated to Anadyr, they were given a two-bedroom flat looking over the harbour, newly renovated with a full Ikea *evroremont* (renovation to European standard). Older than many of the inner-circle modernizers but with a body of professional experience behind him, he seemed less visibly than Kapkov to emulate the Abramovich style. He imported from his previous setting his editorial tweed blazer and brown leather dress shoes, eschewing the cotton-blend pullovers, jeans, and running shoes of the younger cadre. Signalling a position in the modernizing hierarchy at one remove from the circles of administration, his official car was a Russian-made four-by-four, not a Land Cruiser, although it still came with a driver. In contrast with Kapkov, Apletin travelled back to central

Russia only once every two or three months, but he was no more settled in the North than his colleagues. Like most young modernizers, he considered his job a launching pad for a career in central Russia, and he and his wife planned to leave before the end of Abramovich's term. Three years after their arrival, they used their earnings to buy a historical flat in central St. Petersburg; Chukotka for them was an intermediate step between one central Russian city and another.

The numbers of incomer specialists at the level of Kapkov, and even Apletin, were limited and knowable; below them spread a much larger pool of incomer recruits whose numbers constantly fluctuated. At this level were found consultant engineers restructuring Chukotka's power-generation system, aviation specialists, computer and telecommunications experts, public relations professionals, and media managers. Some were based in the administration's Moscow offices, making only the occasional trip to Anadyr. Others shuttled continually: these included a number of lawyers assigned to "handling" the okrug Duma and specialists supervising particular infrastructure projects – hotels, the cinema, entertainment complex, and internet café, the shopping centre, and the experimental windfarm. Due to the nature of their work, other senior modernizers shuttled less often out of the North; for example, the disc jockeys at the administration-funded radio station Purga and the manager of state television and radio could leave their posts only occasionally.

Inhabiting a lower rung within the modernizing community was a population of young graduates recruited from Moscow and other major cities and placed within priority areas of state function. These were television, radio, and print journalists, hotel and retail managers, the brewmaster in the new pub, international relations, public relations, and legal specialists in the administration, and many of those helping to manage the Regionstroy resettlement program from the districts. These people had less loyalty to the modernization project and little personal investment in the culture of nepotism found in closer proximity to the governor. Perhaps because of this, many of them drew some inspiration from the exotic surroundings in which they suddenly found themselves. Whereas the shuttling lifestyle, the exhausting work culture, and the tight insularity among inner-circle modernizers blinkered them from the realities of life in Chukotka's settlements, the foot soldiers of the modernization were more likely to have been recruited anonymously, and so were on the periphery of modernizer networks. Some sought companionship with local people, upon whom they relied to introduce them to the northern landscape; to take them fishing or for *shashliki* (BBQ) on the tundra. In mid-2002, as I was travelling by coal ship up the coast from Anadyr to the port settlement of Egvekinot, I encountered a twenty-two-year-old history graduate from Moscow who by chance had landed a job with the administration organizing the collection of the vast volume of industrial scrap metal in the Egvekinot district (Iul'tinskii Raion). Over the ensuing weeks, I occasionally ran into him as he walked between Egvekinot's local administration offices, petitioning its minor potentates for help in ferrying metal to the town's port. He reminded me of Conrad's Marlow, sent alone to a distant corner of the Belgian Congo in the vain hope that he might have some success in sorting out a fairly unimportant problem for the company. After I spent months observing the lifestyle of key modernizers in Anadyr, people such as this struck me as remarkable for their interest in northern life and in particular their ability to talk with local people on equal terms. Two weeks after I arrived by ship, I returned to Egvekinot from the tundra on my way back to Anadyr and found my acquaintance drinking with the mechanics at the local public works garage, quite oblivious to his scrap-collecting assignment and enthusiastically looking forward to a mushroom-picking trip with his new friends that evening.

Finally, modernization brought a large number of foreign workers to Chukotka, from highly paid specialists recruited in Canada, Iceland, Germany, and the US to cheap but skilled Turkish construction workers. Despite the insular culture of loyalty within Abramovich's inner circles, foreign specialists had privileged access to them, a reflection, first, of their common fate as middle-class urbanites distant from home and, second, of the perception among young Muscovites that certain foreigners embodied a lifestyle to which they aspired. Foreigners were naturally gradated into a hierarchy of esteem by the Russian core of modernizers – some enjoyed the personal confidence of Abramovich himself, others mixed only with administration modernizers in Anadyr's most expensive bars and restaurants, and still others, in particular the Turkish labourers, were viewed largely with racist disdain by modernizers and locals alike, and they kept to their prefabricated barracks in the interests of self-preservation.

Abramovich's habit of travelling the planet to enlist expertise and modern technology in service of his projects helped to explain the particular influence certain foreigners held in administration circles. These included the manager of a Canadian construction company, which won a number of high-value building contracts throughout the okrug, an Alaska-based academic who advised the governor on international affairs, and the senior managers of Yamata, the Turkish contractor renovating and rebuilding most of Anadyr. As large as the foreign presence became after 2000, it remained highly parcellized into national cliques, since few foreigners, regardless of their status and pay, felt any inclination to cultivate relationships with the core Russian modernizers. Language difficulties aside, they were in Chukotka to do a job and leave with the proceeds. Nevertheless, the sudden arrival of large numbers of foreigners made a significant impression on local people, for whom internal divisions within the modernizing community were largely invisible. From the outside, the international complexion of the governor's komanda, along with the modes of conspicuous consumption its members practised, communicated in a very forceful way the social distance that separated outsiders from the local population.[21]

Modernization in the Storming Tradition

The twentieth-century historian Moshe Lewin (1987) called Russia a "culture in a rush." He was referring to a perennial pattern of storming, campaign-like development, and waves of modernizing revolution visited on a traditional rural nation by a cosmopolitan elite frustrated at Russia's economic and socialist backwardness. Before Stalin's industrialization policy of "catch and overtake" *(dognat' i peregnat')* and the institution of the Five-Year Plan, there were the modernizing programs of Petr Stolypin and Sergei Witte, Aleksandr II, Peter I, and Ivan IV, each an assault on the structure of Russian society in an effort to remould, drawing on Western European models.[22] To explain these periodic campaigns of modernization, economic historians such as Aleksandr Gerschenkron (1970) have invoked the determining influence of Russia's peripheral geography, a position in contact with – but not within – the zone of greatest innovation and productivity (Western Europe). For historian Teodor Shanin (1985), Russia's peripheral position next to industrial Europe's dynamism made it the original "developing nation." Yet, the same unbalanced relations between metropolis and periphery have for centuries been present *within* Russian territory. Indeed, since Prince Dolgorukii gathered the lands in the twelfth century, wealth and political power have been highly concentrated in Moscow (and St. Petersburg), creating in the metropole a unique platform for the foment of new technologies, ideologies, and tastes. Slavophile notions of Russia as the Third Rome may have been at odds with the Europhile dream of Russia as a Western power, but both tendencies simply added urgency to the task of civilizing the Russian hinterland and expanding imperial influence. Particularly after the Petrine reforms of the eighteenth century, the socio-economic resources deriving from extreme privilege enabled the urban Russian elite to easily absorb nation-building ideas from the more developed nations of Western Europe (and latterly the US). But the prospect of implanting these technologies and beliefs in a rural peasant nation presented an insoluble dilemma. For the modernizing elite, Russia seemed caught in conditions of perpetual *otstalost'* (fallen-behindness), out of which emerged a dualistic self-regard in the Russian identity, by turns rejecting and embracing the project of Western-oriented transformation, a tension symbolized by Russia's polar emblems: the Bronze Horseman and the Mongol-Tatar yoke.[23]

Just as economic and cultural separation has generated the conditions for modernizing campaigns throughout Russia's history, the stark gap dividing the modernizer and the local in post-2000 Chukotka provided the moral impetus for the campaign of catching up at issue here. The modernizing incomer stands on one side of the still-persistent gulf between the provinces and the metropolis in Russia, delineating class divisions and the geographic differentiation of privilege. In the post-Soviet era, Moscow and a few other cities benefited from the spectacular stratification of wealth and the emergence of a free market. Macro-economic "transition" reforms have enabled the Russian metropolitan core to pull even further away from the provinces and peripheries than they had been in Soviet times, resulting in a national socio-economic fracturing. The educated inhabitants of the big cities were propelled into contact with a new, more Western way of life, transforming the workplace, the pace of life, the use of leisure time, perceptions of success, and patterns of consumption. In offices such as those of Sibneft, a new Russian middle class emerged, increasingly confident it understood how to "live to good purpose under capitalism," partly as a result of routine contact with Western models of the good life.[24] But Moscow-centric liberalization mostly failed to penetrate the vast provincial domain, and in this regard Chukotka was exemplary: a place that was impoverished, disconnected, and depopulated. Indeed, in the first decade after the Soviet collapse, Chukotka was a zone of exceptional otstalost', a condition of stasis Governor Aleksandr Nazarov actually intended to preserve: independent business and civil society were stifled, power was monopolized by the former communist elite, and neither foreigners nor outside Russians could penetrate its bureaucratically enforced borders to form lasting partnerships. So, while Russia's growing urban middle class tasted the first perquisites of the new economic order, settlers in Chukotka experienced "transition" as life within a frozen, institutionally neo-Soviet domain, with the economic and ideological lifeblood drained from its veins. For settlers, the only reference points to a decent way of life were located in the Soviet past, around which a particularly potent realm of nostalgic discourses materialized and recirculated.

Circumstances of the Moscow-centred oligarchic political economy propelled Abramovich to Chukotka and recommended a well-publicized program of development, but problematically, they also brought into contact two spectacularly different social realms. This form of "development" was never likely to entail a project of class levelling, one that might have sought to redistribute decision making (political power) and decision implementing (economic power) from the centre to the local, for this would warp Russia's metropolitan-biased geography of privilege.[25] Instead, the modernizing elite enlisted advanced technology and methods of management in order to revolutionize living standards and administration without seriously unsettling their position as the sole agents of modernity. This arrangement invites comparison with colonial systems of administration in other parts of the world peripheral to the metropoles of technological and political power. Like those in the earlier Soviet era of settler-led osvoenie, Abramovich's modernizing newcomers represented a neo-colonial regime of domination characterized by a rigid separation between its imported agents and its local targets.[26] Of course, only because Abramovich's experts were so young did they miss the fact that among their local targets were yesterday's modernizers of the North. Had they been older, they would have been in danger of recognizing this remarkable state of affairs and of terminally upsetting the arrangement by empathizing with the objects of their modernizing project.

The modernization of Chukotka was similarly a campaign of extreme technical innovation. With his election, Abramovich adopted an approach that had previously proved effective in transforming Sibneft's productive capacities – hiring foreign consultants, project managers, and technology.[27] In his private Boeing 767, he travelled the globe in search of technical solutions to ameliorate the conditions of life in Chukotka's communities. In Iceland, he contracted a geophysical consultancy to exploit thermal springs near the Bering Strait settlements of Lorino and Lavrentiia for heating and vegetable growing. In Canada's Northwest Territories, he found an engineering company with expertise in building for the extreme north and handed it contracts to erect new schools in many of Chukotka's remote villages. He contracted a Ukrainian ICBM missile plant to build wind turbines and brought MDM Bank to the okrug to introduce debit cards and cashless pay systems for reindeer herders. Of course, a fascination with foreign technology is a perennial mainstay of Russian and Soviet campaigns of catching up. Even under the Bolsheviks, the technological prowess of the industrialized West was celebrated. Stalin imported expertise, machinery, principles of management, urban design, and even technologies of hygiene in service of the forced march to industrial modernity (Kotkin 1995).

In a traditional Russian campaign of catching up, if the technologies of modernity are harnessed to compress development timeframes, the notion of compression is conceivable only if time itself becomes a flexible resource. Human capacities must be stretched in such a way that month-long tasks are accomplished in a week. The ostensibly rational practice of the Soviet Five-Year Plan did not in fact sanctify the measured, rationalized use of time, but instead created a framework within which production goals were forever indexed to impossibly short time-windows. Reflecting on the nature of the post-Soviet inheritance, Ken Jowitt (1992, 291) remarked, "Leninist parties ... were overwhelmingly concerned with targets and outcomes, with ends, not means; and they acted in a storming-heroic manner to achieve them. What no Leninist regime ever did was create a culture of impersonal measured action. The result is an Eastern European population more familiar with sharp disjunctions between periods of intense action and passivity than with what Weber termed 'methodical rational acquisition.'"

In other words, the experience of the Soviet factory floor *reinforced* a particularly uneven pattern of production, which Stephen Kotkin (1995) has compared to peasant traditions of work.[28] The hortatory language pervading the socialist workplace encouraged disdain for routine. "Storming" production schedules, racing to over-fulfill the norm or out-produce the neighbouring work collective, became part of a normalized pattern of work. Indeed, Moshe Lewin (quoted in Kotkin

1995, 5) argued that the "peculiar jerky rhythms, a tendency toward frenzied immoderation, and an in-built sense of permanent crisis" were the very defining features of Soviet-style "modernization."

In pace, just as in its technological obsessions, Abramovich's modernizing program followed the storming tradition. Life in Chukotka was to be transformed within the period of a single five-year gubernatorial term (2001-5).[29] Not only was the modernization compressed within a finite window, but also, the spectacular level of investment Abramovich brought to the region crowded the available five years with an impossible volume of projects and reforms. Yet time, and in particular "northern time," could not be bent to suit the plan. Investment, however massive, could not alone defeat the myriad fixed obstacles that modernizers met in Chukotka. In the first year, specialists imported to Anadyr lacked even living space: senior officials shared bare, salvaged flats. Abramovich had a prefabricated house flown to Anadyr from Canada to serve as the governor's residence. The Canadian company contracted to build new infrastructure in Anadyr and more remote settlements spent all of 2001 simply establishing a local office and assembling building materials shipped from Vancouver.[30] A Turkish company given a much larger set of contracts to rebuild Anadyr managed only to establish a base for its twelve hundred imported labourers by summer 2002. Unexpected (but from a local point of view, inevitable) delays created a problem of chronically slipping deadlines. The Turks were to have repaved and landscaped Anadyr's streets by the end of the 2002 construction season, but they began work only in September, with the first snows falling. Flying to Anadyr to begin fieldwork, I met a twenty-three-year-old Muscovite supervising the renovation of Anadyr's Poliarnyi cinema, which she promised would be complete within a month. It opened seven months later.

The pace of activity arose not only from the desperate need to accomplish a revolution in five years, but also because those tasked with its execution were based na materike. This had the effect of fragmenting working life into a series of short, overlapping work campaigns, as modernizers came and went. Because their homes and friends were located elsewhere, they treated the North purely as a zone of work. Periods of intense effort coincided with the presence of department heads and other key outsiders, a rhythm of life that naturally penetrated to the local domain via the resident workers attached to modernizing institutions.[31] Locals within the administration and its affiliated structures found that, when their superiors were in Chukotka, all time belonged to the office. I occasionally called at the Red Cross, whose director and senior staff commuted from Moscow for two- or three-week periods. When they were present, the local staff would be in the office from morning until the early hours of the next day, some even sleeping on the floor at night, their eyes permanently bloodshot and vacant. These periods were so exhausting that, with the director's departure, the office would be abandoned for days as local staff returned to their families and recovered at home. A regular and delimited working day, particularly for the modernizers themselves, was anathema to the patterns of the campaign: to fulfill Abramovich's norms, private time was banished. Administration staff, always sporting expensive mobile phones, would be called away late in a social evening to attend to pressing matters elsewhere. The modernization likewise expected "stormlike" dedication from its foreign contractees: the Turks who were responsible for Anadyr's reconstruction worked in revolving shifts around the clock, even in the dark Arctic winter. Canadian carpenters were on a seventy- to eighty-hour working week, over shifts lasting four or even six months.

Despite the chronic slippage of impossible deadlines and the perversely poor results of so much rushed work, there was logic in the frantic pace Abramovich's modernizers set. Every revolution fears its Thermidor, and so any program of radical change must very quickly produce results and, on the basis of them, entrench the belief in a successful transformation. Ironically, as Abramovich's first term drew to an end in 2005, it became clear that his komanda was desperately trying to forestall a reaction, one that threatened to come not from Chukotka's electorate, but rather, from Moscow (a theme discussed in the concluding chapter). But if the storming tradition in the history of Russian "development" perennially produces less than promised, this too is a factor in the steady persistence of this kind of work. As Joseph Brodsky examined to great effect in *Less Than One* (1986), the dismal results of any "storm attack" on a failing plan create such conditions of deficiency that only another campaign of desperate catching up can be the remedy. This may not have been Abramovich's conscious intention, but his own plan played out on a territory already witness to a century of storming attacks, and it too promised to leave so much undone that future ones were already in sight.

Kul'tura: Modernization as Imperial Acculturation

In 1963, when Anadyr was still a town of two-story wooden barracks crowding along the mouth of Kazachka Creek, a new House of Culture (Dom kul'tury) was built high above, on one side of a new city square it would soon share with the Party headquarters, the post office, and Chukotka's largest department store. "Cultural work" had from the beginning of Soviet power been a critical thrust of the settler presence in the okrug. A network of culture bases (*kul'tbazy*), where Russians taught reading and hygiene, and promoted Soviet ideology, spread throughout Chukotka in the decades preceding industrialization and the collectivization of herding and hunting. Anadyr's new Dom kul'tury was the ultimate symbol of Soviet acculturation and a space in which the burgeoning migrant population could rehearse elements of a "cultured life." For almost forty years, this building played a vital role in animating the settler community, hosting myriad hobby groups, musical ensembles, social events, and special celebrations. In January 2001, soon after his inauguration in the Dom kul'tury, one of Governor Abramovich's first acts was to order its demolition. In its place, towering over the Gulf of Anadyr, rose a new Turkish-built Multi-use Cultural Centre constructed in the form of a sleeping polar bear. This building, much larger and more comfortable than the old Dom kul'tury, was only one of many new facilities in Anadyr (karaoke bars and brew pubs, fitness centres and spas, internet cafés and espresso bars) through which Abramovich's administration planned to redefine the "cultured" life.

Russia's campaigns of catching up have always been as much cultural as economic or geo-political projects, driven by the desire of its privileged classes to civilize and acculturate. In this tradition, the urgency and profligacy of Abramovich's program betrayed an urbanite anxiety about the parochialism of Chukotka's rural-provincial compatriots: the old settler-modernizers, along with their indigenous counterparts, had fallen behind. The impulse to remake the peasant, the worker, or the native in the image of the middle classes is consistent with past modernizations in Russia's history. All were processes of intentional and directed *cultural diffusion,* initiated by a socio-economic elite and codified in programs of "cultured" behaviour for the provincial masses.[32] Any deliberate project of cultural diffusion requires that targeted peoples be relegated to a "primitive" rung on an evolutionary ladder, so that their ways of life (usually reflecting long-term adaptation on a particular landscape) are converted into modes of backwardness. In a critique drawn from South Asia, the anthropologist Piers Vitebsky (1993) argues that, in the post-colonial age, Western or imperial civilizations have redrawn their conquest programs by applying them within frameworks of development assistance. Despite this relabelling, the violence visited on local knowledge by development and modernization projects remains as characteristic of the process as during the colonial era. According to Vitebsky (1993, 107, 108), if any knowledge system that is exported beyond its sociocultural boundaries is to survive, it must be treated as a universalizing truth and perforce mutates into a kind of intolerant intellectual totalitarianism. He adds that "The very nature of 'development' is to declare an essence in someone else, in order to end their previous state of knowledge by transmuting it into ignorance." This was the manoeuvre Soviet settlers performed in "civilizing" Chukotka's natives, and it returned as a vital logic for Abramovich's cultural modernization.

Campaigns of cultural enlightenment are part of a long Russian tradition. In the era of Russia's Great Reforms (1861-1904), a missionary intention arose among the urban middle and upper classes to bring education and culture to the newly emancipated rural peasant majority, materializing in the *zemstvo* schools and their liberal teachers.[33] Their idealism aside, this process played its role in Russia's rapid military and industrial awakening, for St. Petersburg recognized that the strength of Western European nation-states was now built on the discipline and literacy of its working classes. Rural enlightenment became a means of increasing the utility of rural people for the nascent industrial economy, a process that competed with the interests of community life and local knowledge resident in the village by, for example, driving the process of urbanization. Vitebsky's mode of totalitarian knowledge was, in the context of the Great Reforms, a package of essential and reduced cultural attributes – a set of behaviours appropriate for an industrial working population. For the first time, it became possible to speak of kul'tura and its derivatives kul'turnyi and kul'turnost', and of *kul'turnaia rabota* (literally, cultured work) undertaken by professional *kul'turniki.* Because these concepts originated within a context of philosophical debate informed by Victorian-era notions of discipline of the body, and were subsequently packaged for proselytizing purposes by a missionary liberal elite, kul'tura came to possess a reified, objective quality. As Vadim Volkov (1999, 212) observes, kul'tura became "a kind of value that could be accumulated, purposefully transferred to and acquired by wider groups of the population." Culture as a ready-made package naturally matches the paradigms of contemporary development, an increasingly uniform set of orthodoxies in which the replicability of models across social contexts is taken for granted.

Just as with Russia's earlier modernizing projects, Abramovich's technological and managerial aspirations in Chukotka were contingent on the successful penetration of metropolitan post-Soviet cultural forms into the local domain. Necessary comportment – discipline and self-restraint, literacy and hygiene, the cultivation of modern tastes and habits of consumption – was as important for this modernization as for the newly emancipated serf after 1861. If Michel Foucault's description of "bio-power" – the Western European shift toward forms of control over the body and the suppression of sexual and other forms of natural abandon in the interests of industrial production – is germane to the transformation of the Russian serf, the parallels are irresistible with the Stalinist project to create *homo sovieticus.* During Soviet industrialization, moving the peasant to newly constructed factories relied on his acculturation to routine work schedules, controlled forms of relaxation *(otdykh),* and new habits of the body: sobriety, cleanliness, and presentability. Hygiene was explicitly linked to efficiency; one slogan of the Stalin-era shop floor read, "The white collar and the clean shirt are the necessary working instruments providing for the fulfilment of production plans and the quality of products" (quoted in Volkov 1999, 219). In the Russian context, we can substitute the project of sobriety for Foucault's repression of sexual freedom (the Repressive Hypothesis). As Stephen Kotkin (1995) described in his portrait of Magnitogorsk in the 1930s, authorities worked tirelessly (and ineffectively) to replace the bottle with board games, books, and circuses. In the terminology of the time, an insufficiency of kul'tura *(beskul'tur'e)* was the enemy of the plan.

In Abramovich's time, the beskul'tur'e prevailing in Chukotka's settlements was similarly named and targeted as modernization's most dangerous enemy. In a 23 May 2002 statement to the national newspaper *Argumenty i fakty,* Abramovich's cousin Ida Ruchina, director of the Red Cross, lamented, "People in Chukotka's settlements can be divided into two groups: the drinkers and the binge drinkers. The average resident of the okrug consumes fifteen litres of pure alcohol a year!" Via the state-controlled media, the administration continually admonished the local population's purported fondness for drink. In his annual address to the okrug, Abramovich (2002, 3) declared:

> As long as people don't take responsibility for their lives and the lives of their neighbours, all the efforts of the government will be for naught. Here is a sample appeal received on the administration hotline: "When is this chaos *[bardak]* going to end? Can someone establish some sense of order? Every time the guys at public works get paid, every one of them gets dead drunk – from the boiler stoker to the chief. They stoke the boiler if it occurs to them, and the heating station is often locked up for days at a time. The apartments freeze, the kindergarten freezes. Please take measures! Can't you do something so that there were in the key posts, if not teetotallers, at least moderate drinkers?!"

In order to instill techniques of discipline, Abramovich's cultural commissars preached in Victorian terms of *zdorovyi obraz zhizni* (a healthy lifestyle) and the necessity of "lifting up rural residents" and "raising the general level of culture." Opening a broad front in the war for cultural refinement, Abramovich's youngest deputy governor, Sergei Kapkov, administered a program of bringing *kul'turnye* forms of entertainment to Chukotka. Faced with a project of cultural refashioning, he and his lieutenants concentrated their efforts on the young. This might have been a reflection of the youth of modernizers themselves. Certainly, the desire to remake the young arose in part from the conviction that, once Chukotka was normalized (developed), its administration could be safely entrusted to a local generation of post-Soviet youth. But incoming specialists were distraught at the high levels of youth unemployment and the culture of heavy drinking and teenage pregnancy. One recalled her first impressions of Anadyr in 2001: "In the settlements and even here in Anadyr, youth could only huddle in vestibules, drink themselves to oblivion. There were no opportunities to occupy themselves in a cultured fashion *(kul'turno otdokhnut')*" [40].

Abramovich therefore empowered his cultural commissars to occupy the young in constructive and improving ways. Much of the new building in Anadyr was clearly intended to create the right environment. The old Dvorets pionerov (Palace of Pioneers) was completely renovated, Anadyr's old Dom kul'tury (House of Culture) was demolished and in 2005 the massive Multi-use Cultural Centre had risen in its place. The renovated Poliarnyi, the most technically advanced cinema in the Russian North, also housed a café serving espresso and ice cream (but not alcohol), a deliberately *kul'turnoe* environment, according to the deputy governor and culture minister Kapkov. In my experience, the traditional social life of Anadyr's young adults revolved around drinking parties in private flats, which, in the brief summer, would pour into the streets and often degenerate into a highly visible bacchanal of brawling, vomiting, and sleeping it off under the midnight sun. Hoping to create a more restrained culture of drinking, Kapkov supervised the construction of a luxurious entertainment centre in the carcass of the main Soviet department store.[34] Instead of drinking in apartment-building stairwells, locals could now lounge in the mock-timber-frame brew pub before moving to the billiards hall and its twenty tables, perhaps ending the evening in the mini-casino on the top floor. Sport was also intended to engage the young on a mass scale, and by 2005, an all-weather ice rink, a renovated gymnasium, a fitness centre, and a health spa had opened. Kapkov also funded a revolving cycle of sports tournaments held throughout the okrug, including traditional Arctic Winter Games events, ending in the Governor's Cup. Chukotka's participation in the circumpolar Arctic Winter Games for the first time in 2002 became a symbol of the renaissance in youth culture.

More than any other of Kapkov's initiatives, the new radio station – Purga (arctic blizzard) – reached farthest across Chukotka's territory and most deeply penetrated youth consciousness, becoming a touchstone of modernizing kul'tura. Maiak, the established state radio station, broadcast a mixture of indigenous and Russian-language programs appealing to a mostly older, Soviet-generation audience. Purga, on the other hand, was run by a team of under-30s poached from commercial stations in Nizhni Novgorod, who created a sound-saturated, music-heavy, flippantly youth-oriented style appealing to young listeners. Purga brought school-age locals into the studio to produce programs themselves, fused indigenous melodies and throat-singing with electronic compositions for its signature jingles, and broadcast phone-in shows such as *Pozdravliaem!* (Congratulations) to involve the listeners. In contrast with the staid tenor of state-controlled Maiak, Purga program hosts used colourful language ("they curse on air!" older locals reported) and touched on topics such as sex and contraception. It was a wild success with its chosen cohort (and indeed beyond it). In the queue at the egg shop, I overheard a young woman say to a friend, "She just doesn't go out with her friends these days, all she does is lie in bed listening to Purga – all day and all night!" A new sense of youth identity seemed to coalesce around the radio station, affording teenagers and young adults a virtual community of belonging, the elements of which were youth, geography (Purga was *Chukotka's* station), and a sense of membership in a new way of life imported from Russia's big cities.

Nevertheless, a yawning line of fracture inevitably opened up between the newest modernizing population and many older members of the established settler community on the question of kul'tura. This was a conflict of generations, of Soviet versus post-Soviet versions of leisure and entertainment, but it also betrayed older settlers' indignation that their modes of civilized life – the daily language of their own modernizing campaign – were now in question. Certainly, what modernizer outsiders, and foremost Abramovich, considered proper forms of kul'tura were more consumerist and less involving than those to which older locals were accustomed.[35] Modernizing forms of leisure reflected the new post-Soviet reality, which called for the rapid, obsessive pursuit of wealth and the consumption of an ever-widening array of devices and spectacles of distraction *(razvlechenie).* Among young, successful Russians such as Abramovich's recruits, the notion of "fun" – a quality of ecstatic non-productivity evoked in the Russian term *obol'det'* – had overtaken the traditional Soviet-Russian idea of recreation as either resting and recouping or engaging in self-improving forms of leisure activity.[36] During my fieldwork in Chukotka, the perspective on kul'tura as "fun" was particularly evident in two events organized and paid for by the governor. Under the new administration, the annual fishing derby – Korfest (smelt-fest) – became a full-service carnival on the Gulf of Anadyr. Kapkov's department organized open-air concerts and Abramovich gave as prizes flats, new cars, and Canadian snowmobiles. For Korfest 2002, five of Russia's top rock bands gave a concert in Anadyr's half-finished ice arena, followed by a spectacular fireworks display.[37] Later in the year, Abramovich was again in Anadyr for the annual Miss Chukotka Beauty Pageant. A team of consultants from Moscow drilled twenty-five finalists, all teenage girls from Chukotka's settlements, in the necessary techniques required of "cultured" women: dance, public speaking, and physical poise (learning to walk in stiletto heels was an accomplishment for teenage girls raised in rubber boots). In the renovated cinema, this cast of bedazzled girls performed with the support of Miss Omsk, Miss Petersburg, and Miss Nizhni Novgorod, two wildly popular Russian pop groups, and the pageant hosts – two Moscow television celebrities. A post-pageant concert in the ice arena included Russia's two biggest rock groups, Mashina vremeni and Voskresenie.[38]

This brand of spectacle was new to Anadyr. Close proximity with Russia's pop-culture elite gave locals the unreal sensation of having shifted from the utter periphery of Russia's geography and attention during the Nazarov era to the very centre. Residents of Anadyr, a town of only ten thousand on the Bering Sea, were now reading about life in their okrug in the national papers. Abramovich had promised to make local standards of life "acceptable," but this felt positively otherworldly. That was the point, for what Abramovich and his komanda were in fact talking about was a project of making life in Chukotka recognizable to themselves, not of enriching or elaborating on what already existed. Standing in the arena a few feet from the stage where Mashina vremeni were performing (their rock ballads of the 1990s were the musical essence of that decade for many Russians), I could glance over my shoulder to see Abramovich mouthing the lyrics. This was his show and local Anadyr residents were his private guests; we had been invited into his domestic world, and we were sharing in his personal idea of normality.

The most intensive and intrusive policies of remaking local youth emanated from a triad of modernizing bodies directly involved in reorganizing the lives of teenagers and children in Chukotka: the first was the Department of Education; the other two, Pole of Hope (Polius Nadezhdy) and the Chukotka branch of the Russian Red Cross, were the governor's charities. All three were administered by women with close (in one case filial) links to Abramovich, and their programs were generously funded.[39] The Red Cross launched a series of initiatives under the catch-all doctrine of zdorovyi obraz zhizni (healthy lifestyle). In Anadyr, no-smoking discos serving milk drinks, summer camp brigades picking up litter from the tundra, and mountain-biking clubs all made an appearance. Because living conditions in the indigenous settlements were considered particularly dire, and because in modernizers' eyes their residents were Chukotka's true (permanent) population, the Red Cross aspired to achieve "rural uplift." It aimed to send pairs of coordinators (mostly young graduates from Omsk) into every village in Chukotka to combat alcoholism, unemployment, and boredom by organizing cultural activities. A first attempt to distract indigenous villagers from idleness and intoxication was proposed in 2002: a "park of health" would be established in Taivaivaam, a mainly indigenous settlement on the site of a closed state farm adjacent to Anadyr. On 27 March 2002, Red Cross director Ida Ruchina explained her plans to a meeting of bemused villagers in Taivaivaam's public hall *(klub):*

> We've come up with an idea together with the Mayor and the Department of Culture (Kapkov) to create a "*park zdorov'ia*." The idea is a response to the lack of places where people can go and enjoy nature. The park will be 22 kilometres from the city, a place where you don't throw bottles and garbage on the ground, where you can *kul'turno otdokhnut'* (relax in a cultured way), listen to outdoor concerts, ride special BMX bikes, and spend time with your families. The area will be alcohol free. We are creating opportunities for people to fill their time, so they have more to do than just get drunk.

Few of Ruchina's bold plans for cultural enlightenment materialized: the organization and its almost exclusively imported staff met intractable resistance in Taivaivaam and other rural settlements. Red Cross outreach workers found themselves locked out of local networks in the villages. Their failures, to which we will return in Chapter 7, were partly the result of their inexperience and fantastic cultural and experiential distance from their missionary setting. The notion that indigenous people in Taivaivaam lacked places to enjoy nature, for example, was a rather idiotic presumption, given the settlement's location in a vast tundra landscape on the banks of the Bering Sea. Indeed, one of the villagers' principal objections to the idea was that in the summer season, everyone would be too busy fishing for salmon and picking berries and mushrooms on the tundra to attend the "nature park."

Ida Ruchina tried, and usually failed, to create spaces of control, where public behaviour would be regulated, made kult'turno. The ambition to separate local people, and particularly the young, from their unregulated home (and tundra) environments and direct them through acculturating institutions was implemented with much greater efficiency by the Department of Education and the charity Pole of Hope. In 2000 (during the gubernatorial campaign), they began organizing structured summer holidays in central Russia for the majority of Chukotka's school-age children. This was originally an improvised program of Black Sea holidays for children, to relieve them from grinding poverty and enforced immobility in Chukotka's settlements. But, by 2002, the department had constructed a comprehensive plan to fulfill Abramovich's dictate that "all children in Chukotka will be organized throughout the summer season."[40] They proposed that every schoolchild be subjected to "year-round programs of labour, development, rest, and recovery," and reported that "our children now go on directed holidays, where even in the context of leisure, they will exist within a continuous pedagogical and acculturative space."[41]

Four thousand children travelled to summer camps (formerly Soviet Pioneer Camps) in 2001, and by 2002, an annual total of 9,100 children were participating in the administration's various "structured" or "specialized" summer camps *(profil'nye lageria),* costing the okrug budget over US$7 million a year. Now renamed New Generation, these programs blanketed the young in institutional arrangements on a permanent basis, particularly in the settlements. Because many rural indigenous children continued to study in residential schools, summer programming, located in camps across central Russia, merely transferred the institutional regime to a warmer setting (which was deemed necessary for "building health" and "vitaminization"). The expansion of the role of the state in the lives of the young was a key innovation under Abramovich: the provision of education broadened to include concepts such as raising (vospitanie), socialization *(sotsializatsiia),* and realizing oneself *(realizirovat' sebia).* While all the new leisure facilities and spectacles in Anadyr were bringing "fun" to the adult population, leisure for children was becoming a much more demanding category of time. *Valiatsya bez dela* (hang out and do nothing) and *tusovatsia* (spin in the wind) – time-honoured pursuits of youth – were in danger of extinction.[42] This was entirely intended. In private conversations, specialists within the key "caring organizations," including education, explained that the effort to institutionalize young people's time grew out of the belief that the alternative environments, namely, the village and the family, were harmful. Deputy Governor Kapkov stated in a meeting with indigenous leaders that "It seems unbelievable, but local people, and particularly natives, do not demonstrate a sense of responsibility even for their own families."[43]

Within the delimited, sealed circles that modernizing incomers inhabited in Anadyr, the discourses of distrust for locals could be intoxicating. They were produced, after all, by powerful, wealthy, young, and motivated people, who located themselves in the "new Chukotka" – the imported way of life they promised to project over the territory. But outside these circles, across kitchen tables in Anadyr and the okrug's smaller settlements, the ways in which the new administration was penetrating the domestic sphere and abrogating the authority of parents and local communities created much unease. Some equated the new paternalism with patterns of pervasive institutionalization in the Soviet era, when generations of indigenous children were raised in residential schools. Many of them decried the practice of removing children from the North over the summer, at just the time when they should be experiencing the northern landscape, and in fact working usefully on it. Natives and settlers alike voiced these complaints. In doing so, they evaded the boundaries traditionally separating their communities, while pointing in solidarity to the new outsiders and their lack of local understanding.

If the modernization placed today's settlers in the same position as newcomers of the Soviet era had once placed native people, the youth of Abramovich's cadre insulated them from the irony of the situation. From their perspective, Chukotka was a zone of Soviet antiquity. Their technologies filled a vacuum. Their "cultured way of life" answered a condition of non-culture (beskul'tur'e). The "fallen-behindness" (otstalost') of local life, it seemed to them, should generate a near cargo-cult condition of receptivity to their vision of modernity. Unsurprisingly, this was not the attitude they discovered. Settlers had first to digest the astonishing realization that Abramovich's young cadre placed all locals, themselves included, in the same meta-category of otstalost'. Then, faced with a new and purportedly modern package of practices and technologies, these settlers were left to chew on the idea that they no longer controlled the discourses surrounding civilization and modernity in the North. And, as the evangels of an older (Soviet) package of civilizing change, settlers naturally recognized that, in this battle of competing cultures they had lost the connection to Russia's metropolitan heartlands that once underwrote their claim to a modern identity. Abramovich's youthful, hypermobile, and affluent "expert" forcefully impressed on settlers, particularly those living in Anadyr, the extent of their immobility and the degree to which Russia had changed while they were busy surviving on its periphery. This was a threshold experience: the arrival of yet another storming campaign of modernization illuminated for settlers their ultimately *local* position, fixed in place, and (like natives a generation earlier) left to contend with a challenge from far away to their accustomed ways of life.

7

Two Solitudes

In July 2001, six months after Abramovich's inauguration but still in the earliest stages of the modernization program, a young journalist recruited from the central Russian city of Nizhni Novgorod by Chukotka's weekly newspaper wrote an article on her first impressions. Intended for publication outside the region, this piece described Anadyr as a petrified forest, a cultural relic preserved since the Soviet period, a grey, oppressive town bearing none of the marks of capitalist dynamism increasingly familiar elsewhere in Russia. Most significantly, she described its mostly settler population as "frozen" *(zamorozhennoe)*. Unfortunately for her, and for the entire modernizing program, this article soon turned up in Chukotka and began to circulate, along with the term itself, through local networks in the capital, emerging as one of the most enduring discourses framing local attitudes to Abramovich's reforms. It may have been controversial, but her response to Chukotka and its settlers was almost universally shared by modernizing incomers, selected for their youth, their specialist skills, and precisely their *inexperience* with the prevailing realities of life outside Russia's metropolitan core.

I have described the Abramovich modernization as a classic campaign of centre-led development – a "lifting up" in emic terms – following a traditional (and deeply Russian) pattern. Within this tradition, cultural distance between the modernizer and the modernized is a constant feature, lending missionary energy to the cause of catching up. This was plainly the case with Chukotka's most recent modernization. The Five-Year Plan to bring an "acceptable way of life" to the region was simultaneously a technical-organizational and a cultural project, cultural because, like any reforming mission, it relied on a logic of local ineptitude and the attendant necessity of charitable aid. The modernizing missionary buttressed this separation by constructing Chukotkans as citizens not only of a distant place, but also of another era: artefacts of the Soviet past stranded in the present. As Johannes Fabian has observed in *Time and the Other* (1983), this manoeuvre of distancing through a denial of contemporaneity in the other, as though time stands still on the edge while moving ahead at the centre, is paradigmatic of the colonial relationship. Bruce Grant (1995) has more recently demonstrated this tactic in the relationship between Soviet-era settlers and indigenous peoples, in his ethnographic history of modernizations on Sakhalin. In the Soviet North, as in colonial settings generally, social hierarchies were organized along ethnic lines. But in this regard, Abramovich's modernization was an exception, for it set up a hierarchy of esteem that stigmatized *residence* in the North's peripheral geography, rather than ethnicity. In other words, all those whom his modernizing incomers encountered, settler and indigenous alike, bore the same identity of left-behindness; the entire region had been frozen in time.

With investment on a tremendous scale, Chukotka's modernizing administration launched Russia's poorest northern region into the ranks of the most affluent, alongside Moscow city and St. Petersburg. It gave the means to resettle to those locals who wished to leave, and it secured a vastly better standard of living for those who remained. In many senses, the modernization returned to Chukotka a level of security and affluence not seen since the Soviet era. Abramovich, or rather the companies he controlled, was paying for this prosperity, and his komanda of specialists had suspended (at least for a time) their comfortable lives in central Russia to help Chukotka along the path of change. At the very least, they expected gratitude from their local counterparts. It was understandably perplexing for them, therefore, that soon after the initial post-election euphoria receded, they began to encounter a groundswell of *ingratitude.* This was particularly the case in the capital – where the modernization played out in its most radical and concentrated forms – which was the base of operations for most of the new modernizing incomers. As local people came to understand the priorities and inclinations of the new modernizing elite, many of them quickly grasped the challenge this project posed to their own authority and way of life. The modernization in fact sparked fierce indignation, particularly among the generation of settlers who themselves once came north from Russia's metropolitan centre to civilize and modernize.[1] I now turn to the seeds of discord implicit in the modernizing challenge, by exploring the middle ground between these two (admittedly heterogeneous) communities – the new incomer and the established settler.

The modernizing project served to strongly delineate, and furthermore perpetuate, the differences between these groups, and deepen their senses of collective identity. The alienation many local settlers felt regarding a project they initially welcomed, and in fact mandated with their votes, created in the capital a condition of *two solitudes,* a characterization borrowed from the Canadian writer Hugh MacLennan (1945), which he used to evoke the mutual disregard of French and English communities in post-war Quebec.[2] Just as settlers, particularly in Anadyr, were excluded from modernizing networks and institutions, so did the middle ground become a dangerous territory, a place of ambiguous identity saturated with discourses of mutual recrimination. Members of the modernizing and local settler communities marked their collective boundaries, and as the euphoria of regime change died away and practices of network exclusion gathered momentum, the polar identities of "local" and "outsider" reshaped the social landscape. This was soon cleaved by the two parallel and irreconcilable domains of the modernizer and the local.

Although the binary separation of two solitudes purports a real social distance *between,* and a relative social unity *within,* the two communities in question, neither group was strictly homogeneous. Had I sought exclusively to inhabit the world of the modernizing cadre, and my plane of focus had fallen on the discourses and practices that might constitute an "internal" definition of its collective identity, the variance of experiences and loyalties to be found there would surely explode any notion of cultural coherence. But, as Barth (1969) and his followers (Cohen 1985; Jenkins 1994) remind us, communities at once look inward and to their boundaries, and by constructing the other they construct themselves. This is particularly true in the circumstances I found in Abramovich's Chukotka, when its established settlers were thrown into a frequently antagonistic relationship with a discrete and socially distant population of newcomers. At the risk of constructing an idea of "normal life," I believe Abramovich's modernization created exceptional circumstances: local people were being asked to alter their working practices and their habits of leisure and consumption, and, in many cases, to abandon their lives in the North. The resulting condition of two solitudes was momentary and intense, and the vivid distinctions between outsiders and insiders calmed for a time the centripetal energies within each community. For a moment, like a herd of musk ox facing a threat from without, all faces turned to meet the "other."

Discourses of Disdain as a Tactic of Separation

By importing specialists originating from within his companies and connected corporate networks, Abramovich was intentionally subordinating pre-existing power structures, particularly at the level of regional administration based in Anadyr, to outsiders embodying the values and habits of his new-model business culture. The okrug administration was transformed to resemble a branch office of Sibneft headquarters in Moscow. Its senior and middle-ranking employees shuttled between Moscow and Anadyr on chartered jets, spending two or three weeks at a time in the North. Much administration business was conducted from a suite of offices on Kursovoi pereulok in central Moscow. Administration staff, even locally based workers, were employees of Sibneft, rather than of the regional government. The resulting sense of common experience contributed to a strict separation of administration modernizers from the local community. Like officers of the British Raj, Abramovich's elite were separated from local people by vast differences in social class and cultural experience. They were outsiders whose only friends inhabited their own transient networks, a situation perpetuated by their shuttling lifestyle and the sense that Chukotka was a zone of work, whereas the rest of life remained strictly na materike. For those with young families in Moscow and Nizhni Novgorod, this was particularly true. The modernizing institutions, particularly the okrug administration, were further removed from the local setting because they worked on Moscow time – phones went unanswered until early afternoon and business shifted into gear only when the mother office in Moscow opened at 5:00 p.m. Shuttling staffers' working and domestic lives were both suspended and insulated from everyday contact with the local domain: they did not shop for food, live in proximity to local people, or even move through local working spaces on a routine basis. They were housed in prefabricated and purpose-built residences, for whom Anadyr's Turkish-run hotel provided a catering service. Chauffeured Land Cruisers and Volkswagen minibuses moved them along prescribed corridors between the administration, the town's principal restaurant, their prefabricated housing, and the heliport linking Anadyr to its airport and to Moscow beyond.

Although it naturally generated a distance of common understanding, the physical separation of local residents from Abramovich's komanda did not by itself explain the mutual resentment directed by each community toward its counterpart. The discourse of a frozen or petrified local type, first generated by an imported journalist, became emblematic of the gap in mutual sympathy. As "commissar" figures, young modernizers not only embodied the dispositions of the new capitalist Russia, they defined themselves in opposition to the values and lifestyle attributed to the Soviet past. This manoeuvre played out in many cases as disdain for older people, for the backward Russian hinterland, and for the newly apparent lower classes. Many times, new modernizers confided to me their conviction that locals, in particular the older "Soviet generations," had, as a consequence of living in Governor Nazarov's hermetically sealed society, fallen so badly behind *(otstali ot nas)* as to be of little use to the present. One young recruit expressed this problem in pedagogical terms: "We often find, as psychologists, that when we have children with special needs whom we want to remove from special classes and integrate into mainstream learning, we just can't pull it off. Once they've spent time outside the mainstream system, they can't reintegrate – they'll always be behind" [39].

Administration specialists, though socially and physically sealed within their administration communities, were nevertheless compelled to work through the local population in order to animate Abramovich's reforming goals. But contact seemed only to harden incomer attitudes and entrench the condition of two solitudes. By the time I arrived, twelve months into the modernization project, the incomers' early wide-eyed enthusiasm had given way to a vigorously circulating body of negative language on the culture of work among locals. Along with the motif of a "frozen people" *(zamorozhennye, zatormozhennye)*, the phrase "people have forgotten how to work here" *(zdes' liudi otuchilis' rabotat')* was on many lips. One senior figure in the administration conceded that, although the projects of modernization should enlist local people whenever possible, he had been "forced to accept" that the level of skill and work habits of locals fell disastrously short of his standards [43]. This became a justification for outside recruitment – a twenty-two-year-old Moscow graduate was preferable to a forty-year-old local with two decades of northern work experience. Indeed, a key modernizing tactic was to flood certain institutions seen as essential to pushing forward the transformation with outsider specialists, people both loyal to the administration and capable of producing change quickly. The okrug newspaper *Krainyi Sever* was one such institution, and journalists and managers were hired in from major papers in Nizhni Novgorod. But, according to its incomer editors, the habits of the remaining local staff nevertheless sabotaged their efforts: "Reporters here think they have the right to leave for home at 5:00 p.m., even with their stories unfinished. At home in my old newspaper office we worked until late at night as a matter of course. People don't understand how to work here – they're spoiled and lazy. People really are frozen (zamorozhennye)" [40].

Another incomer, who at twenty-two was hired to oversee the renovation of Anadyr's new cinema, complained that middle-aged local staff resisted new methods and technologies. She and other administrators described an ingrained "Soviet mindset" in locals, who combined a mistaken sense of pride in their abilities with a contempt for the tempo and technologies of the modern post-Soviet workplace. Faced with these difficulties, modernizers were empowered to spend their way to a solution and replace locals with incomers. The director of the Red Cross and her incomer deputy from Nizhni Novgorod began operations in 2001 with a locally recruited staff, including a paralegal to run a legal aid program and a culture worker to organize drug- and alcohol-free discos. Two years later, they were gone and only three locals remained in a much-expanded organization. Such conflicts between local settlers and modernizing incomers in the workplace were ubiquitous, and they pointed to a vital difference in their respective perceptions of work itself. The modernizers wanted total commitment; Abramovich's Five-Year Plan required *udarnyi trud* (shock work). Most locals, on the other hand, still understandably bore the habits of survival under Governor Nazarov, when the real work of getting by – casual labour, food gathering, participating in the economy of mutual favours – took place *outside* the workplace. They did not yet realize how thoroughly re-animated the formal workplace had become.

Within modernizing networks, discourses of disdain acted in an orientalizing manner to widen the physical separation between newcomers and locals, and to reinforce the top-down logic of the modernization campaign. As Abramovich's cadre first imagined and then fixed in language the deficiencies of the settler, they inscribed on their local counterparts a state of ignorance only the metropolitan expert could counteract. This naming practice duplicated the postures of an earlier era, when Soviet settlers themselves justified the colonization of Chukotka by naming it a primitive frontier. For the northern migrant of the Soviet era, according to Nikolai Ssorin-Chaikov (2003), the indigenous domain was subject to a "technology of signification" that reduced its peoples to a Hobbesian State of Nature – a condition of internecine chaos requiring the intervention of a higher political agency, the *Leviathan*. Projects of colonial administration inevitably rest upon such discursive frameworks, which have in the past excused forms of apartheid-like racial separation and social hierarchy by labelling the local as "lazy, shiftless, cruel, playful, naïve, dissolute, duplicitous, incapable of abstract thought, impulsive, etc" (Alatas 1977, 112). The discourse of laziness of course provides an entry point for modernization, and like other categorizations of this kind ("efficient," "hard-working," or, conversely, "out of date"), it conceals the power relations lying under the surface of any project of imposed development.

In naming yesterday's incomer-experts as frozen, modernizing newcomers were of course setting up an opposite category – the identity of mobile and progressive expert. If the modernization was a neo-colonial exercise, best understood in terms of antagonistic socio-economic classes, it must be said that social classes remained still-nascent categories in post-Soviet society. I have already observed that the young and newly affluent beneficiaries of market dynamism in Russia's biggest cities inhabit a fluctuating identity; they are a parvenu social formation still unsure of how best to define their position in the emerging class society. Indeed, many of the young Muscovite *eksperty* hired to manage Chukotka's modernization were new arrivals to privilege, having, through some combination of luck and merit, vaulted out of grinding post-Soviet hardship in the 1990s to positions within Abramovich's extremely powerful circle of oligarchic associates. If the practice of conspicuous consumption in Moscow helped to reinforce their new social distance from the ordinary Russian, so too did the exercise of power within this modernization project. Many of Abramovich's cadre were yet unaccustomed to their identities as modern experts, and so, if naming practices set up a discursive framework placing the conflicting moralities of mobility and rootedness into opposition, this simply reflected the fragility and uncertainty of the modernizers' own self-perceptions. They were newcomers in more ways than one.

Network and Nepotism: Everything New Is Old Again

The extent to which the Abramovich modernization followed a pattern deeply ingrained in Russian cultural practice, and thus revealed traditionalist impulses just as it mouthed a revolutionary rhetoric, was abundantly clear in the nepotistic instincts of its representatives. As a twenty-three-year-old assistant to the director of public relations in Abramovich's administration, Yulia[3] was precisely the kind of dynamic and skilled local whom the reforming komanda might have hoped to leave in place to order the "new Chukotka." The generational gulf was evident in her own settler family: her father had been deputy director of a series of reindeer-herding sovkhozy, but during the Nazarov-era crisis in agriculture, he descended into alcoholism. Her mother was a bookkeeper for a local military regiment, but expected to lose her job as a consequence of further demobilization in the okrug. They both planned to resettle to Smolensk Oblast to live on their state pensions.

Yulia, who was born in Anadyr, graduated from School No. 1 in 1997 but was unable to continue studies on the materik when the 1998 currency crisis wiped out her family's savings. Returning to the North, she finished a degree in finance and auditing by correspondence before joining the new okrug administration in the months after Abramovich's election. She was one of a small group of locals working there, most of whom were young graduates with rare skills such as English fluency or a legal education.

When we first met, Yulia was clearly luxuriating in her environment, which was so patently different from a typical office in Anadyr. Her colleagues were young, energetic, well educated, and they came from the big cities in which she still aspired to live and study. She made a lot of money by local standards: $550 a month. And she had access to the closed world in which her incomer colleagues lived: she could go to the karaoke bar, occasionally use a chauffeured Land Cruiser on business, and fly to Moscow on the administration charter for holidays. Yet, Yulia was constantly reminded that she never fully inhabited this world. She invited me to come along to an office BBQ (shashliki), but then called at the last minute to say her colleagues had changed their plans without telling her. In mid-2002, a deputy governor celebrated his birthday in Anadyr, and Yulia spent two days compiling the guest list, preparing and sending invitations, arranging presents and tribute cards, and planning the banquet. Then she realized that although all the Muscovite and Nizhni staff in her office were going, she wasn't invited. She called another local she knew in the administration, and learned he wasn't either. When she first came into the administration, Yulia hoped that it might be a stepping stone to a job in Moscow, perhaps in Sibneft headquarters, but after a year, she saw invisible barriers isolating her from the incomer networks around her.

In the end, Yulia was fired. Taking the Sibneft charter to Moscow for her first summer holiday, she followed the example of her colleagues and took advantage of the free service to send a microwave, some crockery, and a hi-fi back to Anadyr. This was common practice for anyone with access to the regular flights, a key perquisite, since Chukotka's consumer goods prices are the highest in Russia. On her return, however, Yulia's director (Deputy Governor Sergei Kapkov) sacked her without ceremony. A week later, she started work with the okrug Tax Inspection (a settler-dominated institution) in a well-paid and responsible job, but she was nevertheless despondent at having been ejected from "the very centre," where she "always knew what was happening in Chukotka before anyone else." The experience of rejection also reshaped her allegiances; now she turned toward planning a life in Anadyr, rather than striving to leave, and by late 2003, she had bought herself a local apartment.

Yulia's is only one illustration of an Icarus pattern I often observed, in which local residents navigated toward administrative and reforming circles, coming to perceive themselves as integral modernizers before ultimately meeting with rejection. For a time, all of them suffered from mistaken hubris, believing their skills and enthusiasm qualified them for a place within the core modernizing community. In the same year, I interviewed the daughter of a Russian settler to Anadyr, who knew others like Yulia. She commented, "These specialists are always flying in and out, while they exploit our own kids like garbage. I have a friend – local – who works [in the administration] and he's there until 1:00 a.m. most of the time. He never gets time off. They take his weekends, his evenings. They take our locals, squeeze them dry like lemons, and throw them away" [47].

The same year, I spent an evening at the Anadyr Restaurant with a party of administration incomers, one of whom, a Muscovite specialist in auditing and finance, was celebrating her twenty-third birthday. A line of shining black Land Cruisers idled in the arctic winter night outside, while I sat at a table with two deputy governors and a few department heads, not one of whom was older than thirty. To my right sat a young history graduate from Omsk, just arrived in Anadyr, responsible for engineering oversight on Anadyr's many new construction projects – until coming north, he worked as a copy-editor for a newspaper. I had a conversation in English with the birthday girl about getting into the London Business School and shared opinions on ski resorts in the Alps with the deputy governor and culture minister Kapkov, three years younger than me. The only grey hair at the party belonged to two other foreigners – construction engineers from Istanbul. On my way out, I stopped for my coat at the wardrobe and struck up a conversation with a dour woman behind the counter. A Russian from the Urals, she came to Chukotka in 1964 as a highly trained geologist and led prospecting expeditions, never marrying because of the demands of the job but eventually rising to the highest ranks of the geological profession. When the Ekspeditsiia was dissolved during the crisis, she lost her job but stayed in Anadyr; she had no relatives outside Chukotka, and after three decades, the North felt like home.

The image of a grey-haired doctor of geology hanging coats for Chukotka's young elite neatly evokes the manner in which the Abramovich modernization was not only a material transformation of place, but was also a process of replacing people. The transition to "modernity" implied a shift of power from hands tainted by Soviet experience to those of Abramovich's own generation. This process of replacement followed a diffusionist doctrine, which the North had seen before. In the Soviet period, the waves of young specialists sent to Chukotka were charged just as deeply with a sense of colonial agency as the contemporary modernizers whose coats hung in the Anadyr Restaurant. Indeed, just as settlers were lately objectified as the embodiment of a dysfunctional social order, whose Soviet mentality precluded their active participation in the new Chukotka, so had those very settlers deployed the same tactics of representation against local (indigenous) people a few decades earlier. I once raised the question of frozen, petrified locals with a Yup'ik elder in Anadyr, and she laughed with evident glee: "Frozen! That's what newcomers *(priezzhie)* used to call us natives. Now they'll just have to swallow the same pill!" [46].

Why could the old vessels of Soviet modernity – the industrial settlers of an earlier era – not be recycled to carry forward a new wave of centre-led change in the North? Russia's geography of expertise and capital, polarized between nodes of the modern and traditional, the urban and the rural, has always been accompanied by an interpretation of modernity as an *embodied* quality. With the diffusion of metropolitan technologies and knowledge systems to the northern periphery came people holding the skills to exploit them. Natives, settlers, and modernizing incomers alike talked unambiguously of the *priezzhii* (newcomer) as a necessary instrument of change and innovation throughout northern history. This implied that without the movement of bodies from the metropolitan centre, progress is impossible. In the rural setting, Soviet newcomers became drivers, mechanics, veterinarians, and sovkhoz managers, whereas herders were forever herders. Patty Gray (2000) remarked on this arrangement as evidence of an "ethnic division of labour" in Chukotka, a feature that, in her opinion, marked the region as a kind of "internal colony." Although both Soviet and post-Soviet development doctrines have officially mandated the acculturation of local people with modern (metropolitan) skills and knowledge, in practice, incomers have always preserved a monopoly on the means of modernity. Even as new ways and ideas diffused from the metropolitan core to native and peripheral peoples, newcomers remained the medium through which successive waves of modern practice were delivered.

The idea of embodied modernity and traditionality reflects a rigid logic of status, in which the adult, once branded by a certain era, becomes incapable of change. Just as in the early years of Soviet power, when insufficiently proletarian class origins forever disqualified a citizen from assuming a leading place in the new socialist society, in the present era, Soviet generations cannot substantiate post-Soviet renewal; they must be replaced, or at the least radically subordinated to young, modern reformers. Yet, this interpretation of change placed the very efficacy of the Abramovich modernization, such as it was, in question. The modernization was, after all, a momentary campaign, to be implemented by outsiders, intended to change the culture of the local community yet built on the idea of the modernizing agent's rapid departure. Abramovich could recruit an army of outsiders, each an embodiment of a technologically and managerially "modern" domain, as long as he paid to maintain their cosmopolitan lifestyle, installing fitness gyms and karaoke bars in Anadyr and providing regular charter flights to Moscow. However, though Soviet settlers before them had been asked to stay in place, Abramovich couldn't follow suit: the North was no longer the zone of relative privilege it had been a generation before. Given the ephemeral quality of this project, what then did it hope to achieve? One possibility is that a sustainable arrangement, in which a truly "modernized" (or "acceptable") way of life was installed in Chukotka, was never really intended. Perhaps the *practice of modernizing,* of entering into a relationship of "development" and thereby establishing a monopoly on the modern identity, was the true reward for Abramovich's new arrivals.

We should not lose sight of the immense opportunities for professional and social advancement afforded to Abramovich's recruits: for them, the modernization was a vast machine for manufacturing privilege. Using the opportunity to climb into stratospheric heights of wealth and influence within Russia's oligarchic political economy was at the very least an important part of the game. The ways in which these incomers monopolized the modernizing identity, excluding locals such as Yulia from administrative circles and effectively replacing an older generation of experts, should be understood in this light. These episodes serve as evidence of the enduring framework of patronage systems and competitive networks within which the modernizing project was firmly set. As the modernization played out, with the influx of specialist labour into Chukotka's tightly knit communities, it became increasingly clear that underpinning the separation of the two solitudes was a struggle for power between outsider and local, a struggle particularly acute in the capital. Chukotka's cellular structure of internally loyal networks remained in place after Nazarov's departure. Modernization in turn led to an influx of new networks. But these, for the local, were almost unbreachable; they were the product of patronage relations over which locals had very little leverage. It was for this reason that many of the projects of modernization that might initially have seemed logical areas of collaboration with local counterparts actually took on a totalizing and paternalistic character. Solutions were delivered into local settings from a great distance, without involving locals. And in many cases, these solutions, although immensely expensive and breathtakingly modern in appearance, competed in damaging ways with pre-existing local initiatives that had grown organically over time.

Abramovich seemed initially to desire a reformation rather than a revolution, hoping to work through administrative structures in place at the time of his election. At his inaugural banquet in early 2001, he promised, "There will be no dismissals; everyone will stay in place and work conscientiously" ("Chukotskii Renessans" 2001). In the following months, only the head of the health service and senior bureaucrats in the education department were removed. But by mid-2001, his inner circle began to favour the idea of importing into regional administration large numbers of specialists from within his own (corporate) institutions, people whose loyalty and effectiveness would be guaranteed. On Abramovich's recommendation, a new law on government was passed, which abolished all existing departments, committees, and divisions, and created four new super-departments, three of which were led by his close associates Andrei Gorodilov, Irina Panchenko, and Sergei Kapkov.[4] This "strengthened the vertical" and concentrated budgetary powers within structures over which Abramovich maintained direct control, while depriving local bureaucrats of the patronage powers of spending they possessed under Governor Nazarov. As this process culminated in a direct administrative role for key komanda figures, they in turn recruited large numbers of lower-level specialists from within their home networks outside the North. Despite an official policy of hiring local people and working within existing structures, incomer recruits flooded into administrative structures in Anadyr. The discourses of disdain for the local and the principle of generational replacement simply buttressed what was essentially patronage unleashed, by justifying the exclusion of locals on grounds of incompetence. The new Sibneft may have cultivated the reputation of a "super-professional" organization (a transparent and accountable meritocracy), but according to sources inside the company, no hiring ever took place without a personal recommendation.

Many settlers in Anadyr hoped Abramovich's wealth and lack of northern experience would insulate his administration from the influence of local elites (in particular Nazarov's remaining allies). It came as an unpleasant surprise that the subsequent appointment of Sibneft outsiders into local power structures created a new network of influence, this one impervious, and even hostile, to local collaborations. This was ostensibly a class of "new professionals," for whom skills and merit were supposedly more meaningful than connections and blat (ideas deeply associated with Soviet life). But the habits of life within the circle (kruzhok) – of loyalty and trust within personal networks – remained enduring and determinant. This confirms Alena Ledeneva's (1998, 210) views on the post-Soviet modification of the rules of blat, particularly within entrepreneurial circles. She found that while Russian society fractured socio-economically and former blat ties were sundered, a new kind of corporatism *(korporativnost')* prevailed in business circles, which determined "whom an opportunity will be given to." For the emergent business elite, this was a key tactic of survival, for which the label of corruption is perhaps too reductive. Indeed, to label behaviour as corrupt is to elevate a certain view of the state-citizen relationship above alternative moralities that, in a Soviet or post-Soviet context, could be more germane. As Akhil Gupta (1995, 388-89) observes, "the discourse of corruption functions as a diagnostic of the state," which is to say, its meaning derives from an arrangement in which "people construct the state symbolically and define themselves as citizens." When corruption is detected and named, it represents a violation of a particular kind of civic relationship in which state agents are at least notionally *accountable* to citizens/voters/the public. Gupta's observations concern India, an established democracy in which public discourses on the state reliably generate definitions of both administrative virtue and corruption. But constructions of the state and citizenship have been altogether more fluid in Soviet and post-Soviet society; in this context, the members of the kruzhok are accountable to each other, but the state is accountable to no one. Indeed, Alexei Yurchak (2002) has observed that the Soviet experience generated "hybrid moralities," so that loyalty to friends and certain practices, which in official bureaucratic-rationalist terms might be construed as corrupt, in fact represent the moral choice.

If korporativnost' is examined ethnographically, therefore, it actually operates as a *moral* practice within a certain social terrain: namely, the rapidly stratifying conditions of Russia's new market society. As wealth has concentrated in the hands of the post-Soviet elite, the value of mixing with people outside one's spending bracket has declined, for only those in proximate social classes are likely to be useful in building a career or advancing a business interest. The post-Soviet state, after all, appears to owe its citizens nothing; the notion of state accountability has yet to stick. In fact, to all those people whom he controlled, Roman Abramovich, who occupied the highest rung of Russia's new class society,[5] represented an alternative form of statehood more accountable than the state itself. He and his young specialists (by virtue of their position close to him) knew they were exceptionally privileged and socially mobile.[6] They may have been recruited to work in Chukotka, but the networks they most valued were situated back on the materik, in Sibneft headquarters and affiliated corporate structures. Accordingly, friendships with local people in Anadyr, a remote and provincial outpost by their standards, could have little social utility.[7] A local journalist writing for *Krainyi Sever* recalled her early attempts to bridge the cultural gap: "these people do their best to avoid talking to me and everyone else who has lived here a long time. It's amazing! They make friends with each other, but they don't spend any time outside their little closed circle. I said to my boss a while ago, 'It'll be Korfest soon – why not spend a little and organize shashliki (grilled meat) for the workers?' He looked at me like I was mad – he mumbled that it might be a good idea, but I could tell he didn't want to eat in my company" [11].

It almost seemed that the members of the modernizing komanda were oblivious to their location in the geographic north; in their conception, they were located within a project that only occasionally migrated outside Moscow's Ring Road. Their journeys to Chukotka were an exotic form of business trip, and like alpinists or explorers, they operated in a completely self-sufficient, self-contained manner, bringing all they needed with them. Pavel Apletin, the editor of *Krainyi Sever*, rationalized his move to Chukotka as a brief adventure lasting no longer than Abramovich's own five-year term as governor. His assignment to transform the regional newspaper gave him the chance to rocket upwards in his profession, and so coming north, he believed, was a worthwhile short-term sacrifice. Indeed, three years after his arrival, he had managed to purchase a historic flat in central St. Petersburg and earn an entry in the Russian equivalent of *Who's Who*.[8] For his part, the administration's young director of economics and planning, a key member of the reforming komanda, characterized the modernization in Chukotka as an "apprenticeship" *(stazhirovka)* for young recruits like himself. Abramovich had given these young graduates "the opportunity to cut [their] teeth" [38] before moving on to positions of real importance in central Russia.

Had specialist recruits like these come to Chukotka for any reason other than to work in proximity to the Abramovich machine and to advance within its hierarchies, more of them might have made long-term commitments. But, unlike the agents of Soviet modernization, the most recent generation of newcomers lacked the time and the opportunities to question their modernizing ideology. Colonial experiences have often generated reflexive feelings of doubt regarding The Project, in parallel with a fascination with the local. Certain colonial regimes even devised systems to contain their agents within exclusive and insulating lifestyles as a way of combating this effect. This was the role of the colonial social club in India and other Asian colonies during the Victorian era – clubs both offered a purely European social life divorced from daily experience in Bombay and Singapore and strongly reproduced the division of the races, since the only local people within them were carrying the whisky trays. Techniques of ethnosocial distancing in colonial India bear a similarity to the patterns of separation maintaining Abramovich's newcomers, who lived in a kind of social suspension during their shifts in Chukotka. As a result, they were cut off from the kinds of local relationships that might have generated a reflexive self-regard, and this left many of them demoralized by the demands of the transient lifestyle after the initial euphoria of the modernizing campaign receded. Even as early as 2003, when Abramovich began to show signs of losing interest in Chukotka, the incomers I knew were openly talking of departure along with the rest of the Sibneft apparatus of administration.[9]

Secrecy as a Technique of Governance

Although the view from outside was of a monolithic social category exemplified for many local residents of Anadyr in glimpses of young, expensively dressed strangers behind the tinted windows of the ubiquitous black administration Land Cruisers, the modernizing community was in fact an internally competitive patronage system. Riven into cliques and gradations of influence, informants in the okrug administration only half-jokingly spoke of the administration building as a territory of competing mafias. Accompanied by an official belonging to Kapkov's Nizhni Novgorod cohort, I walked along a corridor between the building's offices. As we went, he remarked "that's Moscow in there, foreign territory ... rather too many from Omsk over there ... ah, safety, we're back in Nizhni" (as we stepped into the public relations area) [21]. Within each modernizing kruzhok (circle), the values of trust and loyalty were as paramount as the assumed fealty to Abramovich. Each network possessed its patron figures, those senior officials who first assembled the circle through nepotistic recruitment and within whose protecting embrace members hoped to advance in Abramovich's larger corporate system.

For a young deputy minister or head of department, an assignment to Chukotka was a trial with enormous stakes. In assembling the army of modernizing specialists, the use of nepotism was simply a conservative, proven means of hedging against uncertainty. Ledeneva (1998, 211) confirms the new role of blat in the emerging capitalist institution, remarking, "the whole institution of 'people of the circle' *(svoi liudi)* functions no less effectively than *blat* networks did in the Soviet era." Writing on the new entrepreneurial class, Harley Balzer (2003) reiterates the importance of personal bonds of trust as a means of mitigating risk in a volatile business environment. Balzer (2003, 20) quotes a thirty-something banker from Novosibirsk who had built up his operation to the point that he needed to open a branch in Moscow and hire Muscovites to staff it: "The hardest thing was having to hire someone I did not go to school with." Indeed, it is possible to view the persistence of blat and patronage, in these instances, as compatible with a more meritocratic (or perhaps Darwinian) post-Soviet arrangement: rather than acting as a distributive mechanism for scarce goods, the post-Soviet kruzhok had become an indispensable instrument of management, and acquaintance the most efficacious guarantee of performance.

The insularity of modernizing networks constricted the flow of information from the administration to the local population. I was particularly sensitive to the gulf between these domains because I was, as an outcome of my research methodology, constantly navigating from one to the other. I understood my position as a participant in both the lives of local residents and the world of the modernizing incomers to be insecure and liminal. As a foreigner and guest of the okrug administration, with special permission to travel freely in Chukotka, I could play my cards as an administration insider when necessary. But the difficulties I experienced in penetrating administration cliques, particularly as time passed and my connections within the resident settler community became evident, simply served to illuminate the insular protections surrounding them. It was vital to have both feet in the modernizing camp, to behave as *nash chelovek* (our man). In order to have access to the discourses of disdain about local people, or the frequent jeremiads on life in "Anadyrka" (a play on "Anadyr" and the Russian word for "hole"), one could not afterwards be seen walking across town to hear the local version. One of my best early informants on nepotistic hiring and internal politics in the administration, a modernizer who frequently shuttled to Moscow, was suddenly nervous and evasive when we ran into each other six months later. She evidently felt uncomfortable over having shared information with someone who, she subsequently came to realize, was connected within local networks and who was, furthermore, openly scrutinizing the modernization project. I often found my loyalties challenged, as when I spent an evening with incomer journalists and the discussion turned to an upcoming *Krainyi Sever* story on Avialesokhrana, the local forest-fire-fighting service with which I built a strong relationship. I was asked to concur with their assessment that the director (a friend of mine) used his official position to screen a smuggling and bootlegging operation in certain interior settlements (see Chapter 5 for details). In a similar way, my relationship with the Red Cross (a key "modernizing institution" upon which I focused my research for a time) soured when its director, a relative of the governor and a new arrival to Chukotka, learned I was also spending time with a summer camp outside Anadyr organized by local settlers.

As time passed, my own problems of access were a barometer of insularity, and it became increasingly clear that of the two communities in Anadyr – local settlers and modernizers – it was the latter that guarded its "solitude" most jealously.[10] Membership in the modernizing community appeared to imply continuous fidelity to its rules of internal loyalty; but the community of settler locals (in Anadyr) was entirely more promiscuous, and membership was more a matter of "join our kitchen table if you want – stay away and it's your loss." Here was a paradox of the two solitudes: if insularity, the "island mentality" (see F.S. Nielsen 2007), korporativnost', and the morality of the kruzhok were characteristics of *traditional* Russian social life, they actually surfaced most clearly in the ostensibly *modern* networks of Abramovich's urban cadre. The northern settler, whom they vilified as hopelessly *otstalyi* (out of date, fallen behind), in fact inhabited a more open and inclusive social landscape than theirs, one that strongly contrasted with the old Soviet "island society." Who was really modern, if modern meant the opposite of Soviet? Sibneft and Abramovich's okrug administration used the terms "transparency" and "merit-based advancement" as signatures of their modern identity, but many settlers, and in fact not a few of the modernizers themselves (in a candid moment), preferred to describe the administration culture with highly Soviet terms, including "the cult of secrecy" *(kul't tainosti)* and "nepotism" *(kumovstvo)*.

Secrecy in particular became a key feature of the komanda's style of governance, evident for example in the relations between the governor's office and the okrug Duma. On the one hand, Abramovich appeared to support a rejuvenated local democracy, building in Anadyr's centre a new home for the Duma that was more impressive than even his own okrug administration on the outskirts. On the other, the program of reform almost completely bypassed the Duma assembly, which remained (as it had been under Nazarov) a rubber-stamping body. The administration laid out its general position and plans for each coming year in the governor's annual address to the Duma, the governor's office passed projected legislation on to delegates, and a group of legal experts imported from Moscow ensured its smooth passage through Duma committees. Despite the appearance of a businesslike legislature, its image burnished by the gleaming new Duma building, delegates were unable to shape policy making. The administration and development of the okrug effectively became a private philanthropic project emanating without legislative scrutiny from the administration komanda alone. The peripheral role of elected delegates should not, perhaps, have been a surprise. After all, the entire modernization amounted to a torrent of personal gifts (whether appreciated or not) from the governor and his companies. Consequently, though budget figures were published annually, most of the line items were paid for with "extra-budgetary funds," a category over which the Duma could exercise no oversight.

However, the modernization was not purely a project of investment. It also mandated reforms, and the wholesale reorganization of the education system prompted a particularly sharp controversy. One of Abramovich's first acts was to appoint a new administration for the Department of Education, led by a personal friend from his boyhood in the Komi Republic and staffed entirely with incomers. Education had been a key domain of the civilizing mission in Soviet-era Chukotka, and it remained so in this modernization, a project assigned to the most trustworthy and expert of the komanda. The Montessori method was introduced for preschoolers, new teachers were recruited from the materik with generous incentive packages (although existing teachers' salaries were frozen), and large investments flowed into building new schools and renovating old ones. As plans to build a new vocational college for Chukotka were finalized, initial plans called for the appointment of managing staff and a director entirely from outside. Another flagship education program involved sending thousands of children and teenagers to educational summer camps in central Russia, thus removing them from their home environment during the summer break from formal schooling. One deputy remarked, "I feel the [education administration] is experimenting on us; they are trying out unproven pedagogical ideas on an obscure population in the north in a way they could never pull off on the materik" [24].

But deputies found it very difficult to press these points effectively: "There is no longer consultation – they decide policies behind closed doors and only send the documents to us for approval. I can no longer go to [the incomer head of education]: now I have to appeal to the administration, they consider my request, and then decide, ok, this once you can have a word" [24].

If Duma deputies complained about this culture of secrecy in Abramovich's administration, they had difficulty projecting their concerns beyond their own private circles. There was little recourse to the media, for it too was monopolized by the governor's komanda. When Abramovich appointed Sergei Kapkov (a political campaign manager, or *p-rshik*, by profession) to handle "information policy," the close management of public information was the likely objective. In fact, the administration treated the media as a key modernizing domain, which they employed to define and delimit their vision of change and modernity, and thereby act as a backstop and cheerleader for administration policy. Journalists, incomer and local, were warned not to "send any criticism whatsoever to the address of the administration" [48]. Many of the stories in the okrug newspaper were produced by Kapkov's own information department in the Moscow offices on Kursovoi pereulok. Even nominally federal media organizations – the okrug television and radio stations (Chukotka and Maiak) – were co-opted when a Kapkov associate was appointed as their general director. Control of the media was subsequently used to manage the most controversial projects of modernization, like those on education reform, village closures and the resettlement of locals to the materik, and the re-establishment of Soviet-style state farms in rural settlements. Other issues were excluded from public discussion altogether. Sibneft's oil and gas exploration in Chukotka, for example, lay under a complete information blanket. Although administration insiders talked freely among themselves about the prospects of finding oil in the region, the insularity of their networks and media control sealed this information from the local population.

Quite naturally, the culture of secrecy and the impenetrability of the modernizing clique generated a body of commentary among Anadyr's settler population. Older settlers tended to view Abramovich's new media, and all the images of modernity they generated, with some ambivalence. They were old enough to recognize what amounted to an "official version." The twenty-six-year-old public relations professional Kapkov – the very embodiment of post-Soviet corporate modernity – was enacting a neo-Soviet information policy. Newspaper articles and television bulletins on the installation of new diesel generators, rising levels of reindeer-meat production, and the progress of street paving were reminiscent of the Soviet era, when *Sovetskaia Chukotka* had filled its pages with production figures and exhortations to fulfill the plan. Media control contributed to the impression of an unknowable policy domain, where invisible motives drove the machinery of administration. Despite the thirst for information about the trajectory of reforms among locals, a sense of conversation between the official administrative realm and the ordinary individual was lacking. Not only was nobody crossing the territory between the local settler and the incomer, neither was there much information travelling this gap. Nature abhors a vacuum, however, and the middle ground was flooded with gossip, misinformation, and accusation, a situation germane in a more universal sense to post-Soviet societies. As Ken Jowitt (1992, 289) has observed, secrecy as a mode of governance removes the possibility of any kind of public debate and elevates "rumour as covert political discourse." He wrote that "The neotraditional secrecy characteristic of a Leninist party; its corresponding distrust of an ideologically 'unreconstructed' population; the invidious juxtaposition of an elite in possession of the real, but secret, truth about the polity, economy, world affairs ... ; and a population living in the 'cave' of political jokes and rumour are legacies that continue to shape the character of 'civil society' in Eastern Europe and the Soviet Union."

So it was in Abramovich's Anadyr. The domain of the kitchen table was indeed saturated with rumour, coloured by an inclination to conspiracy theory. Both the

В Анадырском порту разгрузилось последнее судно навигации Чукотки-2002

ФИНАЛЬНЫЙ АККОРД НАВИГАЦИИ

Несмотря на сложную ледовую обстановку, в назначенный срок – 10 ноября – у причала Анадырского морпорта ошвартовался теплоход «Василий Бурханов», подошедший из Приморского порта Восточный. На его борту было 4,76 тысячи тонн грузов, в основном в адрес ООО «Сибнефть-Чукотка», ГУП «Чукотснаб» и ЗАО «Чукотская торговая компания». В числе грузов довольно много строительных материалов, оборудования и автотехники - мобильные подъемные краны, автомобили, автобусы и даже пожарные машины. Ровно в полночь 11 ноября первые грузы поступили на берег. Разгрузка «Василия Бурханова» происходила в сложных условиях. Большие ледовые поля, спускающиеся с верховьев реки Анадырь представляют опасность для судна, стоящего у причала. Во время отливов судно вынуждено было работать главным двигателем, чтобы избежать риска быть оторванным от причала.

Тем не менее, забрав порожние контейнеры, «Василий Бурханов» уходит обратно. Это последнее судно навигации 2002 года. Всего в этом сезоне портовики обработали 85 судов, а в 2001 – лишь 63. Соответственно, значительно больше принято грузов. Вспомним также, что навигация-2002 началась, как навигация-2001 – 18 июня, и примерно в такие же сроки завершается.

Норман ПОДГОРЕЦ, фото Василия ЛЕОНТЬЕВА

За девять месяцев текущего года поголовье оленей в Чукотском автономном округе увеличилось на 815 голов

ОЛЕНЕЙ СТАЛО БОЛЬШЕ

Всего в этом году в ЧАО на 1 ноября насчитывалось около 106 тысяч оленей. «Увеличение поголовья происходит во многом благодаря стабильному финансированию федерального и окружного бюджетов», – отметил **Игорь Тогошиев**, главный специалист Управления сельского хозяйства. В соответствии с принятым окружным законом по государственной поддержке развития северного оленеводства в рамках окружной программы по стабилизации АПК оленеводческим хозяйствам оказывается материально-техническая и финансовая помощь.

«230 миллионов рублей в этом году предусмотрено выделить из окружного бюджета на развитие сельского хозяйства ЧАО, включая оленеводство и морзверобойный промысел. 85 процентов от этой суммы уже освоено», – отметил **Евгений Марочкин**, заместитель начальника Управления сельского хозяйства. Сегодня все двадцать три действующих оленеводческих хозяйства ЧАО готовы к зиме. Все бригады оленеводов обеспечены продовольствием, оружием, получены снегоходы «Буран».

Поголовье оленей в этом году увеличилось в основном за счет успешной работы оленеводческих хозяйств МУП СХП «им. 1 Ревкома Чукотки» и МУП СХП «Канчаланский» Анадырского района, ОАО «Анюйский» и ОАО «Турваургин» Билибинского района.

В оленеводческих хозяйствах МУП СХП «Анадырский», ОАО «Ильгувеем», филиале Конергинского ИУМАПО «Востокагро» - поголовье оленей за прошедший год снизилось.

Пресс-служба правительства ЧАО, фото Константина ЛЕМЕШЕВА

В НАВИГАЦИЮ 2002 ГОДА НА ЧУКОТКУ ЗАВЕЗЕНО СКОЛЬКО НАДО УГЛЯ И ДАЖЕ НА 10 ПРОЦЕНТОВ БОЛЬШЕ

Как сообщили в Управлении промышленности, транспорта, связи и топливно-энергетического комплекса Чукотского автономного округа, в бюджете округа на мероприятия по подготовке объектов жилищно-коммунального хозяйства к осенне-зимнему периоду 2002-2003 гг. заложено более 90 млн. рублей.

На приобретение топлива для предприятий ЖКХ округа затрачено 865,9 млн. рублей; 87,2 млн. рублей - на подготовку предприятий ОАО «Чукотэнерго» к работе в осенне-зимний период. Это на 21, 8 млн. рублей больше, чем в 2001 году.

По словам заместителя начальника Управления промышленности, транспорта, связи и топливно-энергетического комплекса ЧАО **Валерия Васильева**, «на 31 из 68 муниципальных котельных проведен капитальный ремонт, установлено 10 новых котлоагрегатов, заменены ветхие тепловые сети на участке округа протяженностью 38,1 км, а также старые трубы на участке протяженностью 21,5 км».

К эксплуатации подготовлены все тепловые сети, для замены устаревших дизель-генераторов на дизельных электростанциях установлен 71 новый.

В навигацию 2002 года на Чукотку завезено 382 тысячи тонн угля (110% от запланированного) и 107 тысяч тонн нефтепродуктов. «Это достаточное количество топлива на зиму для работы энергообъектов ЖКХ и предприятий ОАО «Чукотэнерго», - отметил Валерий Васильев.

Соб. инф.

Soviet-style reporting in the modernized regional newspaper *Krainyi Sever:* (TOP) “A grand finale for the navigation season: the last ship of 2002 has unloaded at Anadyr’s port,” 1 October 2002; (RIGHT) “Reindeer numbers increase over the past nine months,” 23 November 2002; (BOTTOM) “Over the 2002 shipping season in Chukotka, winter coal quotas have been fully delivered – and even exceeded by 10 percent!” 4 August 2002.

resettlement program and the mass removal of children to central Russian summer camps were viewed as elaborate rackets for money laundering, a perception reinforced when news filtered back to Chukotka of poor management and disappointed participants. So large were the sums invested in the modernization and so many were the "specialists" imported to manage the spending, that in some cases funds certainly were misappropriated; this was especially common when incomers were given responsibility for purchasing equipment and services in Moscow. But the few reliable snippets of information on misspending simply fuelled a rumour mill that, for locals locked out of the administration's informational domain, tainted the entire modernization. As much as it damaged the cause, the culture of secrecy was instinctive, an automatic reflex of governance, and it enhanced the mystique of power surrounding the governor's komanda in an abstract way, just as, in a concrete sense, the black-tinted windows of the administrative Land Cruisers evoked a sense of awe in the local bystander. Secrecy, as Georg Simmel (quoted in Wolff 1950, 336) wrote long ago, is an important ingredient in the mystification of authority and naturally enhances the charismatic powers of any non-democratic regime. To cloak the affairs of governance in secrecy is to underline the distance between the ruling and the ruled: "the secret gives one a position of exception ... everything mysterious is also important and essential."

Yet, secrecy in governance was also an outcome of Chukotka's capture by a corporation, in this case Sibneft. After all, commercial confidentiality is implicit to the culture of the corporation, and this is particularly true of publicly listed natural-resource companies dealing with sensitive exploration-related information. Sibneft was involved in complex transfer-pricing and other tax-efficiency arrangements during Abramovich's time as governor, which, in the context of Putin's post-2000 campaign against the oligarchs and tax evasion generally, created the need for obsessive information control within Abramovich's financial operations. Because the modernization of Chukotka, including the financing of the okrug budget, was in fact only one among Sibneft's many complex internal transactions, budgetary transparency was impossible. The funds invested in Chukotka's modernization reached the region only after a journey through one of the most sophisticated systems for achieving "tax efficiency" operating in Russia at the time (see Chapter 6).

All the same, the opacity of administration and the prevalence in the local kitchen-table domain of misinformed rumour circled back to a central fact of the modernization: it was produced by a sealed, non-local patronage network, whose interests were unquestionably advantaged by its monopolistic control over the project. Chukotka was, for the imported modernizing cadre, a kind of phantom stage for enacting a networking dance that began and ended elsewhere: Moscow, Nizhni Novgorod, or Omsk. Information (about oil exploration, education reforms, resettlement, and other issues at the heart of the reforms) could be understood as a form of currency, a *tovar*, circulating among the modernizers as they fought for power. Pieces of knowledge were symbols of esteem, indications of proximity to Abramovich's inner circle, and so, status was reflected in the amount one knew about Abramovich's plans, doubts, frustrations, and affections. In an earlier era, Governor Nazarov was forced to engage with local actors and to build a locally based patronage regime. For this reason, I found it relatively easy to unearth within established local networks detailed and compromising information about his methods of administration. At that time, information leaked into the broader local community because locals were implicated into the networks at the heart of Nazarov-era governance. But Abramovich's inner circle was a hermetically sealed informational domain.[11]

Settlers Invent a Language

By the era of the Abramovich modernization, settlers in Anadyr and beyond had completed a remarkable journey. Within a single generation, a population once dedicated to establishing colonial power on the northern frontier had transformed into a rooted community now resisting, and trying to influence, a renewed colonial project over which it lacked control. It is therefore worthwhile to briefly revisit the earlier modes of settler identity in Chukotka and to recall how they related to prevailing historical circumstances. In the Soviet era, settlers naturally derived a sense of collective identity largely from their place in the colonial order. Settlers then considered themselves a Soviet labour elite, but they also defined themselves in opposition to the local indigenous population, and transience in the North was an important feature in their plans and self-image. At that time, the term priezzhii – meaning "incomer" or "newcomer" – described settlers aptly enough; they were a "flowing population" (Leksin and Andreeva 1994, 307). Soviet air transport effectively collapsed the Soviet Union's huge distances, and both the ability to regularly imbibe at the cultural spout in Leningrad and Moscow and the relative ease of transporting metropolitan cultural life to the North were vitally important props for the settler lifestyle. Cultural power was also projected onto local natives, and mastery of the North was in part a project of acculturating primitive peoples – the imposition of Great Russian *kul'turnost'*. Finally, high pay and the fantastic (and subsidized) supply of food and household goods in Chukotka's shops elevated the settler to a distinctly privileged social class.

Prosperity, mobility, and colonial agency – these attributes of the Soviet settler idyll disappeared after 1991. Some residual northern benefits still accrued, including longer holidays and early retirement. But these entitlements did nothing to protect the notion of the "privileged settler"; poverty, unemployment, the collapse of northern supply, and extreme isolation converted Chukotka's settlers into an exceptionally *unprivileged* population in post-Soviet Russia. Nevertheless, if we examine the fate of the settler in the decade of crisis (1991-2000), clearly there existed within the settler community the social and political capital, and the skill, to recreate new forms of privilege and domination. And not only did particular settlers with key skills and valuable contacts capitalize on the new arrangement, but also, the Soviet collapse did not entirely end the *kul'turnost'* project in the minds of many settlers. In relation to indigenous people in Chukotka, there remained both a structure of settler dominance (through employment, access to capital, access to transport) and an abstract disposition that the North remained a colonial domain.[12] Essentially, settlers remained at the top of a much-reduced pile, particularly those living in the relative comfort of Nazarov-era Anadyr.

But, at the turn of the millennium, Chukotka and its settlers abruptly shifted to a different path, diverging radically from other northern regions in Russia (perhaps even setting a path others would follow). Abramovich's unprecedented and unheralded modernization knocked settlers from whatever comfortable assumptions they still preserved about their neo-colonial status. His campaign effectively completed the emasculation of their old colonial identity, by excluding locals from the community of core modernizers and, critically, by repositioning settlers as targets, rather than agents, of this most recent project of development.

My ethnographic work began as the new administrative apparatus took shape, continued as the first major programs of modernization were implemented, and ended at a point when individual locals were beginning to understand the consequences of all this change for themselves. One year into Abramovich's first term, a range of concrete indignities and more general complaints about the modernization were circulating through settler networks in Anadyr and beyond into the settlements. The discourses of disdain and distrust had leaked from within closed administration circles into the local community, the practices of exclusion and the recruitment of so many outsiders to the region were arousing bitterness, and finally, the delivery of programs and facilities without local input was creating a sense of alienation from the "new Chukotka," a concept and place locals often referred to with foreboding. Furthermore, for long-time residents, discarding an allegiance to what came before – to the "old Chukotka" – was not uncomplicated. A journalist with fifteen years in the region explained, "We came to Chukotka because we love her as she is. You don't need to drastically transform things. It's fine to make life a little more comfortable [laughing], but it seems to us here that [the modernizing komanda] wants to recreate Petersburg, or Omsk, or Nizhni" [11].

As Turks and Canadians constructed a "new Chukotka" in Anadyr, local settlers often expressed doubts that they had a place in it. The shining new capital, where the regional newspaper boasted about the most advanced cinema, shopping complex, and cultural centre in the entire Far North, reflected a Russia locals knew little about. Abramovich was building a new capital in his own image, a place for an elite class of new Russian professionals. Local settlers spoke openly of a new class society setting up around them, characterizing the new buildings as palaces for the governor's komanda. A twenty-year-old Russian local remarked, "I just don't understand why they build these places – casinos, expensive restaurants, the luxury suites in the Hotel Chukotka. I know my friends and I will never go in and spend our money. When the komanda leaves, these buildings will stand empty. All we want is a nice place you can go, have a drink, meet a girl, and eat something without having to leave your monthly paycheque behind" [50].

If younger locals viewed the emerging Anadyr as inaccessible, their older counterparts viewed much of the new construction as an effacement of the Anadyr they had a hand in building. For them, reconstruction came at an emotional cost. A museum curator complained, "It was really so unpleasant when they renovated the Poliarnyi [cinema] because they just covered up a beautiful wall mural. That mural was done by Istomen, a member of the Union of Artists. They've done this everywhere, in fact, and I think it was so much more interesting when our buildings had their old murals, Lenin or no Lenin. Now it's all monotone, brand new, blinding ... That seems to be their approach to culture" [47].

The arrival of an extraneous threat to the accustomed privileges of settlers in the capital transformed for a time the implicit idea of a settler identity into something reified and clear. The modernization caused settlers to think for the first time about the *nature* of the community to which they belonged. If modernizing newcomers were defining local within a rhetoric of otstalost', it became necessary for settlers to produce a counteracting language of identity. A necessary ingredient of any collective identity is the marking of difference, so that the outsider becomes discernible to those established within the circle. Fredrik Barth (1969) viewed the "cultural stuff" enclosed by the boundary as unhelpful in understanding the character of group identity, but we cannot escape the fact that native (by which I mean local) cultural practices are the very instruments of marking difference. They stand as evidence of the community's rootedness in and inextricability from the very landscape to which it is local. It was certainly the case that for settlers in the capital and beyond, the arrival of Abramovich's newcomers and their program created the impetus to understand "northernness" no longer as a neocolonial role, but rather as a locally rooted attribute. Not only were settlers marking the boundaries of the local with discourses of difference from the outsider, they were also reaching into the toolbox of local practice (or "tradition") in order to express that difference in concrete terms.

Just as this campaign of reform was manufacturing a new elite within Abramovich's modernizing networks, so was it refashioning the identities of its targets. Thus it was that by finally unseating settler privilege, the modernization catalyzed a sense of *native* identity in settlers. Despite their loss of privilege and agency as a result of the Soviet collapse, many settlers possessed a body of locally rooted attachments rich enough to enable them to reconstitute a post-Soviet sense of themselves in the North as that of people with legitimate claims to residence in their Chukotkan communities. Indeed, the settler identity did not emerge barren from its post-Soviet emasculation; valorizations of the "northern type," along with modes of sharing and openness, fluency on the landscape, and nativizing practices of engagement with the "indigenous" Chukotka, remained relatively intact. This carapace of social norms and individual habits enabled the settler community to persist in conditions of isolation and climatic extremes. But, as a form of cultural ballast, this *habitus* of the settler life likewise predetermined the constraints to change. Any program promoting a radical departure from the habits of community interaction and discourses on what it meant to be a northern settler perforce contended with some resistance. This interruption is precisely what Abramovich's project sought to accomplish, and so the character of his reforming challenge, and the frictions on change this challenge subsequently met, animated for a moment a remarkably clear language of belonging and local authority among settlers.

This brand of localism abandoned its former colonial features not for altruistic reasons, but because the layering of a new neo-colonial modernizing population above the established settler left only a *local* moral claim available. Settlers, for whom mobility and the brokering role had been a way of life and a touchstone of identity, began to claim authority on the basis of their rootedness. Settler senses of group identity reconstituted themselves by making explicit reference to land use, local kin and friendship, and long tenure in the North. Paradoxically, settlers in Chukotka's urban areas were often those most vigorously claiming "native" entitlements, resisting pressure to depart Chukotka on the resettlement programs just as they protested their hostility to various modernizing projects. This was a defensive posture, and unfortunately for the settler population, it neatly coincided with modernizers' characterizations of the settler as frozen and out of touch with modern Russia. As so many histories of colonization and development show us, the claim to rooted indigeneity is a kind of last stand, a subaltern position that betrays the loss of other sources of authority and power. And of course, in performing the localist shift, settlers in Chukotka were adopting many of the discourses hitherto the preserve of the indigenous population.

Talking Local

At the heart of any development project bringing outside experts into contact with local people is a conflict of knowledge regimes. Upon the sites of development, the contrasting knowledges of the outsider and the local lock in struggle, as entrenched positions of authority and power are upset. Ways of knowing in fact operate as proxies for insider and outsider interests, competing in a zero-sum fashion presaging the triumph of either "modern ways" or "tradition." Outsider and insider identities are likewise ideas propped up by ways of knowing: knowledges mark the boundaries.

In Chukotka, locals faced a campaign of modernization imposed from a distant metropolis by strangers confident of the superiority of modern, post-Soviet practices of work, leisure, and consumption. As in the previous era of Soviet osvoenie, Abramovich's modernizing solutions to local problems were expensive, imported, and technologically advanced. Moreover, their applicability to new settings in the North was assumed; they reflected modes of knowledge that were deemed universal and, therefore, by definition, sought replicability across an array of social contexts. For settlers facing a developmentalist campaign on their own territory, a principal means of marking a local identity was the declaration of authority for systems of knowledge native to their community and its environment. Naturally, these very settlers had once themselves imported to the region various regimes of "universal" knowledge, but now, unlike the contemporary modernizer, they could also exploit the experience of decades in the North to produce an alternative.

The myriad adaptations necessary to live and work in Chukotka's extreme conditions – to deal with the harsh climate, the region's isolation, the vast distances between settlements, and the long polar night – were cast as a kind of exclusive code referred to as *severnaia spetsifika* (the special circumstances of the North). This was promoted by settlers, even those inhabiting Chukotka's most urban spaces, as an accumulated knowledge, transmitted not through abstract learning, but through experience in the North. Imported technologies, ways of relating to others, and habits of travel, work, and rest must be adapted to local circumstances. Outsiders are asked to bend their will to the fact that "things are different here." I interviewed a member of the okrug Duma who spent three decades working as a construction engineer in Provideniia and Anadyr. He warned that disregarding settler expertise by relying on flown-in construction labour was a disaster in northern conditions. It seemed to him that Anadyr's new building projects were started out of season and too often used the wrong techniques and materials: "You can't erect the same buildings here as in Moscow – it's like asking Africans to build houses for Russians" [27]. In 2002, a Turkish company contracted to pave Anadyr's streets with concrete was still pouring as the arctic winter began in October, and the deputy was not alone in believing the new streets would crack apart in the following spring thaw. (They did.)

Building on permafrost was considered rather a black art – a prime example of severnaia spetsifika – on which long-time locals claimed a monopoly. The Red Cross, a reforming institution staffed by outsiders, imported summer camp volunteers from Moscow. They chose a patch of tundra outside Anadyr as their new "ecological" camp territory – a place where they intended to teach local children how to care for the environment – and levelled the area by stripping the turf with a vezdekhod. This peeled the insulating layer from the permafrost below and created a vast meltwater pond, an episode wryly remarked upon across local kitchen tables the following winter. A cameraman in the local television studio described the frequent visits of documentary film crews from Moscow and abroad who invariably arrived without special polarizing filters for filming in the harsh arctic

Imported technology adapted to local conditions – a Zaporozhits rebuilt for northern conditions
Photographed by Linda Rosenstrom Chang

light – he kept a private collection of camera equipment and made a tidy profit equipping naïve visitors. There was a sea of other such stories in circulation, to do with building to withstand winds roaring off the Bering Sea, wearing the proper type of fur hat while ice-fishing, protecting the eyes while travelling over snow in the spring, and the best cure for nausea during the massive barometric pressure shifts that affect the coastal areas.

In Chukotka, the rhetorical ubiquity of severnaia spetsifika stood as confirmation that no community can exist without knowing things about its local setting that have served it well in the past. This is the essence of agency and identity, for the group and its members. But, if a development initiative is to project its solutions into the places of backwardness that it aims to transform, it must make convincing truth claims that subvert pre-existing (and by definition local) ways. In the process, competing forms of local knowledge must be impugned, converted into a state of ignorance. The capacity of local people to apply experience in resolving the problems they face must be somehow obscured or cheapened by the modernizing arrival – the development worker, the expert, the missionary, the bureaucratic official. As Piers Vitebsky (1993, 105) has observed, the denial of local knowledge is the essential manoeuvre of a modernization: "Persons who previously knew something, withdraw or are pushed out from faith in their own competence to know, in relation to others who 'know' better." Knowledge regimes thus play an instrumental role in setting up the hierarchies natural to development projects, which typically come to be framed by the polarities of "modern" and "dynamic" versus "traditional," "static," and "out of date."

This observation comes through vividly in the writing of Anthony Cohen (1982, 7) on the Shetlands fishing community of Whalsay, which in the 1970s and 1980s faced bureaucratic pressure from mainland authorities to modify its traditional fishery in accordance with scientific findings on fish stocks. Faced with an avalanche of directives and reports from "outside," locals bolstered their "fierce desire for self-determination" with "the community's certain knowledge that it is more expert in resolving its own affairs than are the politicians and bureaucrats of the ... central government." Knowledge became a critical device for the marking of these boundaries. Thus, as Cohen (1993, 33) put it, "One of the ways in which [Whalsay] islanders express their distinctiveness from people elsewhere is by suggesting the ephemeral, superficial and usually bogus nature of Expert knowledge."

In Chukotka, "specialists" *(spetsialisty),* "young experts" *(molodye eksperty),* "modernization" (modernizatsiia), "development" *(razvitiia),* and a "dignified lifestyle" *(dostoinyi obraz zhizni)* were all employed by administrative incomers as normative terms, as though their basis in metropolitan regimes of knowledge signified their irreproachable value. For locals skeptical of imported notions of development, however, these terms could be reversed in a language that, just as in Whalsay, dismissed the possibility of a relevant outsider expertise. Here are some local variations on the concept of the modernizing expert in Chukotka:

> They come in as specialists from Omsk. Well, what are they talking about – they are specialists but we aren't? Pardon me?! We have lots of intellectuals here, people with experience! [47]
>
> The fact is, the young specialists coming here from the materik are having a hard time understanding the unique requirements of the North *(spetsifika severa).* They project standards imported from the materik on a reality they don't know. [27]
>
> Why are we hiring specialists for education from the materik? You say there are no specialists here? Come on, we have well-qualified people here. [24]

Despite their personal stake in the modernizing projects of an earlier time, some settlers perceived in Abramovich's modernization the duplication of mistakes made under Soviet policies of osvoenie. I spoke with a retired Russian sovkhoz director who spent two decades in the coastal settlement of Uelen managing its indigenous sea-mammal-hunting economy. Looking back on his experience, he warned, "Even with the best of intentions, anyone thrown in [to manage local people] from some city in central Russia is going to have a difficult time and is going to make it difficult for everyone around him. You absolutely cannot send in some economic expert with a management degree who can think in eight currencies. If a person comes in and launches a string of reforms, wants to change everything overnight, he can do more harm than good" [52].

It was deeply ironic to witness a former paragon of the Soviet civilizing mission – once a key player in the process of "rationalizing" traditional economies – resituating himself as a spokesperson of local knowledge. He was a man who once drew (quite considerable) authority as a manager among native peoples from his modern, Soviet education, now elevating the value of grounded learning over the imported expertise Abramovich's specialists brought with them to Chukotka. But a lifetime of working and living in small northern settlements nevertheless taught him to attenuate book learning with what local people know. He died a year after we first met, and he devoted that remaining time to writing a genealogy of great Chukchi herding families in his district, hoping it would prove inspirational to the youth in his village.

Because my perspective was that of an outsider, it was easier for me to discern the importance of the severnaia spetsifika discourse for its powers of signification, its ability to mark collective boundaries. I could see that the sense in doing things the local way was as much tied to considerations of affiliation as to the issue of finding a practical solution. As a former "white settler" from the Canadian North, I couldn't help but compare the local ways in Chukotka to the knowledge I imported from my own northern background. Very often the claim of superiority for "traditional" or "local" ways was, if judged strictly on utilitarian grounds, absurd. Local knowledge could never be automatically superior to imported alternatives. It was, on the other hand, automatically better for drawing boundaries between insider and outsider. Even the most anachronistic dispositions of severnaia spetsifika were mustered for a specific effort of self-definition, and so, in a moment of two solitudes, they were eminently useful.

Here are some examples. Modern Anadyr was rapidly built in the last decades of the Soviet era, and in its oppressive uniformity of design it became indistinguishable from any other city in northern Russia. Most of its residents lived in standard five-story apartment blocks built in long lines channelling the bitter winds off the Bering Sea. This was the Arktika model – a monolithic, mass-produced concrete-panel design raised on concrete piles above the frozen earth to prevent permafrost melting and subsidence (see Fig. 2.2). Most are now weathered far beyond their years, but the poor standard of Soviet materials and building practices meant that since the time of their erection, they have existed in parallel states of not-yet-finished and already disintegrating. One evening, I was sitting with a middle-aged settler acquaintance in his own Arktika flat. In a lapse of tact, I began to describe the new Canadian-built hotel on Anadyr's main street: unlike a typical Soviet structure, in which a mass of dangling utility pipes snaked among the concrete piles supporting the building, their exposed position making them vulnerable to freezing, the hotel had enclosed its piping within a crawlspace. He cut me short and gripped my arm across the kitchen table to tell me the Arktika design held the Order of Lenin because it was the only kind of building that could endure

Chukotka's extreme conditions. He promised that the wooden stick framing of the Canadian-built projects and the stucco plaster Turkish workers were using to renovate Anadyr's crumbling facades would all be ripped away in the winds of the next autumn storms. In the same spirit, he denounced the new wind turbines towering over the Gulf of Anadyr, built by a Ukrainian contractor: "So they want to catch the wind? Well, when they catch our winds and end up on their sides, then maybe they'll start listening to us!" [53].

These opinions were common among older settlers. I interviewed a former construction foreman who dismissed the Canadian builders: "In my day we were putting up eleven Arktika buildings a year in Anadyr. But your guys have been building that one row of terrace houses on [the main street] for over a year – what is that? I don't think they know what they're doing" [14]. Abramovich hired the Canadians because they could construct purpose-built structures in Chukotka using techniques developed in their own Arctic. To an outsider like me, these commissions seemed to offer settlements such as Anadyr the opportunity to move away from the monotone brutality of concrete-panel construction, a way of building that produced the same standard spaces regardless of particular requirements. I wondered how local settlers could be so attached to their Arktika homes and offices.

Particular controversy surrounded the laying of a high-voltage cable between the north and south shores of the Gulf of Anadyr. This would unite Anadyr's massive Soviet-era power station with the north shore and its airport, link the newly built windfarm to the larger grid, and result in the closure of twelve costly and polluting diesel generators. The cable project was the first step toward the conversion of power generation for the area to clean-burning and locally produced natural gas, replacing shipped-in coal and petroleum. But many locals were convinced this cable would create a magnetic field blocking the annual salmon migration past Anadyr to interior spawning grounds and driving away the beluga whales that hunted these waters.[13] Moscow-based consultants hired by the administration to conduct an impact assessment published assurances in the okrug newspaper that the cable would be safely buried deep under the seabed, and the Texan company hired to lay the cable reported that analogous projects elsewhere had never compromised local fish migrations. Nevertheless, locals claimed to know better than experts, flown into the okrug to make judgments about a water-body they had never seen before.[14]

These examples of what appeared, to both the modernizing "expert" and the ethnographer, to be anachronistic resistance to sensible projects illuminate the *proprietorial* character of local knowledge. Knowledge becomes appropriate when it comes from "us," is earned and owned by "us," and expresses "our" vested interests. Whereas local senses of understanding are intrinsic and preserve the integrity of local arrangements of power, extraneous knowledge must undergo a process of political sterilization, whereby it becomes detached from outside interests and converts into the property of local actors. Human activity, even strictly economic activity, as Maurice Godelier reminds us in *Rationality and Irrationality in Economics* (1972), is rarely rational on the basis of material considerations alone. The anthropological literature is rich in such observations. In his study of the settler and Inuit communities of Labrador, John Kennedy (1982) reported a wide vocabulary of behaviours to which one group or the other lay claim, not all of which possessed a clear functional utility but that nevertheless played a part in maintaining group distinction. Settlers rejected the sensible Inuit technique of harpooning killed seals to prevent their bodies from sinking into the ocean, preferring instead the time-consuming and often unsuccessful method of retrieving sunken seals with fishing line and jigs. Cohen (1993) provides an analogous example, describing the decision by Whalsay fishermen in the 1970s to invest millions of pounds in new purse-seiners for the notoriously unpredictable pelagic fishery (herring and mackerel), going against the grain of grim government projections on fish stocks. These fishermen may have been acting in contravention of science, but they were loyal to the superiority of their own knowledge and experience. On this basis, Cohen (1993, 37) remarks that "Knowledge does not commend itself locally by intrinsic merit, nor by the subtlety and ingenuity with which it is disseminated, nor even by the congruence with what else is known locally, but rather, by its appropriateness to the ways in which things are known locally."

Thus it was the case that in Anadyr, imported innovations became amenable to local ways of life at the pace by which their possession shifted from the hands of intruding and foreign actors to the dominion of the established community. In my interviews, settlers would often say, "all these new buildings are not meant for us" or "the old shops are perfectly good – why do we need a shopping centre?" But the amenities springing up on every corner – the cinema, cultural centre, fitness gym, ice arena, internet café, and shopping centre – were intended in principle, if not in practice, for local people. What Abramovich's komanda failed to perceive, however, was the manner in which the "grey" *(seroi)* and "frozen" *(zamorozhennyi)* Soviet town they were rebuilding was in fact an inhabited space imbued with personal meaning and serving as a material correlative to the community's collective past. It was an intersubjective environment, in which local people had acted out their lives, and that carried within its forms all the referents to a deep and shared personal history – the town, in this sense, supported its people by carrying their pasts. Anadyr's old House of Culture (Dom kul'tury, or more commonly, the DK) was one such space, built in 1963 and thereafter drafty, cold, dark, and structurally unsafe, yet for decades dearly loved by the town's residents as the site of talent shows, dance classes, choir recitals, and discos. Along with the Poliarnyi cinema, it was one of the only public meeting spaces in Anadyr. By 2000, the building was subsiding down the riverbank into the Gulf of Anadyr, and so Abramovich ordered its destruction and contracted the Turks to erect a grand new cultural centre in its place, another of his generous gifts to the okrug. I arrived as the old DK was being demolished and found many townspeople distraught, despite Abramovich's promise; one local had stopped using the street on which it sat because he could not bear to see the building disappear. A former culture worker *(kul'trabotnik)* in the DK recalled the day they emptied the old building, when one of the workmen pointed to a faded wooden bench in the theatre and said, "I met my wife on that bench over thirty years ago, just after I came here, and now we have grandchildren in Anadyr" [54].

When Anadyr's Novomariinsky shopping centre opened in late 2002, there were long queues of locals eager to see inside the gleaming edifice and experience self-service shopping. Thereafter, among the middle-aged informants who bitterly contested the arrival of "unnecessary" amenities "for the elite," some continued to frequent the Soviet-style *gastronom* (general food shop), whereas others began to visit the new cinema or the gym. Many younger locals had always been enthusiastic about the new Anadyr, despite the misgivings of their elders, and they took jobs as hotel receptionists, security guards, and waiters. Local settlers and incoming modernizers continued to live in a state of two solitudes, but the established community nevertheless began to inhabit Anadyr's new spaces, to make the conveniences they offered indigenous to their local way of life. For, just as they knew that, in time, the modernizers themselves would return to their distant metropolitan lives, they recognized that, also with time, the material geography of the modernization would become a native one.

8
Conclusion: Practices of Belonging

After two years away, and almost four years since I first came to Chukotka, I returned in the summer of 2005. In Anadyr, I ran into Grisha, the young Russian accordionist who returned from studies in Vladivostok as the Soviet Union collapsed and supported his wife and daughter by going out on the land (see Chapter 5). Over pints of locally brewed lager in one of the city's new pubs, he told me about the changes in his life. In 2002, he landed the first steady job he had ever had, as a youth worker for one of the governor's charities, the Red Cross. Until then, it was a good month when his family could buy sugar for their tea. What money he made was from his hunting on the tundra, fishing for smelt and salmon, and freelancing as a music teacher. Not once during the 1990s did they leave Chukotka to visit their relatives on the materik. Now, he flew often to Alaska for the Red Cross and took annual holidays to visit his brother in St. Petersburg. Earlier in the year, he had fulfilled a long-time dream to have his jaw reset and his teeth straightened in Moscow. In fact, he complained that his monthly income of 20,000 rubles (roughly US$800) still left him a little short. When we first met, Grisha told me he could never leave his northern birthplace and that the land had become so much a part of him that he could sense the weather changing a week in advance. Now, he was divorcing his wife, taking evening classes in management and finance at Anadyr's new college, and preparing to emigrate to Canada.

I timed my return to Chukotka to witness the final months of Abramovich's Five-Year Plan, a point when, he once promised, locals would finally have an "acceptable way of life." By this time, he had invested the equivalent of over US$2 billion in the okrug, spread among a permanent population of roughly fifty-five thousand, and the effects were dramatic.[1] Anadyr bore little resemblance to the crumbling, grey city it was before the modernization; in places, the transformation was so complete that only the layout of the streets recalled that past. The central city square, once delimited by the old Communist Party Headquarters and the House of Culture, was now a vast plaza of interlocking paving stones, flowerbeds, and imitation antique street lamps, all built by Turkish shift workers. Next to the gleaming four-story cultural centre stood a timber-and-log Russian Orthodox cathedral, the largest of its kind in the country (and a gift from Deputy Governor Andrei Gorodilov). Where once a four-metre granite statue of Lenin stared out to the Gulf of Anadyr now towered the bronze figure of Saint Nikolai the Miraculous, his arms raised to the waters.

Statue of Saint Nikolai the Miraculous looking over the Gulf of Anadyr, 2005
Photographed by V. Sirtun

Life in the capital had assumed a new pace. Four years earlier, people used the shattered and frost-heaved city streets as their walking paths, and the rare vehicles would have tempted fate had they gone much faster. Now, the streets were smoothly paved, the centre was clogged with traffic, and a stoplight had been installed on the corner of Otke and Rul'tytegina. At MDM Bank, a Western Union cashier served long lines of shift workers sending their money to relatives in central Russia, the Caucasus, and Central Asia. The Novomariinsky supermarket across the street now competed with several other renovated stores. The average monthly income in the capital had risen to 15,000 rubles (roughly US$600), and business was brisk. Anadyr was clearly prospering: my friends were buying their own cars, renovating their flats, eating out in restaurants (at Moscow prices), and flying on holidays to the Black Sea, Turkey, Bulgaria, and Egypt. When I first came to Anadyr in the winter of 2002, Chukotka was served by one weekly flight from Moscow; now there were six.

With this new prosperity, the social texture of life in the capital had also developed in radically new directions. As surprising to me as it was to the locals, the barriers that once divided them from the newcomer modernizer were dissolving. The extended kitchen-table jeremiads on the arrogance and vulgarity of the modernization campaign were much less common, as my friends were gradually recruited into the projects of reform themselves. If the rhetoric of the two solitudes had been most fiercely voiced by those urban settlers with the most to lose in the confusion of Abramovich's arrival, it was they whose skills and knowledge the modernizing administration now most required to expand and perpetuate its

Otke Street in Abramovich's new Anadyr, 2005
Photographed by author

policies. These were, for the most part, well-educated settlers in the capital, and it seemed that Abramovich's expert incomers had softened their earlier disdain and acknowledged in Anadyr's settler establishment their true affines.

The shift was eminently pragmatic. By 2005, the accelerating pace of investment and the massive expectations it fed had generated a long backlog of ambitious tasks to carry out and had resulted in a great deal of employment. Now, people were busy; friends once happy to spend a weekday afternoon chatting over tea at their desks had moved into a new kind of workplace, one with greater demands and better pay. This was evident, for example, at Anadyr's new vocational college, opened in September 2003. It had once appeared that the college instructors and director would be entirely recruited from outside Chukotka. At that time, a great deal of antagonism toward Abramovich's administration from within settler circles in the capital was based on this controversy, particularly since the idea of a college for Chukotka was first proposed by a highly qualified local woman with three decades of teaching experience in the North. In the event, settlers won the battle. She was appointed director, and almost half of her teaching staff was recruited locally. This victory, a public and highly visible recognition that locals could also be experts, mirrored similar episodes throughout Anadyr. Among my settler circles, I encountered local geologists hired to work in the reviving mining industry, journalists returning to the newspaper and television and radio stations, and disaffected teachers returning to the schools on new, and much better, contracts.

As the din of confrontation between Chukotka's settler establishment and Abramovich's newcomers receded, and as the two populations began in fact to interpenetrate and work together, the nativist discourses of rootedness and belonging seemed also to attenuate. In their place had emerged a more complicated language of accommodation, more welcoming to the promise of change without entirely disowning the authority of local knowledge and long residence in the North. For a certain privileged class of urban settler, a stridently localist position was yielding to a new neo-colonial consciousness, as elements of the old Soviet-era settler way of life were recovered. With the return of mobility came the reanimation of the brokering role that settlers in varying degrees had lost to the immobilizing effects of the Nazarov-era crisis. Figures such as the director of the vocational college had decisively returned to the familiar status as intermediary between the power of the distant state and the immediate domains of northern life. In a throwback to the Soviet era, Abramovich's Moscow-based administration had begun to rely on Chukotka's embedded settler elite to enact its policies. Finally, not since Soviet times had Chukotka's settlers enjoyed such a degree of control over their manner of departure from the North. Because the modernization had created employment and restored high pay and northern benefits, they could once again support their children's education in central Russian universities, use their northern wages to buy property outside the North, and look forward to retirement on an elevated northern pension. As a consequence, settlers like Grisha, who might have claimed a *native* identity a few years earlier, were now making preparations to leave: strategies of transience were once again shaping the lives of settlers.

Yet, not all settlers were partaking in this reappraisal. When the momentary condition of two solitudes was most acute, it reified the idea of a monolithic settler identity and signalled a shared sense of northern belonging across this population. But it also concealed the myriad ways in which the experience of living for years in the North had *differentiated* Chukotka's population of in-migrants. The solidarity among settlers in adopting a common language of localism and practices of marking boundaries between outsider and insider amounted to a defensive posture. This language offered a temporary home for people buffeted by the hostile naming practices of their modernizing counterparts and unsure of their material well-being in the future Chukotka. The localist identity, rooted in claims of connection to the natural landscape and its climate, was for many well-educated, urban settlers an unnatural and contrived position. But then, in a storm, any port will do. In retrospect, it was clear that the localist claim, like the discourses of disdain emanating from Abramovich's komanda, was an entry point, a practice of representation used to stake a claim at the outset of an uncertain period of modernizing change. As such, this brand of localism was bound to be as ephemeral as the challenge that awakened it. With this in mind, rather than viewing the discourse of local knowledge as a diagnostic of practical rootedness in the North, we should instead read it as an indication of how thoroughly unavailable was the opposite identity – that of the mobile and modern civilizing agent – when it was monopolized by Abramovich's powerful new arrivals.

Although, a generation earlier, one could speak of a settler population in monolithic terms, this is no longer possible. On the one hand, there are many settlers, particularly in the capital, with only a shallow allegiance to northern life, whose way of life increasingly converges with the most recent generation of in-migrant newcomers. Few plan to stay in the North forever. On the other, the experiences of adaptation, and more importantly of survival during the post-Soviet crisis, have produced a population of non-natives for whom belonging in the North has become a natural and unadvertised fact of life. They hardly existed in the early years of the last great campaign of modernization – the Soviet project of osvoenie – for at that time they were in-migrant "specialists" themselves. But now, this class of settler lives within intimate relationships, to both the natural environment and the local communities, that generate a practical and continually exercised condition of rootedness. Some live in the villages, but others live in Chukotka's capital and its larger towns. Some have ascended to the top of local power structures, others are only getting by. Some have married indigenous partners and have raised children with them. Some are so accustomed to hunting and living on the land that any other kind of life seems repugnant. It was often these settlers who, when I first met them three years earlier, made the least of their local knowledge in rhetorical terms. But then, they were likewise the least likely to view the modernization as a challenge to their way of life, for much of that life played out in spaces of tundra and sea where the changes had no impact.

When this kind of settler voices the language of localism and the discourse of severnaia spetsifika, it is not contrived. We might be tempted to judge settlers' claims to authority on the land as an opportunistic self-presentation, particularly now that many in Chukotka have lost interest in the localist position. After all, if people like Grisha, who once made such robust expressions of attachment to Chukotka's northern landscape, are now looking to their own departure, what credibility remains in the notion of the rooted settler? The answer became evident only with time, as the shock of the modernizing challenge gave way to the complicated processes of accommodation, and each settler made individual peace with the new arrangements in his or her own way. Only at this point was it apparent that the language of local belonging was disingenuous solely for those who appropriated it as a momentary defence. For others, these discourses are in continual use, narrating a way of life that is irreducibly local and rooted in the North. They too require a rhetorical structure to make sense of the lives they lead and to mark the boundaries of their collective and individual identities. As the social texture of two solitudes died away in Anadyr, and settlers and modernizers situated themselves outside of these momentary and simplistic polarities, enduring attachments to life in the

North remained a palpable current within the settler experience. The language of belonging, regardless of the changing cast of characters laying claim to it, persisted.

Practical Attachments

Kolia came to Chukotka from Vladivostok after army service, and for two decades he piloted barges up the Anadyr River to supply the interior settlements of the Anadyr district.[2] During the summer spawning run, he often worked for the fish-processing plant, netting salmon and splitting their stomachs to retrieve the golden roe. A bachelor and alcoholic, he was left in his tiny Anadyr flat with few prospects in Chukotka and none outside of it when the economy collapsed. To survive, he turned to full-time subsistence fishing – smelt in the winter and salmon in the summer – trading a little cured fish on the side for vodka or homebrew and picking up the odd patch of waged work repairing Anadyr's dwindling barge fleet. His flat, with barely room to move between the lines of dryfish, piles of nets and floats, barrels of salmon in brine, and empty bottles, belied the facile dichotomy of urban and rural, and the respective economic domains of the monetized versus traditional-subsistence. Kolia's life was little changed by Abramovich's arrival; the adaptations that ensured his survival in the Nazarov era had become a way of life, replete with networks for barter and a continually exercised intimacy with the land. He epitomized the "economically inactive" "human ballast" that modernizing incomers targeted for removal, yet, in his conversations with me, Kolia talked obsessively about his attachments to the landscape, in both practical and emotional terms. If he could, he would stay.

Recent ethnographic accounts set in the post-Soviet North have almost universally focused on some aspect of the indigenous experience (see Introduction). To the extent that we see European settlers in this literature, they offer themselves as a foil against which are built rich descriptions of indigenous lifeways, identities, and cosmologies. The "Russian" in the North is the "perpetual outsider" (Kerttula 2000), a kind of spectre only half-present, a living remnant of the Soviet colonial order whom we frame within a condition of being out of place. These outsiders, moreover, fail to engage in their local surroundings with anything more than a purely opportunistic brand of land use; the tundra is a vast backyard of natural resources, devoid of cultural or spiritual meaning. They use it, but ultimately long "to be anchored to one site and to walk among monstrous and immovable structures" (Gray 2005, 130) as though northern towns were a proxy for the southern cities of their nostalgic dreams. Certainly, these accounts capture a particular kind of settler experience in the North, but they do not make space for a very different set of non-indigenous identities that are increasingly evident in remote regions such as Chukotka.

This is the most serious deficiency in the existing literature: a failure to disaggregate the category of newcomer into the diversity of experiences and allegiances it contains (admittedly, this was never the goal of indigenous-centred accounts). The very fact that, in most writing, non-natives are still described as newcomers, with an exception made only for the descendants of European migrants of the seventeenth to nineteenth centuries, should raise concern.[3] Recent developments in Chukotka, where the arrival of a new generation of post-Soviet migrants (modernizers) has rendered the pre-existing population of Soviet-era incomers local, provides a forceful illustration of how doubtful this term and its Russian colloquial equivalent, priezzhii, have become.

Although appropriated in an opportunistic way by some with only superficial commitments to the northern setting, the body of knowledge that settlers in Anadyr referenced to symbolically demarcate the boundaries between outsider and insider was based on a practical familiarity with local landscapes that many in fact possessed. This was true of certain settlers even in the capital. For them, the severnaia spetsifika was rooted in an understanding of appropriate behaviour in Chukotka's *natural* conditions, of how to adapt to its extremes. Whereas Abramovich's modernizer imported the built environments of a distant urban way of life – prefabricated housing, designer cafés, luxury air-conditioned vehicles – as a form of insulation, many of those settlers remaining in Chukotka after the out-migration and crisis of the 1990s viewed the natural landscape as an organic extension of the built landscape, as much home as their urban flats. Part of their "ideology of localism" was a celebration of local foods, which were not only viewed as ecologically pure *(ekologicheskie chistye)*, but also testified to competent harvesting practices – the ability to hunt, fish, and gather locally. When I lived in the capital, I often visited an older Russian couple, both former high Party officials. On one occasion they delivered a detailed and enthusiastic explanation of the many discrete salmon runs up the Anadyr River, each of a different species. They described the different tastes and textures of each flesh, and how each kind of roe had to be prepared in its own way. The contrast may not have been intentional, but they then proceeded to tell me about Abramovich's eating habits (they had a friend working in the kitchen of his Anadyr residence): "Everything is brought in – he arrives in his plane and they unload crates of bottled water. This water is from France, I think. And then they unload his food. Everything, meat, milk, bread – it's all from Moscow" [23].

For most settlers, travelling out of the urban or village space, moreover, was not simply an act of subsistence harvesting. This was evident in the fact that, even as budget stability and well-stocked shops returned under Abramovich, urban-based budzhetniki (state employees) persisted in spending their free time on the land, gathering berries, fishing, and hunting. In part, this is because fresh and nutritious foods have always been difficult to obtain in Chukotka's shops for any price – everything but local fish and reindeer is flown across nine time zones from Moscow or shipped forty-five hundred kilometres from Vladivostok. But this also reveals how land use is usually more than strictly a utilitarian practice, even for

Russians. In local settler accounts, going out on the land is good for the soul *(dusha)*, it "ennobles and renews," and for many, it is a movement to a *natural*, as opposed to the artificial, environment. I encountered a Ukrainian builder supervising the rebuilding of Amguema, a remote Chukchi settlement in the interior, who had lived in the district since the 1960s: "They sent me to Moscow to learn about building these kottedzhy, and I had to live in a flat for three months – it was utter hell. How can people live like that? Russians have returned to their troglodyte origins, living in those concrete caves. I couldn't cope anywhere but here; this is my home. When I fish these rivers I feel like a whole person" [56].

The construction of "nature" as an alternative to "civilization," as a place that exists "out there," belongs within a long tradition of Russian romance narratives, particularly as they have been adapted for the North. But in the case of long-term settlers, essentialized views of nature tended to collapse as intimacy with nature grew. When settlers talked of their attachments to Chukotka's natural landscape while sitting in their urban flats, they often framed their perceptions of nature in romantic and essentializing terms, much as Alexander King (2002) has observed. But when I travelled with these same settlers through the landscapes to which they referred, the romantic gloss fell away to reveal the ways in which their pasts were written on the land. I took frequent trips into the interior with the director of Avialesokhrana, Chukotka's wilderness-fire-fighting service (see Chapter 5), as well as several of his senior staff (base managers, parashiutisty, and *nabliudateli* [smokejumper spotters or crewleaders]). On one three-day journey by riverboat up the Anadyr River to the inland settlement of Vaegi, I sat with him in the wheelhouse as he related a succession of personal stories attached to the various locations we passed. We pulled into a bay on the Anadyr estuary, where he showed me a two-metre iron cross, a memorial he had erected to his former accountant, a mixed-descent local from the village of Markovo who drowned nearby in a storm during a berry-picking trip. We poured a libation of vodka before continuing upstream. Later, he pointed to the mouth of a creek, in which he and his closest friend almost died when the vezdekhod they were driving broke through the spring ice. They survived by scooping grease out of the axles to burn in the cabin. On day three, he indicated a hilltop towering over the river, where he made his first landing in Chukotka as a young smokejumper in the 1980s. As we sailed up the river, the director's life in the North emerged as a narrative inextricable from the landscape, made practical and specific, and not at all romantic, by each familiar landmark.

Such accounts reveal an interpenetration of place and person typically witnessed in ethnographies of *indigenous* belonging. Mark Nuttall (1991, 39) has made a compelling argument, based on his research on Greenlandic cultural identity, that senses of belonging to a place emerge through a process of use in which individual and community experiences are "written" on its features. The "hunting places" locals use intensively come to bear the script of collective memory: "The locality is a

Memorial to a lost friend on the tundra near Krasneno, 2003
Photographed by author

memoryscape, a cultural landscape revealed through its place names, which are not merely descriptive but tell of subsistence activities that inform us of a multitude of other close human associations with the natural environment." Nuttall's version of human interpenetration with a landscape is more secular than the indigenous mode that King and Kerttula have described, but as many settlers attest, it contains a force of gravity just as vital. Former geologists who worked on the tundra, while holding professional perspectives on the northern landscape that were by definition utilitarian, were particularly apt to read the land as a "memoryscape." For example, one of them associated a certain mountain face, upon which lie the remnants of a wrecked helicopter, with the eleven geologist friends who perished in the crash. In the willow brush along a certain river, another camped with his new bride in her first year in the North, and he taught her how to fry *blini* on an open fire. She fended off a hungry brown bear with her pan. Certain peaks may hold veins of wolfram, but as an elder Chukchi herder has related, they are also the silhouettes of ancient reindeer. As settler experiences came to be "written" onto the landscape, personal attachments became irrevocable. I interviewed a woman in Moscow who grew up in the settlement of Ust'-Belaia on the Anadyr River, and whose father remained in Chukotka when she left for the materik shortly after the Soviet collapse. He worked as an *okhotoved* (a foreman for the hunting brigade of a state farm) on a large territory in the middle ranges of the Anadyr. An island, where for decades he set his winter camp, came eventually to bear his name in the Chukchi vernacular. When I asked the daughter why her father remained in the North, she said, "I was young when I left and I knew I could start again in Moscow. But Dad is part of that tundra – they [local people] write his name on their maps" [57].

Tundra Vastness and the Existential Moment

It was not immediately evident why certain urban settlers, to whom all the conveniences of the capital were available, would nevertheless attach such value to a continually rehearsed intimacy with the tundra landscape. The former Party official with a thorough knowledge of salmon species was married to a woman originally from Kaliningrad; he preferred to remain in Chukotka when she travelled there on her annual leave. He would spend this time hunting and fishing in the interior west of Anadyr, often staying out for weeks at a time. He knew this landscape; he had come to Chukotka in the late 1960s, and for fifteen years he worked as a geologist on season-long expeditions. He often told me he was more at home on the tundra than in the town. One evening, he explained, "When I'm walking, I always stop to listen. I lie down in the gorse and listen to the silence until my ears ring. You realize you are alone – if you never got up, no one would come to your aid. You realize your human powers, but also your true weakness. You're relying completely on yourself. I live for that sensation" [23].

This could be interpreted as the repetition of a well-worn geologist's cliché about the "silent tundra," reflecting a romanticizing pattern contrasting the urban with nature. But in fact this geologist transcended that formula to end on a more profound note, pointing to the existential condition of the solitary traveller on the vast tundra. On another occasion, he described the tundra as "beautiful, but harsh and indifferent" *(krasiva, no zhestka i ravnodushna),* a place where "you can find everything you need, if you know her" *(dlia tekh kto ee znaiet,' vse v nei pod rukoi)* [23]. With these statements, this man described his movement onto a landscape to which he both submits himself and on which he knows himself to be masterful. His presence in that space, in contrast with the town, is wholly the outcome of an individual act of will. In this manner of using the land, there is a remarkable echo of Tim Ingold's (2000) notion of "enskilled dwelling": the manner in which the geologist knows the land emerges from a long personal history of movement through it.

For those settlers who often left the town and knew how to travel on the land, movement afforded a release from the regimes of control and structure that shaped everyday lives in the urban setting. Driving out onto the tundra from the city in vezdekhody, passengers would choke on dust and exhaust fumes in the rear cabin until, as the concrete landscape receded behind, they could safely pile onto the roof and ride in the open air, beyond the purview of the traffic police *(gaishniki)*. Anadyr was a place of ordered existence and standardized regimes of work, and also a site of effective surveillance, where authorities of many kinds operated the apparatuses of compulsion and sanction. Yet, the city was surrounded by tundra and sea, a terrain over which it could extend little control; the unsettled landscape was therefore its natural foil. Continuous acts of self-liberation through departure from the urban setting were not fuelled by anarchic impulses, however. Instead, submission to the "indifferent" tundra devolved a heightened responsibility onto the person. Distinct from their indigenous counterpart, settler notions of land use were pregnant with ideas of freedom from institutional authority, the unlimited expanse *(prostrantstvo)*, spaces unordered and unsettled *(neustroennost')*, self-realization, and individual agency. These properties coalesce in a single Russian word – *volia* – with its origins in *vol'nitsia* (to achieve liberty), a reference to the flight of serfs and Cossacks from servitude to resettle in Siberia. John Givens (1993, 177) points to the existential character of volia as something more than simply "freedom": "*Volia* implies a conscious willing, an exercising of freedom, an act or action." For the philologist Dmitrii Likhachev, volia is "freedom plus wide open spaces" (quoted in Givens, 180), while the late-Soviet writer Vasilii Shukshin, whose entire opus centred on the particularly Russian aspiration to volia, described the condition as a "holiday of the soul" *(prazdnik dushi)* (quoted in Givens, 188). Shukshin joined in a long literary tradition of manufacturing the idea of Siberia and *sibiriaki*, a tribe of settlers less constrained and more resourceful than the inhabitants of the city. Certainly, the notion of volia penetrated settler self-perceptions, but the search for it also informed behaviours of land use in ways that, far from re-enacting a literary abstraction of volia, reflected personal anxieties and dispositions grounded in concrete circumstances.

An illustration: The employees of Avialesokhrana, the firefighting service, were constantly in motion between "surveilled" and "free" domains – the urban sites of administrative and material resources (Anadyr, Bilibino, Markovo, and Vaegi) and the tundra, where they did their work. As I explained in Chapter 5, its employees evolved complex and locally grounded systems that kept the collective afloat in unpredictable circumstances. If, for example, Avialesokhrana used its resources to transport commercial goods to inland settlements, this simply deepened its social capital in those locations and secured its prospects of working effectively through the coming fire season. Meanwhile, its many techniques of survival pitted the organization against Anadyr-based interests. Avialesokhrana was locked in competition with the okrug branch of the politically powerful Ministry of Emergency Situations (MChS), whose allies – the tax authorities and the Federal Security Service (FSB) – persecuted the firefighters incessantly. I was fortunately not in their vezdekhod when, leaving Anadyr on a three-day journey to Vaegi to deliver a new base manager and supplies, they were apprehended on the outskirts by a team of masked and armed FSB agents who stripped their machine and interrogated the firefighters through the night. The agents said they were trying to prevent the "abuse of state resources" *(netselevoe ispol'zovanie gosudarstvennikh resursov),* and it was widely known that Avialesokhrana often carried extra passengers and goods; Vaegi, like many settlements, had no other regular access to transport. Two months later, with the spring breakup in mid-June, Avialesokhrana sent its 150-ton riverboat to deliver pumps and fuel to its bases upriver in Markovo and Vaegi. My wife and I took this opportunity to travel upriver, but when the day of departure arrived, we were puzzled to be told that we would be leaving Anadyr at 2:00 a.m., as the midnight sun skimmed the horizon. When we stepped on board, we saw that the large passenger cabin was stuffed to the ceiling with boxes of food, its windows curtained. As soon as the silhouette of the sleeping city had faded into the distance and we were alone on the open river, the mood on the boat relaxed, and we cleared the cabin, stacking hundreds of boxes of tinned food, juice, chocolate, and soap on the decks. Later in the journey, I glimpsed into the cargo holds below and saw what I later learned was over a ton of beer.[4] Atop the wheelhouse was fastened a collection of items hardly connected with firefighting: a new Canadian snowmobile won by a Vaegi man in the last ice-fishing derby, a leather office chair for the mayor, a chest freezer, and two perambulators. We weren't even transporting firefighters. Apart from us, the only other passengers on the boat were two Chukchi men from Vaegi who had been stranded for months in Anadyr after medical treatment and were unable until now to return. When we reached the village three days later and unloaded the boat, I counted two cylinder pumps and a few pairs of rubber boots, the sum of our delivery to the firebase.

Here we see that although distance imposes a heavy burden on the lives of northern, and particularly rural, settlers, for those who know the landscape, distance is also a resource. For a settler at ease on the landscape, remoteness affords opportunities of escape from urban-centred structures of control. The tundra is a repository of volia; its unsettledness (neustroennost') affords the individual person control and agency. In practical terms, distance is precious to those with the power to overcome it, for they can dominate those who lack mobility and operate in ways less constrained by the authority of the state. For this reason, there is a strain of settler discourse in which the extremes of climate and isolation in Chukotka attain a positive aspect. They are the necessary conditions for forging the "northern type" – a person in touch with the full extent of his capacities. Avialesokhrana's director described to me a thousand-kilometre journey he took alone by snowmobile from Kamchatka to Anadyr:

> It was early March, intensely cold *[sobachii kholod]* and clear, and the only way I could get back to Chukotka was overland. So I bought a *buran* [Russian snowmobile] and set off. I knew the route – I'd flown the territory by helicopter so many times. I tell you, I was never afraid out there, I was at peace. If the machine had broken down, I would have died and no one would have found my body. But that was *my* problem – I had to make it through, and I did in ten days. Ever since then, I take any opportunity to travel overland in the winter – it strengthens me. [25]

Travel strengthened him because it was a rehearsal of the act of moving and surviving beyond the supporting props of the urban setting. This story follows a narrative pattern I heard many times, in which the solitary individual is brought to the brink of death by some vicissitude of nature and at that point experiences a kind of existential epiphany. When the tundra is most indifferent, the challenges of life in conditions of northern isolation become clearest. The epiphany that such experiences trigger is essentially a self-realization not only of fallibility, but also of power – the skill and experience to move on the land, bridge its distances, and thus accomplish what so few others can.

At the same time as these experiences produce a sense of individual agency, they paradoxically reinforce collectivist loyalties within a select community of northerners. Often, when settlers narrate stories of survival on the land, they identify in such experiences a critical threshold, across which they passed from transience to rootedness in the North. As part of this process, social boundaries imported from mainstream Soviet life dissolve. Settlers detach themselves from their past homes and communities na materike and draw toward their immediate colleagues. One former geologist, who came to Chukotka in 1970 as a Party member, related an epiphany of this kind, when he survived an autumn storm on the tundra in the company of a former convict:

> A terrible blizzard hit and they couldn't get a vezdekhod out to us. We had gone out to visit a drill site for a twelve-hour shift, but it turned into five days. We were in a canvas and wood shelter with no roof, since the drill tower was too high to accommodate – our tower just rattled in the wind and I'm amazed it wasn't carried away. The two of us were stuck there, slowly burning the wood walls for heat, burning our sample trays, the peat insulation between the walls ... In the end, we had to cling to each other for warmth. Before this, he'd said about me, "I'll kill that red shitbag" – I was in the Party since I'd been recommended during army service. And in the end, he and I worked together for two years and I wouldn't have anyone else for a partner. [16]

On the other extreme, Abramovich's imported modernizers insulated themselves from this mode of transformative contact with the environment. The karaoke bar, fitness gym, luxury sauna, cinema complex, internet café, and ice arena in Anadyr were built to duplicate a lifestyle familiar to them. They were constructed as distractions from northern hardship and, in fact, to remove the modernizer from contact with hardship altogether. Many young modernizers accepted northern contracts because of the beguiling exoticism of their destination: remote Chukotka. But their hypermobile and cushioned expatriate lifestyle prevented them from drawing personal lessons from the setting. I initially came to Chukotka as a guest of the Red Cross, an institution staffed by imported experts and strongly identified with outsider-led modernization. Meanwhile, the Avialesokhrana work collective I came to know defined itself as a rooted organization largely through its associations with the natural landscape. My firefighter friends at Avialesokhrana rejected the idea that I could "study life in Chukotka" by spending time at the Red Cross, which they viewed as a kind of artificial and disconnected social space, alien to the non-urban essence of local life. They often told me, "Forget the Red Cross and the [okrug] administration. If it's Chukotka that interests you, only we can help you!"

Like Fredrik Barth's (1969) "idioms" of collective identity, movement into the spaces of volia, where the regimes of urban protection and control were stripped away, reinforced a sense of collectivity and marked the boundaries of difference from the outsider. Whereas, from the outsider's perspective, modernization entailed the enlargement and elaboration of the urban space and its lifestyles, the local way of life required the constant transgression of the imported (and therefore artificial) urban domain. Locals spoke rapturously about fishing in the Gulf of Anadyr during the salmon runs, a form of recreation that involved donning Soviet-era chemical warfare suits and wading far out into the frigid waters to set shore-fast nets (people drowned every season when water entered through puncture holes in the suits, anchoring them out from shore in a rising tide). Danger is implicit in any movement beyond the urban space, just as volia itself implies both personal freedom and responsibility. In contrast, when the modernizing elite ventured into nature, they could not sever their technological umbilical cords. Vice-Governor Gorodilov celebrated his birthday in 2002 by flying upriver with a hundred colleagues in a fleet of helicopters for a day of fishing.

Acting Local, Rural Settlers

If, out of a deep and continually renewed relationship with Chukotka's landscapes, certain settlers drew a sense of themselves as northern people, this was a condition and experience most acutely felt *outside* urban spaces. From Anadyr, getting out to the tundra takes some effort. Many, probably most, residents of the city, busy with the routines of urban life and office work, lived without any kind of genuine and practised intimacy with the land; for them, this relationship was often only rhetorical. This was particularly the case under Abramovich, as the capital's accelerating economy began to demand ever-greater levels of professional commitment from urban settlers. The conditions of life in the villages, in contrast, continued to situate settlers in direct and practical contact with their natural surroundings. Rural isolation enforced a commitment to cultivating the natural and social capital most immediately at hand, and lifting the burden of distance still required knowledge of local places.

Three years after my first visit, I returned to the village of Vaegi once again. It was late August, after the peak bug season, and I joined the "Prince of Vaegi," Viktor Bogorev, as he once again piloted the fire service's riverboat seven hundred kilometres up the Anadyr and Main Rivers from the capital. As always, the decks were stacked with all the sundry necessities of daily life in the interior, and the holds were packed with a season of goods for Viktor's general store: women's nylons, fishing nets, pirated DVDs, Chinese thermoses, tarpaper, and, of course, beer. On the first day, we came upon three moose swimming the still-wide river – a cow and a pair of two-year calves – one of which Viktor shot and quickly butchered on the riverbank, fearful of being spotted by a hunting inspector so close to the capital. Later, at the confluence of the Main and the Anadyr, we stopped at his older brother Sergei's fishing camp a collection of weathered barracks built in the last century by a collective farm downriver and later abandoned. After sharing a bottle of vodka to break the chill of the early morning, Viktor handed over moose meat dried in strips on the boat rigging, and Sergei reciprocated with a three-litre jar of salted salmon roe harvested only the day before. We spread a little on our dwindling supply of bread from Anadyr, downed one more glass "for the road," and sailed south up the blue-green waters of the Main.

The Main River village of Vaegi is only about eighty kilometres south of the larger town of Markovo on the Anadyr. In the stretch between these two communities, the rivers braid and splinter, and a vast labyrinthine expanse of wetlands and twisted channels lies between the main currents. The landscape is low in this part of Chukotka, and an unchanging mass of alder and willow clinging to the banks obscures the view of any mountain that might serve as a landmark. In this place, the power of both rivers is diluted into uncountable detours, pocket lakes, and grassy sloughs, and without a strong, deep current, a boat is constantly in danger of grounding, as attested by the occasional rusting scraps of Soviet barges moored on invisible shallows. To travel safely between Vaegi and Markovo, most boats stay on the largest channel of the Main down to the confluence, and then travel up the widest channel of the Anadyr. This is a journey of almost four hundred kilometres, first east, and then back west again. But for those with exceptional knowledge of the wetlands, there is a much shorter way directly through them, for the labyrinth can be navigated by following a series of winding, shallow channels linking the rivers far upstream of their main confluence. This is always an uncertain route, particularly as the water level falls in the late summer, but for those with the experience, going into the wetland maze can shorten the journey to half a day in a small, fast motorboat.

As we slowly ascended the Main, with the wetlands on our right, a small boat with a single figure at the wheel shot from the mouth of one of these channels. Its speed told us that it had an expensive imported outboard motor fastened to its stern, and so it was no surprise that as it neared, Viktor's youngest brother, Nikolai, stood from behind the windscreen and shouted a few fondly meant expletives. Nikolai, who lived in Markovo, had missed our pull-in at the fish camp, where he had hoped to intercept us; Viktor had promised him a new Korean washing machine and a chest freezer, both still perched on our afterdeck. We pulled into a quiet eddy at the riverbank, wrestled the appliances onto Nikolai's boat, its gunwales now only a handsbreadth above the waterline, and shared some dried moose over a fresh bottle of vodka. Most of what Nikolai had to say concerned his hunting over the past weeks – the freezer would soon be put to use. The salmon were running well, and he expected to spend a few days at Sergei's fish camp in hopes of filling his own pantry and getting a cut of the profits from the jars of roe the brothers would send back with the riverboat on its return journey to Anadyr in a week's time. Neither the hunting nor the fishing was, strictly speaking, legal.

Nikolai Bogorev, younger brother of the "Prince of Vaegi," Viktor, on the Main River, 2005
Photographed by author

But Sergei himself was the wildlife inspector, and there were no others but the brothers in these stretches of river. Not only did they know the labyrinth better than most locals in Markovo and Vaegi, they were the only ones with outboard motors powerful enough to operate so far from the villages. The bottle empty, Nikolai gingerly dropped down into his seat and sped off, quickly disappearing back into the narrow channel that brought him to us.

We reached Vaegi late that evening, and I stayed behind when the riverboat began its journey back to the capital a few days later. As September began, the first signs of autumn appeared. In amongst the aspen and birch forests surrounding the village, scattered stands of larch now perforated the green with their yellow needles. Shoals of mottled salmon slowly circled in the calm waters of the lagoon, their journey to spawning grounds almost complete. Summer's vegetables, with the exception of potatoes and beets waiting to sugar up in the first hard frosts, were ready to harvest. There had been no reindeer meat from the herds in months, for they were high in the mountains on the border with Kamchatka, but huge volumes of cabbage, chives, carrots, cucumbers, and tomatoes were going into pickling jars for the coming winter. One day, Viktor's older brother, Sergei, returned from his fish camp downriver, weary from weeks of netting salmon and scooping their roe into salting vats but pleased with the healthy run this season.

I was waiting for him. The riverboat would not return before freeze-up, and, since it was a wet year without tundra fires, the fire service had no excuse to send a helicopter to the village. There was a scheduled flight from the capital in two weeks, but I needed to be in Anadyr sooner to join a hunting trip. My only way of getting there in time was to catch the weekly flight from Markovo, and only Sergei and his powerful motorboat could take me there. He agreed to do it the next day, but not for free. I might be a guest of his brother the mayor, but I would have to pay him three hundred dollars. The fuel alone would cost a third of that, the trip was difficult in such low water, and in me, Sergei had a captive market. I agreed, relieved after a week of waiting.

We planned to leave before dawn. As the first light began to pinken a low band of clouds to the northeast, I found Sergei in the midst of his vegetable patch. He was stuffing a plastic bag bearing the blank, staring face of Eminem with fistfuls of fresh dill, sheep's sorrel, and soil-covered radishes. He then waded through the thigh-high potato greens to a tool shed, from which he emerged with an armful of reindeer skins and a semi-automatic rifle. He had the price he had asked for, and the haggling was forgotten; now we would make the best of the day and enjoy the trip. As we shuffled down the riverbank to his waiting boat, I could hear the familiar clink of bottles in the bag beneath the freshly plucked dill. It was a crisp September morning, but, with reindeer skins on the seats and over our legs, and the sun beginning to paint the mountain peaks at the edges of the valley, we sped off downriver in comfort.

Touched by the cold night air, the warmer water of the river sent up wisps of mist that, as the morning brightened, still hung along the banks in quiet inlets and eddies. As we turned a bend, we passed a golden eagle standing on a shoal of pebbles and clutching a bloodied salmon, glaring down oblivious as the fish's tail flopped weakly on the rocks. A few bends farther, fresh moose prints made a meandering track along a sandy shoreline and then disappeared in the water, but the animal had made already its crossing and moved into the forest on the far side. Sergei passed me a bottle of bittersweet compote, made from lowbush cranberries he and his wife picked on the bluffs above Vaegi. He produced a box of still-steaming dumplings, stuffed with cabbage and sorrel from his garden, ground reindeer meat, and homemade curd from the dairy cows in the village. His wife had made them in the night before our departure. We grazed on this feast as he told me the story of each bend, mountain, and in-flowing stream. There was the almost overgrown monument to a Soviet-era barge captain who died of a heart attack while skinning a wild reindeer on the riverbank. There was a crumbling cliff undercut by the river's current, where clear blue ice, once deep in the earth, now hung above the water and yielded a rich crop of mammoth tusks. Further downstream, we passed an eroding bank of silo-like hoodoos, which the local Chukchi called the Twenty-one Sisters. Just as the sun's beams finally reached our boat on the water, we passed into the shade of Algan Mountain, whose slope defined the river's eastern bank and still cupped a remnant of morning mist to chill us. Sergei told me this mountain had always been sacred to herders in the area, a guardian visible for great distances in every direction. There had been a plan to build a radio repeater on its peak in the 1980s, but the barge carrying the equipment from Anadyr went aground when the water unexpectedly dropped, and the mountain remained pristine. As we emerged from the shadow, the mouth of the Berezovaia River met our current from the south, and Sergei pointed to the vivid line where its clearer waters met the silty green of the Main.

To our left, the land flattened out and small inlets and channels began to pierce the riverbank – we had come to the labyrinth. Sergei produced a bottle of vodka, which to my surprise we had not yet touched this day, and without a word filled two generous teacups. We toasted, already to friendship, and reached for the radishes. Again we drank from the cups, and my travelling companion told me, with some wisdom I thought, that vodka out in the fresh air could clear the mind as easily as obscure it. With that, he revved the motor and we sped from the Main into the tea-coloured water of a small channel no different in appearance than any of the others we had passed. At times there was a current, but as we wove through the maze we were driving against it as often as with it. Sergei unlocked the outboard on the transom, so that when we hit the shallows it could buck up without breaking a propeller blade. We both donned our rubber hip waders. In one small channel, we walked alongside the boat, pushing it until we found deeper water, and Sergei worried aloud that the autumn waters might have fallen too low to allow even his small boat to pass. We heaved the hull over pebble shoals and walked out to search for deeper water. I could discern no current, one way or the other. The labyrinth was quiet. But we found our way out, in the end. As the sun passed into the western sky, we finally made the main channel of the Anadyr River, a clear and broad current from which the red and silver bodies of salmon arched and slapped on their way upriver. Soon after, we reached the town of Markovo, where I climbed ashore, thanked my friend with one more drink from his teacups, and walked off to the airstrip. He turned his boat back toward the wetland maze. He might reach Vaegi by nightfall.

Since the three Bogorev brothers first came to fight forest fires in the 1980s, the stories concerning them in Chukotka comprise a rich narrative of the settling experience. These men bring nuance to the false polarities of local and transient, fixed and mobile, that so often shape our expectations of the northern newcomer. Sergei and his brothers illustrate belonging in a place to be a subtly graduated condition, one that is continually reshaped by experience and chance. They show that staying in the North and longing to leave can be impulses that occur in the same person. As for certain long-established settlers in the capital, the ability to move over the land comprised a vital source of self-understanding and agency. But, much more than in the capital, the power of mobility is power itself: without local knowledge, they would be immobilized; without mobility, they would lose their knowledge.

With Sergei, the ideas he has of his place in life and his ways of moving on the land interweave in surprising and contradictory ways. He never meant to stay in Vaegi. Like generations of Cossack trader-adventurers *(promyshleniki)* of past centuries who travelled to the Siberian frontier to make their fortunes collecting fur tribute (iasak), he (and later his brothers) initially saw this remote village as a domain where they could operate in freedom. At some point during the Soviet collapse, he promised his Russian wife they would leave when they could afford to, but not before they had paid for the university education of their two children. Staying, at that point, was still a strategy of controlled departure. By the time we met, his eldest son was studying medicine in the most prestigious military academy in the country, due in no small part to Sergei's prodigious ability to pay bribes. Sergei generated this money because he knew what resources the land and the waters around Vaegi could afford him, and because he possessed the technology and experience to exploit them. In summer, he harvested caviar and smoked salmon, hunted moose and wild reindeer, and moved goods and people between Markovo and Vaegi by boat. In the autumn, he hired local women to gather berries, which he sold by the jar to the capital. As winter set in, he and his brothers hunted (and still occasionally obtained a few reindeer from the village herds) and traded the meat on to Anadyr. All year round, he brewed his moonshine and sold it in the village (angering his younger brother, Viktor, who was now mayor). Equally important were the steps he and his wife took to save money by living on their large vegetable patch, the berries and fish they preserved for the winter, and Sergei's hunting. Their lives were still shaped by a residual sense of transience, but it was their children who were leaving while they deferred their own departure. The fact was, neither Sergei nor his wife could any longer imagine a different way of life.

Back in the capital, settlers contended with the challenges of Abramovich's modernization by employing the morality of local belonging, using both discourses and behaviours to mark the boundaries of a distinct northern identity. They claimed to be a special breed, as though the old sense of settler community still transcended the vast distances between Chukotka's towns and villages and bound this population together within common creeds of northern life. Many urban settlers indeed substantiated aspects of this claim through their intimate relationships with the landscape. But really, Sergei and others like him in Vaegi felt little in common with Russians in Anadyr, regardless of whether they were newcomers or established settlers. In the new Chukotka, settler identity was no longer so confederate; little popular sense of identification in a regional Chukotkan identity remained.[5] Now, the most meaningful loyalties rested on solidarity within literal, rather than imagined, places. Just as relationships with the landscape were practical (and local), rather than mediated by romantic images of nature, the imagination of a broader pan-settler identity had foundered on the more palpable reality of literal communities and their immediate natural surroundings.[6]

For people in the village, settlers and natives alike, a common manner of professing local attachments was to direct some sort of slight at the city. Mirroring a general enmity many Chukotkans in the capital held for the megacentre, Moscow, there was a strong current of disdain in Vaegi for Anadyr, which for villagers embodied bureaucratic indifference, metropolitan arrogance, and a flippant disregard for the real challenges of living close to the land. There, in the words of Anthony Cohen (1982, 305), lived people "who have no experience of the local situation but who wield decisive powers over it." Any sense of common cause between city-dwellers and villagers broke apart upon this perception, namely, that urban folk had no true understanding of how masterful villagers were at surviving in the difficult conditions of extreme isolation and an arctic climate. Instead, an ideology of the village emerged that simultaneously valorized knowledge of local surroundings and directed mistrust at the outsider.

In Vaegi, the Bogorev brothers spoke in this language. It also came through vividly in the views of a less powerful but equally rooted member of the settler community, a Cossack named Volodya, who came to the village in the late 1970s as an itinerant labourer.[7] While working as a builder, he met a young Koryak woman just finishing studies at the residential school and settled down to raise a family. When we met, he still officially worked for the public works office as a mechanic, fixing the diesel tractor and maintaining the village generator. But in the summer months, he spent most of his time far from the village. Like practically all those settlers who lived on in Vaegi, Volodya had developed a fluent knowledge of local hunting grounds and the stretches accessible from the Main River. Most days, he travelled up and down the river in a small motorboat with a Chukchi sled dog on its forepeak, checking his salmon nets and gathering mushrooms and berries. It was his native wife, working in the village administration, who earned the cash the family required, while Volodya tended the gardens and built up the larder in preparation for each winter. In this way, they had survived the crisis years passably well, although he had not seen his family in southern Russia since his last visit fifteen years earlier. This is a quote from one of his best stories:

> I had a Chukchi friend who was hunting upriver, and he was attacked by a polar bear. This is totally unexpected in the taiga – this bear was a long way from its home territory and was really desperate. Anyway, my friend was a tough guy. He was just getting tea-water from the river when the bear attacked him, so he only had his hunting knife with him. He got properly mauled and the bear took both his ears off with his paws, but he didn't give up. He was almost dead, but he managed to reach his knife and kill the bear by going in from the belly. So a few weeks later, he's lying in the clinic here in the village and these two bureaucrat parasites fly in from Anadyr and arrest him in his bed for killing a protected animal! That's the kind of shit we put up with from those "nature protectors." They just warm their office chairs in Anadyr for a living. [60]

Typical of the settlers in the village, Volodya blamed Anadyr for the failure of air transport and barge supplies in the 1990s, but he more deeply resented its bureaucratic intrusions into his way of life. They had survived the post-Soviet crisis not thanks to, but *despite* the Anadyr-based administration. It was common in the settlements to encounter a view of the capital as a nest of bureaucrats who fed on the rural hinterland. Anadyr "eats the fat off our backs – those parasites just eat the settlements away!" rued a police officer from the district centre of Beringovskii. This perception deepened in the 1990s, when Governor Nazarov cut services and wage payments in the settlements and concentrated state resources in Anadyr, his true patronage base. Residents of Beringovskii, whose coal mine supplied Anadyr with fuel for heating and power, were themselves without utilities for several years. But bureaucratic parasitism was itself a locally grounded system of survival, a way of life for thousands of settlers who migrated from productive employment to state jobs as the economy collapsed.

On one journey up the Anadyr River to visit Vaegi, I travelled with Chukotka's head inspector for small vessel safety, who toured rural Chukotka every summer extracting licence fees and fining boat owners for "safety infractions." He stayed in Vaegi for a week before moving on to Markovo, and I watched him collect his fines without returning any service to boat owners. In time-honoured style, the rural inspector was simply collecting his rents. In Vaegi, he epitomized the intruding outsider in the village setting, where he wielded punitive authority yet lacked the necessary knowledge to produce anything useful. One morning, as I was setting out with Volodya to check nets on the river, the inspector walked down to the shore and gave him a fine because his Soviet-built Vikhr outboard motor lacked an engine cowling. The inspector failed to see, or possibly contrived to ignore, the obvious explanation: the engine required constant restarting by manually winding a length of twine around the starter wheel and wrenching it into motion. A cowling would have only gotten in the way. In fact, I thought it quite an impressive achievement that Volodya was still using an ancient Vikhr to get up the river. Such ingenuity was certainly beyond the reach of the inspector (although, to be fair, the inspector's facility for collecting his rents was an exquisite talent in its own right).

Encounters like these coloured the outsider with a taint of danger and produced a local conviction that only within the village was the code of the North (based on principles of mutual respect and generosity) properly observed. What mattered in Volodya's moral frame was the accumulation of experience in the local setting, and by extension sympathy for the adaptations that survival there required. This was apparent within the domain of local land use, and the localist claims to identity he staked somewhat dissolved the ethnic divide across which stood his indigenous counterparts. When I suggested that the most difficult thing about living so far from Anadyr must be the lack of fuel, he answered, "It's hard, but I tell you, if there was more fuel around, all the Chukchi men back here in the village would have taken boats and snowmobiles and hunted down every living thing in the area. They're mostly useless, the ones who've lost touch with herding and just hang around here. They don't know how to hunt with respect" [60].

So Volodya rejected both the abstract conservationist extremism of urban inspectors and those practices in the local domain that upset the natural balance he claimed to know intimately. He was not a herder – a profession still the preserve of Chukchi men – but he sorted out friends from enemies not according to ethnicity, but rather within a rubric of proprietary concern for the security of the land and its resources.

Here, I wish to avoid the suggestion that village settlers elevated a Russian mode of land use above and distinct from what they perceived to be indigenous practices. Many settlers in fact professed deep respect for indigenous traditions of land use. In the remote settlement of Vankarem on the Arctic coast, I listened to a Russian vezdekhod driver describe one of the few other remaining settler men as "a really gifted hunter, as good as the old Chukchi" [61]. For him, a notion of the "true Chukchi" served as a kitemark of skill on the land, a model for young natives and settlers alike. Indeed, settlers themselves often took on board the accusation levelled by indigenous activists at the "newcomer" – that Europeans hold a consumerist attitude to the land – but redirected the complaint toward the outsiders of the present, Abramovich's incomers. In this manoeuvre, they consciously positioned themselves in the company of Chukotka's indigenous population (and in particular its older, more "genuine" representatives), whose traditions they might have romanticized into an ideal of sustainable land use, but in whose local rootedness they identified.

In Vaegi, with its mixed population of Chukchi, Koryak, Russian, and métis inhabitants, ethnicity was losing its power as a predictor of native belonging – it wasn't always the indigenous villagers who wanted to stay. Moreover, as the lives of Volodya and the Bogorev brothers testify, an intimate knowledge of the land and, indeed, a propriety respect for it were no longer strictly indigenous attributes. The forces of modernization under Abramovich perpetuated a long-standing set of policies that, regardless of their intention, were levering rural youth out of the village and into distant institutions of higher learning. For Vaegi's young, summer camp programs in central Russia, free spaces in Anadyr's residential college, and perhaps most forcefully of all, employment in Anadyr's booming service and construction industries conspired against a future in the village and out on the tundra. In 2005, locals were calling another settlement downriver, Ust'-Belaia, the "village of orphans." There, scores of working-age indigenous villagers had left their children in the care of grandparents to take jobs in Anadyr.

Few of these younger native villagers either knew how to live on the tundra or wished to know. Vaegi's traditional herding economy had more or less collapsed, and an entire generation had grown up almost completely divorced from the herding and hunting way of life. The vulnerability of indigenous people during the collapse was based on their long-standing dependency on the state to support lives of movement between tundra and village; the ruin of the state-farm system immobilized them in the latter space. Meanwhile, as a class of entrepreneurial settlers like the Bogorevs capitalized on the retreat of the state (and the weakness of their indigenous counterparts), the resources and knowledge needed to travel on the tundra and harvest sustenance from it became concentrated in their hands. So it was that in the deepest years of crisis, the Bogorevs occasionally sold the meat of wild reindeer and moose they had hunted to indigenous villagers who could no longer hunt for themselves. Among village youth, it was the children of these settlers who, due to their superior access to transport, invariably possessed the deepest knowledge of Vaegi's natural surroundings. In the end, they might not choose to stay in the village, but by virtue of experience their sentiments of belonging would extend beyond its edges and into the tundra and waters of the area.

The Density of Community

> Many may remain where they were born out of habit or spiritual duty, but the staying itself is conducive to life because the lived-in land then becomes an extension of the self, the family, the group. Deborah Tall (1996, 112)

Just as practices of land use and discourses of rootedness shape and mark settler identity, senses of belonging also emerged out of a density of relationships and kinship ties within Chukotka's small communities. Since mass settlement began in the Soviet era, the social life of these communities has been at once a powerful source of settlers' belief in their own exceptionality and a compelling cause of their decisions to stay on in the North. It is out of the particularly intense tissue of mutual entanglement and reciprocal helping in northern life that the idea emerged of settlers as a "better people," more honest, generous, and loyal than their central Russian counterparts. Although post-Soviet hardship somewhat emasculated the old norms of community life, at the same time, strategies of survival, whether in Anadyr's urban-bureaucratic networks or remote settlements like Vaegi, still perpetuated long-established patterns of reciprocal aid. As we now see, with the passage of time, those patterns of reciprocity are often concretized in marriage and perpetuated through multiple generations, before their local memorialization in death and the collective memory.

In 2001, advertisements promoting the new administration's campaign to resettle residents of Chukotka to central Russia began to flood the local media, often carrying this publicity mantra:

> They leave because they've given Chukotka all they could!
> They leave for the sake of their children!
> They leave because a new life awaits them! Others await them!
> The Resettlement Program – choose your region!
> Life begins there!

Resettlement comprised a key plank of cost-cutting reform; the administration projected an ideal population of thirty to thirty-five thousand (down from seventy-four thousand in 2001) and proposed the closure of "non-viable" (besperspektivnye) towns and the amalgamation of several districts (see Chapter 6). Many non-indigenous locals took the offer of resettlement, and in the first three years after Abramovich's election, Chukotka's population dropped by twenty thousand. But this was not so large a drop as planners hoped for. The population remaining after the mass out-migration of the 1990s proved less amenable to restructuring than they anticipated. Belying predictions of large "delayed demand" for out-migration (Kontorovich 2000; Heleniak 1999), the resettlement program was in fact undersubscribed in its first three years of operation. Moreover, precisely those kinds of locals whom the administration wished to resettle – middle-aged and older pensioners, the region's so-called human ballast – were often those least interested in departure. Abramovich's investment in resettlement, intended to increase the proportion of young, healthy, and working-age residents to the retired or invalid, and thus to lower social-care costs to the state, appeared to be producing the opposite effect.

The reluctance of pension-aged settlers to leave Chukotka – a total inversion of administration modernizers' expectations – becomes intelligible when local people are considered in terms of the sociality within which they are knitted. Studies in two neighbouring regions bear this out. In an investigation of resettlement in Sakha Republic, Piers Vitebsky (2000) found that settlers without local kinship resources were the most likely to leave for southern Russia, whereas those set in local networks of family and community would often remain, even if they had reached pension age. John Round's (2005) study of gulag survivors in Magadan Oblast suggested that the desire to remain (rather than resettle to central Russia), which development agencies viewed as irrational, was a natural reflection of the relative security these pensioners enjoyed within their local mutual aid network. In 2003, I spent several months interviewing resettlers from Chukotka now living in central Russia. This research revealed that, in the absence of overwhelmingly compelling factors such as community closure or extremely poor health, pensioners tended to resist resettlement from the North unless they were following the earlier out-migration of children. Leaving kin behind in Chukotka was very difficult, both emotionally and in terms of its effects on pensioners' domestic economy and chances of survival. Among my interviewees in central Russia, three pensioner couples whose children and grandchildren remained in Chukotka deeply regretted their decision, particularly when they learned that their right of residency (*propiska*) in Chukotka had been permanently revoked as a condition of resettlement.

A common belief among Chukotka's settlers was that leaving the North to live in a temperate or hot climate after a long period (at least ten years) is medically harmful, and in fact often deadly. Many could point to friends who had left for warmer regions only to drop dead within a year. The human organism, they claimed, adapted irrevocably to the North over time and should not again be transplanted. Indeed, they even claimed that the abundance of vitamins in the fresh foods available in the south was toxic to a "northern organism." I could find no medical or statistical evidence to support this claim, but locals nevertheless treated the notion as a medical fact. It did, however, seem to be true that resettlers often fared poorly, and those of a pensionable age often died within one or two years of moving south. The actual causes of this mortality, as some northerners reflected, might rather be linked to the psychological stress of displacement and the practical consequences of losing family and community support. One older settler, a former sovkhoz director in the coastal settlement of Uelen, framed his own choice to stay in Chukotka after retirement in these terms: "My children and grandchildren were born here – they have no attachment to my old home in Ukraine. So how can I leave if my children stay behind? Sure, I'll live in a comfortable climate, I'll eat fresh vegetables and fruit, I'll never have to worry about blizzards and the long arctic winter. But I'll sit there alone, and I'll be lonely without my children. That is what kills the pensioners who leave, you know" [52].

He continued this observation in more poetic terms: "The old-timers *[starozhiltsy]* who leave must maintain a connection to the North, even if only symbolic: if they lose touch altogether, they're walking corpses. Their souls will be eaten away and they will cease to be fully human" [52].

Abramovich's resettlement program was one of the principal causes of local settler resentment to the modernization. Many perceived resettlement and the liquidation of settlements as proof that the new okrug administration was a corporate division of Abramovich's oil company, Sibneft, staffed by managers who viewed local people as mere economic factors. As the marketing campaign for resettlement gathered momentum, the old Anadyr was demolished to make way for the new, and thousands of imported shift labourers undertook local construction work. I detected a widespread conviction among long-term settlers that modernization was "squeezing us out" *(nas vyzhimaiut)*. A former Party official from Anadyr who loved to hunt on the tundra alone remarked, "That advertisement for resettlement – it's so blatant *[naglyi]*! I know people who have to run into another room whenever they hear it. It's clear – we're not wanted here any more" [23].

Over the course of decades, like many older locals, this man had built relationships within his local community that now eclipsed those he left behind na materike, even those of kin. He explained, "What do I have na materike? Well, I grew up there, studied, served in the army, but then I came straight to the North. As they say, I spent my best years here. Now both my parents are dead. I have a stepfather in Nakhodka [near Vladivostok] with a dacha and garden, a car, a motorcycle – he calls me to tell me it's all mine. But it's not mine – I couldn't imagine setting up a new life there among strangers" [23].

In her ethnographies of life in the northern Welsh mining town of Blaenau Ffestiniog, Isabel Emmet (1982, 207) wrote of the density of community life that, over time, engenders a fixity of social identities and simultaneously defines community belonging: "Those who have grown up in the town have such a wealth of knowledge of each other as to make each encounter densely elaborate." Social "density," though possibly suffocating to the young, was exactly what older settlers in Chukotka feared to lose by leaving. I interviewed a sixty-five-year-old in the district centre of Egvekinot, a former underground tin miner from the liquidated town of Iul'tin and now an alcoholic bachelor living alone in an abandoned flat.

He told me, "They want me to leave – for my health they say. But I'll die soon wherever I am. There [in a central Russian city] people will just see another grandpa, some old fool with no name. But here when I walk on the street, people see [informant's name], they remember who I was. They know I helped build this place, that I was strong and beautiful" [34].

Another feature of the social density of settler society in Chukotka was its increasingly multi-generational profile. The emergence of families of two and three generations living in the same northern towns created affective bonds that cut in both directions, and members of the younger generations often joined their older counterparts in opting for security in local networks instead of the opportunities offered by resettlement. Along with retirement, the moment of school graduation and movement into higher studies was a point at which settlers were particularly likely to permanently migrate from Chukotka. Until 2003, the okrug administration funded the higher education of hundreds of local school graduates in universities throughout Russia, providing tuition, maintenance, and transport. Many working-age locals who planned to out-migrate deferred their move until their children were able to commence higher studies outside the North. Nevertheless, many locally raised youth chose to remain in the North, eschewing higher learning or opting to study by correspondence. Those who did study away often returned to join their networks of kin and friends after taking their degrees. They spoke of the importance of *rodnye steny* ("native" or "home walls"), the "common understanding of what northern life is" among northern friends, and the "pull back home" *(tiaga domoi)*. Several former students who studied na materike explained that while in Moscow or St. Petersburg, they recreated northern networks of mutual aid by working closely with other Chukotkan students. They also preferred to share university residences with fellow northerners, because "we speak the same language," an expression conveying an almost ethnic sense of difference from "mainlanders" [44] [45].

A final key process of local assimilation for settlers was intermarriage. Soviet-era in-migrants typically came to Chukotka without family networks, but since their arrival, many of the most rooted settlers have developed extensive kinship ties within local communities. Piers Vitebsky (2002) has described the marriage of settler labourers to native women in rural Siberia as a corrosive force, denaturing village communities by marooning native men, often nomadic herders, in a purgatory of bachelorhood. In the village of Vaegi, almost all of the approximately thirty settler men who had a long history there were married to native women. Whether a corrosive presence or not, these were settlers with strong attachments to the village, remaining there after a decade of settler out-migration. Most had children in the community. Few planned to leave in the future. The sentiments of Volodya the Cossack suggest that these people could be deeply protective of local resources, even at the expense of their indigenous counterparts.

The Russian graveyard in Vaegi after the Day of the Ancestors, 2005
Photographed by author

As so often occurs in Russia, kinship was also felt with the deceased. The need to identify a *rodina* (homeland) partly arises from the practical concern that individuals should be buried in their true community, where the living can visit and care for their graves.[8] Anxiety about burial thus continually haunts Russians in a state of migrancy, and burial choices are a clear indication of primordial attachments. When settlers died in Soviet Chukotka, they were almost always flown back to the materik for burial. Long-time settlers recall the ever-present, brightly shining aluminium caskets laid out on the Anadyr airport apron beside passengers embarking for Moscow. But in the 1990s, as the cost of airfare to Moscow surpassed the value of a two-room flat in Anadyr, this practice virtually ceased. The small local cemetery quickly reached its limits, and within a decade, a new field of graves sprouted in the tundra beyond the town. Now settlers in many parts of Chukotka observe a ritual, which, according to my informants, was never before part of Soviet life in the North: on the Day of the Ancestors (literally, Parents' Day – *roditel'skii den'*), locals visit the graves of their loved ones to drink, eat, and care for the spirits of the dead. The former high Party official told me that after a week of hunting he was walking back to Anadyr through the new cemetery. He stopped for a drink and, looking about the tombstones, each bearing a small portrait of the deceased, he was struck by the fact that almost every face was known to him. His gaze then fell on the black-and-white features of a good friend, exactly his age but dead for five years, and he noticed how well the grave was tended. He was struck by the thought, almost unthinkable before, that his own grave should be among these, cared for by the friends he had made in his northern life. He remarked, "Morally, I'd be better off lying out there in the cemetery" *(Mne moral'no budet normal'no esli by ia lezhal tam)* [23].

By choosing a local burial, settlers in Anadyr were not only staking a final claim to belonging there, they were inscribing themselves on the local landscape, hopeful that the living would perpetuate their memory within their adopted community. The norms of community exchange thus passed into the domain of death – a well-tended grave remained a testimony to a settler's achievement in building a social "density" of some durability. Abramovich's modernization, in many of its forms, would erase such achievements of belonging while failing to discern their existence, or even their possibility.

A Man Settles Down

The ingredients of belonging are many, and they exist in Chukotka's most committed settlers in as many combinations as they have stories. The density of community life, the powers that come from knowing the land, the kinship felt with the living and the dead, and the accumulated habits of localized survival – they are only some of what constitute practical belonging in the North. Sometimes belonging to a place amounts to a benign and socially enriching way of life, but sometimes to stay in place is a privilege settlers have fought for in the most predatory and internecine fashion. Most often, there is a mixture of both in the individual stories settlers tell about getting by, although it might take an anthropologist many visits to realize this. In whatever way settlers have made their peace with life in Chukotka's still-remote towns and settlements, and whatever are their daily practices of belonging, they are logics of remaining in place surpassing in solidity and longevity the symbolic jousting of boundary marking. There is no way of knowing this, and of judging the rhetoric of identity with detachment, other than to watch over time the progress of individual human lives in Chukotka. So, let us return to the Bogorev brothers in Vaegi a final time.

In the early 2000s, there were at least twelve Russian men living in Vaegi, most married to Chukchi and Koryak women, who might be thought of as fully settled. They were all likely one day to welcome burial in the Russian graveyard in the birch grove on the northern edge of the village. In their company, Viktor Bogorev, who came to the North in the footsteps of his brother Sergei to smokejump tundra fires when the Soviet Union was already fracturing, was a new arrival. Leaving ailing parents in a village near Smolensk, he came to try his luck in Chukotka at a very unlucky time. Perhaps it was a sense of coming late to the party, or perhaps it was his intuition to make a virtue of necessity, but Viktor and his two brothers chose to make their stand in Russia's enveloping crisis by staying. They owed nothing to anyone, they were three without kin, and they came north with few romantic aspirations. In fact, Viktor and his brothers could hardly have preyed on Vaegi and the lands surrounding it without holding some measure of hatred for the place (a hatred possibly born of the bitter disappointments that came with the collapse of the prosperous North and the destruction of the forest-fire-fighting service). I have already related how the Bogorev brothers created of Vaegi in the 1990s a kind of private fief, which they proceeded to parasitically bleed of its modest resources in the most imaginative and mercenary ways (Chapter 5).

When I first travelled to the village in 2002, little had changed since the desperate years of crisis under Nazarov: the village shop was still practically empty, and the clinic had no medicines or even a nurse. Everything from the boarding school to the kolkhoz to the power plant was falling to pieces. There were no scheduled flights out, and villagers still died every year when even medical evacuation flights failed to reach them. Viktor's brother Sergei was the biggest bootlegger and moonshine brewer in the village, but he had plenty of competition. Although Abramovich was now governor, and the modernization was proceeding in other parts of Chukotka, the okrug administration in Anadyr was unsure that rebuilding so remote and poor a village as Vaegi would be a good investment, or even possible.

But in the village, one thing had changed: Viktor had run for mayor against the Chukchi incumbent and won. As a consequence, I soon realized, my visit came at a watershed moment, both for Viktor personally and for Vaegi. He sensed that the time for predatory survival tactics had ended, that there could be a future for Vaegi if somehow he could reach out to Anadyr and make himself known to the governor's people. He knew that Abramovich, very unlike his predecessor Nazarov, was a teetotaller and that the drinking culture in the villages was one of the governor's principal complaints. It must not have been a coincidence that, much to his brother's surprise, Viktor suddenly rounded on Vaegi's moonshine brewers. It started with a warning, but then one brewer's teenage son was beaten bloody in a shack, apparently by the local police constable (and Viktor's ally). Viktor was also making changes in his own life. He moved out of the house he had long shared with a Russian woman in the village, and into another left abandoned by a departing schoolteacher. He had been spending time with a pretty young girl, a member of Vaegi's largest and most powerful Chukchi clan, and now she was pregnant. Despite his misgivings, Viktor (who was now in his forties) had decided to raise a family with her.

When I returned to Vaegi three years later, Viktor was again piloting the Avialesokhrana riverboat on the three-day journey up the river, and he told me about his work. He said he'd travelled the great distance between village and capital so often that he'd contemplated moving his family to Anadyr so he could see them more. He made a point of telling me that he was one of the only village heads to have met Governor Abramovich on his rare visits to the okrug – several times. Apparently, he had been hunting the governor and his ministers with the same merciless determination that he poached the moose and reindeer in the lands around Vaegi, and with the same success. Against all expectations, the okrug administration did not choose to liquidate Vaegi's kolkhoz and amalgamate its remaining reindeer with Markovo's herds. To combat the belief that Vaegi was too isolated and difficult to reach to be included in the village modernization campaign, Viktor personally piloted supply barges up the river and led truck convoys overland in the winter months (so few shipments had reached the village in the 1990s that Viktor was practically the only person in Chukotka with the knowledge to navigate the journey). Meanwhile, he made a point of broadcasting news of the new sobriety in Vaegi. Taking advantage of his old networks, he visited kommersanty in Anadyr who in the past had organized bootlegging flights and informed them they were never again to set foot in his village.

What Viktor said was interesting enough, but the physical transformation of the village in only three years was astounding. Families were moving out of their old tarpaper shacks and into newly built houses with sealed windows, central heating, and running water. The school was under renovation, and Viktor had convinced several new teachers and a director from Ulyanovsk to move to Vaegi. Before, those who wished to wash did so in water heated on a stove; now the old sauna, closed for a decade, was working again. Viktor had already used the prospect of a modern new house, the improved school, and free vegetable plots to lure specialists to the kolkhoz, and now he was secretly negotiating with Ust'-Belaia's only two doctors in the hopes they would relocate. Pay was still poor at the kolkhoz, but it was reliable, and herd numbers were rising. Meanwhile, to exploit Vaegi's unique growing conditions, the kolkhoz had planted experimental cabbage and potato fields. They were producing such an abundant crop that Viktor was making preparations to start shipping vegetables to settlements downriver in the coming year. There was also a new flash-freezer for storing reindeer meat, which would be driven by vezdekhod to market in the capital after freeze-up.

There were changes in Viktor's life as well. His family had grown with the birth of two more children, and they had moved into one of the newly built houses. Outside, next to his Soviet vezdekhod, stood an even bigger six-wheeled all-terrain vehicle. He was almost finished renovating his sauna buildings, which would now house a two-room "hotel." And in 2005, he fought a hard campaign and was re-elected mayor, an event that pleased him almost as much as Abramovich's decision to remain in power for another term.

In light of the scale of modernization throughout Abramovich's Chukotka, the changes in Vaegi were not unusual. Many settlements were rebuilt in their entirety. But the modernization was a selective process, destroying the besperspektivnye in some places as it rebuilt the villages and towns of the "new Chukotka" in others. A tiny village of several hundred, almost without reindeer, lying far up a

Viktor Bogorev and his Chukchi wife, waiting for the Avialesokhrana helicopter in Vaegi, 2005
Photographed by author

shallow, braided river nearly impossible to navigate, and soaked in alcohol, Vaegi looked to be one of the doomed. Viktor, one of the architects of its destruction during the 1990s, had in the following decade made an extraordinary effort to save the village from that fate. I do not think he was driven by altruistic loyalty, but rather (as always with the Bogorev brothers) by shrewd calculation. It suddenly became clear that so deeply intertwined were his interests with those around him, and with the land beyond, that the future of the village would be his future. His parents in Smolensk were dead, his brothers were here, and now there was a family. As he said to me, "I used to dream about taking my children away from the North, settling in a big city – now that I have them, I dream they'll stay here with me. There is nothing I can teach them about that isn't here in the North." Viktor, he realized himself, had settled.

9
Afterword

The settler story springs from a history of modernizations and their intervals, periods of stagnation, poverty, and colonial unravelling. In the late-Soviet period, policies of northern development (severnoe osvoenie) were policies of settlement. The culture of the development campaign saturated the self-understanding of its modernizing participants; that is why, long after they came to the North, they still called themselves newcomers (priezzhie). Settling down, on the other hand, was a coping strategy in times of demodernization, when northern people were left behind by the retreat of the state. As settlers were detached from their colonial-modernizer identities by this collapse, many came to think of themselves as local people, belonging to the place they inhabited.

The dominant interpretations, however, disguise this process. In the Chukotka of Roman Abramovich, absentee governor, the myth of the man and his modernizing projects concealed the deeper and more historically significant reality of settler belonging. One of the most ardently communicated ideas attending his arrival was the claim that a modernization like his had never been seen before. His modernization sought a special status on that basis, putting its agents and techniques on the far side of an unbridgeable divide separating the new and the old. The achievements of the settler, so similar in their time to those of Abramovich's experts, were by this logic erased. Having appropriated the "modern" identity, the new arrivals assumed the authority to declare Chukotka's settlers not only backward and neo-Soviet, but also lacking affinity to the North – a removable population. Believing in modernization without precedent is, of course, dangerously like believing in the end of history. It is as mistaken as the notion that certain people will always be modern – more powerful, more mobile, more expert than others. But, as the people of the Russian Far North can attest, campaigns of modernization come and go, and anyone standing in their tidal wash is likely to experience many different variations of participation and exclusion, agency and emasculation.

If we are to understand the settler story up to the present day, we need to separate the Abramovich modernization from its rhetorical dressing, place it within a history of modernizations, and put our finger on what it changed and what it left untouched. Conveniently, we are already examining this enigma in the past tense, for although President Putin appointed Abramovich for a second gubernatorial term in October 2005, by that time the attention of the man (and with it the reformative zeal of the campaign) had already departed. Clearly, the modernization of

Chukotka was less innovative and more derivative than its rhetoric promised. Despite its claims to a transcendent *post*-Soviet modernity, this was at heart a very Soviet project of catching up, replete with the mass arrival of newcomer experts, the hortatory language of impossible endeavours made possible, impressive capital and technological investment, and an endless glossing-over of the inadvertent damage caused by its crusading methods. To cap it all, so inexperienced were Abramovich and his missionary-like cadre of new arrivals with this kind of work that they ultimately resorted to Soviet models as the objective of their reforms. Thus, their "post-Soviet" mode of rural development amounted to the effective reconstitution of the Soviet state farm, supported by a reconstituted Soviet system of subsidized air transport and Soviet incentive measures for encouraging higher output. To address the low level of vocational skills among indigenous youth, the new education authority returned to the Soviet model of residential education, in many cases removing the young from their homes year-round. On a material level, after a difficult decade under Governor Nazarov, the improvement of living conditions was a true transformation. But in other domains, the language of new directions – of a non-derivative modernity – was irreconcilably distant from the various actual forms this campaign produced. The Abramovich "modernization" was, effectively, not what it claimed to be.

In the first years after Abramovich's election (2001-3), contrary to the overwhelming consensus (in the international media, within academic circles, and in popular Russian opinion) the logic of the campaign did not rest solely on the need for charity. Instead, the governor's arrival in Chukotka was a matter of financial enrichment and political survival under political circumstances increasingly hostile to his larger interests. In Chapter 6, I described the mechanisms by which, between 2001 and 2005, transfer-pricing arrangements and a privileged tax regime in Chukotka made a fortune for the Sibneft-Millhouse industrial structure. I also described how, by very aggressively advertising his efforts to reconstruct Russia's most impecunious northern region, Abramovich protected this fortune, just as President Putin destroyed his closest oligarchic analogue Mikhail Khodorkovsky through the courts. Even now, it is difficult to judge who in 2000 – the people of Chukotka or Roman Abramovich – was more gravely threatened. Whatever the case, through their mutual embrace they saved each other.

With this in mind, we should view Abramovich's modernization as an epiphenomenon of struggles and strategies playing out far away, in the places where power is concentrated in Russia, and having very little to do with the needs of people native to the region. To an endangered oligarch, the poorest corner of the Russian Arctic presented a timely opportunity: Governor Nazarov's ailing edifice of patronage was waiting to be toppled, and the dismal state of life in the region invited intervention. Once captured via the ballot box, Chukotka's administration was joined to a larger corporate structure, and its identity and nature shifted from sovereign public bureaucracy to private branch office. It had always been Abramovich's style to recognize under-performing assets, buy them at a discount, and reform them into highly profitable enterprises. Under his leadership, this was precisely Chukotka's path. Experts from the mother corporation troubleshot and directed investment in the region, and Abramovich came out much wealthier and considerably more secure. However momentous the changes seemed to people in Chukotka, they were mere side effects of a pan-national struggle, amounting to a strategy for navigating the highly volatile political economy of Putin's Russia. To be successful, it needed to be short-term, decisive, and packaged for media consumption – the most transient mode of development Chukotka had yet seen.

This raises the question of sustainability. If the campaign's core objective was the preservation of oligarchic power and wealth in an era of state persecution and creeping nationalization, what can be said of the prospects for sustainable improvement in Chukotka? Very little, for when we pause to consider Abramovich's arrival, and then his departure, it is clear that his modernization truly was like those that came before. On a territory of such geographic scale and social inequality as Russia, intermittent campaigns of transformation are as intrinsic a part of the cycle as periods of stability and stagnation, and of entropy and collapse. Places such as Chukotka, an exemplary frontier utterly peripheral to Russia's most powerful sites of cultural and economic production, experience the extremes of collapse and reformation in their most momentary forms. Because they bear the stigma of an ultimate frontier – zones of exceptional "fallen-behindness" (otstalost') – their native people have particularly little power to intervene. In the abstract, "modernization" is really a euphemism denoting moments of interruption by forces of metropolitan cultural evangelism – the missionaries of lifting up. The notion of sustainable modernization is as oxymoronic as the idea of permanent revolution; campaigns come and go, washing out to the limits of Russia's territory and then draining away like tides.

Here is the paradox – *there is sustainability* in the structure of the cycle itself. The tidal pattern of campaign and stagnation, whereby the metropole suffers a kind of amnesiac compulsion to return again and again to the peripheral sites of its past efforts of reconstruction, is effectively a permanent characteristic of Russian society. It is as though the modernizing spirit has its own powers of regeneration. The failure of one modernization to achieve its ostensible aims, and remake the site of its attentions, presages another campaign in the future. Failure prepares the ground for the next.

But this is a metalogic of little concern to the actual agents of modernization. They have more personal and immediate needs, which the campaign serves regardless of its nominal failure to transform. Chukotka, the site of successive waves of reformative change, Soviet and post-Soviet, shows us precisely how projects of modernization are ultimately far more about making and remaking their missionary agents than they are about transforming the site of their activity. This was true in the Soviet past, when migrants to the North were transcending the deracinating experiences of dislocation, surveillance, and ideological anomie on the materik to become privileged members of a colonial master class in the North. (Even convicts of the gulag forbidden to leave their northern exile after Stalin's death could eventually recover a sense of positive citizenship in their adopted home.) In a more recent era, those young graduates whom Governor Abramovich selected to rebuild Chukotka were negotiating their passage to a nascent post-Soviet managerial class. Heeding the call to go north, they were actually cementing a status of privilege for use back in the new Russian metropolis. Modernization, it seems, is mainly a reflexive phenomenon, an activity of self-change.

Inasmuch as history in the Arctic basically repeats itself, there are also innovations. Although Abramovich brought another Five-Year Plan *(piatiletka)* to Chukotka and reactivated Soviet life in many of the specific acts of modernization, his was actually a different – let us say *post*-Soviet – approach to northern development. To paraphrase the words of Alexei Yurchak (2005), in the world of the Soviet piatiletka, "everything was forever" – permanent, repetitive, ossified. After the present Five-Year Plan another would follow, in a predictable pattern that seemed infinite. The late-Soviet modernization of Chukotka appeared to migrants of the era to be a permanent and irreversible campaign. Although it ultimately was unsustainable, the fragility of severnoe osvoenie was hidden to all but the most skeptical. In contrast, Abramovich (borrowing from the current ideology of global development) promised limited-time modernization, a project of "building capacity" and leaving behind a "sustainable heritage." If permanent nourishment was the Soviet model, Abramovich believed in a one-off inoculation against future crisis. In fact, to push the pace of reform, he wielded the prospect of his departure after five years like a threat. The hypertransience of his campaign, moreover, shaped the minds of its modernizing agents. Unlike the migrants of the Soviet era, these experts hardly landed. Rather than "giving their best years to the North" (to paraphrase a Soviet slogan), they operated like management consultants everywhere, staying only long enough to leave behind a blueprint. They fired, hired, built, and liquidated, but because they planned to leave with the governor, they would be gone before they could test the suitability of their reforms.

By appointing Abramovich to a second term running until 2010, federal authorities may have thought they could resuscitate the modernization itself. In reality, the spirit of the campaign had already ebbed away. Abramovich had for some time been only a pro forma governor, deputizing responsibility to his associate, Andrei Gorodilov. With the 2005 sale of Sibneft and the removal of its tax revenues from Anadyr to St. Petersburg, the era of exceptional investment had also

Anadyr's old Communist Party Headquarters with statue of Lenin, 1980s
Unknown photographer, Archives of the Heritage of Chukotka Regional Museum

ended. So, soon after one transformation, Chukotka now stands on another threshold, and we now see more clearly that Abramovich's time there was only another chapter in a "century of *perestroikas*" (Grant 1995). Looming ahead is, quite probably, another "demodernization," an experience quite familiar to peripheral regions in a globalizing world. Globalization, as James Ferguson (1999) reminds us, is a force that, even while it connects places in increasingly sophisticated and instantaneous ways, acts to disconnect others, leaving them behind as it reorganizes the global geography of privilege. There is little to suggest that Chukotka should be any different. Its people, natives and settlers alike, may be cast back into the ranks of the disconnected and left behind just as suddenly as they were lifted from them after 2000.

With this in mind, the most meaningful interpretations of this exceptional episode arise not from the specific edifices and programs that modernization produced, but rather, from the ways in which they shaped and challenged settler identities. Ironically, the arrival in Chukotka of another wave of modernizing outsiders provided an unusually rich opportunity to examine their settled counterparts. In the process of so vigorously defining themselves, Abramovich's youthful, hypermobile, technologically obsessed, and out-of-place newcomers vividly illuminated their opposite. As they marked their modern identity, the lens was focused on the position of locals, and in particular Soviet-era settlers, in all their contrasting poverty, technological backwardness, and rootedness to place. Before

Restoring the Party headquarter's statue of Lenin in front of a renovated children's leisure centre, 2003
Photographed by Linda Rosenstrom Chang

Abramovich, the passage from migrancy to settledness was proceeding, as everywhere across the Russian North, at its own gradual pace, based on the necessity of localizing practice and knowledge in post-Soviet conditions. By that time, settlers had already completed a remarkable journey in the process of rebuilding a sense of themselves as northern people amidst the wreckage of the failed project of northern mastery that once defined them. But the dramatic and unexpected arrival of a new modernization took from Chukotka's settlers whatever comfortable neocolonial assumptions they still preserved, eliminating the remaining elements of the old settler identity. With this shift, settlers were no longer the agents (even residually) of metropolitan modernity: they were its obstacle.

So it was that an extraneous challenge to the privileges and self-understandings of this population, particularly those in Chukotka's capital, reified the settler identity for a time. Being local became a category with boundaries and characteristics, the nature of which settlers now passionately debated. A language of belonging emerged in counterpoint to the modernizing challenge, just as

Abramovich's newcomers founded their own authority on the idea of settler ineptitude. Settlers, for whom mobility and the brokering role had been a way of life and a touchstone of identity even into the era of crisis and collapse, began to claim authority on the basis of their immobility. Indeed, faced by newcomers so undeniably representative of the distant Russian metropolis, settlers found *localist* moral claims to be the only available alternative. This ideational realignment, in turn, brought settlers into the rhetorical territory hitherto inhabited by indigenous people alone. Mirroring the reactions of indigenous Chukotkans a generation before, many settlers now called themselves natives *(mestnye)* and faced new arrivals to the North armed with the authority of rooted people: knowledge of the land, local kin and community, and long tenure in the North.

Like Roman Abramovich's attention, the vigour of the modernization could not be sustained. With the passage of time, the idea of the rooted settler also lost some of its power. Resistance to certain aspects of the modernization soon attenuated the threat to settlers and even enabled their selective co-option. This was particularly the case in the capital, where the boundaries between Abramovich's outsiders and the established settler elite soon blurred. All the same, it was the momentary clarity of those boundaries – the strength of feeling that elevated the symbols of difference and the ideology of localism into plainest view – that encouraged me to explore its origins in practice more fully. Unlike Fredrik Barth and his followers, I do not believe that collective and individual identities are strictly a matter of symbolic differentiation. Not all practices are symbolic, although all practices possess symbolic potential, available if needed to mark a boundary. At the risk of introducing a positivist perspective, this is why we must still look to the everyday "content" of collective identities – in this case, the practical basis for settler belonging in northern places. After all, urban settlers trapped within the polarities of two solitudes were developing their language of localism from the raw materials of a truly existing way of life. The intensity of community and the sustaining powers afforded by knowing the land (that certain settlers already enjoyed when Abramovich arrived) are an enduring foundation of practice. This mode of belonging, perhaps not always self-conscious, has the power to endure quite independently of the tidal fluctuations of the modernizing cycle.

This is why an examination of the history of migration and the practices of survival in the hard years preceding Abramovich's time is required not only to understand the settler response to modernization, but also for making predictions about the settler life after his withdrawal. Through a historical portrait of changing collective identities, we can view a past in which the settler had less need to define the boundaries of the group, and we can anticipate a future in which this is again the case. Ultimately, settlers in Chukotka have taken a journey away from migrancy and toward settledness that is common throughout the Russian North. Their story is unusual only in the speed and urgency with which they travelled this path, facing the particular challenges of an extreme modernization. And this is precisely why the universal question of settling in the Arctic was best tackled in the context of Abramovich's Chukotka.

In the opening pages of this book, I ventured that there was more to be gained through an ethnographic scrutiny of the settler experience than through the anthropological conquest of a hitherto unexamined population. The story of the settler, I argued, would also enrich the anthropology of the Arctic with unexpected theoretical and practical insight. It would help to heal the parochialism of Siberian and northern studies, by providing new bridge-points to the broader field of anthropology. This study may be a beginning. After all, until recently, our manner of thinking about "whites" in the Arctic has been structured by highly impoverished characterizations. The Canadian-centric and out-of-date portrait of whites as a sequestered neo-colonial officer class (Brody 1975), the assumption of white transience in northern settings, and the figures of white patrons and brokers (Paine 1971, 1977) persist in perceptions of the Canadian North. There is some sense in this, but these frameworks are also projected into other circumpolar settings where they fall very wide of the mark. In northern Russia, already the site of much ethnographic scrutiny, the non-indigenous figure is just as poorly understood. There, the role reserved for "newcomers" is still a mere foil for a panoply of richly rendered descriptions of the indigenous experience. Naturally, such objectification disguises the emerging reality of settledness to be found among the remnant populations of Soviet-era migration. There is now in Chukotka, and I predict throughout the Russian Arctic and Subarctic regions, a population of "natives" who are neither indigenous nor newcomers. They are people whose senses of belonging in the North have not been described, or even predicted as a possibility. Their stories reveal the process of settling as, in its various moments, a rhetorical aspiration, a process of self-renovation, a strategy of survival in conditions of state collapse, and simply an outcome of living for a lifetime in a northern place. Most promising of all, settler stories show how coming to rest in a place is ultimately a journey of fundamental benefit to the North. Settling down changes the view, away from the dream of departure and all its corrosive behaviours, and toward a sense of responsibility to what is local.

Appendices

Appendix 1: List of Informants

[1] M/50s, Russian. Migrated to Chukotka in early 1970s. Former geologist and gold prospector, museum curator. Egvekinot.

[2] M/40s, Chechen and Yup'ik. Born in Chukotka. Freelance artist. Egvekinot.

[3] M/50s, Russian. Migrated to Chukotka in late 1970s. Geologist and museum curator. Anadyr.

[4] F/60s, Byelorussian. Migrated to Chukotka in early 1960s. Seamstress, art teacher, and textile artist. Anadyr.

[5] M/70s, Russian. Migrated to Chukotka in late 1950s. Former senior geologist/director. Resettled from Anadyr to Lipetsk.

[6] M/40s, Byelorussian. Migrated to Chukotka in early 1980s. Public works engineer. Anadyr.

[7] F/40s, Russian. Born in Chukotka. Schoolteacher. Anadyr.

[8] M/60s, Russian. Migrated to Chukotka from Kazakhstan in late 1960s. Geodesist. Anadyr.

[9] M/70s, Russian. Migrated from Kazakhstan to Chukotka in late 1960s. Resettled from Anadyr to Voronezh. Former vezdekhod driver and garbage collector. Voronezh.

[10] M/50s, Russian. Migrated to Chukotka in mid-1970s. Resettled from Bilibino (Chukotka) to near Lipetsk. Russian. Former electrician. Lipetsk.

[11] F/40s, Russian. Migrated to Chukotka in early 1980s. Former communications engineer, translator, journalist. Anadyr.

[12] M/50s, Russian. Migrated from Kyrgyzstan to Chukotka in late 1970s. Senior academic/director. Anadyr.

[13] M/50s, Russian. Migrated to Chukotka in 1969. Dentist. Anadyr.

[14] M/40s, Russian. Migrated to Chukotka in mid-1970s. Former construction engineer, government safety inspector. Anadyr.

[15] M/70s, Russian. Exiled to Chukotka in late 1950s. Son of a political prison labourer, former geologist. Retired to Smolensk.

[16] M/50s, Ukrainian. Migrated to Chukotka in 1970. Former geological drill technician, marine communications officer, newsreader, musician, photographer, environmental activist. Anadyr.

[17] M/40s, Russian. Migrated to Chukotka in mid-1980s. Former geologist, photographer/journalist. Egvekinot.

[18] F/40s, Ida Rutchina (public figure). Russian. Director of the Chukotka branch of the Russian Red Cross. Moscow and Anadyr.

[19] F/50s, Russian. Migrated to Chukotka in early 1970s. Radio dispatcher. Anadyr.

[20] F/30s, Tatar and Chukchi. Born in Anadyr. Physician. Anadyr.

[21] M/30s, Russian. Temporary administration recruit from Nizhni Novgorod. Senior public relations specialist. Anadyr.

[22] M/20s, Sergei Kapkov (public figure). Russian. Former Deputy Governor, Culture Minister, and public face of Abramovich's administration from 2001-4. From 2004, Chukotka's Deputy to the Federal Duma. Anadyr and Moscow.

[23] M/50s, Russian. Migrated to Chukotka in late 1960s. Former geologist and senior Party official in okrug Executive Committee, administration official. Anadyr.

[24] M/40s, Petr Klimov (public figure). Chukchi and Russian. Entrepreneur and okrug Duma deputy. Born in Anadyr. Former Komsomol leader and Soviet Party official. Anadyr.

[25] M/40s, Albert Klimentiev (public figure). Tatar. Migrated to Chukotka in late 1980s. Director of okrug forest-fire-fighting service. Former parashiutist. Anadyr.

[26] M/40s, Chukchi. Born near Anadyr. Former culture worker with itinerant agitprop brigade, indigenous political activist. Anadyr.

[27] M/50s, Russian. Migrated to Chukotka in early 1970s. Former construction engineer, Duma deputy, and administration official under Governor Nazarov. Anadyr.

[28] M/50s, Russian. Migrated to Chukotka in early 1970s. Former geologist, senior tax inspection official. Anadyr.

[29] M/50s, Russian. Migrated to Chukotka in late 1970s. Filmmaker and journalist. Anadyr.

[30] M/40s, Chukchi. Born on Chukotka's Arctic coast. Former sovkhoz director, political activist, and senior official in agriculture department. Anadyr.

[31] M/60s, Chukchi. Born in Chukotka's interior. Long-time indigenous political activist, official in Nazarov administration. Okrug Duma deputy. Anadyr.

[32] M/50s, Russian. Migrated to Chukotka in late 1960s. Resettled from Anadyr to Smolensk. Former senior geologist. Smolensk.

[33] M/50s, Altai Cossack. Migrated to Chukotka in early 1970s. Former fish-processing-plant director. Anadyr.

[34] M/60s, Ukrainian. Migrated to Chukotka in early 1970s. Former underground tin miner. Egvekinot.

[35] F/50s, Russian. Migrated to Chukotka in mid-1970s. Resettled from Anadyr to Voronezh. Former military accountant. Voronezh.

[36] F/40s, Russian. Migrated to Chukotka in late 1970s. Resettled from Anadyr to Leningrad Oblast. Former schoolteacher. Leningrad Oblast.

[37] M/30s, Russian. Born in Anadyr. Musician, community outreach worker, former entrepreneur, and hunter. Anadyr.

[38] M/20s, Russian. Temporary administration recruit from Moscow. Senior economic planner in Abramovich administration. Anadyr and Moscow.

[39] M/30s, Pavel Apletin (public figure). Russian. Director of administration-supported regional newspaper and press, senior member of Abramovich administration. Temporary recruit from Nizhni Novgorod. Anadyr.

[40] F/20s, Russian. Temporary administration recruit from Nizhni Novgorod. Editor. Anadyr.

[41] M/50s, Turkish. Recruited from Istanbul. Hotel manager. Anadyr.

[42] M/30s, Canadian. Manager of Canadian-run construction projects in Chukotka. Anadyr and Edmonton, Canada.

[43] M/50s, Russian. Former military officer. Senior public relations expert for okrug administration. Moscow.

[44] M/20s, Chukchi and Russian. Born in interior Chukotka. Bank manager. Anadyr.

[45] M/20s, Russian. Born in Anadyr. Police lawyer. Anadyr.

[46] F/60s, Yup'ik. Born in Bering Strait area. Yup'ik- and Chukchi-language broadcaster for okrug radio station. Anadyr.

[47] F/40s, Russian. Born in Anadyr. Former horticulturalist, museum worker. Anadyr.

[48] M/20s, Russian. Temporary administration recruit from Nizhni Novgorod. Television reporter. Anadyr.

[49] M/30s, Chukchi. Born in interior Chukotka. Native activist, community worker. Anadyr.

[50] M/20s, Russian. Born in Anadyr. Television station technician. Anadyr.

[51] M/30s, Russian. Born in Anadyr. Cameraman for television station. Anadyr.

[52] M/60s, Russian. Migrated to Chukotka in late 1960s. Former state farm director, amateur historian. Ust'-Belaia.

[53] M/40s, Russian. Migrated to Chukotka in early 1980s. Former KGB bureaucrat, police legal assistant, legal aid worker. Anadyr.

[54] F/40s, Russian. Migrated to Chukotka in late 1970s. Culture worker. Anadyr.

[55] F/40s, Chukchi. Born on Arctic coast. Radio broadcaster, native activist, community worker. Anadyr.

[56] M/50s, Russian. Migrated to Chukotka in late 1960s. Construction foreman. Amgeuma (Iul'tinskii District).

[57] F/30s, Russian. Born in interior Chukotka. Resettled from Ust'-Belaia to Moscow. Cosmetics salesperson. Moscow.

[58] M/40s, Viktor Bogorev (public figure). Russian. Migrated to Chukotka in early 1980s. Former parashiutist, trader, entrepreneur. Head of village administration. Vaegi (Anadyrskii District).

[59] M/50s, Russian. Migrated to Chukotka in mid-1970s. Former pipefitter. Radio technician. Anadyr.

[60] M/40s, Kuban Cossack. Migrated to Chukotka in late 1970s. Former construction worker. Subsistence hunter, fisherman, part-time mechanic. Vaegi (Anadyrskii District).

[61] M/40s, Russian. Migrated to Chukotka in late 1970s. Former sovkhoz mechanic. Freelance vezdekhod driver. Amguema (Iul'tinskii District).

[62] M/18, Russian. Born in Egvekinot, Chukotka. Student at teacher-training college. Anadyr.

[63] F/20s, Russian. Born in Anadyr. Former administration employee, tax inspection auditor. Anadyr.

[64] M/50s, Russian. Migrated from central Russia to Egvekinot in early 1970s. Former geologist. Reporter. Anadyr.

[65] F/50s, Russian. Migrated to Chukotka in early 1980s. Former geologist. Museum curator. Anadyr.

[66] M/70s, Armenian. Migrated from Armenia to Beringovskii in late 1960s. Resettled from Beringovskii to Voronezh. Former underwater welder. Voronezh.

Appendix 2: Glossary of Russian Terms

Entusiasty: In the context of northern settlement, these were willing recruits from outside the Soviet North to the tasks associated with industrializing, settling, and taming the North. Often used to denote a "true believer" in Soviet northern policies. Usually settlers of the 1950s and 1960s.

Glava administratsii: Head of administration, the term for mayor in towns and villages.

Gulag: System of prisoner-labour camps in the Stalin-era Soviet Union.

Koeffitsient: A multiplier or factor used to determine the monthly income of northern workers, the size of which grew with length of residence. The maximum factor in the Soviet North (and in Chukotka) was three (times base income).

Kolkhoz: Soviet collective farm, the result of collectivization of agricultural and traditional activities in the Soviet era. Still used colloquially to refer to the agricultural conglomerates controlling herding and hunting in Chukotka's villages.

Komanda: "Team," referring in this text to the large group of individuals recruited through personal networks by Governor Roman Abramovich to execute his program of modernization of Chukotka.

Kommersant: Private trader, in the North an individual engaged in private and often unlicensed sale of goods in remote villages at a large mark-up.

Komsomoltsy: Members of the Komsomol, the youth branch of the Communist Party in Soviet times.

Kooperativ: In the context of the Soviet North, a term referring to apartment buildings in central and southern parts of the country; northerners had the right to commission their construction on a private, for-hire basis. These became their destination upon retirement from northern work.

Krysha: Lit. "roof," a term referring in Russia to connections that can protect and shelter a person or an organization from persecution. Often associated with the protection racket.

Kul'tura: Lit. "culture," referring in Russia to a relatively defined set of cultural characteristics. Equivalent to the English "civilized behaviour" or "civilization."

Materik (na materike): "The mainland," used in the North to refer to central and southern regions of Russia.

Nadbavka: A sum added to the base monthly income of northerners in Soviet times, the size of which grew with length of residence in the North.

Osvoenie severa: "Mastery of the North," a term referring to Soviet, and sometimes Russian, programs to settle and industrialize the North.

Otstalost': A condition of being left behind, made obsolete.

Parashiutist: Professional forest-fire fighter, trained to parachute from small aircraft into remote fires.

Po-blatu (blat): Coll. "through connections" or "through the back door."

Priezzhii: Lit. "recently arrived," colloquial term typically used to refer to a non-Aboriginal in the North. "Newcomer," "incomer."

Priezzhii mentalitet: Mentality of the newcomer non-Aboriginal in the North.

Prostota: In the context in which it is often used, as a positive quality in people, this term denotes simple honesty or sincerity.

Raspredelenie: The Soviet-era system of distributing university and college graduates to positions throughout the country, and sometimes to the North.

Rodina: Homeland or motherland.

Romantika severa: Romance of the North.

Samizdat: Literature not sanctioned by the Soviet state, and published clandestinely. Lit. "self-published."

Severnyi muzhik: Coll. a bonafide man of the North, salt of the earth, someone with true masculine characteristics.

Shabashniki: Itinerant freelance labourers in the Soviet era, often engaged in construction trades.

Sovkhoz: Soviet state farm, the result of amalgamating collective farms and intensive investments in production.

Ukrupnenie: Amalgamation, referring to the closure of small villages and the concentration of Aboriginal populations in larger centres in the Soviet era.

Vedomstvo: Generic term for a government department, often used to denote any institution in a Russian setting.

Vezdekhod: Military-surplus heavy tracked personnel carrier, used widely in the Russian North for overland travel.

Vyzov: In the context of the Soviet North, an official summons to work in northern regions

Zamestitel' (zam-gubornator): Deputy (deputy governor).

Zamorozhennyi: Frozen, paralyzed.

Zhilploshchad': Living quarters, private living space.

Notes

Introduction

1 The few authors to directly address the problem of "newcomers" or "whites" in a northern setting include Hugh Brody (1975), Robert Paine (1971, 1977), and Evie Plaice (1990), all of whom worked in the Canadian North.

2 The most common words used in English-language accounts to refer to russophone non-indigenous residents of the North are either the untranslated emic term priezzhii, or "newcomer" (D. Anderson 2000; Kerttula 2000; Rethmann 2001; Krupnik and Vakhtin 1997), "incomer" (Gray 2000), or "non-native" (Schindler 1997).

3 I do not capitalize the term "native" in this text, because one of my central arguments is that the quality of "nativeness" cannot be conflated with "indigeneity." To be a native person, I argue, is rather to have a deeply felt and much practised way of relating to place.

4 The "cognac zone" (*zona koniaka*) is a term several settler informants used to convey the conditions of prosperity they recall in the late-Soviet North. I have not encountered it in literature from the period.

5 The most comprehensive and policy-directed expression of this view is Fiona Hill and Clifford Gaddy, *The Siberian Curse: How Communist Planners Left Russia out in the Cold* (2003). See also Tim Heleniak (1999) and Vladimir Kontorovich (2000).

6 In the popular press, examples include Steven Myers, "Siberians Tell Moscow: Like It or Not, It's Home," *New York Times,* 28 January 2004; S. Sataline, "Welcome to Vorkuta: It's 10 Degrees in This Former Prison Town in Russia's Far North. So Why Can't the Government Even Pay People to Leave?" *Boston Globe,* 23 May 2004. Scholarly examinations of resistance to resettlement include my own publications (Thompson 2002, 2004) and John Round (2005). Information on a major European Science Foundation sponsored research project into this problem, called "Moved by the State: Perspectives on Relocation and Resettlement in the Circumpolar North (MOVE)," can be found at, http://www.alaska.edu/boreas/move.

7 Nikolai Vakhtin, Evgenii Golovko, and Peter Schweitzer's *Russkie starozhily Sibiri* (Russian Old Settlers in Siberia) (2004) represents a notable exception within post-Soviet ethnography in its examination of Old Settlers (a métis population, with a centuries-long presence) in the Far North, including Chukotka. Subsequently, some of this material became available in a condensed form in English, as Schweitzer, Vakhtin, and Golovko, "The Difficulty of Being Oneself: Identity Politics of 'Old Settler' Communities in Northeastern Siberia" (2005).

8 Although some would argue that "settler" is not itself an ethnically neutral category, but rather is equivalent to "Slavic" or "Russian," my point relates to the manner in which professional Soviet, and later Russian, ethnographers viewed indigenous groups as *etnosy* (ethnic formations) and therefore worthy of ethnographic study. Russians, in contrast, were thought to belong to a *narod* (a people or nation).

9 To be fair, both Gray (2005) and Habeck (2005b) have endeavoured in their recent work to dismantle the ethnic rigidities of the Soviet ethnographic tradition, both by examining the reifying effects of ethnic categories and, in Habeck's case, pointing to the manifold means beyond ethnicity that northern people have of expressing who they are.

10 The intersubjectivity of landscape and human within indigenous senses of identity is a familiar theme in many ethnographies from regions outside the Russian North. See, for example, accounts of the Dene (Sharpe 2001) and the Cree (Brightman 1993).

11 English-language sources on tsarist-era Chukotka and the Chukchi Wars include T. Armstrong (1965), J. Forsyth (1992), and J.J. Stephan (1994). Non-English-language sources include B. Nielsen (2005), N.N. Dikov (1989, 1974), S.B. Okun (1935), and I.S. Vdovin (1965).

12 I have not discovered any written sources of information on these episodes. In 2002 and 2003, in the interior settlements of Vaegi and Amguema, I interviewed seven elder Chukchi who had witnessed or participated in the resistance that occured in the region in the early 1950s.

13 The Chukchi Autonomous Okrug was an administrative subunit of Magadan Oblast from 1953. From 1951 to 1953, the region was subordinate to Khabarovsk Krai, and previous to this, it had been a subterritory of Kamchatka. Chukotka was first designated an autonomous region in 1930 (Dikov 1989).

14 In a revised version of his PhD thesis, Finn Sivert Nielsen (2007) provides a fascinating discussion of this question.

15 Moshe Lewin (1985), for example, describes Russia's traditional dual geography, containing nodes of extreme intellectual cosmopolitanism and technological innovation and a vast hinterland of conservative rural peasants. An alternative reading of fragmented and differentiated space can be found in B. Ruble, J. Koehn, and N. Popson (2002).

16 The best-known proponents of the *totalitarian* trend, which focused on state ideology and structures of power, and which held Soviet ideology to be inherently flawed and unsustainable, were Merle Fainsod, Hannah Arendt, Zbigniew Brzezinski, and Richard Pipes. The *revisionists* attacked this trend on both methodological and substantive grounds, and argued that a deeper analysis of society (a "ground-up" approach) and a focus on class was necessary for understanding the nature of the state and its powers. The principal members of this school were Robert C. Tucker, Ronald G. Suny, Moshe Lewin, Sheila Fitzpatrick, and Gail Warshofsky Lapidus. Finally, this revisionist trend has come under attack from a *post-revisionist* school, which proposes a closer examination of everyday practices based on anthropological methods; its best-known members are Stephen Kotkin, Julie Hessler, Peter Holoquist, Jochen Hellbeck, Yuri Slezkine, and Alexei Yurchak.

17 This view of the fragmented Soviet society is well represented in Ken Jowitt (1992), as well as the more recent works of Caroline Humphrey (2002), Katherine Verdery (1996), and Finn Sivert Nielsen (2003).

18 In his 2005 book *Everything Was Forever, Until It Was No More: The Last Soviet Generation,* Alexei Yurchak refutes Vladimir Shlapentokh's (1989) famous argument, proposing (partly on the basis of his own experience) that the Soviet state in fact seemed to its citizens enduring and awesome, and that its official "authoritative discourse" was embodied and reproduced *without* any clear sense of its weakness or immorality.

19 Any discussion of survival in the post-Soviet context should acknowledge the work of S. Bridger and F. Pine (1998) in Poland, Emma Wilson (2002) in Sakhalin, and Petra Rethmann (2001) in Kamchatka. However, whereas these studies have identified a measure of resistance and political agency in the "practices of everyday survival" (see Scott 1985, 1990) or the "hidden transcripts" (Humphrey 1994) of their subjects, I view the political content of survival as oblique at best. I would concede only that practices of survival are productive of localist attachments and thereby of a strengthened collective identity, which may *in time* serve as a starting point for political expression.

20 See these discussions on the nature of indigenous status and identity in three recent volumes of *Current Anthropology:* A. Béteille (1998), A. Kuper (2003), and M. Asch et al. (2004).

Chapter 2: Northern Settlement and the Late-Soviet State

1 Major revisionist social and state histories include Vladimir Shlapentokh (1989), Ken Jowitt (1992), Sheila Fitzpatrick (1999), Katherine Verdery (1996), and Caroline Humphrey (2002).

2 A particularly detailed explanation of this process can be found in Gerald Easter (2000, 168), as well as Jowitt (1992).

3 See N. Aitov (1983) and V. Shlapentokh (1989).

4 Nielsen's text, entitled *The Eye of the Whirlwind: Russian Identity and Soviet Nation-Building – Quests for Meaning in a Soviet Metropolis,* is also available in print in a Russian version entitled *Glasburi: Russkaia identichnost' i sovetskoe natsional'noe stroitel'stvo* (St. Petersburg: Aletei, 2003).

5 Similar descriptions of an atomized social texture can be found in Ledeneva (1998) and Jowitt (1992).

6 On this model, see Harold Innis (1995).

7 This phrase is familiar to most long-term residents of Chukotka, serving as one prop in settlers' discourse of self-justification.

8 The record of northern development in Canada, perhaps the most geographically analogous territory to the Russian North, is much more conservative; no comparably grand project to ameliorate the conditions of life in the Arctic and embark on large-scale settlement ever materialized in Canadian northern policy. There, cost-benefit approaches to northern investment led to smaller, more transient migrant populations consisting of industrial shift labour or the service personnel for Canada's evolving system of "welfare colonialism," as the state's relationship with the native peoples of the North has been characterized (Paine 1977). As a consequence, unlike in the post-Soviet North, indigenous peoples remain in the majority in most of Canada's northern territory. Just over half of the residents of the Northwest Territories are Aboriginal (statistics on ethnicity and population can be found at http://www.gov.nt.ca/research/facts/index.html), whereas 85 percent of the population of the Territory of Nunavut is Aboriginal (statistics on ethnicity and population can be found at http://www.gov.nu.ca/english/about/ourland.pdf).

9 Evidence that the Soviet leadership preferred to base osvoenie policies on production needs rather than the principles of charity emerged early in the Soviet period. The Committee of the North, with its aims of gentle cultural convergence (the "soft" policy on native peoples), was abolished in 1935 in favour of ministries and government agencies with hard production targets, such as Glavsevmorput, Dalstroi, and the Ministry of Mines (McCannon 1998; Slavin 1961, 1972, 1982).

10 In Chukotka's Amguema and Pevek regions, where uranium, tin, tungsten, and gold were mined from the 1940s, the collectivization of reindeer herding was carried out by gulag authorities (administered by Dalstroi) to secure meat for the growing industrial population [1][3]. In the Anadyr River basin, Soviet authorities established collective farms between 1945 and 1955 to supply reindeer meat and fish to the growing military bases and the civilian settlement of Anadyr in the first years of the Cold War. The experience of Yuri Rytkheu, who was sent to study philology at the elite Herzen Institute for training indigenous students in Leningrad, was rare; most promising young natives continued their studies in vocational institutes in Magadan, where they learned technical skills for application in the new state farms.

11 Among the best analyses of the Stalinist-era system of "closed distribution" are Sheila Fitzpatrick (1999, 2000) and Elena Osokina (2001).

12 The original phrases are *My idem k izobiliyu!* and *Zhizn' stala luchshe, tovarishchi, zhizn' stala veselee!* Detailed portraits of the Stalin-era culture of consumerism can be found in Stephen Kotkin (1995), Julie Hessler (2000), and Fitzpatrick (1999, 2000).

13 The geographical arrangement of privilege was possible only once the old tsarist system of internal passports was reintroduced in 1932, which made the propiska a mandatory condition of residence and allowed authorities to control internal migration.

14 Another well-known closed city was Akademgorodok, a central Siberian research colony that opened in the early 1960s and was envisioned as a sort of scientific utopia for the nation's brightest researchers. This was the first elite research facility created outside Moscow and Leningrad, and it was conceived as a campus where talented scientists would enjoy superb living conditions as an incentive to working more productively. Living space, or *zhilploshchad'*, was a perennial concern for Soviet citizens because it was always particularly scarce. So, in Akademgorodok, students and scientists received flats larger than the Soviet average, and senior scientists received their own detached houses. The colony had its own bakeries, food shops, and services, all of which were much better than could be found in a typical Soviet city (Ledeneva 1998; Josephson 1995).

15 Information on the regulations governing access to the Far North in the Soviet period is condensed from interviews with long-term settler residents of Chukotka.

16 The identities of all informants, other than prominent public figures, are protected using an anonymizing system. See Appendix 1: List of Informants for basic descriptions of each informant corresponding to number codes used here.

17 General Secretary Nikita Krushchev (1956-64) launched a national construction campaign to increase the stock of available housing, which finally gave average Soviet families the opportunity to obtain flats of their own.

18 This idea, for example, became a received piece of wisdom with the publication of Terence Armstrong's influential *Russian Settlement in the North* (1965), and it is perpetuated in more recent literature on the region (Heleniak 1999; Kontorovich 2000). Armstrong's view reflected a broader tendency among Sovietologists of the era to view income as a primary indicator of hierarchy and privilege, and therefore to closely examine wage differentiation in the Soviet labour market. For example, see David Lane (1982).

19 In the 1980s, it was quite common for northerners to spend their large savings on expensive black market goods obtained while on holiday. A former geologist related how in 1986 he flew to Moscow and spent thirty-five hundred rubles on a Western-manufactured video player. At the time, this amounted to three years' pay for his father, a coal miner in western Ukraine [64].

20 For older Russians who were adults when the Soviet Union collapsed, a recurrent feature of their accounts of that time is the loss of ruble savings to hyperinflation. But these informants now live in a monetized economy, in which cash has been the ultimate convertible value for well over a decade. I believe this often retroactively inflates the importance of the old Soviet ruble, as informants remember the low prices and the abundance of money, and forget the difficulty of actually finding useful things to buy with it. This is illustrated by the fact that by 1980, private savings accounts held 200 billion rubles, more than three times the official value of all Soviet goods in circulation (Birman 1980; Kornai 1992).

21 In her analysis of connections and "pull" in late-Soviet society, Alena Ledeneva (1998) explores the process of "obtaining" (*dostovat'*) in the shortage economy.

22 In other publications, I have described this as the "moral economy of sacrifice." For a detailed explanation, see Niobe Thompson (2003).

23 For example, the geologist from Iul'tinskii District who bought a Western-manufactured video player in the eighties obtained it through an employee of the state export-financing agency, who used foreign travel privileges to smuggle Western goods into the country.

Chapter 3: Arctic Idyll

1 After Tönnies (1957) and Durkheim (1964), important later theorists of the official and unofficial public domains in the Soviet context were V. Shlapentokh (1989), K. Jowitt (1992), S. Boym (1994), I. Pilkington (1994), T. Cushman (1995), L. Ionin (1997), O. Kharkhordin (1999), and S. Zdravomyslova and V. Voronkov (2002).

2 Kharkhordin (1999) describes how Soviet citizens participated in the radical circumscription of their private life through practices of mutual surveillance and admonition, ritual confession and self-criticism, and collective efforts of correction, all aimed, from the perspective of the state, at achieving social discipline and eliminating opportunities for subversion. Stephen Kotkin (1995) also treats this subject.

3 Ethnographic descriptions of sexuality in late-Soviet society can be found in Finn Sivert Nielsen (2003) and A. Rotkirch (2000).

4 On the tusovka in late-Soviet society, see S. Zdravomyslova (2002), H. Pilkington (1994), and T. Cushman (1995).

5 The Russian terms *chistota* and *prostota* are translated here as "purity" and "simple honesty."

6 "Za tumanom" was released in 1966 by the bard-poet Yuri Kukin. The full Russian text can be found at Little Russia in US, "Yuriy Alexandrovich Kukin," http://www.russia-in-us.com/Music/Artists/Kukin/.

7 The most famous episode of the period in fact took place off the northern coast of Chukotka in 1933-34. Otto Schmidt, the country's best-known living northern explorer and the head of Glavsevmorput (1932-39), attempted a complete traverse of the Northern Sea Route in the *Cheliuskin* with a crew of 112 specialists. Caught in the ice, the ship sank in the East Siberian Sea, and the crew was forced to weather the winter on the open ice. In the subsequent months, a group of daring aviators, partly supported from Alaska, succeeded in ferrying the entire crew by small plane to the Chukotkan villages along the coast. In one of these, the village of Vankarem, the primary school and the hospital are still housed in wooden buildings built by members of the *Cheliuskin*'s crew as a mark of gratitude.

8 Native peoples had already been recruited to serve in earlier Stalin-era romance narratives, offered as a kind of noble savage simultaneously jealous of the advantages of modernity and harbouring a moral aptitude for the communist way of life. Tikhon Semushkin was the foremost northernist among this generation of writers, and his stories of socialist conversion among the Chukchi set in the interwar period earned him the Lenin Prize for Literature in 1949.

9 Rytkheu's *Son v nachale tumana* (1968) is now available in English translation as *A Dream in Polar Fog* (2005).

10 Almost all indigenous employees within the rural state and collective farm system also worked in shift systems, since their workplace was the village, and hunting, herding, and fishing practices were not amenable to a regular eight-hour-day working pattern.

11 So many of the settlers in present-day Chukotka were once geologists because, in the last decades of Soviet power in the region, the geological survey (Ekspeditsiia) was one of the largest employers. For example, Egvekinot's district survey branch alone had roughly seven hundred employees by 1985.

12 Examinations of kul'tura in Soviet official public life include Vadim Volkov (1999) and Kotkin (1995).

13 A particularly rich description of the uses of hortatory rhetoric for Soviet labour discipline is Kotkin (1995).

14 Bruce Grant (1993, 231) defines *kult'bazy* as "all-purpose social service centres serving as the main avenue for information collection and programme implementation." In Chukotka, krasnye iarangy were mobile agitprop initiatives, which visited nomadic herder encampments and dispensed political education, literacy lessons, health care, and other services.

15 In describing this new romantic modesty before the indigenous native, Slezkine (1994, 360) is referring to the indigenous Nanai guide of Vladimir Arsen'ev's early twentieth century novel, eponymously named *Dersu Uzala:* "When a new generation of Russian romantics arrived in the taiga, the old pathfinder was brought back to do his job."

16 Alexia Bloch's (2003) book on the institutionalization of indigenous children in Soviet residential schools offers a perfect illustration.

17 In two early studies of whites in the Canadian North, Robert Paine (1971, 1977) examines this two-way mediation role (brokering) as fundamental to white hegemony in the arctic Inuit village in the era of "welfare colonialism."

18 This dualistic theory of community draws both on Fredrik Barth's (1969) constructivism and older structuralist traditions: a community is simultaneously characterized by internal similarity or "culture in common" and by relational difference mediated by group boundaries. As far as a working definition for "group identity," I share Anthony Cohen's (1985) belief that this merely refers to the capacity of people in a community to maintain a reflexive consciousness, an awareness of both the content and the boundaries of the community to which they belong. Perhaps it is enough to point to a lexical feature of the term: identity reflects the place and the people with which one *identifies.*

19 Shlapentokh (1989, 178) evoked this shift with the phrase "death of the neighbour in Soviet society." The Soviet novelist Valentin Rasputin dedicated his best-known novel, *Fire* (1985), to an examination of this problem.

20 This informant's father, having returned from Stalin's camps in the late 1950s, died while his son was serving in the army. As a son of a convicted "political," he was deprived of the right to leave service and attend the funeral.

21 This notion corresponds to the "law of the tundra" *(zakon tundry)* observed by herding peoples across the Russian North (see Stammler 2004).

22 In neighbouring Magadan, by comparison, former prisoners of the gulag who survived into the post-Stalinist era lived under a stigma, probably resulting less from the suggestion of their past criminality than from the fact that they were *not* the selectees of the northern-residence vetting process.

23 In the late-Soviet period, Chukotka had no facilities for long-term incarceration, so those convicted of a crime by the courts were sent to southern cities such as Khabarovsk to serve their sentences [8].

24 Informants reported that some criminals were in fact able to find sanctuary in Chukotka, where they hoped to locate themselves beyond the reach of the law. They point in particular to migrants from the Caucasus, and a former director of the geological survey recalled that sophisticated Chechen and Georgian gold-smuggling organizations were uncovered in the 1980s [5].

25 Foreigners visiting Russia often observe that in many spheres of public life, courtesy and politeness are ineffective and inappropriate tools for interaction. On this count, Finn Sivert Nielsen (2007, 42) writes, "There is no art of compromise. Instead, there are polarised modes of behaviour, between cold insistence on barriers and warm subversion." In other words, you are in or out.

26 I do not claim that these qualities differentiate a northern variant of the Russian muzhik; I simply record that these northerners made a distinction. The ideal of the muzhik is of course also valorized on the materik. However, it seems that in the conditions of the North it is more likely to be realized.

27 These terms all relate to informal means of obtaining scarce goods and special favours; they could be translated variously as "by connections," "through the back door," or "between friends."

Chapter 4: Idyll Destroyed

1 This letter was finally printed in a special edition of the Russian monthly *Ogon'ek* in 2001 and made its way back to Vaegi. I visited the village for the first time in 2002. Many of the

local residents confirmed the veracity of this description, and as that time receded into the past, they cherished this printed letter as a concrete piece of evidence testifying to the difficulties they survived in the nineties.

2 This was a strategy of state-enterprise reform that Polish political scientist Jadwiga Staniszkis observed early in the pre-collapse era of perestroika. He employed the term "political capitalism" to describe how bureaucrats and enterprise managers created "profit-centres" within larger state enterprise by hiving the most promising assets off from the mother institution. Jadwiga Staniszkis, "Political Capitalism in Poland," *East European Politics and Societies* 5 (1991): 129-30.

3 The first was a small gold-mining company based in distant Khabarovsk, with no ties to Chukotka, and the second was an appliance shop in Anadyr with ten employees.

4 I have discussed the "moral economy of sacrifice" in settler life in more detail in Niobe Thompson (2002).

5 Michel Foucault has characterized this mode of rule as "without metaphysical considerations, nor any serious attention paid to goals beyond that of the prince's power" (quoted in Dreyfus, Hubert, and Rabinow 1982, 136).

6 The Russian Constitutional Court upheld Chukotka's Declaration of Independence in 1993 (Gray 2005; Mote 1998).

7 The declaration of sovereignty is titled in Russian *Reshenie Soveta Narodnykh Deputatov Chukotskogo Avtonomnogo Okruga XXI Sozyva ot 28 sentiabria 1990-ogo goda "O provozglashenii Chukotskoi Sovetskoi Avtonomnoi Respubliki."*

8 Patty Gray (2005, 166), who produced the only thorough examination of this episode in Chukotka's history, notes, "Etylin for his part still openly avowed the strengths of a socialist system ... while Nazarov claimed to whole-heartedly embrace democratisation and privatisation."

9 A new elected body was later created, the okrug Duma. However, it never achieved the influence of the old Soviet and remains almost completely subordinate to the governor's office.

10 President Yeltsin's instinctive strategy of inviting yet greater regional autonomy, manifest in his 1990 call to "take as much sovereignty as you can swallow" (quoted in Mote 1998, 141), should be understood in this context. Just as Brezhnev leveraged his regionally based authority in order to unseat the centrist Krushchev, so Yeltsin destroyed central Soviet power by accelerating the regions' already evident centrifugal tendencies.

11 Nazarov's success in capturing a regional administrative territory and accumulating power within it to a near-feudal degree was certainly not unique in post-Soviet Russia. An example close at hand was the governorship of Evgenii Nazdratenko in Primorskii Krai. Nazdratenko constructed a personal fiefdom through the open use of graft and patronage, while defying the attempts of first Yeltsin and later Putin to rein him in. When his refusal to raise regional utility tariffs in the 1990s led to a catastrophic energy crisis in the winter of 2001, he embezzled for personal use the emergency funds that had been transferred to the region by the federal government to alleviate the crisis. Only by engaging in a dedicated effort to publicly humiliate Nazdratenko and by buying him off with a lucrative post in the federal fishing-quotas authority was Putin able to remove him from power (Hill and Gaddy 2003).

12 Verdery and Humphrey both view the emergence of local bosses in these terms and characterize the post-socialist "mafia" as the outcome of this process of "privatizing power." Verdery (1996, 218) writes, "In earlier times, socialism's bureaucracy operated through networks of reciprocity, both vertical and horizontal, that were built up over decades and enabled production to take place despite severe shortages. With the collapse of the party-state, the vertical ties became less valuable, as superiors could no longer guarantee deliveries and investments; subordinates therefore abandoned their vertical loyalties so as to cement local,

horizontal relations that might serve them better. These horizontal ties of reciprocity, sometimes culminating in violence, are what constitute 'mafia.'"

13 Examples of new government agencies established in Anadyr as a consequence of Chukotka's secession include the Pension Fund, departments of social service such as health care, education, and welfare, the customs and immigration service, environment and natural resource departments, and legal and administrative departments in the new okrug administration.

14 In a similar vein, the sociologist Vadim Volkov (2000) writes of the "patrimonial rationality" of the Russian state, and Ken Jowitt (1992) describes the "neotraditional" aspect of the Soviet regime, noting the survivals of pre-revolutionary governance in the post-revolutionary era.

15 For descriptions of patron roles in traditional mafia society, see J.P. Schneider (1976) and A. Blok (1974) on the Sicilian mafia.

16 Writing on politics in southern Italy, Sidney Tarrow (1967, 69) drew a distinction between formal feudalism and informal clientalism: "In feudal society, social relationships were formalised, hierarchical and legally sanctioned ... Clientelism on the other hand is shifting and informal and has no institutional recognition in concrete institutions."

17 A good summary of the generic structure of patron-client relationships can be found in S.N. Eisenstadt and L. Roniger (1984) and C. Clapham (1982).

18 Paine (1971, 9) asserts that since the value of the services and goods flowing between patron and client is constantly and mutually audited to ensure commensurality, patronage relationships naturally tend to flatten social hierarchies.

19 The natural parallels between the functions of the market and the criminal mafia are irresistible, as Vadim Volkov (2002) has observed in his analysis of "entrepreneurial violence" and the Russian mafia in the "transition" era. The strenuous efforts companies make to "capture market share," which governments counteract with anti-trust regulation, mirror the manner in which patron figures in a mafia setting act to defend their territory and destroy, often through violence, their competitors. Volkov characterizes Russian criminal organizations in the 1990s as nascent corporations, using violence to capture markets for their services (foremost among them the provision of a *krysha,* or "protection"). Equilibrium was possible only if criminal gangs dominated discrete patches of economic turf in which they faced zero competition from contending forces; violence was the outcome of competition within a single territory.

20 For an example of extreme optimism regarding a Russian transition to democratic capitalism, see Anders Aslund (1995).

21 This contention is based on the statements of several informants, two within the post-2000 Abramovich administration who dealt directly with the FSB (successor to the KGB) and were involved in the abortive attempt to lift the border regime when Abramovich began his tenure [21] [22], and three with close links to former Party networks and the Nazarov administration [23] [24] [25]. Patty Gray (2005) also provides a discussion of the border regime policy and in particular its effects on foreign visitors in the 1990s.

22 In the official proposal that led to the multi-million-dollar USAID-funded Alaska Chukotka Development Program in 2001, Anchorage-based Professor Vic Fischer (2001, 3) wrote, "Melting of the 'ice curtain' between the neighbour regions came with Gorbachev's *perestroika* ... Hundreds of Alaskans travelled to Chukotka to help improve healthcare, establish new businesses, set up new air and telephone connections ... During the 1990s, this wave of assistance was slowly choked off by the corrupt, repressive regional administration. Visas became difficult to obtain. Shipments of aid were held up in customs. Movements of medical supplies and services were reduced to nearly zero. Most fledgling business partnerships disintegrated."

23 Only a handful of foreign researchers succeeded in conducting fieldwork outside Chukotka's principal towns over the 1990s, including Debra Schindler, Patty Gray, Virginie Vaté, Anna

Kerttula, and Michael Dunn. However, according to Gray, they faced increasing bureaucratic restrictions on movement as the decade progressed, were subjected to monitoring and harassment from the security services, and even found themselves the targets of denunciations in the regional press. By 1998, regulations were published that officially required anyone not resident in Chukotka to obtain permission to visit its border regions, although such restrictions had existed in practice from 1994 (Gray 2005). My own experiences after Nazarov's removal from office in 2000 illustrate that there was actually great latitude in the interpretation of border regime regulations. With the help of Governor Abramovich's administration, I had no difficulty obtaining the permissions necessary to conduct research in every region of Chukotka during the years 2001-5. However, since Abramovich's administration failed to ameliorate the existing border regime legislation [21], it remains to be seen whether the new openness to foreign researchers proves more than a temporary relaxation.

24 Among my sources on this point were news journalists from the national broadcaster RTR and the national newspaper *Nezavisimaia Gazeta.* Their experience was also confirmed by three well-known photographers, one Ukrainian and two Russians based in Moscow, who worked in neighbouring Sakha, Magadan, and Kamchatka throughout the 1990s but never succeeded in getting permission to shoot in Chukotka.

25 The security services enforcing the border regime were nominally subordinate only to their superiors in Moscow, but a large number of informants insisted that local FSB and Border Guard commanders were deeply implicated in informal network arrangements with Governor Nazarov. At a time when Yeltsin-led reforms were dismantling and under-financing the old security apparatus of the Soviet state, local bosses found their relationships with the okrug administration (with which they had no formal ties) more meaningful than their confused and unpredictable connections with superiors in Moscow. Indeed, by lobbying federal authorities to maintain Chukotka's border regime as neighbouring regions opened up, Nazarov helped preserve a role for the local security-service bureaucracy. In return, it appeared that the governor's office possessed an informal power to act through the security services, admitting or refusing outsiders to the okrug by influencing the FSB-administered vetting procedure. Several informants who occupied administrative and managerial positions in the 1990s reported that local FSB commanders sometimes falsified their reports to Moscow to conceal their involvement, or at least acquiescence, in activities such as the smuggling of retail goods to avoid taxation, poaching of fish and reindeer, and the liquidation of state assets for private profit.

26 This information was collected in interviews conducted in January and February 2003 with former residents of Beringovskii resettled in central Russia, including former employees of the local post office and the police, both of whom were personally involved in censoring correspondence.

27 On several occasions, residents of Beringovskii collectively raised the money to send a local to central Russia: ostensibly "on holiday," these travellers were actually couriers for their messages.

28 Only in 2001, after Nazarov was removed from office, did Etylin win a seat as Chukotka's representative to the federal Duma. He lost his seat in the 2003 parliamentary elections, replaced by Irina Panchenko, a close associate of then governor Roman Abramovich and a shareholder in his oil company Sibneft.

29 I make this observation on the basis of my 2002-5 experiences. Patty Gray (2005) also describes the relative health of these two organizations in Nazarov-era Chukotka, pointing specifically to their proximity to Alaskan partners and isolation from the okrug administration in Anadyr as factors critical to their survival.

30 Only in late 1997 was a branch of the Central Bank established in Anadyr to handle these disbursements, depriving the administration of control over budget funds and consequently

reducing the opportunities for embezzlement. Meanwhile, taxation responsibility was devolved to the okrug from January 1996, and because the severe economic crisis thereafter resulted in low local tax revenues, the okrug administration was left with far fewer resources than previously [25].

31 Again, performance theory alerts us to the importance of *audience* in a ritual such as this. In the villages, Nazarov's acts of benevolent distribution were in fact set-piece performances packaged for consumption in Anadyr and Moscow, where his key constituencies were located. In reality, he persecuted the rural domain through a policy of near-total neglect. I got to know the local filmmaker whom Nazarov hired to shoot his occasional rural visits, and he related how in 2002 he was paid to produce each into an hour-long "documentary," complete with a custom-produced musical score and professional editing. Although it rather sickened him to produce these advertisements for the governor, this was practically the only paid film work to be had in Chukotka during the 1990s.[29]

32 This information, supplied by the member of the okrug Duma who chaired the Committee for Agriculture in 2002, was corroborated by senior officials in the department [30] [31]. In contrast to the 5-million-ruble budget of 2000, the 2001 budget (in Abramovich's first year) was over 200 million rubles, delivered to the department as actual funding.

33 An English-language description of the kormlenie principle can be found in B. Lincoln (1994). For a more extensive Russian-language examination, see S. Pushkarev (1993).

34 Ken Jowitt (1992, 288) writes, "I distinguish individualism and personalism in the following manner: individualism is ego restrained by both impersonal norms and an internal discipline of deferred gratification. Personalism is ego unrestrained by anything except external obstacle or internal disability."

35 A very important source of information about the corrupt practices of Governor Nazarov and his inner circle is recorded in a self-published, so-called fictional historical account written by informant number [28] under the pseudonymn P. Kholostov: *Na l'dine: Pochti istoricheskoe povestvovanie* (On ice: A near-historical account) (Anadyr: Anadyrskoe izdatel'stvo, 2001). No information from Kholostov's account is reproduced in this book unless it has been confirmed independently by two or more informants.

36 Former geologists with an intimate knowledge of Chukotka's gold potential in fact report that by this time, no easily accessible surface deposits remained in Chukotka; Nazarov was apparently not inclined to believe the scientific prognosis [32] [5] [3] [1]. On Nazarov's expectation that secession would prevent Magadan from skimming Chukotka's wealth for itself, see Igor Krupnik and Nikolai Vakhtin (2002).

37 Respectively, these were the Valunistoe and Kara'veemskoe deposits [1] [3] [5] [32].

38 This is not a joke: these actually were the names given to the two companies.

39 According to the 24 May 2004 issue of *Nezavisimaia Gazeta*, Nazarov's administration received special federal loans in 1994-95 worth US$190 million. This information was corroborated by the head of special loans at the Moscow-based Bank Vozrozhdeniia, who was seconded to Anadyr in 2002 to investigate the affair of the missing funds. Some of these details also appeared in Petr Mikhailov, "Chukotka – ostrov nevezeniia," *Ogon'ek*, 11 November 2000.

40 Stories also circulate about the obscene spending habits of Nazarov and his closest lieutenants, particularly outside the okrug, at a time when residents of Chukotka were surviving on Red Cross humanitarian aid packages. Alaskan sources recall profligate shopping trips for the governor's family to Anchorage. Associates of Nazarov, including several deputy governors, purchased luxury *kottedzhy* (literally "cottages", but actually mansions) on the outskirts of Moscow. The governor maintained a football team in Moscow, representing the okrug in Russia's premier league. At the time of Nazarov's defeat in 2000, his wife owned an exclusive jewellery outlet on Ulitsa Tverskaya in Moscow, one of the world's most expensive shopping streets.

41 For example, an erstwhile member of Governor Nazarov's administration who later moved to the okrug tax inspectorate was scathing regarding the manner in which the geological profession was dismantled under Nazarov's watch. This informant was prepared to reveal sensitive information about Nazarov's administration because he had been a professional geologist for two decades in the Soviet Ekspeditsiia, and regardless of his later involvements, his loyalties in 2002 still lay with the old project of northern geology [28].

42 In late 2000, Nazarov withdrew his candidacy in the gubernatorial elections and conceded to Roman Abramovich. It appears he was compensated with an appointment to the Federation Council and to chair the federal Committee on the North and Indigenous Affairs.

Chapter 5: Surviving without the State

1 This was a far-reaching discussion carried on in the national (and local) media, but the best-known landmark article was A.I. Pika and B.B. Prokhorov's "Bol'shie problemy malykh narodov" (1988), followed by Nikolai Vakhtin's *Native Peoples of the Russian Far North* (1992), an English-language publication that effectively internationalized these issues.

2 Robert Putnam (2000), a theorist of social capital, would call this pattern of association "bonding social capital," one that binds together groups of natural affinity, such as clans or work collectives. What is missing in such a situation, according to Putnam, is "bridging social capital," which transcends the natural cleavages of association to form inclusive networks and a sense of common cause.

3 Many informants frequently drifted between professions in the Soviet era. A senior dentist spent a year captaining ferries across the Gulf of Anadyr "to get away from teeth for a while" [13]. A geologist took a job as a radio operator in a coal ship to experience Chukotka from the sea, before becoming a news anchor for the okrug television station [16].

4 The closure was announced in February 1995, the plant closed in May, and by the end of June, Iul'tin's water, heating, and electricity were disconnected. Except for some holdouts, the population of roughly five thousand was evacuated before the first snows in September.

5 The case of Egvekinot's total capture by a single institution in the 1990s appears to mirror Governor Nazarov's patronage machine in Anadyr. There is a significant contrast, however. Egvekinot's administration preserved the material assets and institutions it inherited from the Soviet era. With the exception of the Iul'tin enterprises, which were never under district control anyway, asset stripping was not the pattern. Consequently, the district's collective farms (reindeer herds), schools, transport infrastructure, and cultural institutions remained intact. The explanation for this apparent fidelity to the local population and commitment to the long-term prospects of the settlement were to be found, I believe, in the particularly strong attachment to place I detected among settlers in *Iul'tinskii Raion*, compounded by a fierce pride in their achievements as builders of the district's industrial complex (mines, road, port). I return to the question of localist attachments in Chapter 8.

6 The relevant Russian laws on the resettlement rights of northern residents, special pay benefits, elevated pensions, and early retirement can be found in V.A. Kriazhkov (1994).

7 The success of the resettlement program was further eroded by incompetent management on the part of the district administration. In several cases, residents of Chukotka were resettled to housing that, in the time it took to travel from the North, was confiscated by local authorities in the destination region or sold on the private market [35] [36]. One family from Anadyr was on the verge of leaving for a new home in Altai when they learned they were being resettled to a town whose own liquidation was imminent [9].

8 Cash loans during much of the 1990s were extremely difficult to secure because, in conditions of high inflation, they were effectively grants. For the most part, banks did not lend in rubles, and so the only source of credit for businesses and state agencies was the state itself.

9 For this reason, life in Chukotka was never quite as desperate as economic indicators suggested. At the level of everyday life in the settlements, the continuing habits of reciprocity – the non-monetized exchange of food and favours – were not reflected in economic statistics in the same manner as the closure of factories and the collapse of tax revenues.

10 All names are changed to conceal the identity of sources.

11 When I describe the circumstances many settlers faced in the 1990s, I use the term "survival" in the most literal sense. I met men and women whose family lives disintegrated over this period, as a result of their inability to raise an income. In some cases, the state labelled them incapable parents and institutionalized their children (for a full account of "social orphanhood" in neighbouring Magadan, see Khlinovskaya-Rockhill 2003). "Survivors" related stories of friends *(khoroshie muzhiki v svoe vremya)* who responded to personal crises by killing themselves, either through design or self-neglect. This appeared to be the case with Grisha's Chukchi hunting partner. In 2003, while interviewing a neighbour of his in Anadyr, I helped pull his unconscious body from his burning flat, where he had fallen asleep with a burning cigarette after a week-long drinking binge.

12 When I visited Iul'tin in September 2002, seven years after its closure, a handful of these characters still resided there.

13 Although the successor to the Soviet-era kolkhoz and sovkhoz in Chukotka was the *unitarnoe gosudarstvennoe predpriiatie* (Consolidated State Enterprise), the former terms are still used in the vernacular.

14 The only equivalent of the Russian parashiutist is the "smokejumper," an American term for the elite forest-fire fighters who parachute from planes into remote wildfires. To this day, despite the legendary standards of smokejumper programs, Russian parashiutisti undergo a more extensive and professionalized preparation in their Moscow academy. It was due to the fact that I once worked as a Canadian forest-fire fighter that I had such unusual access to the lives of the men of Avialesokhrana.

15 At that time, the Chukchi Autonomous Okrug was still subordinate to Magadan Oblast, and the regional Avialesokhrana headquarters was in the city of Magadan.

16 This refers only to permanent staff – bookkeepers, pilots, radio operators, senior firefighters, warehousemen – who stay throughout the year. Like any firefighting operation, Avialesokhrana hired large numbers of temporary firefighters in the summer months, in response to fire conditions.

17 Chuvantsy are the descendants of seventeenth-century Cossack settlers and the indigenous population of the middle and upper reaches of the Anadyr River. Currently, most live in the Anadyr River settlement of Markovo (see Vakhtin, Golovko, and Schweitzer 2004).

18 The local, rooted, and partly indigenous character of Avialesokhrana's workforce was also an outcome of out-migration from Chukotka over the previous decade. The Soviet-era service was staffed by professional firefighters and managers trained at a central institute in Moscow and thus usually outsiders; this is Director Klimentiev's story. Pay was once extremely high for firefighters (parashiutisty), and the job held a romantic allure. In the 1990s, the work became more difficult (since resources such as air support were scarcer) and pay dropped. As a result, locals, particularly those accustomed to working in a tundra environment out in the settlements, filled the shoes of departing newcomer recruits.

19 On several occasions during the 1990s, Governor Nazarov personally urged Avialesokhrana's director to engage in "privateering" rather than to expect funding from the okrug administration. There was some irony in this because, at other times, Nazarov attempted to wrestle Avialesokhrana's federal funding into the okrug budget.

20 His position was formally the head of administration (glava administratsii), which in the Soviet era had been of equal importance to the chair of the village Soviet. Once the latter

post was abolished after 1991, the only other administrative positions of real influence in the village were the head of the kolkhoz, the director of public works, and perhaps the school headmaster.

21 On the rare occasion when potentially troublesome visitors made the trip, the Bogorevs were standing by to ensure that they left with the right impression. In August 2005, I witnessed the visit to Vaegi of an Anadyr judge. At that time, Vaegi's policeman, who would naturally be on hand to meet him, was new to the village. Feeling that he was not yet a reliable ally, Viktor ensured that this encounter never took place: acting on his instructions, two young village women spent the day before the visit drinking with the policeman, who then slept through the entire following day and never emerged from his house to meet the guest. As for the judge himself, Viktor ensured speedy transport back to Markovo as soon as official business was completed.

22 When regular pay returned under Governor Abramovich, several settler informants visited relatives on the materik for the first time in over a decade.

Chapter 6: Modernization Again

1 The 1989 Soviet census enumerated 164,700 residents in Chukotka, not including military personnel, whereas the 2002 census counted 54,000 residents, a drop of roughly 68 percent (FSGS 2004).

2 In its 2007 survey, *Forbes Magazine* listed Roman Abramovich as Russia's richest citizen and the sixteenth wealthiest in the world, with an estimated net worth of over $18.7 billion. He built his fortune as the majority owner of Sibneft, a major Russian oil company, which he sold to the Russian state-owned Gazprom in 2005, earning $13 billion. He has also held shares in some of Russia's largest aluminium, auto, airline, and media firms, and he is the owner of the Chelsea Football Club in London. The term "oligarch" gained currency in the mid-1990s to describe the small number of very wealthy Russian businessmen who enjoyed access to political power. President Vladimir Putin (since 2000) has largely detached the oligarchs from political decision making and, in certain cases (Berezovsky, Gusinsky, Khodorkovsky), has destroyed their business empires, but several of them, Abramovich included, have thus far escaped serious persecution.

3 Officially, Abramovich won 92 percent of the vote, but rumours persist that, unlike his predecessor Aleksandr Nazarov, who manufactured election results to stay in power, Abramovich deflated his own polling numbers to create the illusion of a good democratic contest.

4 In its messianic impact, Abramovich's arrival in Chukotka might be compared with Lenin's entry by train at Petrograd's Finland Station in 1917.

5 This figure is based on the 2002 census population of 54,000. In the intervening five years, the in-migration of labour has roughly compensated for continuing high rates of out-migration, with the effect of stabilizing the population.

6 By 2000, public infrastructure in Chukotka was indeed in a state of general collapse. The value of assets in the public sector – housing, public works, social infrastructure, administration, transport – was less than 10 percent of its 1991 equivalent. Furthermore, over 70 percent of state-owned enterprises were in a condition of virtual bankruptcy (Abramovich 2001).

7 This statement appeared throughout the Russian press and was found on the official website of the Chukotka administration, http://www.chukotka.org. In apparently accepting a distinct basket of rights for the Chukchi, Yup'ik, and other local indigenous peoples, Abramovich followed a pattern of "oligarchic liberalism" detected by David Anderson (2002) in other northern regions recently captured by resource-capital interests. Departing from Nazarov's style of malevolent disregard for the indigenous population (see Gray 2005, 2000), Abram-

ovich embraced the notion of "original peoples," whom he excused from the calculations of cost-efficiency applied to settlers in Chukotka.

8 Despite the opening of Anadyr's vocational college, Chukotka remains the only territory of the Russian Federation without an "institute of higher learning" (*VUZ*, or university).

9 Abramovich's developmentalist approach to the indigenous population echoes the "soft policy" of gentle enlightenment advanced by the Committee of the North immediately after the 1917 Communist Revolution (McCannon 1998). At that time, idealistic Russian ethnographers took advantage of a period of official uncertainty regarding the role of northern natives in the socialist project to shape state policy. This window of opportunity soon closed, however, when Stalinist industrialization recast natives in the role of labour support for northern mines, military installations, and fishing enterprises.

10 There were obvious parallels in this program with the late-Soviet practice of *ukrupnenie*, a policy of amalgamating indigenous populations into large agricultural settlements, where economies of scale and centralized management of herding and hunting were meant to modernize the traditional native economy.

11 President Putin openly supported this approach in a 2004 speech he made in Salekhard. *Nezavisimaia Gazeta*, 30 April 2004.

12 State resettlement programs in the 1990s and the Soviet era were never so explicitly informed by a cost-benefit ideology. Rather, resettlement rights were typically perceived as the fulfillment of a moral contract between the state and northern residents, whose sacrifices in the North merited concrete rewards and privileges.

13 For details on this program, see Niobe Thompson (2002, 2004).

14 Officials treated thirty to thirty-five thousand as an ideal population, a figure they calculated as supportable based on the levels of federal subsidy anticipated in the future. They also estimated that the cost of resettlement within the Regionstroy program would be recouped by subsidy cost savings within five years.

15 The first signs of industrial investment returning to the okrug strongly suggested a shift toward the future use of transient labour: Sibneft's oil and gas exploration program relied on workers from the Omsk region, and a new Canadian gold mine in the interior imported labour from Magadan, with specialists from Canada.

16 For details on the oligarchs' rush to the provinces, see A. Barnes (2003).

17 Sibneft's transfer-pricing arrangements became widely known from mid-2003. For example, see "The Boy Done Good," *Economist*, 3 July 2003; Catherine Belton, "Yukos, Market Suffer New Hits," *Moscow Times*, 19 November 2003; and Catherine Belton, "Sibneft Hit with $1bn Tax Claim," *Moscow Times*, 3 March 2004.

18 Although the figure of the New Russian is emblematic of life in the turbulent 1990s, a large body of social research and popular discourse has struggled to characterize its place in society (Humphrey 2002; H. Balzer 2003; Graham 2003). Popular perceptions of the newly affluent fluctuate between moral indignation and grudging admiration for their practices of Veblenesque consumption. Fifteen years into the free market experience, a sense of illegitimacy still haunts the pursuit of profit, so that on the "Russian street" one still finds entrepreneurs conflated with corrupt bureaucrats and racketeers. As Caroline Humphrey (2002) has observed, conspicuous consumption emits very ambiguous signals in post-Soviet conditions of moral and economic flux, and so the display of wealth often comes across as strained and ridiculous, if not altogether obnoxious.

19 Moscow, where Sibneft had its headquarters, was naturally the biggest recruiting ground, but so was Omsk, the home of key Sibneft operations as well as of Abramovich's ally Governor Leonid Polezhaev. From Nizhni Novgorod, which produced leading reformer figures throughout the 1990s (Boris Nemtsov, Sergei Kir'yenko) came virtually the administration's

entire cohort of media and public relations specialists. From Syktyvkar, where Abramovich spent his childhood, came the team running Chukotka's Department of Education.

20 Of the five deputy governors in 2001-3, three were former Sibneft executives with large share holdings.

21 In 2002, Canadian plumbers and electricians working in Chukotka earned roughly US$9,000 a month, at a tax rate of 4 percent.

22 Trotsky viewed the unequal stages of social development in which the provinces and the metropole found themselves on the eve of the Communist Revolution as a justification for "telescoping change." Stalin, whose program of forced industrialization was the concrete manifestation of this belief, viewed his efforts as part of a reforming tradition and in fact welcomed comparisons with Peter I and Ivan IV (Tucker 1990).

23 This impulse is often accompanied by a simultaneous revulsion at the decadent superfluity of the urban middle-class lifestyle, and so urban attentions to the rural have often been a search for communion with uncorrupted and eternal Russian roots. Leo Tolstoy evoked a literary epiphany of this nature in *War and Peace*, when his aristocratic protagonist scythes a field of autumn wheat with his own serfs. The derevenshiki movement of the late-Soviet period, of which Valentin Rasputin was the best-known writer, similarly identified a salvation for middle-class urban Soviet youth in the disappearing "true Russian village."

24 The quotation in this sentence is a conscious reference to a similar phrase of Caroline Humphrey's (1983, 375) – "to live to good purpose under socialism." Waves of emulatory modernization in Russia have always left a footprint in the vocabulary of technological and cultural change, as witnessed in the new Russian professions of *ekspert po auditing* (expert in auditing), *menedzher* (manager), and *p-rshik* (public relations specialist).

25 Devolving power in the context of Russia's rigidly hierarchic polity has always been a delicate process. In assessing Russia's Crimea defeat (1856) at the hands of Western nations, Aleksandr II believed that to match the military power of Britain and France, universal military training for peasants and a professional armed forces would be required. However, Nicolas I before him had already discarded this proposal, since to empower the peasantry with such training would have seriously endangered the supremacy of the land-owning gentry (see Rieber 1966).

26 In theoretical terms, modernization appeared to follow the pattern of "internal colonialism" (Hechter 1975) or "colonialism without colonies" (Osterhammel 2002) witnessed in the relationship England maintained with its "Celtic fringe" (Wales, Scotland, Ireland).

27 In the first years after Abramovich acquired Sibneft, he was heavily reliant on the multinational oil-field service company Schlumberger to exploit the resources Sibneft controlled. Although Sibneft's reserves were enormous, it lacked in-house expertise and access to the latest technology, as was typical of all the formerly state-owned resource conglomerates. In Chukotka, Schlumberger was contracted to run the oil exploration program on the marine shelf of the Gulf of Anadyr; Sibneft itself had almost no direct involvement.

28 Kotkin (1995, 203) argues that the patterns of work native to the rural setting were imported to the industrial workplace as a consequence of forced urbanization and industrialization. He writes, "Construction work during the Five-Year Plan was performed in rushes, or 'storms,' a style that, although it has been likened to the very old, rural, rhythm-setting work cry *(vziali)*, was christened with a new term, shock work *(udarnyi trud)*."

29 After his inauguration in 2001, Abramovich stated that he would not run for a second term and would leave Chukotka (he was rarely there in any case) by the end of 2005. However, on the eve of his departure, President Putin persuaded him to remain for another term running until 2010. This situation arose for two reasons: by this juncture, regional governors were appointed by the president rather than elected for office, and Putin now held extraordinary influence over the activities of the remaining oligarchs. Personal communication with

governor's assistant, Aleksandr Borodin; "Oligarch Governor Says He Won't Seek Second Term," *RFE/RL Russian Report*, 1 May 2002; *Trud*, 26 April 2002.

30 In order to link its office to the phone grid, the company trenched a dedicated line through Anadyr to the telephone exchange. A critical shipload of building supplies reached Anadyr too late in the season and was stranded beyond the shorefast ice. It was redirected to Vladivostok, forty-five hundred kilometres to the south, and its contents were then loaded onto long-distance cargo planes and flown to Chukotka.

31 In this regard, Abramovich, whose infrequent visits to the region rarely exceeded four days, led by example. His presence in Anadyr was signalled by a particular intensity of helicopter traffic overhead and fleets of black Land Cruisers navigating the cratered streets even faster than usual.

32 Norbert Elias, in *The Civilising Process* (1978), described the evolution of Western European societies as partly a transition of acculturated behaviour from "constraint by others" to "self-restraint," a process of self-disciplining. Only with the appearance of these widely held habits of self-discipline – codified manners, rules of hygiene, forms of intercourse – could less violent and more productive and complex societies emerge.

33 The *zemstvo* was a form of local government instituted in 1864 during the liberal reforms introduced by Tsar Aleksander II. They were abolished after the 1917 Communist Revolution.

34 Its generic name, the *razvlekatel'nyi tsentr*, may be translated literally as "distraction centre"; distraction was precisely the intention.

35 A typical comment on pre-Abramovich modes of kul'tura, which older settlers claimed were always highly participatory and constitutive of their sense of community, comes from a veteran journalist: "Chukotka was always unique in the sense that there were few artists and performers in settler circles, so everyone was compelled to develop his own artistic capacities. It's more interesting for people to be involved in their own creative productions than to watch passively as other people perform" [11].

36 This quality of leisure time is captured in the Russian expression "kul'turno otdokhnut'" (to spend free time in a civilized and constructive way). Otdokhnut' translates literally as "to catch one's breath," and recuperation is certainly part of its generally accepted meaning, yet it is the stand-in term expressing the activity of filling time away from work.

37 The event was not unmarred: during the performance of Night Sniper, a local threw a bottle at the lead singer, which smashed into her forehead, and their drummer was assaulted on the street after the show. Abramovich was dismayed by this display of beskul'tur'e and personally visited the performers in their hotel to apologize. His deputy Sergei Kapkov then published a letter in *Krainyi Sever* strongly admonishing the local spectators, which he concluded with the words "Insanely annoying and extremely shameful!" *Krainyi Sever*, 26 April 2002, 3.

38 Two full-sized Tupolev passenger jets were required to transport the entourage from Moscow to Anadyr.

39 The role played by these (mostly female) transmitters of kul'tura finds a remarkable parallel in the Stalinist industrialization campaign: the mobilization of senior engineers' and managers' wives to coordinate the mass civilization of everyday life. This national movement published a journal called *Obshestvennitsa*, and its rank and file were known as *obshestvennitsy*. With backing from the Ministry of Industry under Ordzhonikidze, they strove to reorganize the life of the industrial workforce according to the principles of kul'turnost', precisely the techniques of self-restraint and discipline required of a more productive and trustworthy type of worker (for more detail see Buckley 1996; Volkov 1999).

40 This quote was ascribed to Abramovich by Dora Poluksht, the director of education and a close associate of the governor, at a strategy seminar on education reforms held in November 2002.

41 These statements were made in the closed planning seminar on education policy I attended in late 2002. They were later published in *Krainyi Sever*, 15 November 2003, 6. Transliterations from the original read, "programmy kruglogodichnogo truda, razvitiya, otdykha, i ozdorovleniya shkol'nikov" and "U nas deti ezdyat po napravleniyam, i dazhe v khode organitsii letnego otdykha detei dolzhno sokhranyatsya edinoe obrazovatel'noe i vospitatel'noe prostranstvo."

42 The rather Maoist maxim of the New Generation program was "Health, Development, Labour," and a pillar of the curriculum in the villages was gathering rubbish, a kind of continual youth *subbotnik* (in Soviet times, an organized, collective work project, usually cleaning public spaces, which was held on Saturdays).

43 This quote was passed from L.I. Ainana, the chairperson of Chukotka's Yup'ik Society (called Yup'ik) to Petr Omrynto, the senior indigenous deputy in Chukotka's okrug Duma. Omrynto later included the quote in an open letter to Sergei Kapkov, published in *Krainyi Sever*, 7 June 2002, 14.

Chapter 7: Two Solitudes

1 Within Anadyr's settler networks, the negative attitudes regarding Abramovich and his projects differed radically from those of most indigenous Chukotkans, the young offspring of Soviet-era settlers, and even of settlers living in rural areas. There are several explanations for this. First, only in Anadyr did locals come into regular contact with modernizing specialists from outside, and only there did the reforms encroach on the authority of local figures. Second, in the villages and district centres, Abramovich brought living standards back from an extremely critical state, which Anadyr never experienced. Finally, the large majority of those living in Anadyr at the time of Abramovich's arrival were *established* settlers with a personal stake in regional power networks.

2 Hugh MacLennan (1945) himself had borrowed the expression from Rainer Maria Rilke, who wrote, "In love two solitudes protect and touch and greet each other." Obviously, MacLennan's two solitudes were very much less in communion than Rilke's, and I follow the spirit of his updated use of the term.

3 This was not her actual name.

4 The new *departmenty* were Industry and Agriculture (Gorodilov); Finance, Economy, and Property (Panchenko); Culture, Youth, Sport, Tourism, and Public Relations (Kapkov); and Social Affairs and Public Welfare (Viacheslav Zolotarev, a local removed from his post in early 2003).

5 This is not in any way to infer that the Soviet Union was a classless society; see Chapter 2 for an exploration of Soviet class and the place of the northerner in the hierarchy of privilege. Post-Soviet flux has simply rearranged and magnified class differences.

6 Almost none of the middle-ranking and senior modernizers outside the very inner circle were wealthy. But, having been recruited into Abramovich's corporate family, they were in close proximity to fantastic wealth. Abramovich and his deputies liked to hold lavish parties for administration staff from time to time. At one, Abramovich began to give away expensive presents. He promised his new four-by-four Humvee, which he had shipped to Anadyr, to the person who, within a minute, could name the most settlements in Chukotka. Apletin, the editor of *Krainyi Sever*, won the contest. When I knew him, he was quite desperate to get the Humvee out of the region and sell it; it was worth over US$200,000, but he couldn't afford to keep it since the cost of its registration alone exceeded his annual salary.

7 The birthday party to which Yulia (the local in the okrug administration) was not invited was open only to those clearly inhabiting the modernizing networks suspended between Moscow and Chukotka. As such, it was a premier networking event and not a place that incomers such as Kapkov wished to crowd with low network-utility locals.

8 This name of this publication, *Luchshye liudy Rossii,* translates roughly as "Russia's best people."

9 The purchase of the Chelsea Football Club in spring 2003 absorbed much of the time and interest that Abramovich had previously devoted to the project of modernizing Chukotka.

10 Over the course of my research, the illusion that my wife and I belonged within the modernizing cadre became untenable. We did nothing to hide our foreign origins, but we nevertheless failed in almost all respects to observe the "techniques of separation" that modernizing acquaintances might have expected as a condition of membership in their tightly knit community. Instead of living in prefabricated administration housing, my wife and I rented a flat in an ordinary concrete apartment building. My wife taught English in School No. 3 and the teacher-training college, and studied Russian with a series of local instructors. We rarely ate in the hotels or the Anadyr Restaurant, which filled up with newcomer experts at every lunch and dinner hour. And whereas the shuttling lifestyle of our administration acquaintances removed them from our lives on a regular basis, we gradually deepened our friendships among a circle of local friends on whom we could always call.

11 To illustrate, whereas the embezzlement by Nazarov's office of federal gold credits was widely known when it occurred (see Chapter 4 for details), I learned of the Chukotka-based transfer-pricing schemes Roman Abramovich was using to avoid taxation on his companies only when, after fieldwork, I returned to Moscow and spoke with acquaintances there who had handled some of the paperwork involved in setting them up.

12 Patty Gray's writing on post-Soviet indigenous-settler relations in Chukotka are the best source of information on this theme, in particular her "Chukotkan Reindeer Husbandry in the Post-Socialist Transition" (2000).

13 Fishing in the gulf waters featured large in the lives of Anadyr's local population; winter ice-fishing for smelt and summer salmon-fishing from the shore formed a pattern of local excursions similar in function to dacha visits in temperate parts of Russia.

14 The project proceeded over the summers of 2002 and 2003 but stalled when, citing security issues, the okrug FSB (Russian Federal Security Service, successor to the KGB) delayed cabling by withholding essential maps of the gulf. Local rumours suggested that disgruntled locals within the security service, concerned about the coming season's catch, were behind this act.

Chapter 8: Conclusion

1 In 2001, Abramovich began to bring two principal sources of new revenue to the okrug. First, he and his business partners donated roughly 6 billion rubles (US$224 million) each year, channelled through a charitable organization called the Territories Fund (simply Territoriia). In the annual okrug budget, these funds are listed as "extra-budgetary." In addition, Abramovich registered Sibneft in the okrug, and its tax contributions also added approximately 6 billion rubles each year between 2001 and 2005. However, Abramovich sold his 72 percent stake in Sibneft to the Russian state (Gazprom) in late 2005, and, for tax purposes, its headquarters were relocated to St. Petersburg, leaving a large hole in Chukotka's budget. My sources for this information include senior okrug administration officials and advisors to Governor Abramovich, 2005-6; Tat'iana Netreba and Tat'iana Bogdanova, "Chukotka – krai alchnykh chinovnikov," *Argumenty i fakty,* 9 August 2006; Valeria Korchagina, "Chukotka Wonders What's Next," and "3 Ways to Survive with No Governor," *Moscow Times* special series on Chukotka, 1-5 September 2006.

2 This is not his actual name.

3 See, for example, Peter Schweitzer, Nikolai Vakhtin, and Evgenii Golovko (2005).

4 The mayor of Vaegi, who was also on the riverboat, told me that shipping beer to his village was his way of combating the influence of vodka bootleggers and screech brewers. He did

not expect that the villagers would ever stop drinking, so he decided they might be distracted from hard spirits with low-proof beer. "Plus," he said, "it fills you up!" [58].

5 This has potentially important political implications. The state-building exercise initiated by former governor Nazarov (see Chapter 4), who intended to create a lasting sense of strictly Chukotkan identity by entrenching bureaucratic interests at the okrug level and severing ties with the former parent oblast Magadan, failed to engender a corresponding popular sense of okrug-level identity. From the time of Abramovich's election, momentum built in favour of a remerging of Chukotka with Magadan, an initiative cynically advanced in 2002 by Aleksandr Nazarov himself, who by that time chaired the federal Committee on the North. "Eks-gubernator Chukotki Aleksandr Nazarov schitaet, chto Chukotskii avtonomnyi okrug mozhet byt' ob'edinen s Magadanskoi oblast'yu," *Krainyi Sever,* 15 November 2002, 12.

6 This finding was apparent in interviews with many settlers in Anadyr who had migrated from smaller settlements to larger ones, a kind of cascading effect that ended in Anadyr, in search of jobs and still-functioning infrastructure. These informants very often complained that Anadyr offered only a pale version of the natural environment and community spirit in the settlements they had been forced to abandon. For more detail on "cascade migration" in the Nazarov era, see Igor Krupnik and Nikolai Vakhtin (2002).

7 Volodya is a pseudonym for this informant.

8 For a general discussion of Russian death and mourning practices, see Catherine Merridale (2000).

References

Abramovich, R.A. 2001. "Poslanie gubernatora Chukokskogo avtonomnogo okruga deputatam okruzhnoi dumy" (Address of the governor of the Chukchi Autonomous Okrug to the deputies of the okrug Duma). Governor's Office, Chukchi Autonomous Okrug.

–. 2002. "Poslanie gubernatora Chukokskogo avtonomnogo okruga deputatam okruzhnoi dumy" (Address of the governor of the Chukchi Autonomous Okrug to the deputies of the okrug Duma). Governor's Office, Chukchi Autonomous Okrug.

Aitov, N. 1983. *Rabochiie khoroshiie i plokhiie* (Workers Good and Bad). Moscow: Sovietskaia Rossiia.

Alatas, S.H. 1977. *The Myth of the Lazy Native.* London: Frank Cass.

Anderson, B. 1983. *Imagined Communities: Reflections on the Origin and Spread of Nationalism.* London: Verso Books.

Anderson, D. 2000. *Identity and Ecology in Arctic Siberia.* Oxford: Oxford University Press.

–. 2002. "Entitlements, Identity, and Time: Addressing Aboriginal Rights and Nature Protection in Siberia's New Resource Colonies." In E. Kasten, ed., *People and the Land: Pathways to Reform in Post-Soviet Siberia,* 99-124. Berlin: Dietrich Reimer Verlag.

"Annual Ranking of Regions." 2000. *Ekspert* 37, 4: "Another Oligarch, Another Investigation." 2004. *RFE/RL Russian Political Weekly* 2, 20.

Applebaum, A. 2003. *Gulag: A History of the Soviet Camps.* London: Penguin.

Argounova, T. 2001. "Scapegoats of Nationalism: Ethnic Tensions in Sakha (Yakutia), Northeastern Russia." PhD diss., University of Cambridge.

Armstrong, T. 1965. *Russian Settlement in the North.* Cambridge: Cambridge University Press.

Asch, M., C. Samson, D. Heinen, J. Kernick, J. Lewis, S. Saugestad, and T. Turner. 2004. "On the Return of the Native." *Current Anthropology* 45: 261-67.

Aslund, A. 1995. *How Russia Became a Market Economy.* Washington, DC: The Brookings Institute.

Balzer, H. 2003. "Routinization of the New Russians." *Russian Review* 62: 15-36.

Balzer, M.M. 1992. *Russian Traditional Culture: Religion, Gender, and Customary Law.* Armonk, NY, and London: M.E. Sharpe.

–. 1999. *The Tenacity of Ethnicity: A Siberian Saga in Global Perspective.* Princeton: Princeton University Press.

Balzer, M.M., and U.A. Vinokurova. 1996. "Nationalism, Interethnic Relations, and Federalism." *Europe-Asia Studies* 48: 101-20.

Barker, A. 1993. "The Divided Self: Yuri Rytkheu and Contemporary Chukchi Literature." In G. Diment and Y. Slezkine, eds., *Between Heaven and Hell: The Myth of Siberia in Russian Culture,* 218-26. New York: St. Martin's Press.

Barnes, A. 2003. "Russia's New Business Groups and State Power." *Post-Soviet Affairs* 19: 154-86.

Barth, F. 1969. *Ethnic Groups and Boundaries: The Social Organization of Cultural Difference.* Boston: Little Brown.

Basilov, V.N. 1994. "Etnografiya: Est' li u nee budushchee?" (Ethnography: Does it have a future?). *Etnograficheskoe obozrenie* 4: 3-17.

Bauman, Z. 1998. *Globalization: The Human Consequences.* New York: Columbia University Press.
Bell, C., and H. Newby. 1978. "Community, Communion, Class and Community Action: The Social Sources of the New Urban Politics." In D.T. Herbert and R.J. Johnston, eds., *Social Areas in Cities: Processes, Patterns and Problems,* 189-99. New York: John Wiley and Sons.
Béteille, A. 1998. "The Idea of Indigenous People." *Current Anthropology* 39: 187-91.
Birman, I. 1980. "The Financial Crisis in the USSR." *Soviet Studies* 32: 84-105.
Bloch, A. 2003. *Red Ties and Residential Schools: Indigenous Siberians in a Post-Soviet State.* Philadelphia: University of Pennsylvania Press.
Blok, A. 1974. *The Mafia of a Sicilian Village, 1860-1960: A Study of Violent Peasant Entrepreneurs.* New York: Harper and Row.
Bogoras, W. 1904-9. *The Chukchee.* Publications of the Jesup North Pacific Expedition. Vol. 7. New York: Stechert.
Bond, A. 1994. "The Non-Energy Mineral Industries of Post-Soviet Russia." *Post-Soviet Geography* 35: 543-55.
Bourdieu, P. 1983. "Forms of Capital." In J.G. Richardson, ed., *Handbook of Theory and Research for the Sociology of Education,* 241-58. New York: Greenwood Press.
–. 1985. *Distinction: A Social Critique of the Judgment of Taste.* London: Routledge.
–. 1990. *The Logic of Practice.* London: Polity.
Boym, S. 1994. *Common Places: Mythologies of Everyday Life in Russia.* Cambridge, MA: Harvard University Press.
Bradshaw, M. 1995. "The Russian North in Transition: General Introduction." *Post-Soviet Geography* 36: 195-203.
Bridger, S., and F. Pine, eds. 1998. *Surviving Post-Socialism: Local Strategies and Regional Responses in Eastern Europe and the Former Soviet Union.* London and New York: Routledge.
Brightman, R. 1993. *Grateful Prey: Rock Cree Human-Animal Relationships.* Berkeley: University of California Press.
Brodsky, J. 1986. *Less Than One: Selected Essays.* London: Viking.
Brody, H. 1975. *The People's Land: Eskimos and Whites in the Eastern Arctic.* London: Penguin.
–. 1981. *Maps and Dreams: Indians and the British Columbia Frontier.* Vancouver: Douglas and McIntyre.
–. 2000. *The Other Side of Eden: Hunter-Gatherers, Farmers and the Shaping of the World.* London: Faber and Faber.
Brubacker, R. 2004. *Ethnicity without Groups.* Boston: Harvard University Press.
Buckley, M. 1996. "The Untold Story of *Obshestvennitsa* in the 1930s." *Europe-Asia Studies* 4: 572-74.
–. 2001. "Chukotskii Renessans: Roman Abramovich pytaetsya obyzdat' svoikh chinovnikov i uvelichit' pogolov'e olenei" (The Reniassance of Chukotka: Roman Abramovich attempts to reign in his public servants and increase reindeer herds). *Nezavisimaia Gazeta,* 26 October.
Clapham, C., ed. 1982. *Private Patronage and Public Power: Political Clientalism in the Modern State.* London: London University Press.
Cohen, A.P., ed. 1982. *Belonging: Identity and Social Organisation in British Rural Cultures.* Manchester: Manchester University Press.
–. 1985. *The Symbolic Construction of Community.* London: Routledge.
–. 1987. *Whalsay: Symbol, Segment and Boundary in a Shetland Island Community.* Manchester: Manchester University Press.
–. 1993. "Segmentary Knowledge: A Whalsay Sketch." In M. Hobart, ed., *An Anthropological Critique of Development: The Growth of Ignorance,* 31-42. London: Routledge.

Coleman, J.S. 1988. "Social Capital in the Creation of Human Capital." *American Journal of Sociology* 94: 95-120.

Cushman, T. 1995. *Notes from the Underground: Rock Music and Counterculture in Russia.* Albany: State University of New York Press.

Dikov, N.N. 1974. *Ocherki istorii Chukotki s drevneishikh vremen do nashikh dnei* (Notes on the history of Chukotka from ancient times to the present). Novosibirsk: Nauka.

–. 1989. *Istoriia Chukotki s drevneishikh vremen do nashikh dnei* (History of Chukotka from ancient times to the present). Moscow: Mysl'.

Diment, G., and Y. Slezkine, eds. 1993. *Between Heaven and Hell: The Myth of Siberia in Russian Culture.* New York: St. Martin's Press.

Douglas, M. 1967. "Primitive Rationing." In R. Firth, ed., *Themes in Economic Anthropology,* 119-48. London: Tavistock.

Dreyfus, M., L. Hubert, and P. Rabinow. 1982. *Michel Foucault: Beyond Structuralism and Hermeneutics.* London: Harvester Wheatsheaf.

Dunham, V.S. 1976. *In Stalin's Time: Middleclass Values in Soviet Fiction.* Cambridge: Cambridge University Press.

Durkheim, É. 1964. *The Division of Labour in Society.* Glencoe, IL: Free Press.

Easter, G.M. 2000. *Reconstructing the State: Personal Networks and Elite Networks in Soviet Russia.* Cambridge: Cambridge University Press.

Eisenstadt, S.N., and L. Roniger. 1984. *Patrons, Clients and Friends: Interpersonal Relationships and the Structure of Trust in Society.* Cambridge: Cambridge University Press.

Elias, N. 1978. *The Civilising Process.* Vol. 1, *The History of Manners.* Oxford: Basil Blackwell.

Elias, N., and J. Scotson. 1965. *The Established and the Outsiders.* London: Frank Cass.

Emmet, I. 1982. "Place, Community and Bilingualism in Blaenau Ffestiniog." In A.P. Cohen, ed., *Belonging: Identity and Social Organisation in British Rural Cultures,* 43-61. Manchester: Manchester University Press.

Fabian, J. 1983. *Time and the Other: How Anthropology Makes Its Object.* New York: Columbia University Press.

Feld, S., and K.H. Basso, eds. 1996. *Senses of Place.* Santa Fe, NM: School of American Research Press.

Ferguson, J. 1994. *The Anti-Politics Machine: "Development," Depoliticization, and Bureaucratic Power in Lesotho.* Minneapolis: University of Minnesota Press.

–. 1999. *Expectations of Modernity: Myths and Meanings of Urban Life on the Zambian Copperbelt.* Berkeley: University of California Press.

Finkler, H.W. 1995. "Health Care in the Russian and Canadian North: A Comparative Perspective." *Post-Soviet Geography* 36: 238-45.

Fischer, V. 2001. "Alaska Chukotka Development Program." Funding proposal, University of Alaska Anchorage.

Fitzpatrick, S. 1999. *Everyday Stalinism: Ordinary Life in Extraordinary Times – Soviet Russia in the 1930s.* Oxford: Oxford University Press.

–, ed. 2000. *Stalinism: New Directions.* London: Routledge.

Fondahl, G. 1995. "The Status of Indigenous Peoples in the Russian Far North." *Post-Soviet Geography* 36: 215-24.

–. 1998. *Gaining Ground? Evenkis, Land and Reform in Southeastern Siberia.* Wilton, CT: Allyn and Bacon.

Forsyth, J. 1992. *A History of the Peoples of Siberia: Russia's North Asian Colony 1582-1990.* Cambridge: Cambridge University Press.

Foucault, M. 1979. *Discipline and Punish: The Birth of the Prison.* Translated by A. Sheridan. New York: Vintage/Random House.

FSGS (Federal'naia sluzhba gosudarstvennoi statistiki) (FSSA [Federal State Statistics Agency]). 2004. *Perepis naseleniia 1897-2002 gg. – Chukotskii avtonomnyi okrug* (General Census 1897-2002 – Chukchi Autonomous Okrug). Anadyr: FSGS.

Gerschenkron, A. 1970. *Europe in the Russian Mirror: Four Lectures in Economic History.* Cambridge: Cambridge University Press.

Giddens, A. 1988. *The Constitution of Society: Outline of the Theory of Structuration.* Cambridge: Polity Press.

Givens, J. 1993. "Prodigal Son: Vasilii Shukshin in Soviet Russian Culture." *Slavic Review* 61, 1: 177-93.

Godelier, M. 1972. *Rationality and Irrationality in Economics.* Translated by B. Pearce. New York and London: Monthly Review Press.

Goffman, E. 1959. *The Presentation of Self in Everyday Life.* London: Penguin Books.

Golovnev, A.V., and G. Osherenko. 1999. *Siberian Survival: The Nenets and Their Story.* Ithaca, NY: Cornell University Press.

Goskomstat Rossii (Chukotka branch). 1998. *Kratkii statisticheskii sbornik – Sotsial'no-ekonomicheskoe razvitie Chukotskogo avtonomnogo okruga v 1991-1997 gg.* Anadyr: Goskomstat Rossii (Chukotka branch).

Goskomstat Rossii. 1999. *Demograficheskii ezhegodnik Rossii 1999* (Demographic Yearbook of Russia 1999). Moscow: Goskomstat.

Graham, S. 2003. "The Wages of Syncretism: Folkloric New Russians and Post-Soviet Popular Culture." *Russian Review* 62: 37-53.

Grant, B. 1993. "Siberia Hot and Cold: Reconstructing the Image of Siberian Indigenous Peoples." In G. Diment and Y. Slezkine, eds., *Between Heaven and Hell: The Myth of Siberia in Russian Culture,* 227-54. New York: St. Martin's Press.

–. 1995. *In the Soviet House of Culture.* Princeton: Princeton University Press.

Gray, P. 2000. "Chukotkan Reindeer Husbandry in the Post-Socialist Transition." *Polar Research* 19: 31-37.

–. 2003. "Chukotkan Reindeer Husbandry in the Twentieth Century: In the Image of the Soviet Economy." In D. Anderson and M. Nuttall, eds., *Cultivating Arctic Landscapes: Knowing and Managing Animals in the Circumpolar North,* 136-53. Oxford: Berghahn Press.

–. 2005. *The Predicament of Chukotka's Indigenous Movement: Post Soviet Activism in the Far North.* Cambridge: Cambridge University Press.

Gray, P., N. Vakhtin, and P. Schweitzer. 2003. "Who Owns Siberian Ethnography? A Critical Assessment of a Re-internationalised Field." *Sibirica* 3: 194-216.

Gregory, P., and R. Stuart. 1986. *Soviet Economic Structure and Performance.* New York: Harper and Row.

Gregory, P.R., and V. Lazarev, eds. 2003. *The Economics of Forced Labour: The Soviet Gulag.* Stanford: Hoover Institution Press.

Gruber, R. 1944. *I Went to the Soviet Arctic.* New York: Viking.

Gupta, A. 1995. "Blurred Boundaries: The Discourses of Corruption, the Culture of Politics and the Imagined State." *American Ethnologist* 22: 375-402.

Habeck, O. 2005a. "Dimensions of Identity." In E. Kasten, ed., *Rebuilding Identities: Pathways to Reform in Post-Soviet Siberia,* 9-25. Berlin: Dietrich Reimer Verlag.

–. 2005b. *What It Means to Be a Herdsman: The Practice and Image of Reindeer Husbandry among the Komi of Northern Russia.* Berlin: Lit Verlag.

Haraway, D. 1989. *Primate Visions: Gender, Race and Nature in the World of Modern Science.* New York: Routledge.

Hechter, M. 1975. *Internal Colonialism: The Celtic Fringe in British National Development, 1536-1966.* London: Routledge.

Heleniak, T. 1999. "Out-Migration and Depopulation of the Russian North during the 1990s." *Post-Soviet Geography and Economics* 40: 155-205.

–. 2003. "The 2002 Census in Russia: Preliminary Results." *Eurasian Geography and Economics* 44: 430-442.

Hessler, J. 2000. "Cultured Trade: The Stalinist Turn towards Consumerism." In S. Fitzpatrick, ed., *Stalinism: New Directions,* 182-209. London: Routledge.

Hill, F., and C. Gaddy. 2003. *The Siberian Curse: How Communist Planners Left Russia out in the Cold.* Washington, DC: Brookings Institute.

Hirsch, E., and M. O'Hanlon, eds. 1995. *The Anthropology of Landscape: Perspectives on Place and Space.* Oxford: Clarendon Press.

Hobsbawm, E., and T. Ranger, eds. 1983. *The Invention of Tradition.* Cambridge: Cambridge University Press.

Horensma, P. 1991. *The Soviet Arctic.* London: Routledge.

Hosking, G. 2000. "Patronage and the Russian State." *Slavic and East European Review (SEER)* 78: 301-20.

Humphrey, C. 1983. *The Karl Marx Collective: Economy, Society and Religion in a Siberian Collective Farm.* Cambridge: Cambridge University Press.

–. 1994. "Remembering an Enemy: The Bogd Khan in Twentieth Century Mongolia." In R. Watson, ed., *Memory, History and Opposition under State Socialism,* 21-44. Santa Fe, NM: School of American Research.

–. 2000. "An Anthropological View of Barter in Russia." In P. Seabright, ed., *The Vanishing Ruble: Barter Networks and Non-Monetary Transactions in Post-Soviet Societies,* 71-90. Cambridge: Cambridge University Press.

–. 2002. *The Unmaking of Soviet Life: Everyday Economies after Socialism.* Ithaca, NY, and London: Cornell University Press.

Ingold, T. 2000. *The Perception of the Environment: Essays in Livelihood, Dwelling and Skill.* London: Routledge.

–. 2004. "A Manifesto for the Anthropology of the North." Plenary paper presented at 5th International Congress of Arctic Social Sciences (ICASS V), Fairbanks, AK.

Innis, H. 1995. *Staples, Markets and Cultural Change: Selected Essays.* Montreal and Kingston: McGill-Queen's University Press.

Ionin, L. 1997. *Svoboda v SSSR* (Freedom in the USSR) St. Petersburg: Fond 'universitetskaia kniga'.

Ivanov, A.I. 1991. *L'goty dlya rabotnikov severa* (Benefits for northern workers). Moscow: Yuridicheskaya Literatura.

Jenkins, R. 1994. "Rethinking Ethnicity: Identity, Categorisation and Power." *Ethnic and Racial Studies* 17: 197-223.

Josephson, P.R. 1995. "New Atlantic Revisited: Akademgorodok, Siberian City of Science." In S. Wolff, ed. *Rediscovering Russia in Asia: Siberia and the Russian Far East,* 89-107. London: M.E. Sharpe.

Jowitt, K. 1992. *New World Disorder: The Leninist Extinction.* Berkeley: University of California Press.

Kaiser, R. 1994. *The Geography of Nationalism in Russia and the USSR.* Princeton: Princeton University Press.

Kennedy, J.C. 1982. *Holding the Line: Ethnic Boundaries in a Northern Labrador Community.* Social and Economic Studies No. 27. St. John's: Institute of Social and Economic Research, Memorial University of Newfoundland.

Kerttula, A.M. 2000. *Antler on the Sea: The Yupik and Chukchi of the Russian Far East.* London: Cornell University Press.

Kharkhordin, O. 1999. *The Collective and the Individual.* London: University of California Press.

Khlinovskaya-Rockhill, E. 2003. "Family Discontinuity and 'Social Orphanhood' in the Russian Far East: Children in Residential Care Institutions." PhD diss., University of Cambridge.

King, A.D. 2002. "Reindeer Herders' Culturescapes in the Koryak Autonomous Okrug." In E. Kasten, ed., *People and the Land: Pathways to Reform in Post-Soviet Siberia,* 63-82. Berlin: Dietrich Reimer Verlag.

Klopov, E. 1985. *Rabochii Klass SSSR (Tendentsii razvitiia v 60-70 gg)* (The Working Class in the USSR [Trends in development during the 1960s and 1970s]). Moscow: Mysl'.

Kontorovich, V. 2000. "Can Russia Resettle the Far East?" *Post-Communist Economies* 12: 365-83.

Kornai, J. 1992. *The Socialist System: The Political Economy of Communism.* Oxford: Oxford University Press.

Kotkin, S. 1995. *Magnetic Mountain: Stalinism as a Civilisation.* Berkeley: University of California Press.

Kotov, A.N., ed. 1995. *Chukotka: Prirodno-ekonomicheskii ocherk* (Chukotka: Natural and economic digest). Moscow: Art-Liteks.

Kriazhkov, V.A. 1994. *Status malochislennykh narodov Rossii: Pravovye akty i dokumenty* (The status of Russia's indigenous minorities: Legal statues and documents). Moscow: Iuridicheskaya Literatura.

Krupnik, I. 1993. *Arctic Adaptations: Native Whalers and Herders in Northern Eurasia.* 2nd rev. ed. Hanover, NH: University Press of New England.

Krupnik, I., and N. Vakhtin. 1997. "Indigenous Knowledge in Modern Culture: Siberian Yupik Ecological Legacy in Transition." *Arctic Anthropology* 34: 236-52.

–. 2002. "In the 'House of Dismay': Knowledge, Culture and Post-Soviet Politics in Chukotka, 1995-96." In E. Kasten and D. Reimer, eds., *People and the Land: Pathways to Reform in Post-Soviet Siberia,* 7-44. Berlin: Verlag.

Kuper, A. 2003. "The Return of the Native." *Current Anthropology* 44, 3: 389-403.

Kuvaev, O. 1982. *Territoriya: Roman, povesti, raskaz* (The Territory: Novel, tales, story). Leningrad: Lenizdat.

Lane, D. 1982. *The End of Social Inequality: Class, Status, and Power under State Socialism.* London: George Allen and Unwin.

Ledeneva, A.V. 1998. *Russia's Economy of Favours: Blat, Networking and Informal Exchange.* Cambridge: Cambridge University Press.

Leksin, V., and E. Andreeva. 1994. "Environmental, Social and Legal Issues in Russia's Northern Policy." *Polar Geography and Geology* 18: 296-326.

Lewin, M. 1985. *The Making of the Soviet System: Essays in the Social History of Interwar Russia.* New York: Pantheon.

–. 1987. *The Gorbachev Phenomenon.* Berkeley: University of California Press.

Lincoln, B. 1994. *The Conquest of a Continent: Siberia and the Russians.* New York: Random House.

MacLennan, H. 1945. *Two Solitudes.* New York: Duell, Sloan and Pierce.

Mauss, M. 1990. *The Gift: The Form and Reason for Exchange in Archaic Societies.* London: Routledge.

McCannon, J. 1998. *Red Arctic: Polar Exploration and the Myth of the North in the Soviet Union, 1923-1939.* Oxford: Oxford University Press.

Mead, G.H. 1934. *Mind, Self and Society from the Standpoint of a Social Behaviorist.* Chicago: University of Chicago Press.

Merridale, C. 2000. *Night of Stone: Death and Mourning in Russia.* London: Granta.

Mote, V. 1998. *Siberia: Worlds Apart.* Oxford: Westview Press.

Mowat, F. 1970. *Sibir: My Discovery of Siberia.* Toronto: McClelland and Stewart.

Nielsen, B., ed. 2005. *Tjukotka i fortid og nutid* (Chukotka in future and present), *Eskimologiskrifter nr. 18* (Publications on Eskimology Number 18). Copenhagen: University of Copenhagen.

Nielsen, F.S. 2007. *The Eye of the Whirlwind: Russian Identity and Soviet Nation-Building – Quests for Meaning in a Soviet Metropolis.* Oslo: Department of Social Anthropology, University of Oslo. This work is available at http://www.anthrobase.com/Txt/N/Nielsen_F_S_03.htm.

Nuttall, M. 1991. "Memoryscape: A Sense of Locality in Northwest Greenland." *North Atlantic Studies* 1: 39-50.

–. 1992. *Arctic Homeland: Kinship, Community, and Development in Northwest Greenland.* Toronto: University of Toronto Press.

Okun, S.B. 1935. *Kolonialnia politika tsarizma na Kamchatke i Chukotke: Sbornik akhivnikh materialov pod redaktsiei J.P. Alkora i A.K. Drezena* (Tsarist colonial policy in Kamchatka and Chukotka: Collected archival materials edited by J.P. Alkora and A.K. Drezena). Leningrad: Izdatelstvo Instituta Narodov Severa TSIK SSSR.

Osherenko, G. 1995. "Property Rights and Transformation in Russia: Institutional Change in the Russian Far North." *Europe-Asia Studies* 47: 1077-1108.

Osokina, E. 2001. *Our Daily Bread: Socialist Distribution and the Art of Survival in Stalin's Russia, 1927-1941.* London: M.E. Sharpe.

Osterhammel, J. 2002. *Colonialism.* Princeton, NJ: Markus Wiener.

Paine, R., ed. 1971. *Patrons and Brokers in the East Arctic.* St. John's: Memorial University of Newfoundland.

–. 1977. *The White Arctic: Anthropological Essays on Tutelage and Ethnicity.* St. John's: Memorial University of Newfoundland.

Pika, A. 1996. "Reproductive Attitudes and Family Planning among the Aboriginal Peoples of Alaska, Kamchatka and Chukotka: The Results of Comparative Research." *Arctic Anthropology* 33: 50-61.

Pika, A., and V. Prokhorov. 1988. "Bol'shie problemy malykh narodov (The big problems of the small peoples)," *Kommunist,* 13 July.

Pilkington, H. 1994. *Russia's Youth and Its Culture: A Nation's Constructors and Constructed.* London: Routledge.

Plaice, E. 1990. *The Native Game.* St. John's: Memorial University of Newfoundland.

Popov-Cherkasov, I.N. 1981. *L'goty i preimushchestva rabochim i sluzhshachim* (Labour benefits and privileges for workers and military personnel). Moscow: Yuridicheskaya Literatura.

Pushkarev, S. 1993. *Obzor russkoi istorii* (Survey of Russian history). Stavropol: Kavkazkii Krai.

Putnam, R.D. 2000. *Bowling Alone: The Collapse and Revival of American Community.* New York: Simon and Schuster.

Radcliffe-Browne, A.R. 1957. *A Natural Science of Society.* Glencoe, IL: Free Press.

Raipon. 2002. *Chislenost' korennykh malochislennykh narodov Severa, Sibiri, i Dal'nego Vostoka Rossiiskoi Federatsii po territoriyam preimushestvennogo prozhivaniya, Vserossiiskii perepis naseleniia 2002 g.* (Population of the indigenous peoples of the Russian North, Siberia, and the Far East by territory of predominant residence, all-Russian census of 2002). Moscow: Raipon.

Rethmann, P. 2001. *Tundra Passages: History and Gender in the Russian Far East.* University Park: Pennsylvania State University Press.

–. 2004. "A Dream of Democracy in the Russian Far East." In M. Blaser, H. Feit, and G. McRae, eds., *In the Way of Development: Indigenous Peoples, Life Projects, and Globalization,* 256-78. London: Zed Press.

Rieber, A.J., ed. 1966. *The Politics of Autocracy: Letters of Alexander II to Prince A.I. Bariatinskii, 1857-1864.* The Hague: Brill Academic Publishers.

Robert-Lamblin, J. 1993. "Socio-Demographic Situation of the Yupik and Inuit Eskimos and Chukhis of Chukotka." *Etudes/Inuit/Studies* 17: 73-96.
Rotkirch, A. 2000. *The Man Question: Loves and Lives in Late Twentieth-Century Russia.* Research Reports 1/2000. Helsinki: Department of Social Policy, University of Helsinki.
Round, J. 2005. "Rescaling Russia's Geography: The Challenges of Depopulating the Northern Periphery." *Europe-Asia Studies* 57, 5: 705-27.
Rozin, B., E. Khlystova, and V. Shchegel'skii. 1975. *L'goty rabotnikam krainego severa* (Benefits for workers in the Far North). Moscow: Profizdat.
Ruble, B., J. Koehn, and N. Popson, eds. 2002. *Fragmented Space in the Soviet Union.* Washington, DC: Woodrow Wilson Center Press.
Rytkheu, Y. 1967. *Vremya tayaniya snegov* (Time of the melting snows). Moscow: Molodaya Gvardiya.
–. 1981. *Izbrannoe* (Selected works). Leningrad: Khudozhestvennaya literatura.
–. 2005. *A Dream in Polar Fog.* Translated by I. Yazhbin. New York: Archipelago Books.
Sahlins, M. 1972. *Stone Age Economics.* Chicago: Aldine-Atherton.
Schindler, D.L. 1991. "Theory, Policy and the *Narody Severa.*" *Anthropology Quarterly* 64: 68-74.
–. 1994. "Competing for Resources: First Nation Rights and Economic Development in the Russian Far East." In B. Johnston, ed., *Who Pays the Price? The Socioeconomic Context of Environmental Crisis,* 99-109. New York: Island Press.
–. 1997. "Redefining Tradition and Renegotiating Ethnicity in Native Russia." *Arctic Anthropology* 34: 194-211.
Schneider, J.P. 1976. *Culture and Political Economy in Western Sicily.* New York: Academic Press.
Schweitzer, P., N. Vakhtin, and E. Golovko. 2005. "The Difficulty of Being Oneself: Identity Politics of 'Old Settler' Communities in Northeastern Siberia." In E. Kasten, ed., *Rebuilding Identities: Pathways to Reform in Post-Soviet Siberia,* 135-51. Berlin: Dietrich Reimer Verlag.
Scott, J. 1985. *Weapons of the Weak: Everyday Forms of Peasant Resistance.* New Haven and London: Yale University Press.
–. 1990. *Domination and the Arts of Resistance: Hidden Transcripts.* New Haven: Yale University Press.
Semushkin, T. 1950. *Chukotka.* Moscow: Gosudarstvennoe Izdatel'stvo Detskoi Literatury Ministerstva Prosveshcheniia RSFSR.
Serkin, V. 1997. "Severnyi nevroz (Northern neurosis)." *NG-Regiony,* 1.
Shanin, T. 1985. *Russia as a Developing Society.* London: Macmillan.
Sharpe, H.S. 2001. *Loon: Memory, Meaning and Reality in a Northern Dene Community.* Lincoln: University of Nebraska Press.
Shlapentokh, V. 1989. *Public and Private Life of the Soviet People: Changing Values in Post-Stalin Russia.* Oxford: Oxford University Press.
Shmyganovski, V. 1997. "Rossiia otstupaet na iug" (Russia retreats to the south). *Izvestiia* 1, 3: 158.
Slavin, S. 1961. *Promyshlennoe i transportnoe osvoenie Severa SSSR* (The industrial and infrastructural development of the Soviet North). Moscow: Ekonomizdat.
–. 1972. *The Soviet North: Present Developments and Prospects.* Moscow: Progress.
–. 1982. *Osvoenie Severa Sovetskogo Soyuza* (The development of the Soviet North). Moscow: Nauka.
Slezkine, Y. 1991. "The Fall of Soviet Ethnography." *Current Anthropology* 4: 476-84.
–. 1994. *Arctic Mirrors: Russia and the Small Peoples of the North.* Ithaca: Cornell University Press.
Slipchenko, W. 1972. *Siberia 1971: A Report on the Visit of the Honourable Jean Chrétien, Minister of Indian Affairs and Northern Development, and Official Delegation to the Soviet Union.* Ottawa: Department of Indian and Northern Affairs.

Smolka, H.P. 1937. *Forty Thousand against the Arctic: Russia's Polar Empire.* London: Hutchinson.

Sökefeld, M. 1999. "Debating Self, Identity, and Culture in Anthropology." *Current Anthropology* 40: 417-47.

Ssorin-Chaikov, N.V. 2000. "Bear Skins and Macaroni: The Social Life of Things at the Margins of a Siberian State Collective." In P. Seabright, ed., *The Vanishing Rouble: Barter Networks and Non-Monetary Transactions in Post-Soviet Societies*, 345-61. Cambridge: Cambridge University Press.

–. 2003. *The Social Life of the State in Subarctic Siberia.* Stanford: Stanford University Press.

Stammler, F. 2004. *When Reindeer Nomads Meet the Market: Culture, Property and Globalisation at the End of the Land.* Halle Studies in the Anthropology of Eurasia. Munster: LIT-Verlag.

Stephan, J.J. 1994. *The Russian Far East: A History.* Stanford: Stanford University Press.

Strathern, M. 1981. *Kinship at the Core: An Anthropology of Elmdon, Essex.* Cambridge: Cambridge University Press.

Tall, D. 1996. "Dwelling: Making Peace with Space and Place." In W. Vitek and W. Jackson, eds., *Rooted in the Land: Essays on Community and Place*, 93-131. New Haven: Yale University Press.

Tarrow, S. 1967. *Peasant Communism in Southern Italy.* New Haven: Yale University Press.

Taussig, M. 1980. *The Devil and Commodity Fetishism in South America.* Chapel Hill: University of North Carolina Press.

Thompson, N. 2002. "Administrative Resettlement and the Pursuit of Economy: The Case of Chukotka." *Polar Geography* 26: 270-88.

–. 2003. "The Native Settler: Contesting Local Identities on Russia's Resource Frontier." *Polar Geography* 27: 136-58.

–. 2004. "Migration and Resettlement in Chukotka: A Research Note." *Eurasian Geography and Economics* 45: 73-81.

Tichotsky, J. 2000. *Russia's Diamond Colony: The Republic of Sakha.* Amsterdam: Harwood Academic Publishers.

Tönnies, F. 1957. *Community and Society.* New York: Harper and Row.

Tucker, R.C. 1990. *Stalin in Power: The Revolution from Above 1928-1941.* New York: Norton.

Vakhtin, N. 1992. *Native Peoples of the Russian Far North.* London: Minority Rights Group.

Vakhtin, N., E. Golovko, and P. Schweitzer. 2004. *Russkie starozhily Sibiri: sotsial'nye i simvolicheskie aspekty samosoznaniya* (Russian Old Settlers in Siberia: Social and symbolic aspects of identity). St. Petersburg: Novoe Izdatel'stvo.

Vaté, V. 2003. "Le rituel de mort volontaire: rendre l'ame pour pertetuer la vie" (The ritual of voluntary death: Returning the heart to perpetuate life). *Chemins d'etoiles* 10: 55-61.

Vdovin, I.S. 1965. *Otcherki istorii i etnografii chukchei* (Notes on the history and ethnography of the Chukchi). Moscow: Nauka.

Verdery, K. 1996. *What Was Socialism and What Comes Next?* Princeton: Princeton University Press.

Vidich, A., and J. Bensman. 1968. *Small Town in Mass Society: Class, Power and Religion in a Rural Community.* Princeton: Princeton University Press.

Vitebsky, P. 1992. "Landscape and Self-Determination among the Eveny: The Political Environment of Siberian Reindeer Herders Today." In E. Croll and O. Parkin, eds., *Bush Base Forest Farm: Culture, Environment and Development*, 223-46. London: Routledge.

–. 1993. "Is Death the Same Everywhere? Contexts of Knowing and Doubting." In M. Hobart, ed., *An Anthropological Critique of Development: The Growth of Ignorance*, 100-15. London: Routledge.

–. 1996. "The Northern Minorities." In G. Smith, ed., *The Nationalities Question in the Post-Soviet States*, 94-112. London: Longmans.

–. 2000. "Coping with Distance: Social, Economic and Environmental Change in the Sakha Republic (Yakutia), Northeastern Siberia." Unpublished report, Scott Polar Research Institute, Cambridge.
–. 2002. "Withdrawing from the Land: Social and Spiritual Crisis in the Indigenous Russian Arctic." In C.M. Hann, ed., *Postsocialism: Ideals, Ideologies and Practices in Eurasia*, 180-195. London: Routledge.
–. 2005. *Reindeer People: Among the Humans, Animals and Spirits in Siberia.* New York: Harper Collins.
Vitebsky, P., and S. Wolfe. 2001. "The Separation of the Sexes among Siberian Reindeer Herders." In S. Tremayne and A. Low, eds., *Women as "Sacred Custodians" of the Earth?* 81-94. Oxford: Berg.
Volkov, V. 1999. "The Concept of Kul'turnost': Notes on the Stalinist Civilising Process." In S. Fitzpatrick, ed., *Stalinism: New Directions*, 210-30. London: Routledge.
–. 2000. "Patrimonialism versus Rational Bureaucracy: On the Historical Relativity of Corruption." In S. Lovell, A.V. Ledeneva, and A. Rogachevskii, eds., *Bribery and Blat in Russia: Negotiating Reciprocity from the Middle Ages to the 1990s*, 35-47. London: Macmillan.
–. 2002. *Violent Entrepreneurs: The Use of Force in the Making of Russian Capitalism.* Ithaca: Cornell University Press.
Wallace, H. 1992. *Pervye dni na zemle Sovetskoi Azii* (First days on Soviet Asian soil). Magadan: Magadanskii oblastnoi krayevedcheskii muzei.
Weber, M. 1968. *Economy and Society.* Berkeley: University of California Press.
Wilson, E. 2002. "Making Space for Local Voices: Local Participation in Natural Resource Management, North-Eastern Sakhalin Island, the Russian Far East." PhD diss., University of Cambridge.
Wolff, K.H. 1950. *The Sociology of Georg Simmel.* Glencoe, IL: Free Press.
Yanitskii, O. 1993. *Russian Environmentalism: Figures, Facts, Opinions.* Moscow: Mezhdunarodnye Otnosheniia.
Yanovskii, V.V. 1969. *Chelovek i sever* (Man and the North). Magadan: Magadanskoe knizhnoe izdatel'stvo.
Yurchak, A. 2002. "Entrepreneurial Governmentality in Post-Socialist Russia: A Cultural Investigation of Business Practices." In V. Bonell and T. Gold, eds., *The New Entrepreneurs of Europe and Asia*, 278-324. Armonk, NY: M.E. Sharpe.
–. 2005. *Everything Was Forever, Until It Was No More: The Last Soviet Generation.* Princeton: Princeton University Press.
Zaslavskaia, T.I. 1984. "The Novosibirsk Report." *Survey* 28, 1: 83-109.
Zdravomyslova, E. 2002. "*Tusovka* of Café 'Saigon': The Segment of the Quasi-Public Sphere of the Late-Soviet Society." In R. Humphrey, R. Miller, and E. Zdravomyslova, eds., *Altered Lives and Broken Biographies: Biographical Research in Eastern Europe*, 141-80. London: Palgrave.
Zdravomyslova, E., and V. Voronkov. 2002. "The Informal Public in Soviet Society: Double Morality at Work." *Social Research* 69, 1: 49-69.
Ziker, J. 2002. *Peoples of the Tundra: Northern Siberians in the Post-Communist Transition.* Prospect Heights, IL: Waveland Press.
Znamenski, A.A. 1999. "Vague Sense of Belonging to the Russian Empire: The Reindeer Chukchi's Status in Nineteenth Century Northeastern Siberia." *Arctic Anthropology* 36: 19-36.

Index

Bold page numbers refer to photographs or figures.

Printed and bound in Canada by Friesens

Set in Helvetica Condensed and Minion by Artegraphica Design Co. Ltd.

Copy editor: Deborah Kerr

Proofreader and indexer: Dianne Tiefensee